BUILDING CANADA

Sponsored by the
Canadian Public Works Association

Norman R. Ball
Senior Editor

Building Canada

A HISTORY OF PUBLIC WORKS

UNIVERSITY OF TORONTO PRESS
Toronto Buffalo London

© University of Toronto Press 1988
Toronto Buffalo London
Printed in Canada

ISBN 0-8020-3449-7

Canadian Cataloguing in Publication Data

Main entry under title:

Building Canada: a history of public works

Includes index.
ISBN 0-8020-3449-7

1. Canada – Public works – History.
I. Ball, Norman R., 1944–
II. Canadian Public Works Association.

TA26.B85 1988   363.'0971   c88-094433-1

Contents

Abbreviations

The following abbreviations are used in captions to the illustrations that appear throughout the text. These institutions have kindly given permission to reproduce material in their collections.

AO Archives of Ontario, Toronto
CIHB Canadian Inventory of Historic Building, Environment Canada
CNR Canadian National Railway Archives, Montreal
CP Canadian Pacific Archives, Windsor Station, Montreal
CPS Canadian Parks Service
CPWA Sask Chapter Canadian Public Works Association, Saskatchewan Chapter
DND Department of National Defence
CTA City of Toronto Archives
GAC Glenbow Archives, Calgary
HQ Hydro Québec
MTLB Metropolitan Toronto Library Board
MTWD Metropolitan Toronto Works Department

MUCTC Montreal Urban Community Transportation Commission
MWRB Province of Manitoba Water Resources Branch
NA National Archives Canada, Ottawa
NPA Notman Photographic Archives, McCord Museum, McGill University, Montreal
NPS National Parks Service Canada
NSM Nova Scotia Museum, Halifax
OH Ontario Hydro Archives, Toronto
OMCC Ontario Ministry of Culture and Communications
OMT Ontario Ministry of Transportation
PAA Provincial Archives of Alberta, Edmonton
PABC Provincial Archives of British Columbia, Victoria
PAM Provincial Archives of Manitoba, Winnipeg
SAB Saskatchewan Archives Board, Regina
TC Transport Canada
VH Victoria Hospital, London, Ontario

Preface

The words 'building Canada' may be the most important words in this volume of public works history. Public works 'comprises the design, construction, and maintenance of structures governments at all levels provide so that services essential to the functioning of organized society are available.' For this reason the history of public works in Canada is the story of 'building Canada.' Yet public works are usually taken for granted by Canadians. They just assume that water will flow when they turn on a tap; the quality of the water is seldom, if ever, questioned. Providing communities with an adequate supply of drinking water should be regarded as an achievement as great as providing electric power.

Modern professional public works engineers and administrators blend their skills with others in allied fields, such as surveyors, scientists, communications personnel, medical health practitioners, business administrators, financial personnel, social workers, and planners, all with a view to manage effectively in a public and often political environment.

Factors that dominate every facet of Canadian life are the country's enormous geographical area – the second largest in the world – and its great range of climates – semi-tropical on the west coast; hot summers and frigid, wind-swept winters on the prairies; more moderate weather in Ontario and Que-

bec, but with tropical summers on the Great Lakes; and the winds of Atlantic Canada; to say nothing of the Arctic conditions in Yukon and the Northwest Territories. In addition, a great variation in topography is accompanied by countless natural resources. Forging a nation out of a wilderness, in the harshest of conditions, was in large measure the accomplishment of public works.

In 1976 the American Public Works Association (APWA) published *History of Public Works in the United States: 1776–1976*, which evoked much interest in Canada as well as in the United States. R.D. Bugher, the executive director of the APWA, subsequently urged members of the APWA's chapters in Canada, the board of directors of the Canadian Public Works Council, and the members of the newly formed Canadian Public Works Association (CPWA) to undertake a companion volume, a history of public works in Canada. He solicited the help of the APWA's board of directors, of which a Canadian, Roger K. Brown, currently serves as president, to support the venture financially, administratively, and editorially. All bodies showed great enthusiasm for the venture, and the result is *Building Canada: A History of Public Works*.

This book was the product of several years of effort and dedication on the part of many people. Public works professionals worked closely with historians throughout Canada to produce this important addition to historical understanding. Local CPWA Chapter Historical Committees have contributed greatly to the history and have helped pay for its production. The members of the Editorial Committee of the CPWA were William D. Hurst, Winnipeg; Dr Robert F. Legget, Ottawa; and Phyllis Rose, Toronto; and Dr Norman R. Ball, chief of research, National Museum of Science and Technology, Ottawa, was senior editor. Dr Howard Rosen, director, Public Works Historical Society, Chicago, was project director.

Special thanks are due to the many institutions that supplied the illustrations which add so much to this book. While it is not possible to list everyone here, special mention should be made of Kenneth Wallace, principal photo researcher, André Bolduc of Hydro Québec, and Joy Houston, Diane Martineau, and Sharon Uno of the National Archives of Canada.

In addition, we must thank the University of Toronto Press and its dedicated and professional staff for their fine efforts on behalf of this book. In particular, we are indebted to John Parry who provided us with the copyediting. Virgil Duff, Peter Scaggs, Will Rueter, and their associates provided us with excellent production and design assistance, and Susan Kent prepared a superb index.

Grateful acknowledgment is made to Environment Canada, Canadian Parks Service, for its support in providing the services of Robert W. Passfield, and to the National Museum of Science and Technology, for the services of Norman R. Ball.

We wish to thank the several Canadian provinces and the federal government which have given generous financial assistance and kindly lent their personnel. In addition, many individuals and firms have been munificent donors and subscribers.

For the past 100 years or more public works professionals have been serving Canada. What follows is their story.

William D. Hurst, CM, CE, P ENG
Chairman, National Editorial Committee
Winnipeg, September 1988

Acknowledgments

GOVERNMENT SPONSORS

The Canadian Public Works Association wishes to acknowledge the vital support of the following government agencies to the financing and preparation of this book:

THE NATIONAL MUSEUM OF SCIENCE & TECHNOLOGY
Ottawa

PUBLIC WORKS CANADA
The Honourable Stewart McInnes, Minister

THE DEPARTMENT OF MUNICIPAL AFFAIRS,
PROVINCE OF NOVA SCOTIA
The Honourable David Nantes, Minister

THE MINISTRY OF CULTURE AND COMMUNICATIONS,
PROVINCE OF ONTARIO
The Honourable Lily Oddie Munro, Minister

THE MINISTRY OF THE ENVIRONMENT, PROVINCE OF ONTARIO
The Honourable Jim Bradley, Minister

THE MINISTRY OF TRANSPORTATION, PROVINCE OF ONTARIO
The Honourable Ed Fulton, Minister

THE MINISTRY OF CULTURE, HERITAGE AND RECREATION,
PROVINCE OF MANITOBA
The Honourable Judy Wasylycia-Leis, Minister

THE CITY COUNCIL OF WINNIPEG
His Worship William Norrie, Mayor

ENVIRONMENT CANADA – PARKS
The Honourable Thomas M. McMillan, Minister

The Canadian Public Works Association wishes to acknowledge
in addition the assistance of:

THE AMERICAN PUBLIC WORKS ASSOCIATION   Roger K. Brown, President
THE PUBLIC WORKS HISTORICAL SOCIETY   Edward B. Rodie, President

INSTITUTIONAL PATRONS

R.V. Anderson & Associates Limited
Willowdale, Ontario

Atlantic Industries Limited
Sackville, New Brunswick

B-A Construction Ltd
Winnipeg, Manitoba

K.J. Beamish Construction Co., Limited
King City, Ontario

Bell Canada
Toronto, Ontario

Browning Ferris Industries, Limited
Toronto, Ontario

Bruell Contracting Limited
Toronto, Ontario

The City of Calgary
Commissioners' Office
Calgary, Alberta

Cambrian Excavators
Winnipeg, Manitoba

Champion Road Machinery Limited
Goderich, Ontario

Chisholm, Fleming & Associates
Agincourt, Ontario

The Consumer's Gas Company
Scarborough, Ontario

D. Crupi & Sons, Ltd
Agincourt, Ontario

The Day & Ross Transportation Group
Hartland, New Brunswick

Dayton & Knight Ltd
West Vancouver, British Columbia

DeLCan Engineering
Don Mills, Ontario

M.M. Dillon Limited
Willowdale, Ontario

City of Edmonton
Engineering Division
Transportation Department
Edmonton, Alberta

Edmonton Water and Sanitation
Edmonton, Alberta

The Equity Development Group, Inc.
Scarborough, Ontario

Fenco Engineers, Inc.
Willowdale, Ontario

Giffels Associates Limited
Rexdale, Ontario

Gore & Storrie, Limited
Toronto, Ontario

Guild Electric Limited
Scarborough, Ontario

Knox Martin Kretch Limited
Brampton, Ontario

Laidlaw Waste Systems
Hamilton, Ontario

N.D. Lea and Associates
Vancouver, British Columbia

MacLaren Engineers Inc. &
MacLaren Plansearch Inc.
Toronto, Ontario

S. McNally & Sons Ltd
Hamilton, Ontario

Marshall Macklin Monaghan Limited
Don Mills, Ontario

Metropolitan Department of Works and
Metropolitan Department of Roads and
Traffic, Toronto, Ontario

M.S.O. Construction Limited
Rexdale, Ontario

PLANMAC Consultants Limited
Toronto, Ontario

The Proctor & Redfern Group
Don Mills, Ontario

Fred Schaeffer & Associates
Downsview, Ontario

Standard Paving Maritime Limited
Halifax, Nova Scotia

Taggart Construction Ltd
Ottawa, Ontario

Taillieu Construction Ltd
Winnipeg, Manitoba

Paul Theil & Associates Limited
Bramalea, Ontario

Totten Sims Hubicki Associates
Whitby, Ontario

Tractors & Equipment (1962) Limited
Fredericton, New Brunswick

Trow Ltd
Brampton, Ontario

UMA Engineering Limited
Rexdale, Ontario

Urban Engineering Consultants
Toronto, Ontario

City of Vancouver
Vancouver, British Columbia

J. Philip Vaughn Engineering Assoc. Ltd
Halifax, Nova Scotia

Willis Cunliffe Tait/DeLCan
New Westminster
British Columbia

Derek L. Wilson, Ltd
Willowdale, Ontario

George Wimpey Canada
Toronto, Ontario

WMI Waste Management of Canada
Weston, Ontario

INDIVIDUAL PATRONS

Allan R. Arbuckle
Etobicoke, Ontario

Aime C. Beaulieu
Peace River, Alberta

R. Clark Brewer
Dawson Creek, British Columbia

Roger K. Brown
Scarborough, Ontario

Norm Coleman
Winnipeg, Manitoba

R.R. Foster
Winnipeg, Manitoba

Joseph David George
Islington, Ontario

Tom Harris
Carbonear, Newfoundland

S.A. Humeny
Calgary, Alberta

William D. Hurst
Winnipeg, Manitoba

Wayne J. Imrie
Winnipeg, Manitoba

E.K. Jerrett
Roberts, Newfoundland

Sean Kavanagh
St John's, Newfoundland

Ivan P. Lieszkowszky
Markham, Ontario

Sean O'Rafferty
St John's, Newfoundland

M.L. Perkins
Richmond Hill, Ontario

W.H. Powell
Winnipeg, Manitoba

Wesley M. Steeves
Moncton, New Brunswick

Paul A. Stephen
Huntsville, Ontario

Bruce Sully
Goderich, Ontario

Daniel Suzuki
Kitchener, Ontario

Marcel Taillieu
Headingley, Manitoba

K.G. Thompson
Truro, Nova Scotia

INSTITUTIONAL SPONSORS

Acres International Limited
Winnipeg, Manitoba

Amalgamated Sewer Services Inc.
Winnipeg, Manitoba

Armadillo Holdings Ltd
Winnipeg, Manitoba

Atlantic Concrete
A division of the Lundrigan Group Ltd
St John's, Newfoundland

Beaudry Construction (1980) Ltd
St Agathe, Manitoba

Beaver Sewer & Water Services Ltd
Winnipeg, Manitoba

L.J. Casavechia Contracting Ltd
Dartmouth, Nova Scotia

J.R. Cousin Consultants Ltd
Winnipeg, Manitoba

Cowin Steel Co. Ltd
Winnipeg, Manitoba

Crosier Kilgour Partners
Winnipeg, Manitoba

Reid Crowther and Partners Ltd
Winnipeg, Manitoba

DeLCan Engineering
Winnipeg, Manitoba

Diamond Ready Mix
Concrete Ltd
Steinbach, Manitoba

Dominion Bridge
Winnipeg, Manitoba

DS-LEA Associates Ltd
Winnipeg, Manitoba

Dyregrov and Burgess
Winnipeg, Manitoba

John P. Enns Construction Ltd
Altona, Manitoba

D.G. Eppler Diversified Construction
  Services Ltd
Winnipeg, Manitoba

W.H.D. Hurst, Architects
Toronto, Ontario

I.D. Engineering Canada Inc.
Winnipeg, Manitoba

Kleysen Transport Ltd
Winnipeg, Manitoba

Lavalin
Montreal, Quebec

MacLaren Engineers, Inc.
Winnipeg, Manitoba

Maritime Testing Ltd
Dartmouth, Nova Scotia

Midland Concrete Products
  (1977) Ltd
Winnipeg, Manitoba

Nelson River Construction
  (1984) Inc.
Winnipeg, Manitoba

Newfoundland Design Associates
  Limited
St John's, Newfoundland

N.I. Construction
Winnipeg, Manitoba

O'Halloran Campbell Consultants
  Limited
Halifax, Nova Scotia

Parkdale Construction Ltd
Winnipeg, Manitoba

Phillips Barratt Kaiser Engineering
Surrey, British Columbia

Pile Foundation ('79) Ltd
Fort Whyte, Manitoba

Poetker Engineering Consultants
Winnipeg, Manitoba

Romaine Construction Limited
St John's, Newfoundland

Scouten Mitchell Sigurdson &
  Associates Limited
Winnipeg, Manitoba

Smook Bros. (Thompson) Ltd
Thompson, Manitoba

Titan Foundry Ltd
Winnipeg, Manitoba

UMA Engineering Ltd
Winnipeg, Manitoba

CANADIAN PUBLIC WORKS ASSOCIATION

BOARD OF DIRECTORS

President
Peter S. Connell
Director, Engineering and Works
Halifax, Nova Scotia

Vice-President
M.A. Bamford
Manager, Engineering Division
Calgary, Alberta

Past Presidents
Jean Fortin
Manager of Utility Coordination (ret.)
Bell Canada – Quebec
Montreal, Quebec

Aime C. Beaulieu
Airport Manager
Peace River, Alberta

Alberta
M.A. Bamford
Manager, Engineering Division
Calgary, Alberta

Atlantic Provinces
Geoff Greenough
City Engineer
Moncton, New Brunswick

British Columbia
Craig Sinclair
Assistant Director – Engineering and
  Works
Burnaby, British Columbia

Manitoba
Harold E. Granke
Supervisor of Streets (ret.), District 3
Winnipeg, Manitoba

Ontario
Bruce Brunton
Commissioner of Works
Etobicoke, Ontario

Quebec
Claude Paquin
Director of Public Works
LaSalle, Quebec

Saskatchewan
James C. McAlister
Director of Public Works
Melfort, Saskatchewan

Secretary-Treasurer
William D. Hurst
Winnipeg, Manitoba

CHAPTER HISTORICAL COMMITTEE CHAIRS

Alberta
Don P. Corrigan
City Manager
St Albert, Alberta

Atlantic Provinces
Antoine J. Richard
Executive Director of Vehicle
  Management
Fredericton, New Brunswick

British Columbia
R. Clark Brewer
Municipal Engineer
Dawson Creek, British Columbia

Manitoba
Ronald V. Houghton
Director of Civic Properties
Winnipeg, Manitoba

Ontario
Michael Gibson
Vice President – Barker Terp Gibson, Ltd
Don Mills, Ontario

Bruce Brunton
Commissioner of Works
Etobicoke, Ontario

Derek L. Wilson
Consulting Engineer
Willowdale, Ontario

Robert G. Ferguson
Deputy Commissioner of Works –
  Metropolitan Toronto
Toronto, Ontario

Quebec
Yvan Brunet
Urban Engineering Consultant
Montreal, Quebec

Saskatchewan
James Duffee
Integrated Engineering Services
Saskatoon, Saskatchewan

Joseph Urbanowski
Town Foreman
Tisdale, Saskatchewan

James C. McAlister
Director of Public Works
Melfort, Saskatchewan

Contributors

LETTY ANDERSON is a professor of economics at Atkinson College, York University. Her main teaching and research interests are economic history of urban service provision and women's labour force issues.

CHRISTOPHER ANDREAE of Historica Research Limited, a historical, planning, and research firm in London, Ontario, has for more than two decades written about Canada's railway and industrial heritage. He is working on a historical atlas of the railways and canals of Canada.

ALAN F.J. ARTIBISE, former director, Institute of Urban Studies, University of Winnipeg, is now director, School of Community and Regional Planning, University of British Columbia. He has written or edited 12 books, served on numerous boards, and received a variety of awards, including the Canadian Historical Association Award of Merit.

DOUGLAS BALDWIN is a professor of history at Acadia University in Wolfville, Nova Scotia. He has written, in addition to numerous articles on the history of Canadian technology and medicine, history and social studies textbooks and other books, including *The Cradle of Canadian Mining: A Pictorial History of Mining Technology* (1978). He is currently

writing a biography of Mona Wilson (1894–1981), a Canadian public health nurse.

NORMAN R. BALL is chief of research, National Museum of Science and Technology, and president, Canadian Science and Technology Historical Association. His most recent book is *Mind, Heart and Vision: Professional Engineering in Canada, 1887 to 1987* (1987). He was awarded the Engineering Centennial Board Silver Medal in 1987 and honorary membership in the Engineering Institute of Canada in 1988.

A.A. DEN OTTER is a professor of history at Memorial University of Newfoundland. A specialist in western Canadian history, he has written *Civilizing the West: The Galts and the Development of Western Canada* (1982).

MARK FRAM, architectural planner and consultant, served as a conservation officer with the Heritage Branch, Ontario Ministry of Culture and Communications. Now an independent consultant, he is the author of *Well Preserved: The Ontario Heritage Foundation's Manual of Principles and Practice for Architectural Conservation* (1988).

JULIE HARRIS is an architectural historian with the Architectural History Branch of the Canadian Parks Service. She is engaged in research on the history of buildings and construction on federal experimental farms and stations.

PAUL-ANDRÉ LINTEAU is a professor at the Université du Québec à Montréal, where he teaches Canadian economic, social, and urban history. Well known for his research on various aspects of urban history in Quebec, he won the Sir John A. Macdonald Prize of the Canadian Historical Association for *The Promoter's City: Building the Industrial Town of Maisonneuve, 1883–1918* (1985).

LARRY MCNALLY is science and engineering archivist, Manuscript Division, National Archives of Canada. He has done extensive research on the industries of the Lachine Canal and is working on a study of Montreal engine foundries in the 19th century.

ROBERT PASSFIELD is a historian with the National Parks and Sites Branch, Cana-

dian Parks Service, and a specialist in canal- and bridge-building technology. His publications include *Building the Rideau Canal: A Pictorial History* (1982).

ARNOLD ROOS is a historian with the Canadian Parks Service. He has served as the president of the Canadian Science and Technology Historical Association and was co-editor of *Critical Issues in the History of Canadian Science, Technology and Medicine* (1983).

PHYLLIS ROSE works in engineering history. A past president of the Ontario Society for Industrial Archaeology, she is a member of the Board of Trustees of the Public Works Historical Society.

JEAN SIMONTON is a conservation officer with the Heritage Branch, Ontario Ministry of Culture and Communications, which identifies, conserves, and manages historically significant public structures owned by the province.

BUILDING CANADA

NORMAN R. BALL

Introduction

In one of the world's many creation myths, the devil looked down in dismay upon the comfort, convenience, security, and joy experienced by mankind and in a jealous rage scratched the earth's surface with his nails. The resultant valleys and ridges separated mankind from fields and crops, kept families apart, and threatened life itself. The angels descended, spread their wings over uncrossable valleys, and in giving mankind its first bridges provided one of the keys to continuing survival.[1] Myths are not intended to provide literal and provable facts; rather they are an expression of the truths by which we live and the values we cherish. This creation myth interprets engineering, bridges, and other public works as gifts of gods or angels that we need because the world we live in is imperfect.

Nations too have their mythology, and Canada's prose, poetry, and songs present numerous, often fanciful tales of great rivers, canals, railways, and highways. One looks harder, perhaps even in vain, to find the sewers, water-supply, irrigation projects, airports, or planners and city engineers. Yet, if questioned, many Canadians would undoubtedly affirm the importance of these public works and their practitioners and understand that they shape and stand as a measure of our society, its achieve-ments and values. Perhaps more is taught in Canadian schools about how the quest for public works shaped the ancient river valley civilizations of the Indus and the Nile than about how it shaped Canada's past and present. And yet colonial relations with both France and England, the Act of Union of 1840, and the British North America Act of 1867, as well as later additions to Confederation, were all heavily laden with public works needs and promises. While public works have been central to Canadian history, they have not been a conscious focal point of historical scholarship, but this is very likely to change. The past is not static: it is re-evaluated and rewritten in light of current concerns. Moreover, a variety of historical disciplines have laid much of the groundwork needed for better understanding of the interaction of public works with Canadian society and history.

While increased historical study would certainly help Canadian public works professionals better to know their field, such rarified motives seldom foster great spurts of scholarly activity. Changing societal concerns are far more effective. Although the present is not the only period in Canadian history characterized by intense environmental and public works concerns, the current sense of worry and quest for understanding is instigating a re-examination of Canada's past. Rewriting history is not a make-work project akin to digging holes on Mondays and filling them in on Tuesdays; rather it reflects the fundamental truth that research and thought are never finished, that there is no such thing as a thorough examination that extracts all that is ever to be discovered. At best one finds the answers to the questions that are asked. With time the questions change to reflect both current interests and cumulative awareness of the narrowness and inadequacies of the previous questions and their answers. Many Canadians are concerned about very serious problems in areas such as water and air pollution and the ageing public works infrastructures, including roads, bridges, watermains, and sewer systems, which will need extensive upgrading or replacement at great cost. Public works history should therefore grow if there is some semblance of a free and unhampered intellectual market-place.

This book is by no means comprehensive, but the list of chapters clearly indicates the range and variety of public works: bridges; roads, streets, and highways; urban mass transit; railways; waterways; irrigation and flood control; electricity; water-supply; sewerage; solid waste; public buildings; airports; and planning. Any one of these chapters might be expanded into numerous books; even single aspects or projects within any chapter could be expanded into one or more books. Necessarily the chapters only begin to hint at the complexity of public works undertakings, the realms of knowledge upon which they draw, and the complex relationships between public works achievement and all levels of government, quasi-governmental organizations, and private enterprise.

There is no shortage of subject matter for public works history; in fact its diversity and quantity make it all too easy and tempting to select a small portion to research and write about, without presenting the larger picture. The chapters in this book certainly reveal diversity of approach and subject matter, but one should not lose sight of the common thread, for each is but a variation on the same theme: the expenditure of public funds to build for the improvement of the common good. Therefore the long-term challenge facing public works history is to encourage the study of discrete areas as well as an awareness of the larger picture and the interconnectedness of the parts and their impact. The narrower studies will be easier and fit in more with past achievements and current styles in historical writing.

Specialization is both a necessary fact and a curse of modern professional life. Any profession's body of knowledge is so wide, and often so difficult to master, that an individual must dwell in a small sub-specialty. It is the same with engineers, chemists, physicists, and physicians; each group is so specialized that it usually lacks sophisticated universal discourse. Historical research displays the same fragmentation, with all its attendant communications problems, but one can turn apparent disadvantage to advantage. Much of the intellectual infrastructure for growth in public works history may be constructed by drawing upon the wide range of articles found in the various sub-specialties of Canadian historical research. Some of the authors in this book have started the process, and it will be a continuing challenge for scholars to draw together works from various sub-specialties, absorb their information and insights, add new research and ideas, and combine new with old to produce a historical literature that will make public works less peripheral to students of Canadian society and history.

The fields from which the public works historian will draw are too numerous to list, but one should not pass by without introducing some of the most obvious, along with samples of the type of work so germane to Canadian public works history.

Many public works projects aim at lessening the incidence of disease, and articles such as Heather MacDougall's 'Public Health and the 'Sanitary Idea" in Toronto, 1866–1890'[2] present research and insights from the history of public health and medicine invaluable to historians of public works. MacDougall's study of the links between public health and public works probes the kind of relationship which is common knowledge but rarely explored in the depth required to add to understanding. Similarly, an article such as John Norris's 'Typhoid in the Rockies: Epidemiology in a Constrained Habitat, 1882–1929' underscores the fundamental role of public works in reducing death tolls from disease.[3] Many hospital histories look inward and dwell on the institution as a distinct unit, but some, such as *Growing to Serve: A History of Victoria Hospital, London, Ontario*,[4] try to fit it into that larger framework which also encompasses public works.

The writings of some urban historians reflect the heavy concentration of major public works in cities and urban centres. There is not a school of writing centred on urban public works, but the subject appears often enough to remind the reader of its importance and, in some cases, to whet the appetite for more studies. In his masterly study, *The Promoter's City: Building the Industrial Town of Maisonneuve 1883–1918*,[5] Paul-André

Linteau, one of the contributors to this volume, has highlighted the crucial role of some public works in promoting the growth of a burgeoning city and the need to change priorities over time and not be stuck in the attitudes of urban youth when the heady years of expansion are over. Each book in the History of Canadian Cities series, published by James Lorimer & Company in conjunction with the Canadian Museum of Civilization,[6] looks at a different city, but the role of public works is often given in frustratingly scanty detail. Other articles by urban historians have looked at a particular problem area and put it in a larger framework, as in 'The Conflagration and the City: Disaster and Progress in Nineteenth-Century British North America' or 'The Second Great Fire of Toronto, 19–20 April, 1904.'[7] But these titles merely suggest the kinds of literature that exist and the type of problems that might be examined; further study of the growing literature of Canadian urban history will richly reward anyone wishing to explore the written histories of public works.

Histories of utilities can be similarly rewarding. These range widely in both coverage and quality. Many smack more of ancestor worship than critical history, but even these provide some clues to further reading and ideas. Three fine studies are E.V. Buchanan, *London's Water Supply: A History*,[8] André Bolduc, *Québec: un siècle d'électricité*,[9] and Clinton O. White, *Power for a Province: A History of Saskatchewan Power*.[10]

This brief introduction is intended merely to note that public works history is not as divorced as one might imagine from contemporary historical scholarship. A far better introduction to the existing sources will come from the notes to the chapters. While introductions to some books seem to vie with individual chapters in length, this editor sees the introduction as fulfilling a different role. Its function is to welcome the reader, briefly set the stage on which the authors have set their pieces, and remind all who enter that a book such as this is a beginning, not an end. Short-term effectiveness will be measured in terms of the enjoyment and intellectual stimulation experienced by readers; long-term success will be measured by studies that follow in its wake. When one is so fool-hardy as to tackle a subject that properly merits many lifetimes of work, one can only hope to encourage others to do the job better. This is a beginning that looks forward to those who will go further.

NOTES

1 I am indebted to Samuel C. Florman, of Kreisler, Borg, Florman Construction, Scarsdale, NY, for bringing this to my attention.

2 Heather MacDougall 'Public Health and the "Sanitary Idea" in Toronto, 1866–1890' in Wendy Mitchinson and Janice P. Dickin McGinnis eds *Essays in the History of Canadian Medicine* (Toronto 1988) 62–87. See also Heather MacDougall ' "Health is Wealth": The Development of Public Health Activity in Toronto 1834–1890' doctoral dissertation, University of Toronto, 1982.

3 John Norris 'Typhoid in the Rockies: Epidemiology in a Constrained Habitat, 1883–1939' in Charles G. Roland ed *Health, Disease and Medicine: Essays in Canadian History* (Toronto 1984) 276–95

4 John R. Sullivan and Norman R. Ball *Growing to Serve: A History of Victoria Hospital, London, Ontario* (London 1985)

5 Paul-André Linteau *The Promoter's City: Building the Industrial Town of Maisonneuve 1883–1918* trans Robert Chodos (Toronto 1985)

6 See, for example, Alan Artibise *Winnipeg: An Illustrated History* (Toronto 1977), Patricia E. Roy *Vancouver: An Illustrated History* (Toronto 1980), John H. Taylor *Ottawa: An Illustrated History* (Toronto 1986), and John C. Weaver *Hamilton: An Illustrated History* (Toronto 1982).

7 John C. Weaver and Peter DeLottinville 'The Conflagration and the City: Disaster and Progress in Nineteenth-Century British North America' *Histoire Sociale / Social History* 13 No. 26 (Nov 1980) 417–49; Fred A. Armstrong 'The Second Great Fire of Toronto, 19–20 April, 1904' *Ontario History* 70 No. 1 (March 1978) 3–38

8 E.V. Buchanan *London's Water Supply: A History* (London 1968)

9 André Bolduc et al *Québec: un siècle d'électricité* (Montreal 1979, 1984)

10 Clinton O. White *Power for a Province: A History of Saskatchewan Power* (Regina 1976)

PHYLLIS ROSE

Bridges

When, in September 1828, Lt.-Col. John By's Chaudière Bridge spanned the raging waters of the Ottawa River between Bytown (Ottawa) and Wright's Town (Hull), it created a short-lived but exciting and apt symbol of public works in Canada. This first substantial span across a major Canadian river stood as a pioneer in public works built to improve transportation and communications and encourage economic development. Conceived as a means of supplying personnel, equipment, and supplies for the building of the Rideau Canal, it provided the only fixed link between Upper and Lower Canada along their long water border.[1]

Design and construction responsibilities for the bridge were shared by Lt.-Col. By and his colleagues John MacTaggart and Thomas Burrowes. The canal was a magnificent piece of frontier engineering for public works, built under the most adverse and trying conditions. Upon its completion, By returned to England, where he was humiliated by unjust, trumped-up charges of cost overruns. Burrowes went on to design and build bridges in other parts of Canada. MacTaggart, his health broken by the overwork, cold, malnutrition, and disease brought on by working in the swamps of frontier Canada, returned to his native Scotland and died soon thereafter.

The Chaudière Bridge consisted of 7 spans: 3 wooden king-post structures of 18.3 m (60 ft) each, 2 stone arches at 14.2 m (57 ft), a wooden arch of 35.2 m (117 ft), and, one of the engineering wonders of the day, a 64.2-m (212-ft) wooden arch span. Greatly admired by contemporaries and captured by artists, the great arch soon paid the price of an underfunded structure at the edge of knowledge and experience. In December 1835 it began sagging and was restricted to pedestrian traffic; it fell into the river on 18 May 1836.[2] Building a replacement was entrusted to the eminent engineer and public works professional Samuel Keefer, and in 1843 a 73.4-m (242-ft) suspension bridge was opened. Even its name was symbolic: the Union Bridge; the provinces had united in 1841. It, too, was a marvel of its time. Much later it was outclassed and outdistanced by the larger suspension bridge that Keefer built over the Niagara River for a railway. Age and increasing load are the curses of bridges, and in 1876 a new and stronger, but less spectacular and more mundane-looking bridge replaced the graceful Union Bridge. Today many cross the Chaudière daily, but few see or understand the remaining foundation elements that link the present to adventurous early efforts in public bridge-building.

The succession of bridges at the Chaudière Falls underscores both the

The Union Suspension Bridge joining Ottawa and Hull, designed by Samuel Keefer and completed in 1843. The approach from the Quebec side consists of a long sloping arched bridge. Both the artist and the printer of this lithograph, as well as Keefer, were public works employees. (NA C-87903)

importance of bridges in Canadian history and the problem of the historian. Bridges run contrary to much of the imagery of Canadian history, which is seen, from fur trader and fishing boat to massive modern freighters, as passing along Canada's waterways and coasts. Bridges bypass or surmount bodies of water: water is an impediment, not an asset. Besides crossing water or deep dry land, bridges come in a stunning array of designs, sizes, materials, functions, and even modes of financing and ownership. How then best to categorize and introduce some of the bridges that have built and symbolize Canadian history? There is no single best way, but as materials are fundamental to the possibilities and help place bridges in a rough chronological framework, they will be the major basis for classification and organization in this chapter. But each material offers numerous choices, and some characteristics are common to different materials, for the bridges of Canada are as varied as its vast terrain and history.

TIMBER

In the design of a modern bridge, engineers must deal with numerous factors, such as dead load, live load, impact, deformation stresses, wind pressure, even temperature stresses and loads during construction. But hovering above all these is availability of three major items: money, materials, and skilled labour. During much of early Canadian history money was scarce, trees were overabundant, and the stonemason was much harder to find than the skilled axeman or carpenter. Travelling through North America in 1838, British engineer David Stevenson pointed out the engineering consequences of this state of affairs. Bridges, he wrote, 'are, in general, constructed entirely of wood. Although good building materials had been plentiful in every part of the country, the consumption of time and money attending the construction of stone bridges of so great extent must have proved too considerable to warrant their erec-

The Union Bridge from the Hull side, 1875, with extensive sawmilling establishments that had grown up at this site. (NA C-30315)

tion. Many of those recently built consist of a wooden superstructure resting on stone piers, and in general exhibit specimens of good carpentry and not infrequently good engineering.'[3]

Timber is the only natural building material that is strong when pulled or in tension. Shaping and joining timber became highly sophisticated before the ready availability of man-made tension materials such as cast and wrought iron, steel, aluminum, and plastics. A timber bridge is constructed of numerous pieces of wood, and the strength and rigidity that come from application of the basic truss element – the rigid triangle – appeared first in wood. Numerous truss forms developed in wood were later translated to iron.

The fundamentals of truss construction were laid down in the writings of 16th-century architect Andreas Palladio. By the late 18th and early 19th centuries, wooden truss bridges spanned American rivers, and they soon appeared in Canada. Until the expansion of railways, with their much heavier load, the same master craftsmen who built factories or mills also erected bridges, carrying on an oral tradition that paralleled formal book learning. In the absence of highway or building codes, their numerous truss designs were the product of experience, intuition, and a feeling for what was right rather than mathematical engineering analysis.

The king-post truss is essentially a vertical post set on a beam supporting

In 1889 a heavier truss structure was built around the Union Bridge, which was then taken down. In this way traffic could continue on a very busy crossing. The masonry arches, incorporated into the new bridge, are still in use. (NA PA-12396, NA PA-33944)

two inclined members. An essential element in timber structures such as barns, it also appeared in bridges in the 20-to-40-ft (6-to-12-m) range in many settled areas. But in contrast to the very handsome mid-19th-century stone buildings across Canada, timber bridges were often carelessly built, rickety structures, regularly washed away in spring floods.

In order to protect the wooden roadway, trusses, bracing, and chords from the alternating cycles of wet and dry, which promote rapid weathering and failure, wooden bridges were often covered with a conventional gable roof and side sheathing. The vertical board siding sometimes stopped short of the roof to admit light but keep out moisture. Famous covered or 'kissing' bridges, such as the Hartland Bridge in New Brunswick and the West Montrose Bridge in Ontario, are logical solutions to structural problems.

Quebec and New Brunswick have the largest stock of surviving covered bridges in Canada. Many of Quebec's were built early in the 20th century by the provincial Department of Colonization, which was responsible for opening new roads. The world's longest covered bridge, at 391 m (1,282 ft), spans the St John River at Hartland, New Brunswick. The original structure, consisting of seven Howe truss spans on cedar cribwork abutments, was built 1898-9 by the Hartland Bridge Co. as a tollway, five cents per person, ten cents per team.[4] The New Brunswick government took it over in 1904 and eliminated tolls.

One of the greatest threats to covered bridges is users' impatience, brought on in heavily travelled areas by their single-lane width. When congestion became a problem on the Hartland, a new concrete structure, the Hugh John Fleming Bridge, was built a couple of miles away. But the covered bridge and the salmon pools below should remain as important tourist attractions for many years to come.

On the transcontinental railway, the numerous wooden trestles constructed in the difficult terrain north of Lake Superior and through the mountains of British Columbia represented an ingenious, economical solution to the challenge of building in rugged environments. Timber trestles were quick and relatively simple to erect, often with local materials, and the design was so straightforward that trestles could be built by unskilled labourers. Low cost and speedy construction were important for both the cash-starved Canadian Pacific Railway (CPR) and the fulfilling of Sir John A. Macdonald's promise to British Columbia. Some very large timber trestles, such as that which carried the CPR over Mountain Creek near Glacier, captured the world's imagination. Designed by W.A. Doans and completed in 1885, its 2 million board feet of lumber made it, at a height of 45.73 m (150 ft) and a length of 326.7 m (1,070 ft), one of the longest wooden trestles in the world.

Covered or not, wooden bridges were still subject to rapid deterioration. When time and money permitted, timber bridges were rebuilt in iron and, later, steel. A surprising revival of timber bridges began in 1930 and continued for about 20 years. Creosote effectively protected timber against decay.[5] Between 1930 and 1950, New Brunswick, with a long tradition of wooden bridges, produced many timber trusses. The highway department had many skilled carpenters on its payroll; there was also a shortage of structural steel during and immediately after the Second World War.[6]

Timber bridges need not be short-lived, and many are still in use; winter road salt, so corrosive to concrete and steel bridges, preserves wood. One of

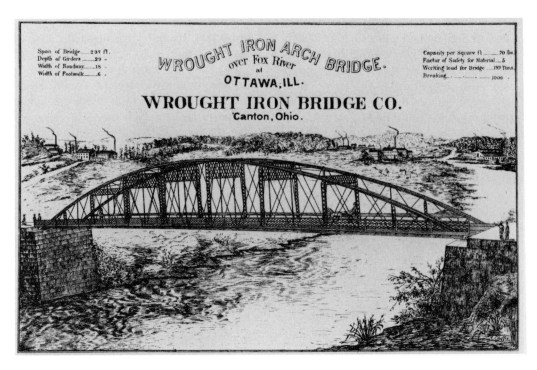

The Wrought Iron Bridge Co. advertised ready-to-assemble bridges in its catalogues. The company supplied the Blackfriars Bridge in London, Ontario, now a local landmark. (NA Barnett Collection, C-35566)

the most notable survivors is the Sioux Narrows Bridge, the largest timber span highway bridge in North America. Located on Highway 71, near Kenora, Ontario, it was built in the 1930s. When wood specialists examined it for decay half a century later, only five pieces of wood (used for overhead framing) in several thousand were recommended for replacement.[7]

IRON

Nineteenth-century engineering relied increasingly on iron for construction. Iron had been used in Greek temples, Roman bridges, Byzantine churches, and Gothic cathedrals but, on account of cost and scarcity, only sparingly for clamps and reinforcement rods. New technology lowered the cost of iron, and

the first iron bridge was erected at Coalbrookdale, England, in 1779. It is still standing.

Bridge engineers soon discovered that iron components strengthened a wooden bridge and speeded assembly. The next step brought bridges made entirely of iron trusses. Of all the bridge building materials – stone, wood, iron, steel, and concrete – iron was used for the shortest time and is the only one no longer used structurally. Canada's age of stuctural iron, transitional between wood and steel, began around 1850 and ended about 1890, when most foundries could no longer handle the increased casting lengths required.

Iron was particularly suitable for railway bridges. Standardized, prefabricated iron components could be shipped by rail from forge or foundry to erection site

Suspension bridge over the Niagara Gorge, designed to carry trains on one level and carriages and pedestrians on the other; first crossed by a locomotive on 8 March 1855 (Private collection)

and readily assembled by a moderately skilled work crew. Iron truss bridges needed neither roofs nor walls and were fire-resistant, an important consideration with steam locomotives belching clouds of smoke and burning cinders. Iron could be fashioned into light and ornamental bridges, with pleasing architectural features. Cast iron was used for the earliest iron bridges. Its brittleness and lack of resilience, however, made it suitable only for certain bridge components. By mid-century, wrought iron, with its high tensile strength, was the standard building material. The iron-working industry's explosive growth and technical prowess soon made wood-

en bridge construction an outdated, rural practice, often relegated to low-cost, temporary structures. Wrought iron was used until it was displaced by steel.

Iron also displaced rope in suspension bridges, beginning in Britain soon after 1800. Bytown's Union Bridge (1843) was Canada's first of this type. Several others were built in the 1850s, some singularly short-lived. The Montmorency Falls Suspension Bridge (1853–6), near Quebec City, designed by Samuel Keefer but poorly built by the contractor, collapsed a week after opening. At Grand Falls, New Brunswick, Edward W. Serrell had better luck in 1859, with a replacement of a bridge that had lasted only three months. He also designed the first suspension bridge at the Reversing Falls in Saint John, as well as the earlier Lewiston and Queenston Bridge, in Ontario.

The Niagara Gorge, site of the famous falls, has seen a variety of spectacular bridges. In the exhibit catalogue *Spanning Niagara: The International Bridges 1848–1962*, Ralph Greenhill speaks of 'the spanning of Niagara' as 'a story of international cooperation and a proud chapter in the history of engineering.'[8] The first suspension bridge there began in 1848, when engineer-builder Charles Ellet jr offered a five-dollar reward to any boy who could fly a kite across the gorge. The kite string was the first of a succession of heavier cords and cables pulled across the gorge. Ellet even pulled himself over in a basket to stir up interest in his project.

John A. Roebling's Niagara Suspension Bridge, built for the Great Western Railway of Canada, is perhaps one of the most famous of the Niagara bridges: graceful and stunningly beautiful, it was also an engineering landmark. The crucial problem was how to support a moving train. Roebling's solution created the world's first wire cable suspension bridge for railways and some essential analysis about safety in all suspension bridges.

Roebling had long advocated stiffening of bridge roadbeds and was worried about frequent high winds in the Niagara Gorge. He adopted a system of trusses and inclined stays. The single 251.46-m (825-ft) span was supported by four cables 25.4 cm (10 in) in diameter, draped over masonry towers 18.28 m (60 ft) high. The unique arrangement of the cables was designed to carry six times their working load. Two were attached to the lower deck, and two to the upper deck. The two levels on the bridge – the 7.33-m-wide (24 ft) upper deck, for a single railway track, and the 4.57-m-

wide (15 ft) lower deck, for carriages and pedestrians – were in turn joined by an innovative system of stiffening trusses, fully 5.49 m (18 ft) deep, which occupied the entire depth between the two decks. The high cost of iron forced Roebling to use traditional timber trusses in what was then a very modern piece of engineering design. In March 1855 the first fully loaded train crossed the Niagara Suspension Bridge. When Mark Twain crossed in 1869 he wrote, 'You drive over the Suspension Bridge and divide your misery between the chances of smashing down 200 feet into the river below and the chances of having the railway train overhead smashing down onto you. Either possibility is discomforting taken by itself but mixed together they amount in the aggregate to positive unhappiness.'[9]

The bridge proved its mettle by carrying heavier and heavier trains, until 1897, when it was taken out of service after consistently carrying three times its supposed capacity.

When the Canada Southern Railway crossed the gorge in 1883, it did so with a cantilever with a 143.26-m (470-ft) central span. It, too, earned a place in engineering history, when it was erected in the short time of eight months.

Other major rivers generated impressive series of bridges. The St Lawrence's started with the well-known Victoria Bridge. The Grand Trunk Railway already had a track from the south shore to Montreal's winter port at Portland, Maine. In the absence of a bridge, however, passengers and freight had to transfer to ferries to cross the river. In addition to facing hazards created by the breadth and roughness of the St Lawrence at Montreal, any bridge there had to overcome three main problems. It needed broad spans to accommodate timber rafts, height to rise above masts of large sailing ships, and piers and abutments to withstand extraordinary ice loads during spring thaws.

Planned in 1853, built 1854–9, and officially opened in 1860 by the Prince of Wales, the Victoria Bridge was notable for its novel form of construction as well as its immense size. *Harper's Weekly* called it 'one of the noblest works of engineering in the world and in its way perfectly unique.'[10] The enclosed tubular bridge, composed of prefabricated wrought-iron plates from England and riveted on site, ascended gradually from either shore to a huge, 100.59-m (330-ft) centre span 18.29 m (60 ft) above the water. Massive stone piers, which flared out on the upstream side to force ice to ride up and break of its own weight, supported the central span, and 12 more on either side, to give the bridge a total of 25 spans, an aggregate length of 1,870 m (6,138 ft), and a weight of 8,250 tons.

The tubular Victoria Bridge was a structural success but a traveller's nightmare. Ventilation was terrible, even when portions of the closed top of the tube were removed. Unsatisfactory as it was, one could no longer envision life without it, and so any modification or additions had to be done with little or no disruption of traffic. A more conventional steel, open Pratt truss, wide enough for a double track, was built around the tube in 1897. The tube itself was then dismantled, and roadways were added.

During the second half of the 19th century, railway construction advanced with rapidly increasing intensity, with two projects – the Intercolonial and the Canadian Pacific – being completed to fulfil Confederation agreements. In 1863 the Canadian government appointed Sandford Fleming, Canada's foremost railway surveyor and construction engineer, chief surveyor of the proposed Intercolonial Railway, from Quebec City to Halifax and Saint John. The celebrated 'battle of the bridges' was the most

Suspension bridge in Grand Falls, New Brunswick, built 1860 for the light traffic of the day: 'Walk Your Horses and Save a Fine of $20' (NA C-132207)

dramatic of the difficulties that complicated Fleming's work. His bridge specifications called for masonry abutments and piers with iron superstructures, but the railway commissioners wanted timber structures, more traditional for initial construction in Canada. Fleming maintained that iron and stone removed the risk of fire and would be cheaper in the long run because, unlike timber, they were permanent. Nerve, willingness to risk being fired, persistence, and connections, plus the fortuitous destruction by fire of some existing wooden bridges, allowed Fleming to prevail. Eight years later he became chief engineer for the Canadian Pacific Railway.

On account of both cost and their general purpose of promoting the public good, most bridges open to public traffic are built by or on behalf of various levels of government; they are public works. There are exceptions, built with private capital to serve the general public. Some, such as the first bridge built in Saint John, are little known, while others, such as the Lions Gate Bridge in Vancouver, are known internationally.

Two private bridges were erected in

Public works structures such as these bridges over the famous Reversing Falls at Saint John, New Brunswick, often adorned postcards used for daily communications. (NA C-132206)

Winnipeg in the 1880s by a Mr Brydges of the Hudson's Bay Company. Winnipeg is cut by two rivers, the Red and the Assiniboine. Its population rose from 241 in 1871 to 7,985 in 1881 and 20,238 in 1886. Such growth demanded an increase in public services, most acutely for bridges. Passage across river ice was easy in winter, and in summer ferries carried residents and freight. During freeze-up and thaw, crossings could be difficult and dangerous. Citizens wanted better service, and the Hudson's Bay Company wanted its property to remain the focus of routes coming into the rapidly growing city from the south and east.

By 1881 the Hudson's Bay Company had erected an iron swing bridge across the Assiniboine and was collecting tolls on a very profitable investment. When the growing population of Fort Rouge, south of the river, began lobbying for both annexation to Winnipeg and free bridges, the city, also in favour of annexation, bought the Assiniboine Bridge for

$45,000. The Hudson's Bay Company built a similar bridge across the Red, which collapsed during construction and even when completed never generated good toll revenues. Twenty years later St Boniface bought it, ending the era of private bridges in Winnipeg. As one historian has written, 'The bridges probably did more to benefit landowners with property in St Boniface and Fort Rouge than the Hudson's Bay Company. Their holdings were given appreciably better access to the city as a result. Regional road access was also improved. The HBC and its bridge company therefore made a significant contribution to the city's infrastructure.'[11]

Most growing Canadian cities used public funds to put up bridges, and many, from about the 1860s until the 1880s, were prefabricated wrought-iron structures made by specialized US manufacturers. Handsome trade catalogues were often accompanied by testimonials and an order form on which the company would base its price. These bridges are an important part of Canadian history, but very few remain, and their numbers are dwindling. One was made for Paris, Ontario, by the Wrought Iron Bridge Co. of Canton, Ohio, in 1877. Between drafting of this chapter and its revision, that 110-year-old bridge was demolished. Not far away, in London, another of the same company's bridges – the Blackfriar's Bridge over the Thames – has had a happier history. Now restored, and strengthened to carry a heavier load, it is an important visual asset and a proud part of the city's self-image and stock of tangible links with the past.

The last girder on the CPR viaduct near Lethbridge, Alberta, being lowered into place, 22 June 1909 (GAC NC-2-306)

STEEL

The 19th century saw dramatic change in both bridge design and materials, and before it ended steel would oust wrought iron from bridge building. Structural steel, with a safe working strength 20 per cent greater than that of wrought iron, came into general use about 1890, and in less than five years wrought-iron shapes were no longer rolled. This change in materials coincided with and ushered in a transformation in Canadian railways.

As the 1890s approached, fire hazards and maintenance problems forced the CPR, and others, to consider replacing timber bridges. To speed up construction and lessen interest charges, the CPR had built some 600 long, high timber trestles, many with timber pile or crib substructures. A 50-km (30-mi) section of the Fraser Canyon contained 100. Beginning about 1883, costs fell when many of the enormous wood trestles were partially prefabricated: the design was standardized and the timber stockpiled, numbered, and precut for shipment and rapid assembly.[12] Even though building costs were being reduced, timber still decayed and the increasing

weight and speed of trains required bridges of great rigidity and carrying capacity. Steel was the answer, and soon steel bridges dominated river crossings and railway viaducts.

Further railway developments introduced heights and spans far beyond anything previously attempted in Canada. One spectacular example, the Lethbridge Viaduct, carried CPR trains for over 1.61 km (1 mi) at heights up to 96 m (315 ft) above the river valley. Steel's great strength allowed more daring designs and encouraged adoption of a new type of bridge, the cantilever truss, used over the Firth of Forth and at Quebec. The bridge is built by extending the superstructure outward to form a pair of piers toward midpoint; the outstretched arms of the cantilever are then linked by a suspended truss of conventional design. Prototypes may be found in a variety of older wooden bridges, including some built by the natives of the west coast.[13]

The transition from suspension to cantilever is well illustrated at the famous Reversing Falls in Saint John. The depth of the river bed in the swift currents of the narrows, plus the fluctuating river height emanating from the highest tides

Lethbridge Viaduct, over 1.6 km (1 mi) long and 96 m (315 ft) tall (GAC N-2-259)

in the world in the Bay of Fundy, pre-cluded building piers in the river. An 1852 suspension bridge spanned the gap but could not carry rail traffic. Conse-quently rail freight and passengers had to be ferried to another train. In 1884 a 248-m (813-ft) cantilever span allowed through rail traffic.[14] In due course, age and the transition from horse to automo-bile required replacement of the suspen-sion bridge with a new cantilever bridge, completed in 1914. In the 1920s, heavier rail traffic and loads led to the replace-ment of the 1884 cantilever with yet another, heavier railway bridge, also a cantilever. All three cantilevers were built by the Dominion Bridge Co.

In some cases corporate rivalry joined increasing traffic as a reason for bridge building. The Grand Trunk crossed the St Lawrence on the Victoria Bridge, but the CPR, unable to lease rights on the

bridge, built its own. The resulting La-chine Bridge, a cantilever, was opened in 1886. One section of the bridge passed over the Mohawk reservation at Caugh-nawaga. The residents, fascinated by the project, kept climbing about the girders and asking the foremen for work. When some were given jobs, it started a tradi-tion: the confident and surefooted Mo-hawk have become well known as high steel men throughout North America.

Even greater rail traffic across the St Lawrence and the structural possibilities of steel led to the opening on 22 August 1919 of the Quebec Bridge. Its 548.6-m (1,800-ft) centre span made it the longest cantilever in the world, but it was built at very great cost. Faulty design calcula-tions and a poor management structure led to the collapse in 1907 of the first attempt, with the death of 75 workmen, many of them Caughnawaga Indians.

For the second attempt, Dominion Bridge and Canadian Bridge pooled resources and produced a heavier and stronger bridge with a different method of construction and an international design team paying particular attention to calculations. Even so, as the centre span was being hoisted into position, a faulty jack failed, and the 5,000-ton span fell into the river, killing 11. By 1917, the Quebec Bridge was at last completed. A longer cantilever truss has never been built. The Pierre Laporte Suspension Bridge now stands next to the Quebec Bridge.

BUILDERS

The history of Canadian bridges merits exploration, be it by material, by design type, by province, by municipality, or by use. It might be looked at in terms of bridge companies, as in a recent history of Dominion Bridge,[15] or through the careers of such giants as Samuel Keefer, Collingwood Schreiber, Phelps Johnson, and P.L. Pratley.

Pratley worked first as a junior engineer on the second Quebec Bridge, later in partnership with C.N. Monsarrat before establishing his own consulting practice. The Jacques Cartier Bridge in Montreal was one of Pratley's early jobs. A second highway bridge to supplement the upgraded Victoria Bridge was needed but delayed by intergovernmental jurisdictional disputes. In 1921 commissioners of the Port of Montreal gained control of the project and chose Monsarrat and Pratley to select a site and prepare a design. The Jacques Cartier cantilever bridge, opened in 1929, is a visual treat, frequently used as a symbol of Montreal and its province. Late in the Depression, Monsarrat and Pratley designed another great symbol: the Lions Gate Bridge, across the First Narrows of Burrard Inlet, Vancouver. The Guinness

brewing interests built it to connect their luxury subdivisions with the city. Additional investment income was generated through tolls, and in 1955 the bridge was sold to the province for $6 million. Tolls were removed in 1963.

The lift bridge at the entrance to Hamilton harbour had long delayed road traffic between Toronto and the Niagara Peninsula. Pratley was commissioned to design a parallel, supplementary fixed bridge, high enough to clear shipping below. Built in 1957, the Burlington Skyway, over 6.44 km (4 mi) long, including approaches, consists of 75 spans, with a cantilever truss directly over the water. Heavy increases in road traffic necessitated building of another, parallel bridge in the mid-1980s.

Pratley was also involved in a number of Canada's other great bridges, including the Angus L. Macdonald suspension bridge connecting Halifax to Dartmouth; the Ambassador Bridge at Windsor, Ontario; and the Ivy Lea Bridge at the Thousand Islands. He was doing early design work on Montreal's Champlain Bridge when he died in 1958. The Champlain Bridge opened in June 1962 as a toll bridge providing six much-needed lanes between Montreal and the South Shore by way of Nun's Island. The section over the St Lawrence is cantilevered; the rest is a series of pre-stressed concrete spans, supported on pillars. Much appreciated by daily users, it attracted considerable notice in technical journals as having the longest pre-stressed concrete spans in North America.

CONCRETE

P.L. Pratley's career started on the world's longest steel cantilever, a bridge used by both railways and automobiles. His last job is more famous for its pioneering work in the use of pre-stressed concrete to meet the needs of automobile traffic. Pratley's career captures and illustrates an important development in 20th-century bridge building: the increasing importance of concrete. Just as the demands of railways had called for steel bridges, the growing need for high-volume, direct, convenient routes for cars, trucks, and busses meant spanning wide, previously unbridged bodies of water and valleys. There concrete played an important role.

Concrete – an ancient concoction of cement, water, and sand and gravel – hardens to become artificial stone. Like natural stone, it is strong only in compression and suited only for massive piers and arches. Its use in bridge construction started slowly in Canada. For example, specifications for the Alexandra Bridge, linking Ottawa and Hull in 1898, allowed concrete no closer to the surface than 6.1 m (20 ft).[16] Toward the end of the century, it was discovered that this man-made masonry might be given strength in tension by incorporating rods of iron or steel. 'Reinforced' concrete was especially suited for highway bridges, and in 1906 a reinforced concrete arch highway bridge was built at Massey, in northern Ontario, and another, Hurdman's Bridge, in Ottawa. Since then, innumerable such structures, in the form of simple beams or girders, viaducts, arches, and cantilever or continuous-span bridges, have been built.

Public works engineers very properly proceeded with caution. On the Ontario provincial highway system, only two reinforced concrete bridges had been built to the end of 1923. In 1924, however, the province built 10 such bridges of moderate size. In Manitoba, short-span bridges – up to 9.1 m (30 ft) – were built before 1915. Lack of a durable, alkali-resistant cement delayed concrete's arrival in Saskatchewan; before the 1920s, practically all important brid-

Middle Road Bridge, Etobicoke, Ontario, 1910, designed by Frank Barber, a pioneer in the use of reinforced concrete in Canada (Private collection)

ges were built in steel.

Towns and rural municipalities across Canada experimented and built many reinforced concrete bridges. The scarcity and high cost of steel during the First World War encouraged longer and longer bridges of reinforced concrete. But railways continued to be cautious except for the radial railway systems expanding around larger cities. Reinforced concrete bridges were ideal for this purpose.

One of the most influential designers to work with reinforced concrete was Frank Barber, engineer for York County, Ontario. In addition to his municipal responsibilities, Barber formed a partnership in 1908 with his civil-engineering classmate, C.R. Young. The practice with Young, later dean of applied science and engineering at the University of Toronto, lasted only three years, but Barber continued the practice on his own. He designed and supervised construction of more than 500 bridges throughout southern Ontario, including 16 of the first 20 reinforced concrete truss bridges in Canada.

In 1909, Barber and Young designed the second structure of this type built in North America – the first in Canada – the Middle Road Bridge, which crossed

Building the falsework and setting reinforcing rods in place for the concrete deck of the
Broadway Bridge, Saskatoon, a relief project during the Depression (CPWA Sask Chapter)

the Etobicoke Creek near Lake Ontario.
The seven-panelled parabolic bowstring
truss featured massive arched compression chords, slim vertical tension members, and a system of counterbraces
acting alternatively in compression and
tension under a moving load. Containing 13 tons of reinforcing steel and
weighing almost 200 tons, the bridge
spanned 24.4 m (80 ft). Poured in one
week and cured for another, the bridge
matured faultlessly. To avoid poor bonding between concrete pours on successive days, the contractor laid bags of
cracked ice on the last pour each night.
The low temperature retarded setting,
and the next morning the concrete
would be as plastic as on the preceding
day. On-site testing was carried out at
the official opening with a moving load
of two tons and a herd of accommodating cattle.

Widely described in technical journals
of the period, the bridge has aged re-
markably well, although it is no longer
used for road traffic.[17] After its success,
use of reinforced concrete for bowstring
or tied arch bridges spread quickly. Adaptable for almost any location, in single
or multiple spans, it was widely used
until the Second World War, especially
on county roads.

Barber was also responsible for the
Ashburnham Bridge over the Otonabee
River at Peterborough. At 71.3 m (234 ft),
this magnificent reinforced concrete
bridge was for many years the longest
concrete arch span in Canada. It is still
used every day, and its pleasing shape
and tasteful decorative elements have
made it a treasured part of Peterborough's working historical heritage. By
1920, when it was completed, reinforced
concrete was completely acceptable for

county roads. The *Ontario Government Standard for County Roads* even specified that 'All bridges and culverts are to be of a permanent type. Steel trusses on concrete substructures of reinforced concrete throughout are the materials favoured.'[18] Concrete had not displaced steel for bridge construction, but engineers generally agreed that each had its place. Reinforced concrete was preferred for spans up to 15.2 m (50 ft) – with sufficient rise, up to 38.1 m (125 ft).

Reinforced concrete bridges were built all across Canada. In Saskatoon, the ten open-spandrel arch spans of the University Bridge over the South Saskatchewan, completed in 1916, made up the most extensive piece of concrete construction in Canada to that time.[19] In 1931, as the Depression deepened, Saskatoon asked for federal relief project money to construct a concrete arch bridge across the South Saskatchewan to connect the main business district with a residential area. C.J. Mackenzie, dean of engineering at the University of Saskatchewan and later president of the National Research Council, rejected steel in favour of a more labour-intensive five-arch span of reinforced concrete.

Unemployed workers were recruited through the relief office and set to work immediately in order to meet the funding proviso of completion within a year. Construction began in January 1932, and even though temperatures fell as low as minus 40 degrees up to 450 men worked round the clock in three shifts. The river's flood stage in June made it impossible to construct much of the falsework in the river until the waters receded. By October temperatures hovered about freezing again. Yet the Broadway Bridge opened in November, eleven months after construction began. It has become synonymous with Saskatoon and with strength in the face of adversity. In 1985, the Canadian Society for Civil Engineer-

ing recognized it as a heritage site.

Another Depression-era concrete bridge was built over the North Saskatchewan about 50 km (30 mi) northwest of Saskatoon. The Borden Bridge, designed by C.J. Mackenzie with research by his students and built 1935-6, is a concrete bowstring arch, similar to the Barber and Young plan for their Middle Road Bridge. Although most of its spans were short, the 64.9-m (213-ft) centre span was one of the world's longest concrete bowstring arch bridges on floating foundations.[20]

Between the world wars, bridge designers focused on development of pre-stressed concrete. Pre-stressing involves creating preliminary compressive stresses in the concrete to avoid cracking under conditions of the working load. The pre-stress is usually applied by stretching steel wires, bars, or cables. The reinforcing steel is said to be pre-tensioned if it is stretched before the concrete is set, post-tensioned if after the concrete has hardened. Pre-stressing permits graceful and slender yet strong bridges, with savings in time and material.

Pre-stressed concrete was developed in Europe, where post-tensioned structures predominated. North Americans' well-established skills in mass production led to rapid development of pre-tensioning for a variety of structures.[21] Bridges of pre-stressed concrete did not arrive in Canada until the 1950s. Building authorities were reluctant to accept this new form of construction without codes for guidance, and many consulting engineers declined to design with a material about which they knew little, and the contractors possibly less. British Columbia was the first province to test the new material. Results of its tests led to construction in 1952 of the first Canadian pre-stressed concrete bridge, over Mosquito Creek in North Vancouver.

The Burlington Skyway Bridge, completed 1958, allowed uninterrupted four-lane traffic on the Queen Elizabeth Way. Raising of the lift bridge to allow freighters into the busy Hamilton harbour had created massive traffic jams. (NA PA-138903)

Alberta followed a year later with the Ross Creek Bridge at Medicine Hat. The number of companies interested in applying pre-stressed concrete began to grow rapidly. So did the number of pre-stressed concrete bridges in all provinces.

NEW DIRECTIONS

In 1945 joy generated by the end of the war mingled with sadness and sense of loss for many who would not return.[22] Profound confidence in Canadian industry and engineering had been generated by Canada's role in meeting Allied needs for crucial materials such as synthetic rubber and aluminum, as well as a wide range of equipment, including ships and planes. Aluminum was destined to be important in post-war Canada, and nothing better reflects the confidence in it than the opening in 1951 of the world's first aluminum bridge.

Aluminum's lightness and strength in aircraft during the war had encouraged the search for other applications. Bridge builders also pursue lightness and strength, and so when a bridge across the Saguenay River was needed in the aluminum centre of Arvida, now part of Jonquière, Quebec, the world's first large aluminum bridge was erected. Its span of 154 m (504 ft) has never been surpassed in aluminum.[23] The bridge has withstood heavy traffic and severe winters, never needs painting, and weighs only 190 tons, compared with the

The Hugh John Fleming Bridge, St John River, New Brunswick, completed 1960 as part of the Trans-Canada Highway (Canada Cement Lafarge Ltd)

430 it would have weighed in steel. It did not, however, start a rush toward aluminum bridges. Aluminum is considerably more expensive by weight than steel, and improved metallurgy and design techniques later made steel bridges much lighter and hence less costly, so much so that aluminum could not compete.

The orthotropic deck bridge provided one of the most significant advances in the pursuit of lightness, which in turn meant lower material costs and greater load-carrying capability. In such a structure, the deck, instead of simply carrying traffic, stiffens and supports the bridge.

Germany pioneered in the use of orthotropic decks as a means of saving material during the massive rebuilding or replacement of the nearly 8,500 bridges bombed during the war.[24] In Canada, the building of the Trans-Canada highway prompted construction of numerous bridges which merit historical study. Where the highway would cross the Fraser River at Port Mann, British Columbia, navigation needs dictated a minumum clearance of 44 m (145 ft) above the main channel of the Fraser, and highway specifications called for a maximum approach gradient of 3 per cent on land. As the vice-president of the consulting engineering firm in charge of design explained: 'To meet the fixed river navigation requirements and keep the length of approaches to a minimum, it was important economically to select a structural type that would provide a minimum of depth between the roadway and the bottom of the main girders. Each additional foot of depth required an additional 30 ft. of approach spans for the stipulated gradient on the north side.'[25] The orthotropic deck on a tied-arch bridge offered this combination. The deck's dual function reduced weight by about 25 per cent and lowered costs. The bridge was functional, cost-effective, and aesthetically pleasing. Its 366-m (1,200-ft) span made it 'the world's longest, high level, stiffened tied arch bridge; ... also the longest in the world with an orthotropic deck, and the first major North American bridge with an orthotropic plate deck.'[26]

In Halifax, another benchmark was created in response to increasing traffic congestion both on land and on the Angus L. Macdonald Bridge which had opened across the Bedford Basin between Dartmouth and Halifax in 1954. A site 2.4 km (1.5 mi) further inland offered ideal conditions for a suspension bridge to 'relieve the growing congestion on the existing harbor crossing and form part of a future ring road system around Halifax and Dartmouth.'[27] Once again there was need to consider both navigation needs – 50 m (165 ft) at mid-span – and maximum allowable grade, this time 4 per cent. The resulting bridge, the A. Murray MacKay, featured the first North American use of an orthotropic steel deck on a suspension bridge. In Quebec City, the radical differences in design and material between the Quebec Bridge, a cantilevered truss structure, and its lighter companion, the Pierre Laporte Suspension Bridge, are immediately evident. It takes a slightly more observant eye to see that A. Murray MacKay Bridge appears much more graceful than the Angus L. Macdonald. The orthotropic bridge which opened in 1970 is approximately 50 per cent lighter than the bridge built only 16 years earlier.

The A. Murray MacKay is a historic structure in terms of wind tunnel testing. Suspension bridges are exceedingly complicated, and as the bridge's engineer, Roger Dorton, wrote: 'No rigorous mathematical theory exists to explain all aspects of [their] aerodynamic behaviour.'[28] Orthotropic bridges use less steel but place a premium on quality of construction; the deck, a large, relatively thin plate, must be designed and fabricated so as not to buckle from compression forces. Particularly in the harsh Canadian climate, fabrication is far easier under shelter on the ground; and so large sections of the deck were to be made on the ground and then hoisted into position. These large, light, relatively thin sections are comparable to a sail in their response to wind, and engineers were concerned about hoisting and the several months between initial placement and final fastening and tightening to form a stable system. They needed good information on how the components and the system would react.

Previously, wind-tunnel testing of bridge models had been conducted in aeronautical-type wind tunnels, which provide a smooth flow of air. But close to the earth's surface, wind flow is turbulent, and this condition could now be duplicated at the recently opened Boundary Layer Wind Tunnel Laboratory at the University of Western Ontario. It was a radical change in bridge testing. It had been customary to test models only of portions of a bridge, and in smooth flow, but Dr Alan Davenport and his colleagues at Western tested a model of the entire bridge, in the much more realistic conditions of turbulent flow. They also tested models representing various stages in construction, rather than simply the finished product, as had

One of the boundary layer wind tunnel models crucial in the design of the A. Murray MacKay Bridge, Halifax (Boundary Layer Wind Tunnel Laboratory, Faculty of Engineering Science, University of Western Ontario)

been the custom. They discovered that turbulent-flow testing of complete models differed significantly from sectional testing in smooth flow, which could misrepresent performance and lead to incorrect or faulty design decisions which would not be made with turbulent-flow testing of full models. This testing was regarded as so exciting, and so representative of the best of Canadian engineering and public works, that blown-up photos of the wind tunnel models were exhibited in Montreal at Expo '67.[29] Such a radical approach to design takes time to be integrated into practice, and its full significance has yet to be appreciated.

The continuing leadership exercised by public works bridges was again recognized in late 1987, when the Award of Excellence in the Canadian Consulting Engineering Awards went to the Vancouver firm CBA-Buckland and Taylor, consulting engineers to the BC Ministry of Transportation and Highways for the Alex Fraser Bridge. It is a cable-stayed suspension bridge of extraordinary beauty and grace. Like the Lions Gate or the Quebec Bridge, it is undoubtedly destined to become an internationally recognized symbol of Canada. Crossing the Fraser River, the same river where CBA-Buckland had introduced large orthotropic deck structures to North Am-

The Alex Fraser Bridge, Annacis Narrows, British Columbia. This award-winning and breathtakingly beautiful cable-stayed bridge has a designed capacity of 6 lanes of highway traffic, or 4 lanes plus 2 tracks for LightRail Transit. At 465 m (1,525 ft), its main span is the longest of its type in the world. (Buckland and Taylor Ltd)

erica, its 465-m (1,525-ft) main deck span is the longest of its type in the world. Important in terms of a number of firsts, it also demonstrates the increasing sophistication of public works projects and the central role played by computer design and monitoring – as well as the benefits: 20 per cent lower cost than earlier North American cable-stayed bridges of smaller spans.[30]

When the Granville Street Bridge opened in early 1954, it was the biggest civic project ever undertaken by Vancouver and the only eight-lane bridge in North America outside New York State. It was also a response to change. K. Vaughan-Birch, Vancouver's director of traffic, observed:

We are prone to forget how recent has been our progress. Probably bridge design illustrates more clearly than anything else how recently the traffic problem was born and how quickly it has grown. To emphasize this growth it might be noted that in the past ten years in Vancouver we have approximately doubled vehicle registration and trebled our vehicle gasoline consumption.

I believe I am correct in saying that it is little more than twenty-five or so years ago when bridge building was generally looked upon only as a structural problem and indeed in the light of the then existing traffic there was little occasion to consider any other aspect. Usually the bridge formed the continuation or link in a main roadway and that was that.

It was not until the number of motor vehicles had grown to the point where they began to tax the capacity of the main roads that new significance was given to bridge building. Today the aproaches to a bridge are equally as important from a traffic standpoint as the main structure.[31]

Vaughan-Birch's attitude was similar to that of the great bridge builders: they embraced change, in materials, designs, or calculations and in design and construction aids, such as wind tunnels and computers.

The stability of modern bridges may appear the antithesis of change; yet they are monuments to change. They are 'a measure of an ability to adapt to the present and anticipate the future.' Bridges stand as a tribute to the engineers who planned, analysed, and designed them and to the daring people who risked, and in some cases lost, their lives in the building. Bridges are also a measure of those who saw the need and then worked to create the climate of opinion in which they could be approved and built. These were the people who ushered them through the often labyrinthine channels and processes, from planning, bidding, and construction to opening and beyond. As one historian of engineering has noted: 'Canadians who are seeking new ways of broadening the understanding of Canadian culture, life and experience might profitably turn to public works in general and bridges in particular. From the humblest county or rural structure to the largest internationally known symbols of Canada, they represent responses to change and change is fundamental to both life and history.'[32]

NOTES

1 Douglas Richardson and Harold Kalman 'Building for Transportation in the Nineteenth Century' *Journal of Canadian Art History* 3 (fall 1976) 25
2 For detailed information on the Chaudière Bridge I would like to thank Rob-

ert Passfield, Canadian Parks Service, Ottawa.
3 David Stevenson *Sketch of Civil Engineering in North America* (London 1838) 224
4 Lyn Harrington and Richard Harrington *Covered Bridges of Central and Eastern Canada* (Toronto 1976) 18
5 David Plowden *Bridges – The Spans of North America* (New York 1974) 37
6 Ibid
7 'Ontario's "Other" Bridges: Built to Last!' *Engineering Dimensions* (March-April 1987) 32
8 Ralph Greenhill *Spanning Niagara – The International Bridges 1848–1962* exhibition catalogue, Buscaglia-Castellani Art Gallery of Niagara University (Niagara Falls, NY 1984) 19
9 Mark Twain 'A Day at Niagara' *Sketches Old and New* (New York 1875) 58
10 Quoted in Richardson and Kalman 'Building' 30
11 John Selwood 'Mr. Brydges' Bridges' *The Beaver* (summer 1981) 21
12 Richardson and Kalman 'Building' 34
13 Ibid 31
14 Doug Fetherling *Vision in Steel 1882–1982 / One Hundred Years of Growth, Dominion Bridge to AMCA International* privately printed by AMCA International (Montreal 1982) 37
15 Ibid
16 C.R. Young 'Engineering' in Royal Canadian Institute *Royal Canadian Institute Centennial Volume 1849–1949* (Toronto 1949) 55
17 David Cuming 'Lost and Found' *Bulletin of the Ontario Society for Industrial Archaeology* 2:2 (1985) 1
18 W.A. McLean 'Government Standard for County Roads' *Contract Record* 24 (Feb 1910) 42
19 C.R. Young 'Bridge Building' *Journal of the Engineering Institute of Canada* 19 (June 1937) 490
20 David Neufeld 'Dealing with an Industrial Monument: The Borden Bridge' *Material History Bulletin* 20 (fall 1984) 53

21 Mark Huggins 'The Beginnings of Pre-
stressed Concrete in Canada' *Prestressed
Concrete Institute Journal* (Nov-Dec
1979) 119

22 I would like to thank Dr Norman R. Ball,
chief of research, National Museum of
Science and Technology, for access to
several as yet unpublished papers by
him on post–Second World War bridge
engineering in Canada.

23 Fetherling *Vision in Steel* 115, 119

24 Plowden *Bridges* 290

25 George W. Lake 'The Port Mann Bridge'
Engineering Journal 46 (May 1964) 29

26 'The Port Mann Bridge' *B.C. Professional
Engineer* 34 (Nov 1963) 26

27 R.A. Dorton 'Design of the Narrows
Suspension Bridge, Halifax' *Engineering Journal* 51 (Dec 1968) 15–26

28 Horman *Engineering Journal* 50 (Dec 1968)
27

29 Based on interviews with Dr Alan Davenport, director, Boundary Layer
Wind Tunnel, School of Engineering,
University of Western Ontario, conducted by Dr Norman R. Ball,
1987–8

30 'Award of Excellence. Alex Fraser Bridge
– Delta B.C., CBA-Buckland and Taylor, Vancouver' *Canadian Consulting Engineer* (Sept-Oct 1987) 29

31 K. Vaughan-Birch 'The Traffic Aspect
of the New Granville Street Bridge'
B.C. Professional Engineer 25 (March
1954) 15

32 Norman R. Ball 'On Understanding
Bridges and Other Public Works' unpublished manuscript, 1

LARRY MC NALLY

Roads, Streets, and Highways

Few people realize the vital role that the construction and maintenance of roads have played throughout Canadian history, even when subservient to waterway or railway transportation. Roads emerged from the dark days of neglect in the late 19th century to dominance by the mid-20th century because of automobiles. The struggle to find appropriate road-building techniques was long and still continues. Just as important as technology was the development of administrative and financial systems for road construction and maintenance. Without the shift from local to provincial responsibility, modern highway systems would not exist in Canada.

Even the terminology presents difficulties. The designations 'roads' and 'highways' are often used interchangeably, and it is common to follow a street name with the word 'road.' For this chapter, however, we will generally consider all urban thoroughfares to be streets, connecting links between urban areas to be highways, and rural arteries to be roads.

EARLY ROAD CONSTRUCTION

Problems

Geography, distance, and climate have made transportation a continuing Canadian preoccupation. For many centuries, water was the only practical form of travel. Canada is well endowed with an extensive coastline and navigable waterways which encouraged water transport. In the Maritimes, numerous sailing vessels reduced the need for a substantial road network. The St Lawrence River and the Great Lakes formed a ready-made transportation route for central Canada. Access to the western Canadian interior was via Hudson Bay and its tributaries. In winter the frozen surfaces of rivers and lakes provide smooth surfaces for sleighing. Only in British Columbia did fast-flowing rivers make water transport difficult.

In spite of the water network, a variety of factors encouraged Canadians to build roads.[1] One was stretches of rapids too rough for water transport or land separating two major bodies of water. The portages of the voyageurs are well known. Examples of historic short-cuts are Yonge Street, between lakes Ontario and Simcoe, and the route between St Jean and Laprairie, Quebec, that linked the Richelieu and St Lawrence rivers. Roads have also been instruments of military policy. Commanders ordered the building of roads in Nova Scotia and Lower and Upper Canada to facilitate the movement of troops for defence.[2] Governments, particularly in the mid-19th century, also used roads to encourage settlement. The Talbot roads of Upper Canada in the 1810s and the colonization roads of the Province of Canada in the 1840s and 1850s were built for such a purpose.[3] Most roads in this period were built for communication, business, and travel.

Many problems faced early road-builders and administrators. Geography made road-building very difficult. Large parts of the country were composed of rock, hills, swamp, and muskeg. Even where terrain was relatively flat, thick forest cover made construction arduous. The climate, with extremes of heat and cold, plus wet springs and autumns, also retarded highway construction. The small population had few resources to overcome the forces of geography and climate. Money and manpower for road-building were limited. Lack of money limited use of professionals to direct road building and the availability of full-time road construction workers.

Road-builders used a variety of solutions to overcome these problems. Many early roads were built parallel to navigable waterways, along established trade routes, or between population centres. The roads from Quebec to Toronto and beyond were built along the St Lawrence and Great Lakes rather than cutting inland. In Quebec, the land survey system, which had narrow farms along rivers, further concentrated settlement.

Because of limited resources, early roads took advantage of the abundance of trees. Trees being felled to open a road were laid parallel and at right angles to the direction of travel, to form a firm surface over muddy depressions or streams. This 'corduroy' principle minimized the need for expensive building materials.[4] However, this type of road was uncomfortable to ride on. The comments of Anna Jamieson were undoubtedly echoed by many others in mid-19th century: 'The road was scarcely passable; there were no longer cheerful farms and clearings, but the dark pine forest

Canadian roads and highways, now world-famous for quality, first gained notoriety through bone-jarring corduroy roads such as this one, through a swamp in Orillia Township, Ontario, sketched in 1844 by Titus Ware. (MTLB T14377)

and the rank swamp, crossed by those terrific corduroy paths (my bones ache at the mere recollection), and deep holes and pools of rotted vegetable matter with water, black, bottomless, sloughs of despond!'[5]

To build roads, early governments conscripted all available men. Statute labour (corvée in Quebec) produced a local force for road-building several days each year.[6] However, this unskilled and unpaid work-force was problematic, especially in the later 19th century, when road-building became more complicated. As well, governments often required settlers with land grants to clear and maintain abutting roads.[7] Throughout the 19th century in Quebec, inhabitants were to keep their roads marked and cleared in winter.[8]

Two Attempted Solutions
By the 1830s, tolerable progress had been made, but much road-building remained to be done. A number of changes in the 1830s and 1840s portended improved road transport. One major factor was development of the plank road: long parallel wooden stringers or beams, with thick wooden planks nailed at right angles to the stringers.[9] Covered with a thin layer of sand, this type of road provided a smooth, fairly durable surface, easily and cheaply built with readily available natural resources.

The first plank road was built 1835–6 on a stretch of highway leading east from Toronto. It so impressed the commissioners of Yonge Street, who controlled the road north from Toronto, that in 1841 they decided to plank various portions of their road.[10] The commissioners had been following the road-construction method devised by John Macadam in Britain: a layer of stones covered by layers of tightly packed and increasingly small gravel. Though it created a strong and durable road surface, it was extremely expensive, since the gravel often had to be made from rock broken by hand. While true macadam roads were rare in Canada, many roads consisted of large stones covered by one or two layers of finer gravel. After 1840, though, plank roads became popular. Private toll road companies, as well as local governments, built and maintained plank roads. In Lower Canada, the first plank road was Chemin Chambly, between Longueuil and Chambly, built in 1841.[11] By 1852, various governments in Canada had built 192 mi (309 km) of plank road and private enterprise 250 mi (402 km). This Canadian innovation was also picked up by the Americans. Soon there were plank roads from Maine to Texas. New York State, for one, had over 2,000 mi (3,200 km) of plank roads by the 1850s.[12]

The popularity of plank roads was stimulated by the writings of Canadian engineers such as William Kingsford and Thomas Roy, describing the principles, construction methods, costs, and economic benefits of such roads. Roy, writing in 1841, figured that the initial cost and maintenance for 24 years of a plank road were twice that of a macadam road. Kingsford figured the cost of construction differently in 1852, showing substantial savings from plank roads. Differences lie largely with the length of maintenance time included. Macadam roads held up better than plank roads over the long run.[13]

Maintenance problems plagued plank roads. Heavily loaded wagons caused thin planks to flex, loosening the nails holding planks to stringers. Horse hooves and wagon wheels wore down the planks half an inch a year. Plank roads did not provide the salvation for overland transportation; Canadians abandoned them soon after the mid-19th century.

In 1841, Upper and Lower Canada were amalgamated into the Province of Canada. In order to improve internal communication, the British government made a £1.5-million ($6-million) loan to the province for public works. The lion's share went for reconstruction of the canal system between Lake Erie and Montreal, but the province planned to spend substantial sums on roads. The government hired professional engineers to build a road system that would link inland areas with navigable waterways, connect major cities, and open up new territories for settlement.[14] One of these engineers was Casimir Gzowski, an exiled Pole. Soon after arriving in Canada in 1841, Gzowski became superintendent of roads and waterways for the London District, Canada West.[15] He built a great variety of roads, including gravel, macadam, and plank, in southwestern Ontario. In the mid-1840s, he built rough colonization roads to Guelph and Owen Sound and others north of Lake Ontario to open up unsettled areas not directly connected to waterways.[16]

The statute creating the Department of Public Works made it responsible for 'provincial roads,' but failed to define this term. Because of this oversight, Public Works became responsible for most public roads in Canada. Originally, $1,286,148 was to be spent in building and upgrading roads between 1841 and 1846.[17] However, lack of central control over public works, especially canals, caused serious overspending, creating a financial crisis. After a detailed review, Public Works was revamped, its budget was slashed, and 'provincial roads' were more clearly defined. Further changes in 1850 allowed Public Works to sell roads to private companies or to local governments.[18] The more profitable roads, particularly near Quebec City and Montreal, were sold to private toll road companies, and other roads to local authorities. By 1853, Public Works claimed that it had sold almost all of its roads, but lack of maintenance by the new owners forced the department to repossess various roads and rebuild and resell them.[19]

At its inception, Public Works was a well-funded department using professional engineers to build a road system for Canada. Work got under way but lack of central administrative control and over-spending crippled expansion. Even substantial resources could not overcome the geographical, administrative, and financial problems of road-building.[20] A smaller Public Works tried to extricate itself from the bottomless morass of local and provincial roads.

Reaction to Failed Solutions

While horrific descriptions of 19th-century roads came from English gentlemen, urban dwellers, and coachmen, farmers, the major users, appeared satisfied with conditions. Land grant holders were to clear and maintain the local road fronting their land as well as being liable for statute labour on roads. Farmers often chose to clear and work their land rather than improve local roads, thus indicating that roads had lower priority.[21] Agricultural products, principally wheat, were transported primarily by sleigh in winter. Frozen rivers and snow trails largely overcame the ill effects of bad roads.[22] Local authorities were once again made responsible for roads in their jurisdiction but had few financial and technical resources. Their limited tax base left them seldom able to hire professional engineers and permanent road workers. Even counties found it difficult to maintain their roads: some spent between 10 and 20 per cent of their budget on roads, and a number were forced into deficit financing to pay off road debentures.[23]

Privately owned toll roads provided an important service, especially around major cities. These roads, which, by provincial law, had to be either macadamized or planked, became popular in the late 1830s. The Municipal Act, 1849, required only an agreement between the municipality or township and a company before a toll road could be built. Private companies purchased some of the roads constructed by Public Works. One recent article describes the Bytown and Nepean Road Co.'s 8-mi (12.9-km) route between Ottawa and Bell's Corners.[24] The road was profitable from its completion in 1853 until almost 1920, when it was purchased by Nepean Township. Its profitability ensured adequate maintenance. Only demands for free access and automobiles themselves

Main Street, Winnipeg, photographed by geologist Robert Bell in 1879. The wide streets found in many early western Canadian cities gave cart and wagon drivers room to manoeuvre among the many ruts. (NA R. Bell c-33881)

finally destroyed this toll road.[25]

Another major cause of the low status of roads was mid-century competition from a new form of transportation: railways. In the past, navigable waterways and roads had formed a complementary system, but the new mode of transportation completely upset this situation. By the later 19th century, railways monopolized the carrying of people, mail, and high-value freight because they connected major cities, as well as linking metropolises to hinterlands, and operated year round. This new transport quickly eclipsed a road system that had been evolving for several decades. Many groups, including engineers, government officials, businessmen, and the general public, believed that railways were the answer to Canada's transportation problems. In the competition for resources among the various modes of transport, railways quickly beat out both water and road. Therefore provinces, counties, and individuals invested in railways rather than in creating a better road network. For many roads, this led to years of neglect and little growth.

ERA OF CHANGE

After Confederation, the provinces quickly turned responsibility for roads over to local governments. For the next quarter-century, roads continued both undeveloped and unappreciated. However, industrialization, urbanization, and western expansion required improved local and national transportation. Roads were one answer.

Cities grew and changed functions in the late 19th century; some continued to be large commercial centres, while others industrialized. All demanded more of street transport. An early method of public transport was to combine horse-drawn omnibuses with elements of railway technology. The first Canadian horse-drawn streetcars riding on rails arrived in Toronto and Montreal in 1861.[26] This advance, however, damaged roads: horses' hooves chewed up the road surface between the rails; horsecars quickly wore down macadam, cedar blocks, and bricks; stone, though durable, was slippery when wet; and cedar blocks, though not slippery, did not last. Many combinations of pavements were tried, and this remained a problem, even after electrification of streetcar lines started in the 1890s. Asphalt and concrete paving would soon solve the problem.[27]

As cities industrialized, freighting (teaming) became increasingly important for bringing in raw materials and shipping out finished goods. Even the supplying of foodstuffs generated high demands on urban streets. Merchants, manufacturers, city councils, and city engineers made adequate street pavements a major concern. By necessity, cities became experimenters in road surfacing. Toronto, for example, tried cedar blocks in the late 1860s, granolithic pavements (concrete) in 1886, asphalt in 1888, and brick paving blocks in 1893.[28] Though little research has been done on the history of pavements in Canadian cities, it can be assumed that cities wrestled with this problem in various ways with differing success.

Sanitation also forced cities to confront street problems. By the mid-19th century the connection between open sewers and cholera had been realized. As the number of horses in cities grew, so did the amount of waste they left behind, which became a major health hazard. The ability to clean different types of pavement easily and adequately became a factor in their selection. Cobblestones fell into disfavour because it was difficult to clean the cracks between the stones.

Wooden block pavements were not sanitary either. With the new century, city engineers and health officials pushed for smooth-surface pavements such as asphalt or concrete, which were easy to clean.[29]

Beside their transportation use, city streets also formed a grid for underground utilities. Pipes to supply clean water, along with sanitary and storm sewers, were installed beneath them. In some areas, electrical, gas, steam, and telephone supply lines were also buried, creating large utility corridors.

Rural Needs

City dwellers were not the only ones to push for road improvements by the turn of the century. Settled rural areas also felt the limitations of poor roads. Urban demand for fresh milk, cheese, butter, and vegetables encouraged development of dairy and market farms. Dairy products especially had to be transported to consumers quickly, requiring suitable all-weather roads. Unpaved country roads, once considered adequate, needed improvement. By around 1900 both main and branch railway lines had been pushed to their economically feasible limits, but many rural villages still lacked rail links. Shipping small amounts of freight (like foodstuffs) over short distances was uneconomical for railways. Better roads were the logical answer.

Pressure for better rural roads also came from newer interest groups. Bicycling, the North American rage of the 1890s, required improved roads.[30] Exemplifying changing attitudes toward rural roads was the formation of the Ontario Good Roads Association in 1894, modelled on similar US groups. It functioned as a lobbying group, uniting progressive farmers, county engineers, merchants, and bicyclists, and pressed governments for more funds and better roads. Results

Scenic country roads such as this, being used by a milk collector for a cheese factory in Vernon River, PEI, were adequate for horse and buggy, but not for motorcars. (NA C-10413)

were not long in coming. In 1896 Ontario appointed A.W. 'Good Roads' Campbell, former city engineer of St Thomas, as provincial inspector of roads. Campbell visited towns and villages throughout Ontario giving lectures on the economic and social benefits of good roads and demonstrating proper road-building techniques on short sections of local roads. These demonstrations were well received and helped shape popular ideas of what constituted an adequate road.[31]

The Automobile

The movement toward better roads antedates the mass-produced automobile. The forces pushing for change in road administration and construction were in place before 1900. Though self-propelled road vehicles date back to the 1860s in Canada, automobile ownership was slow to develop,[32] restricted originally to the rich or very adventurous. The first Canadian automobile statistics, in 1903, showed only 178 passenger cars. Ten years later, 54,380 vehicles were registered in Canada.[33]

In the early stages of motoring, automobiles were largely an urban phenomenon. Cities had the support systems needed by drivers: repair garages, mechanics, places selling gasoline and other products – and miles of paved streets. Once outside cities, motorists encountered unimproved dirt roads, easily converted into a series of mud holes by rain, or 'improved' gravel or macadam roads that still left much to be desired. Other obstacles were very sharp turns and narrow, high-crowned roads. With their steep slope, designed to facilitate drainage, drivers had to travel down the

Logging roads were often coated with ice in order to reduce friction with sled runners and enable specially shod horses to haul heavier loads: Crooked River, Saskatchewan. (NA C-38358)

centre of the road, leading to many confrontations between fast-moving cars and slow-moving horse-drawn wagons. Cars also had a disastrous effect on existing paved country roads. Macadamized roads, with their layers of carefully compacted crushed stone, worked tolerably well for horse-drawn vehicles, but the fast-turning wheels of cars tore through the carefully prepared layers of gravel, quickly destroying the road.[34]

Early motorists banded together in local associations to provide mutual support and lobby for better roads. The Hamilton Automobile Club (1903) was followed by others in Toronto (1903), Montreal (1904), and Winnipeg (1904). Soon afterward, local associations grouped together to form provincial organizations such as the Ontario Motor League (1907) and the Manitoba Motor League (1908), which provided many services, including route numbers and signposts, guide books, and promotion

of safe driving.[35] Wealthy and influential people were often made honorary members and helped lobby institutions and governments for improvements.[36] Ten years after formation of the first local associations, a meeting was held on 30 December 1913 to create the Canadian Automobile Federation. The following year, the name was changed to the Canadian Automobile Association (CAA), and the headquarters moved to Ottawa.[37]

The Good Roads movement had a similar history. Initially, provincial organizations were set up, with more professional members (road builders, municipal and county engineers, and other public officials) than the automobile clubs. In May 1914, the first Canadian and International Good Roads Congress was held in Montreal. This meeting facilitated formation of a national organization, and the Canadian Good Roads Association (CGRA) was set up in 1917

Dirt roads became quagmires in spring and dustbowls in dry weather. In the spring of 1914, seemingly on the eve of modernity, a Toronto Electric Light Co. wagon passes a sign advertising Dunlop Clincher Automobile Tires at the corner of Yonge and St Clair. (CTA James 26)

'to collect and distribute information concerning highway legislation, construction and maintenance ... to stimulate and encourage in all ways the improvement, construction and maintenance of roads, the whole from an educational and practical standpoint.'[38] Though less well known than the CAA, the CGRA was quite influential in Canadian highway development.

Government Response

In 1901 the Ontario legislature passed the Highway Improvement Act, which made road building grants available to county governments.[39] Though townships and municipalities, which had greater road responsibilities, failed to get financial aid, a precedent was set. Across Canada, the problem was the same: roads could be improved only when provinces made funds available to local governments. In each province, this evolution had to take place before there could be significant change.

Local rural officials still needed to improve their roads. With increased financial resources, counsel from govern-

ment road engineers, and numerous articles appearing in engineering and other journals, county engineers and their road superintendents learned how to build better roads. Common gravel roads were improved with proper drainage, flatter road crowns, wider road surfaces, and straightening of superfluous curves.[40] Horse-drawn graders replaced split log drags and gave better control over road surfaces. Steam-powered rock crushers increased the supply of crushed stone, and steam rollers were also introduced. Of equal importance was the development of permanent road-building crews, by both contractors and local governments. Rural roads gradually changed for the better.

The application of urban-type surfaces to highway construction began about 1910. The first long-distance concrete highway in Canada was a 10-mi (16-km) stretch between Montreal and Ste Rose (now part of Laval) built in 1910.[41] In 1914, work began on a similar highway between Toronto and Hamilton, but expropriation problems and escalating costs delayed completion until 1917.[42] When finished, it was one of the longest stretches of inter-city concrete highway in the world.

These new roads required vastly increased financial and administrative resources. New provincial-government bodies had to be created to set standards, approve projects, and distribute grants. The first provincial highway organization was set up in Quebec in 1912. A road division, headed by a deputy minister, was formed in the Quebec Department of Agriculture to administer road funds, provide education, and build selected highways. In Ontario, the Royal Commission on Public Roads and Highways (1913–14) led to creation of a Department of Public Works and Highways in 1917. At first, its duties were administrative,

Snow-covered roads could be rolled, instead of ploughed, to give a smooth surface: Ottawa, 1908. (NA C-25616)

Horse-drawn street sweepers removed dust, manure, and a certain amount of domestic garbage: London, 1918. (NA PA-70970)

but it gradually acquired responsibility for road construction and maintenance, initially on 47 mi (75.6 km) of Kingston Road east from Toronto. It built more highways, but Ontario lacked a coherent highway system until 1920, when federal legislation forced its creation. To the already existing 422 mi (679 km) of provincial highways, 1,402 mi (2,256 km) was added, covering most of southern Ontario.[43]

In western Canada, road-tending was difficult. Saskatchewan, for example, tried various administrative alternatives. Before 1912, building of roads and bridges was part of the mandate of the province's Department of Public Works. In that year, because of the urgent demand for roads, a three-member Highway Commission was set up. Public Works made $3 million available to rural municipalities on a matching-funds basis to build and improve roads. Saskatchewan municipalities, eager for better roads, spent their allowances without following the commission's guidelines and failed to provide for future maintenance or to follow construction standards. Two years later a provincial board began directly overseeing the road expenditures. The board identified 'designated main roads' through consultation with municipal officials, members of the legislature, and other interested groups. Either the board's own crews or contractors hired by individual municipalities completed the road work.[44]

A DEVELOPING SYSTEM

Automobiles became an accepted part of life between the two world wars. Proper roads, vital to automobile culture, became important to motorists and governments alike. Provincial highway departments, set up to govern and build highways, became increasingly influential.

First the sheer volume of horse traffic, and later buses, trucks, and automobiles, necessitated road surfaces that were easier to clean and lasted longer than dirt or gravel. In 1905 workmen on the Esplanade in Toronto lay stone blocks –'cobblestones' – probably made of granite. (NA PA-55729)

Automobile Culture
Improvements in the standard of living, larger disposable incomes, and a significant decrease in the price of American mass-produced automobiles enabled many Canadians to own their own cars. The total number of vehicles in Canada rose from 342,433 in 1919 to 1,232,489 in 1930.[45] Rural residents as well as city-dwellers owned automobiles. Though the geographic distribution of ownership was uneven, the car was a significant force everywhere.[46] Trucks began to compete with railways to move freight.

The expanding road system was hard pressed to match the growing number of automobiles. While there was little growth in the total mileage of roads, the length of surfaced roads in Canada (gravel, asphalt, and concrete) grew from 49,000 mi (78,800 km) (1922) to 82,100 mi (13,210 km) (1930). The

A brick road: Sheridan Avenue, Toronto, 1903. The large template on the left gives the base a crown, or curvature, for proper drainage of the road surface. (NA PA-55303)

Asphalt blocks: Victoria Street, Toronto, 1904. Individually formed asphalt blocks were laid in similar fashion to paving blocks of stone, brick, or wood. (NA PA-55333)

Hot asphalt paving: Jarvis Street, Toronto. Note the long-handled hand roller, familiar steam roller, and numerous workmen with shovels, rakes, and brooms. (NA PA-55181)

Concrete roadway: the intersection of Côte d'Abraham and St Réal in Quebec City being converted in 1928 in response to the growing number of automobiles (Canada Cement LaFarge Ltd)

amount of paved road always remained a small fraction of the surfaced total. By 1930, there was only 3,800 mi (6,114 km) of hard-surfaced highway in Canada.[47]

The car culture of the 1920s and 1930s was more than the sum of vehicles and mileage. The automobile came to represent a new way of life. In cities no longer dependent on streetcars or radial railways, people with cars were much freer to live and work where they wished. This further encouraged development of suburban areas with detached housing. Factories could move to new, lower-cost industrial areas. Gas pumps, service stations, car dealerships, and other car-related services were much in evidence. The smooth flow of traffic became so important that a new branch of engineering and urban planning developed. Besides producing street plans for new suburban areas, traffic engineers widened narrow downtown streets, regularized traffic patterns, and pushed for paving of more streets. As well, there were traffic lights, traffic regulations, speed limits, and parking regulations to standardize.[48]

The effect of automobiles on rural areas was less visible. Rural residents now had their own independent means of transport. The isolation of rural life was ended by easier access to urban markets and services, including stores, schools, and health resources.[49] Better roads, even snow removal, meant a better life for many rural residents.

Another facet of Canadian automobile culture was American tourism. Great numbers of newly motorized Americans visited Canada in the 1920s, spending significant amounts of money. In 1929 alone, some 4,508,808 American cars crossed into Canada. According to one estimate, based on four people to a car spending five dollars a day each, these Americans spent $397,806,760 in Can-

Before hot asphalt or paving blocks could be laid, the road base had to be prepared. The process often started with ploughing, as at 3rd Avenue and 24th Street in Saskatoon, 1926. (CPWA Sask Chapter)

ada.[50] Provincial governments were quick to realize the potential benefits from tourism and began to improve their roads. As early as 1912, Quebec built a highway between Montreal and the New York border. Ontario highways such as the Toronto–Hamilton Highway (1913–17) and the Queen Elizabeth Way (1939) also brought tourism.[51] Some Canadian cities were the unofficial terminuses of early American highways: the Meridian Highway from Laredo, Texas, and the Jefferson Highway, from New Orleans, terminated in Winnipeg.[52] Manitoba responded by surfacing the highway between Winnipeg and the Minnesota border in 1924. American tourism resulted in construction of north-south links rather than east-west Canadian roads.[53] Federal and provincial governments spent money creating scenic highways for tourists.[54] Economic benefits from American tourism pushed Canadian road-building probably beyond what was required domestically.[55] North-south routes reflected the importance of US trade, as well as tourism.

Grading road near Abee, Alberta, in 1922, apparently after ploughing (NA PA-19093)

Government

By the late 1920s, fully fledged provincial highway departments had developed. In true bureaucratic style, each department was a well-defined hierarchical structure, headed by a cabinet minister or at least a full-time deputy minister. Below was a professionally trained staff, including a chief engineer of highways, assistants, surveyors, and bridge designers.[56] Most provinces had district engineers, who directed new road construction and day-to-day maintenance.[57]

Responsibilities of highway departments were roughly the same. They designed new highways to relieve the congestion on older, less adequate roads. Then, as now, much of their energy went into upgrading existing routes – surfacing and widening existing roads and reducing steep grades and sharp curves. Often they set road and construction standards for county and municipal governments. Highway departments differed because of varying provincial populations, size, and wealth. The western provinces, with large territories and relatively few people, or the economically distressed Maritimes, did not have the same resources to construct roads as central Canada. Canadian provinces spent a total of $884.1 million on road construction and maintenance from 1919 to 1936: Ontario $377.2 million, Quebec $169.9 million, and the other provinces less than $85 million each.[58]

By the early 1930s roads had become expensive. Even a province with a modest highway system such as New Brunswick spent $7.5 million on roads in 1930.[59] Funds to support highway programs came from general provincial revenue and automobiles themselves: sales taxes, licence fees, fines, and so on. The most lucrative source was the gasoline sales tax. Alberta was the first province to adopt this tax, in 1922, and by 1928 all provinces had done so. By 1930 across Canada this tax was worth $22.7 million

The theory behind toll roads was that the users would pay and the owners would maintain the roads properly. At this toll gate near Bradford, Ontario, in 1917, 'automobilists' could pay tolls and purchase 'filtered motor gasoline.' (NA RD 220)

in revenue.[60] However, taxes and fees collected from motor vehicles provided only 41 per cent of money spent by provinces on roads between 1919 and 1930.[61] Clearly much of the funding came from general provincial revenues.

The situation was further complicated because local governments were still responsible for most roads. Since their revenue base was limited, they were much harder pressed in road matters. Provinces developed different systems for dealing with secondary and local roads. All provinces took care of provincial highways. Some, such as Quebec and Saskatchewan, did only that; others, such as Nova Scotia and New Brunswick, also handled municipal roads.[62] Since adequate roads had to be built, provinces devised subsidy plans for local governments. Ontario started subsidizing county roads in 1901 and those in townships in 1904. By 1920 townships received a 20 per cent subsidy.[63]

The federal government, though not constitutionally responsible for roads, did make several brief but significant intrusions. In 1912 and in 1913, Robert Borden's Conservative majority in the House voted to make money available to provinces for road construction. The Liberal majority in the Senate, however, refused to pass the bill both times.[64] Because of the First World War, it was 1919 before the Borden government could provide aid to highways. The Canadian Highway Act provided $20 million 'to encourage the construction and improvement of highways.' The federal government was to pay 40 per cent of the cost of building and maintaining main and market roads. This forced each province to rationalize its main and secondary road systems before it could apply for a subsidy. Originally designed as a five-year program, the act was extended an additional three years so that road projects under way could be finished. By 1928, provinces had constructed or rebuilt over 25,000 mi of highways under this program.[65]

Though the federal Department of

Railways and Canals had a Highways Branch, it restricted itself to compiling statistics and producing reports on topics such as the cost of hauling farm produce to market and ideal technical specifications for roads.[66] The department did not get involved in road research or building.[67]

Depression and World War
By early 1930, provincial governments began to feel the effects of the Depression. Some extended or speeded up road-building to employ as many people as possible. In Saskatchewan 'the government decided that this was not the right time to cut down on useful and much needed public works, which would provide work for many who would otherwise be unemployed.'[68] The use of road construction and maintenance as make-work projects became a familiar practice throughout the 1930s. The federal government also provided relief funds that were used for road-building by the provinces. For road projects, it generally paid 50 per cent of approved costs. From 1930 to 1940, $44.5 million was provided through this program, but it was not a consistent source of funds: $11.2 million (the largest payment) in 1931, but only $1.1 million in 1932. As well, not all provinces had enough money to build roads in order to get federal funding. Ontario got just over 50 per cent of the total, but none of the other provinces got more than $3.5 million.[69]

The Depression affected far more than road financing. It also decreased automobile registrations. From a high of 1,061,500 cars in 1930, registration declined to 919,917 in 1933, a fall of 14 per cent. Saskatchewan suffered the most, losing one-third of its registrations.[70] However, by 1936, the total number of vehicles surpassed 1930, enhanced by the continued growth of commercial ve-

hicles, which reached 187,770 by 1936.

In comparison with the First World War, which seems to have little affected Canadian cars and roads, the Second World War had a much greater impact. Production of civilian vehicles ceased in 1942, to allow the building of badly needed military equipment. Overuse of the existing automobile stock caused a fall from 1,281,190 cars (1941) to 1,161,337 (1945).[71] The road and street system, already weakened by the Depression, was further abused. There was no money for new highway construction (except for military roads) and precious little for repairs, yet roads were essential to the war effort.

Technology
Road technology made great progress in the 1920s. Better road materials developed largely for urban streets could now be applied to inter-city and rural highways. One of the preferred surfaces was concrete, particularly useful for heavily used urban streets and inter-city highways. It produced a strong and durable surface, but it was expensive and required a large construction crew. Concrete construction in the 1920s emphasized the quality of cement and road bed. Large-scale use of mechanized equipment helped increase output and decrease costs.[72] According to figures from the Canada Cement Co., 28,691,607 sq yd (about 24 million sq m) of concrete paving had been laid in Canada from before 1912 through 1930. Between 1927 and 1930, over 3 million sq yd (2.5 million sq m) a year were laid. Ontario had been the heaviest user of concrete (21.5 million sq yd [18 million sq m]), followed by Quebec (3.7 million [3.1 million]) and British Columbia (2.1 million [1.8 million]). The other provinces had laid less than 1 million sq yd (0.84 million sq m) each.[73]

Asphalt – a group of substances –

Cars and trucks, with their greater speed and weight, needed improved roads. Scenes such as this, on the Ottawa-Morrisburg highway, now Highway 31, with horse-drawn graders and steam rollers, were common. (NA C-36973)

By the 1920s tar sands were becoming a source of road bitumen. In Manitoba in 1930 a bitumen and aggregate mixture is being spread by a towed road grader. (NA PA-17490)

became even more popular as a road surface. One of the most common types was sheet asphalt. Trucks dumped hot asphalt in piles which was spread either manually or by motorized graders and then compacted by rollers. Other asphalt mixtures included retread surfaces – a light asphaltic oil poured over the existing surface of a gravel road, bonding together the small pieces of gravel. A stronger bond was obtained with penetration asphalt – a hot asphalt mixture poured over 2-to-3-inch-diameter (5.1-to-7.6 cm) gravel. The final type was the so-called mixed macadam – 1-to-2-inch gravel (2.5-to-5.1-cm) thoroughly combined with hot asphalt in a mixer and spread over the road and rolled. Mixed asphalt became popular because of its hardness, its durability, and especially its flexibility, important in a Canada's extreme climate.[74] For lower-cost roads, tar could be substituted for asphalt and applied to existing surfaces or mixed with new gravel and spread. The use of tar appears to be an English development imported to North America.[75]

Gravel and earth roads remained very much evident in Canada during the inter-war years, where traffic demands or financial resources were not sufficient. Depending on traffic, these roads were 24 to 36 ft (7.3 to 11 m) wide and had a flatter profile (a quarter-inch [0.64 cm] slope per foot) than the old high-crown macadam roads. Road engineers were advised to super-elevate, or 'bank,' outside portions of curves and provide adequate drainage.[76]

One particular Canadian problem was how to deal with snow. For many years after introduction of the automobile, highways closed down for the winter. However, economical methods of removing snow from streets had been developed in cities where economic activities were too important to be interrupted by snow. Motorized snow-re-moval equipment, such as rotary snow-blowers and vehicles with conveyor belts to put snow into dump trucks, were used in cities by 1918. Economic justifications could not be applied to rural areas in the same way. However, by the late 1920s, the automobile was so important that year-round road operation was becoming necessary. Quebec cleared 87 mi (140 km) of provincial routes in the vicinity of Montreal and Quebec in 1928–9. Direct costs were calculated to be an average of $200 per mi ($124 per km). On the basis of fuel tax revenue, 600 vehicles a day had to use a road in winter before it became economically viable to clear it of snow.[77] By the early 1930s, the technology to clear roads existed, but economics determined when and how often.

A MATURE SYSTEM

When the production of civilian automobiles resumed in August 1945, there was enormous pent-up demand. Three-quarters of a million additional cars clogged the roads within five years. As the economy and the demands of consumers grew, so did the number of cars. By 1956, the number of cars reached 3.2 million, and by 1960 it was over 4.1 million.[78] Growth has continued almost unabated through recession, inflation, and sharp fuel price rises. In 1982, there were 10.5 million cars in Canada, 3.3 million trucks and buses, plus 486,000 other vehicles.[79] There were approximately three vehicles for every five Canadians, making this country one of the most motorized in the world.

The whole infrastructure of Canada expanded to adapt to this proliferation of vehicles. The number of gas stations, car dealerships, shopping centres, parking lots, and road regulations had to increase proportionally. Financial institutions, urban planners, highway engineers, as well as municipal and provincial politicians have all paid heed to this mechanical hoard.[80]

The highway network responded slowly to this stimulus, but it was much easier to manufacture and acquire a car than to build new roads or repair old ones. Though total mileage decreased by 26,000 mi (41,834 km) between 1946 and 1975, surfaced road rose from 150,100 (241,511) to over 434,600 mi (699,271 km). In 1946, only one-sixth of surfaced roads were concrete or asphalt; most were gravelled. During the next 30 years, the amount of hard-surfaced road rose to better than half of the total.[81] In 1983, all three levels of government plus the private sector spent $4.52 billion on highway, road, street, and bridge construction. Of this, 77.5 per cent was for construction and 22.5 per cent for repair.[82]

In 1970, Canadians travelled about 110 billion passenger miles; 85 to 90 per cent of all travel was over roads.[83] Half of Canada's $30-billion transportation investment was in cars, roads, and related facilities. Canada has a higher per capita investment in roads than the United States.[84] Besides reflecting the enormous size of the country and the higher cost of building roads, it also indicates the high priority that Canadians have given to their roads.

High-Speed Divided Highways
The design of surfaced roads has changed dramatically in the last 50 years. High-speed divided highways are one innovation in these years. The earliest work on limited-access divided highways came after T.B. McQuesten became minister of highways for Ontario in 1934. From his experience with Hamilton road planning and the Niagara Parkway, McQuesten pushed his department to integrate two different road concepts. One was the parkway, a scenic highway through attractive countryside; the other, a high-speed divided highway with controlled access.[85] He first tried out these concepts in southern Ontario. The Queen Elizabeth Way (QEW) opened in June 1939 between Toronto and St Catharines.[86] It was the longest divided highway in the world and had public lighting for most of its length. A high level of design applied to bridges, light standards, and even the landscaping along the route.[87] The first grade-separated cloverleaf in Canada was built at the Port Credit interchange.

One problem not immediately solved concerned access roads. Because the highway was built from existing roads, numerous streets and private driveways connected with the QEW. At first, highway engineers tried permits to limit access points, but legal problems emerged concerning abutting property rights. Major reconstruction, 1948–57, reduced access points and provided grade separation at intersections. In the 1960s, the whole highway was widened to three lanes in each direction. Highway engineers widened the road to four and even five lanes in the 1970s and constructed more complex interchanges. In each succeeding rebuilding, more of the original parkway features, such as landscaping and decorative touches, disappeared.[88]

The lessons learned from the QEW were applied to the new generation of Ontario highways. Highway 400, built 1947–52 between Toronto and Barrie, was divided throughout its length with complete grade separation at all intersections and limited access points.[89] Ontario also constructed the Macdonald-Cartier Freeway (the 401), which spans the 510 mi (832 km) from Windsor to the Quebec border. Engineers conducted careful surveys and planning to find the route that least upset the existing road system and local communities.[90] Despite these precautions, the 401 has profoundly affected development in southern Ontario.

Proliferation of automobiles led to urban sprawl and increasingly busy and complex highway systems. Highway 401 north of Toronto is the busiest route in Canada. The Avenue Road/401 interchange (June 1961) looks almost abandoned by today's standards. The nearby Queen Elizabeth Way/427 interchange (May 1969) displays the graceful curves and concrete work that make such structures things of beauty. (OMT 1317 and OMT 1177A-F)

New growth has sprung up between existing urban centres and the 401. In Toronto, traffic generated by growth around the 401 strangled high-speed travel. The Toronto bypass has been enlarged several times, from 4 to 12 lanes and more, yet crossing Toronto on the 401 remains a problem at rush hours.

Urban areas have been greatly affected by increasing traffic densities. Many planners claimed that the answer was urban high-speed divided highways. Montreal built numerous urban expressways. Mount Royal made east-west travel difficult, and therefore the province built a major elevated expressway behind the mountain. Metropolitan Boulevard, finished in 1960, was one of the first urban expressways in Canada.[91] A spate of construction took place just before Expo '67, which included the depressed Decarie Boulevard and a westward extension of Metropolitain Boulevard, known as the Trans-Canada, which eventually connected to the 401 at the Quebec border.[92] The government also built major bridges and autoroutes to the Laurentians and to the Eastern Townships. The last link built was the Ville-Marie Expressway, in the mid-1970s, which went east-west close to downtown Montreal. Local community and environmental groups provided stiff opposition to the construction. Also, many people questioned an extremely expensive expressway when Montreal's subway system was expanding.

The Trans-Canada Highway

The idea of a road across Canada antedates the transcontinental railway. The notion languished, however, in the years after completion of the railway.[93] The modern concept of a transcontinental highway came from the Canada Highway Association, an organization of western motorists formed in 1910. It was an ambitious dream, since there were no roads north of Lake Superior or through the Rocky Mountains. To promote its goal, the association sponsored a transcontinental motor contest. Not until 1947 did Brigadier R.A. MacFarlane and Kenneth Gilliverary claim the medal by driving their Chevrolet over 4,743 mi (7,631 km) of Canadian roads.[94]

Since the First World War, the federal government has aided construction of roads that might eventually form a highway across Canada. The Canada Highway Act, 1919, provided subsidies to the provinces for road construction and rationalization of highway systems. In the early 1930s, the federal government again made available to the provinces highway money, which was often used as unemployment relief. Valuable roadbuilding was done in northern Ontario and the Rockies.[95]

In 1949, Parliament passed the Trans-Canada Highway Act. An estimated $300 million was to be given to the provinces to construct a 4,860-mi (7,820-km) all-weather surfaced road from St John's to Victoria. Ottawa would pay 50 per cent of the cost. The federal government also set the standards: two lanes (24 ft [7.3 m]) in width, with 10-ft (3.0-m) gravel shoulders, 6-per-cent maximum grades, clear lines of visibility, and completion in 1956. Both time required and cost of building proved greater than anticipated. The subsidy for building new roads was raised to 90 per cent of cost and a new completion date set for 1960.[96]

Construction of the Trans-Canada Highway resembled building of the Canadian Pacific Railway (CPR) 70 years before. Both followed a route along Canada's southern boundary and received heavy federal subsidies. The two areas that gave the CPR problems also troubled the Trans-Canada builders: the Canadian Shield north of Lake Superior and the continental divide in the Rockies. By the late 1950s the eastern section was complete except through the ancient granite, muskeg, mountains, and rivers in northern Ontario. In 1958–9, a big push was made to finish the last 165 mi (265 km). A few contractors even worked through that winter. Low temperatures and the remoteness of some sites challenged contractors and contributed to high costs. However, with up-to-date mechanical equipment and innovative solutions to engineering problems, the northern-Ontario section was opened in September 1960.[97]

In the Rockies, the few existing roads were narrow, full of sharp turns, and vulnerable to rock and snow slides. The government required a safe 60-mi-per-hour (96.5-km-per-hour) road through the same terrain. Engineers achieved this goal with massive earthworks, numerous tunnels, and many bridges. In Rogers Pass, where there was great danger from snowslides, long stretches of snowshed were constructed to protect the highway. The Trans-Canada Highway opened there, along one of its most difficult and spectacular sections, on 3 September 1962, two years behind schedule.[98] The final cost of the highway to the federal government was $825 million.[99] The system is owned and operated by the provincial governments. Much of it, except around major cities, remains two-lane, undivided highway. Upgrading to divided multi-lane highway is unlikely because of the enormous cost.

Northern Road-Building
Canada faces one road-building problem encountered by few other countries: extreme cold. In northern Quebec, the four western provinces, Yukon, and the Northwest Territories, vast distances with little or no habitation, long and severe winters, and permanently frozen ground (permafrost) test the skills of highway engineers. For many centuries, the canoe was the only means of practical travel during the short summer. By the turn of the century sternwheel steamboats were in place on navigable waterways such as the Yukon, Mackenzie, Athabaska, and Great Slave rivers. The Klondike Gold Rush fostered an extensive network of wagon trails – 500 mi (804.5 km) by 1913, mostly between Whitehorse and Dawson, but not linked to the outside world.[100] After the First World War, the airplane played a greater role in northern transportation.

The Second World War changed this picture dramatically. The United States feared a Japanese invasion through the Aleutian Islands and Alaska. Needing a secure overland route to supply Alaska, the US military decided to build the Alcan Military Highway (the Alaska Highway) from Dawson Creek, British Columbia, to Fairbanks, Alaska. Construction of this 1,523-mi (2,450-km) road required 11,000 US military personnel and 16,000 Canadian and American civilian workers and contractors. Work started in March 1942 at several points, and the road advanced at a remarkable 8 mi (13 km) a day. A mere eight months after starting, the Alaska Highway was officially opened on 20 November 1942. Shortcuts were used in construction; the road avoided crossing muskeg wherever possible, temporary wooden and pontoon bridges were built in place of permanent structures, and the road wound around mountains to avoid rock removal.[101] Throughout the rest of the war, the US Army Corps of Engineers upgraded the road and began to put in permanent structures.

In 1946, the Canadian portion of the Alaska Highway (1,221 mi [1,965 km]) was turned over to the Canadian army, which in turn relinquished control to the federal Department of Public Works in 1964. Since construction, the highway's steep grades have been reduced, and

Although some snow could be ploughed aside and left to melt, cities could remove snow from the streets and dump it elsewhere. Well-dressed onlookers on Bay Street, Toronto, 17 March 1931, suggest an equipment demonstration. (NA PA-98350)

better bridges and culverts put in; damage from spring floods and landslides has been repaired, and more gravel added.[102] At present, over one-third of the route in Yukon has been paved with asphalt, over one-third covered with bituminous surface treatment (hot asphalt poured over the gravel), and only a small percentage of the original gravel road remains.[103] The Alaska Highway, originally built as a military route, has proved its worth many times over as a year-round commercial highway.

A particular problem in the north is building roads on permafrost. If not properly constructed, a road can crack badly as a result of frost heave or even sink into a swamp created by the melting of permafrost. In order to build better and cheaper roads, the National Re-

search Council, the federal Department of Public Works, and provincial governments have done significant research. The main problem is understanding the freezing and thawing cycle of permafrost. Researchers have found that permanently frozen ground provides a good road bed. Insulation between ground and road surface lets the permafrost remain frozen, thus providing an adequate bearing surface.[104]

The first push for roads in the Northwest Territories came in the late 1930s, with discovery of gold at Yellowknife, on the north shore of Great Slave Lake. Until then, supplies could come only by water, during the short summer shipping season. In March 1939, however, a team of three caterpillar tractors, each pulling six heavily laden sleighs, left

Grimshaw, Alberta, and followed a rough bush trail up the Hay River to the southern side of Great Slave Lake and then straight across the frozen lake to Yellowknife. Gradually the road between Grimshaw and Great Slave Lake, known as the Mackenzie Highway, was improved so that trucks could use it. However, it was not until 1957 that the federal government constructed a crude 300-mi road around the lake to Yellowknife, providing that town with a permanent overland link with the rest of Canada.[105] The main branch of the Mackenzie Highway has been gradually pushed up the Mackenzie Valley, past Fort Simpson, and now terminates in Ogilvie.[106] Eventually this highway will reach Inuvik in the Mackenzie Delta, not far from the Beaufort Sea.

Another major northern road is the Dempster Highway, which opened in 1979 between Dawson and Inuvik. This was the first Canadian highway to cross the Arctic Circle.[107] Its origins lie with the 'Roads to Resources' program of John Diefenbaker's Conservative government (1957–63) to encourage oil and mineral exploration in the Mackenzie Valley. Construction started in 1958 and followed an old Indian and Royal Canadian Mounted Police trail. By 1959, 30 mi (48.3 km) had been built, but changing government priorities and the cost of northern road-building slowed work. The project built only another 45 mi (72.4 km) in the 1960s and ground to a halt. The Dempster came to life again in 1969 with the search for oil and gas in the Mackenzie Valley. The federal government renewed funding and completed the highway.[108]

CONCLUSION

Canada's highway needs have changed dramatically over time. The history of Canadian roads began with crude dirt and corduroy trails. Improvements such

Sometimes the plough had to be rescued by the simplest of snow removal equipment – men with shovels: Regina, 1936 and 1937. (SAB R-A5850[1], SAB R-A5851[3])

as plank and macadam roads were found inadequate. Because of special urban requirements, city engineers developed concrete and asphalt road surfaces. Provincial governments applied these improvements to inter-city and rural highways in the early 20th century. Because of increasing numbers of automobiles and rising expectations, the simple two-lane road was also found inadequate. So highway engineers developed the high-speed, limited-access divided highway. These highways are now standard for large urban areas and certain major inter-city routes in Canada.

Roads played an important role in early Canada, even when they were adjuncts to the canal and waterway systems. In the 1840s, the Department of Public Works of the Province of Canada unsuccessfully attempted to build an ambitious national system of roads. However, railways made long-distance highways redundant and reduced roads to a local concern. The automobile fuelled the rebirth of Canadian highway-building in the early 20th century. Provincial governments started granting funds to local governments to build and maintain highways. Each government slowly developed subsidies, construction practices, and regulations. The federal government subsidized provincial road-building in the 1920s and 1930s and again in the 1950s and 1960s, for the Trans-Canada Highway. Still, there is no national road system, only a collection of provincial systems. Making sure that provincial highway regulations and networks are compatible remains a major difficulty.

NOTES

1 Two general books on Canadian roads are E.G. Guillet *The Story of Canadian Roads* (Toronto 1966) and G.P. de T. Glazebrook *A History of Transportation in Canada* (Toronto 1964). Numerous articles have been written on local roads; see, for example, W.H. Breithaupt 'Dundas Street and Other Upper Canadian Roads' *Ontario Historical Society Papers and Records* 21 (1924) *Ontario History* 49 (1957) 1–17 and M.E. Waterston 'Travel Paths in Canada: Nineteenth Century' *Waterloo Historical Society* 57 (1969) 5–9.
2 Guillet *Story* 49, 57–9, 179–89
3 See Marilyn Miller *Straight Lines in Curved Space: Colonization Roads in Eastern Ontario* (Toronto 1978) and A.E. Hoekstra and W.G. Ross 'The Craig and Gosford Roads: Early Colonization Roads in the Eastern Townships of Quebec' *Canadian Geographical Journal* 79:2 (Aug 1969) 52–7.
4 Guillet *Story* 59–61

5 Ibid 62
6 Ibid 15
7 T.F. McIlwraith 'The Adequacy of Rural Roads in the Era before Railways: An Illustration from Upper Canada' *Canadian Geographer* 14:4 (winter 1970) 355
8 Guillet *Story* 15
9 On plank roads see W.M. Gillespie *A Manual on the Principles and Practices of Roadmaking Comprising the Location, Construction and Improvement of Roads ... and Railways* (New York 1868) and William Kingsford *History, Structure and Statistics of Plank Roads in the United States and Canada* (Philadelphia 1852).
10 Michael S. Cross 'The Stormy History of the York Roads, 1833–1865' *Ontario History* 54:1 (March 1962) 8–9
11 Guillet *Story* 67
12 Kingsford *History* 10
13 Thomas Roy *Principles and Practices of Road Making as Applicable to Canada* (Toronto 1841) 25–9
14 J.E. Hodgetts *Pioneer Public Service: An Administrative History of the United Canadas, 1841–1867* (Toronto 1955) chap 11 and 12 and Douglas Owram *Building for Canadians: A History of Public Works, 1840–1960* (Ottawa 1978)
15 Ludwik Kos-Rabcewicz-Zubkowski and William Edward Greening *Sir Casimir Stanislaus Gzowski: A Biography* (Toronto 1959) 27
16 Ibid 38–40
17 Owram *Building* 16
18 Ibid 54
19 Hodgetts *Pioneer* 181
20 The department spent $2,204,721 on roads between 1841 and 1867: Canada *Sessional Papers* Department of Public Works (1866–7) Appendix 19, 172.
21 McIlwraith 'Adequacy' 355–6
22 Ibid 356–7
23 Michael S. Cross 'Some Aspects of Road Financing and Administration, 1791–1901' unpublished ms, Ministry of Transportation and Communication Library, Downsview, Ont., 1961, 30–1

24 Nancy B. Bouchier 'A Broad Clear Track in Good Order: The Bytown and Nepean Road Company – Richmond Toll Road, Ottawa, 1851–1875' *Ontario History* 76:2 (June 1984) 103–27

25 Ibid 122–3

26 Thomas F. McIlwraith 'The Influence of Street Railways upon Street Engineering: The Toronto Experience, 1860–1890' in R.A. Jarrell and A.E. Roos eds *Critical Issues in the History of Canadian Science, Technology and Medicine* (Thornhill, Ont. 1983) 218–27

27 Ibid, especially table on 224

28 Guillet *Story* 124

29 Clay McShane 'Transforming the Use of Urban Space: A Look at the Revolution in Street Pavements, 1880–1924' *Journal of Urban History* 5:3 (May 1979) 279–307

30 Anita Rush 'The Bicycle Boom of the Gay Nineties: A Reassessment' *Material History Bulletin* 18 (fall 1983) 3–4

31 Guillet *Story* 155

32 For an account of early self-propelled road vehicles see Hugh Durnford and Glenn Baechler *Cars of Canada* (Toronto 1973) chap 2.

33 F.H. Lacey *Historical Statistics of Canada* 2nd ed (Ottawa 1983) Series T147–T194

34 Cars were a factor that led to the end of private toll roads in Ontario, though the last one (Sarnia–Florence) did not disappear until 1926. See Bouchier 'A Broad Clear Track' 120–2 and Ontario Ministry of Transportation and Communication *Footprints to Freeways: The Story of Ontario Roads* (Toronto 1984) 49.

35 Durnford and Baechler *Cars* 292–3

36 Denis Methot 'The History of CAA in Quebec, Part I (Quebec City)' *Touring* 64:4 (Sept-Oct 1986) 7

37 Durnford and Baechler *Cars* 293–5

38 Roads and Transportation Association of Canada (RTAC) *The Way It Was, 1914–1974* (n.p., n.d.) 1. This association is the renamed Canadian Good Roads Association.

39 Marion J. Duncan 'Some Aspects of Road Financing and Administration, Pt. 2, 1901–1958' unpublished ms, Ministry of Transportation Library, 1961, 50

40 Road engineers spent much of their time repairing bad road designs of the past. See for example E.L. Miles 'Road Building in Ontario' *Engineering Journal* 13:10 (Oct 1930) 578.

41 Guillet *Story* 155

42 Ontario Ministry of Transportation *Footprints to Freeways* 68–9

43 Ibid 71–4

44 Charles W. Dill 'Development of Saskatchewan's Highway System' *Canadian Engineer* 38:8 (19 Feb 1920) 222–5. For the social side of Saskatchewan motoring, see G.T. Bloomfield ' "I Can See a Car in That Crop": Motorization in Saskatchewan' *Saskatchewan History* 37:1 (winter 1984) 3–24.

45 Lacey *Historical Statistics* Tables T147–T150

46 Gerald Bloomfield 'The Automobile and the Canadian Landscape: A Retrospective View' Canadian Historical Association paper, Winnipeg, 1986, 8, 29–30

47 Canadian Tax Foundation *Taxes and Traffic: A Study of Highway Financing* (Toronto 1955) Tables 3–5, pp. 10–13

48 The effect of the automobile on Canadian life has only begun to be explored. Recent articles include Donald F. Davis 'Dependent Motorization: Canada and the Automobile to the 1930s' *Journal of Canadian Studies* 21:3 (1986) 106–31 and Bloomfield 'I Can See a Car.'

49 Davis 'Dependent' 123

50 Miles 'Road Building' 578

51 Davis 'Dependent' 125

52 F.L. Paxton 'The Highway Movement, 1916–1935' *American Historical Review* 51 (Jan 1946) 242

53 Davis 'Dependent' 125

54 See J.M. Wardle 'Highway Work in the Canadian National Parks' *Engineering Journal* 8:9 (Sept 1925) 382–4.
55 Davis 'Dependent' 126
56 For organizational charts of provincial highway departments see *Canadian Engineer* 59:13 (23 Sept 1930) 164–74.
57 See the reports of the provinces for their 1930 activities in ibid 264–70F.
58 Canadian Tax Foundation *Taxes* Table 19, p. 30
59 D.A. Stewart 'New Brunswick' *Canadian Engineer* 8:9 (Sept 1930) 269
60 Canadian Tax Foundation *Taxes* Table 42, p. 46
61 Ibid 43
62 Adapted from the accounts of provincial highway activities in *Canadian Engineer* 8:9 (Sept 1930) 264–70F
63 Duncan 'Road Financing' 61–4
64 Guillet *Story* 158–9
65 Ibid
66 A.W. Campbell (1863–1927), after leaving the Ontario government in 1910, became deputy minister of the federal Department of Railways and Canals. Later he was the federal commissioner of highways and responsible for implementation of the Canada Highways Act.
67 The federal government's role in road research is very different from that of the US government, which did considerable road research and testing. See Bruce E. Seely 'The Scientific Mystique in Engineering: Highways Branch Research at the Bureau of Public Works, 1918–1940' *Technology and Culture* 25:4 (Oct 1984) 798–851.
68 A.C. Stewart 'Saskatchewan' *Canadian Engineer* 8:9 (Sept 1930) 270
69 Canadian Tax Foundation *Taxes* Table 54, p. 69
70 Lacey *Historical Statistics* Tables T147–T194
71 Ibid
72 E.M. Fleming 'Trend of Practice in Concrete Paving' *Canadian Engineer* 8:9 (Sept 1930) 253–5
73 See ibid, table, p. 256.
74 E.H. Scott 'Trend of Practice in Asphalt Paving' *Canadian Engineer* 8:9 (Sept 1930) 257–8D
75 G.E. Martin 'Trend of Practice in Tar Construction' *Canadian Engineer* 8:9 (Sept 1930) 258E–F
76 H.A. Lumsden 'Gravel and Earth Construction Trend' *Canadian Engineer* 8:9 (Sept 1930) 258I–J
77 A. Fraser 'Maintaining Winter Roads in Quebec' *Canadian Engineer* 8:9 (Sept 1930) 150–2
78 Lacey *Historical Statistics* Tables T147–T194
79 *Canada Year Book* 1985, Table 13.10, p. 426
80 The best historical analysis of Canadian automobiles, roads, and society has been done by Dr Gerald Bloomfield of the University of Guelph. His unpublished papers include: 'The Adoption of Motor Vehicles in Canada' and 'Canadian Highways and the Automobile' Reports 21 and 22 for the Historical Atlas of Canada project (1983) and 'The Automobile and the Canadian Landscape.'
81 Lacey *Historical Statistics* Tables T142–T146
82 *Canada Year Book* 1985 Table 13.8, p. 425
83 About 5,200 mi (8,368 km) of the 6,000 mi (9,656 km) travelled by the average Canadian per year are on roads; Transportation Development Agency *Highway Systems in Canada* (Montreal 1976) i, 11.
84 Ibid 2
85 John C. van Nostrand 'The Queen Elizabeth Way: Public Utility vs Public Space' *Urban History Review* 12:2 (Oct 1983) 1–2. Also see Ministry of Transportation and Communication *The Queen Elizabeth Way: Ontario's First Superhighway* (Toronto n.d.).
86 Van Nostrand 'The QEW' 5

87 Ibid 9

88 Ibid 13–18

89 Ministry of Transportation and Communication *Highway 400: Ontario's Vacationland Freeway* (Toronto 1976) 1–5

90 Ministry of Transportation and Communication *'401': The Macdonald-Cartier Freeway* (Toronto n.d.) 1–5

91 Ludger Beauregard 'The Automobile and Its Impact on Montreal' in L. Beauregard ed *IGU Montreal Field Guide* (Montreal 1972) 171–3

92 Ibid 172

93 Guillet *Story* 219

94 Ibid 227 and Bloomfield 'Canadian Highways' 3

95 Guillet *Story* 223–4

96 Ibid 227–9

97 'Last 165 Miles Toughest of Them All' *Engineering and Contract Record* 72:9 (Sept 1959) 96–9

98 Guillet *Story* 229–30

99 Bloomfield 'Canadian Highways' Tables 2 and 3, pp. 17–18

100 Guillet *Story* 179

101 Ibid 182

102 Ibid 183–7

103 Information from J.M. Crawford, director, Highways, Public Works Canada, June 1987

104 A.I. Wallace and P.J. Williams 'Problems of Building Roads in the North' *Canadian Geographical Journal* 89:1 and 2 (July-Aug 1974) 40–7

105 George E. Inglis 'The Mackenzie Highway: Driveway to Canada's Future Land' *Canadian Geographical Journal* 79:3 (Sept 1969) 85–7

106 Information from J.M. Crawford, June 1987

107 Allen A. Wright 'Yukon Hails the Opening of the Dempster Highway' *Canadian Geographic Journal* (June-July 1979) 16–21

108 Ibid

PAUL-ANDRÉ LINTEAU

Urban Mass Transit

Moving people within Canadian towns was not a major problem in the 19th century when communities were merely mercantile outposts. The journey to work was often very short. Many merchants, artisans, and apprentices lived and worked in the same building. Others walked only a few blocks. Churches, stores, and other services were close to most homes. The affluent could use their own horse or carriage, or hire a cab driver, but these costly services were beyond the means of the ordinary citizen. The mercantile city was a walking city.

In the second half of the 19th century, rapid industrialization transformed cities into busy commercial metropolises and hubs of inter-regional transportation systems. Montreal, for example, grew from 27,000 inhabitants in 1831 to 100,000 by the time of Confederation, and at the turn of the century city and suburbs housed 325,000. In the mean time, the radius of urbanized area expanded from 1 to 4 mi (1.6 to 6.4 km). The combined expansion and sharper specialization of urban space led to a clearer separation between home and work-place and a longer journey to work, which called for new modes of transportation.

Canada drew upon earlier British and American experiments in urban transportation. Having been importers of

ideas and technology for more than two centuries, Canadians were prepared to borrow and adapt the solutions and devices invented elsewhere. Thus the history of urban mass transport in Canada cannot be understood without reference to experience elsewhere, particularly in the United States.[1]

There is no single representative Canadian city. One must take into account the marked difference in size separating the two large cities, Montreal and Toronto, from the numerous medium-sized and small towns and cities. The British North America Act, 1867, vested authority over local and municipal undertakings in the provinces and left the way open for diverse regional situations and policies. If the history of urban mass transport reveals striking common features nation-wide, it shows also significant local differences in organization and regulation. Even in a national survey, one has thus to develop 'a sense of time and place.'[2]

STREETCARS

Although other systems had been tried earlier, inauguration of horse-drawn streetcar systems in various cities in the early 1860s marked the official beginning of urban public transport in Canada. A version of the horse-drawn carriage, the omnibus (a French invention that spread

Before the use of electricity, streetcar companies (here, in Montreal) had three types of horse-drawn transport: wooden-wheeled carriages for the mud of spring, rail cars for summer and autumn, and sleighs for winter. (NA C-48734)

through the United States in the 1830s) emerged in some Canadian towns. In Toronto, for example, H.B. Williams began operating, in 1849, a 2-mi (3.2-km) omnibus line from St Lawrence market to Yorkville. His first carriages carried six passengers, and later vehicles could accommodate ten.[3] The story of the omnibus in Canada has not been well recorded, and it is difficult to draw an overall picture of an industry made up of various small-scale operators. A ride on an omnibus was not always pleasant. As most streets were not paved and were generally dusty and poorly maintained, passengers had to endure frequent bumps and rough driving conditions.[4]

The safer and smoother steam railway, which was introduced to Canada in 1836 and grew rapidly in the early 1850s, provided a popular solution for long-distance travel. It was, however, ill adapted to urban transport: smoke generated air pollution, sparks and burning embers created a fire hazard, noise frightened horses, and exclusive rights of way were needed. Urban steam railways linked outlying communities

Canada's first public streetcar system (opened 1861): car no. 23 posed in front of St Andrew's Presbyterian Church in Toronto (MTLB E4-51f)

only with downtown central stations.

The horse-drawn streetcar took features from both systems. The iron wheels and rails of the railway joined the carriage design and animal traction of the omnibus. Rails permitted a smoother and steadier ride than omnibuses on rough streets, while reduced friction enabled larger vehicles with more passengers to travel at higher speeds. The standard carriage had 10 to 12 transverse seats, with an open side and a step, permitting passengers to go in and out; closed cars with a rear entrance were also in use. The vehicles were drawn by two horses and rolled at a pace of 5 to 7 mi (8.0 to 11.3 km) per hour. In winter, straw was spread on the floor and passengers were provided with horse blankets.

The first streetcar system in Canada was inaugurated in Toronto, on 10 September 1861. Two months later, Montreal's system was put into service, while Quebec had to wait until 1865. Gradually, similar service was introduced in other cities, including Halifax, Hamilton, Ottawa, Saint John, and Winnipeg.

The new services were an immediate success; in 1864, for example, the Montreal system carried a million passengers. 'During the early days the cars were run in a rather happy-go-lucky fashion. Time was of little object. The cars would stop anywhere to take up passengers, and if one wanted to get off and talk to a friend or do a little shopping, the obliging conductors would wait and give their horses a rest.'[5] But stricter schedules and procedures were soon to be introduced.

Within 30 years the Montreal company grew from 8 cars, running on 6.5 mi (10.5 km) of track, to 30 mi (48.3 km) of track, 300 cars, and stables for 1,000 horses.[6] In 1892 it carried 11.6 million passengers. Despite such expansion, the streetcar was not fulfilling the needs of most of the population. Most people could walk to work, and workers earning six or seven dollars a week could not afford a 5-cent ride twice a day. Historians C. Armstrong and H.V. Nelles have calculated that the number of riders as a proportion of Montreal's labour force rose only from 5.4 per cent in 1881 to 10.6 per cent in 1892. Regular streetcar use was a middle-class privilege in Montreal. Toronto was different: there the index rose from 8.4 per cent to 25.7 per cent during the same period, and, despite a smaller population, streetcars carried 19 million passengers in 1892, 64 per cent more than Montreal. The gap is probably due to a number of factors, including differences in economic, occupational, and housing structures. Montreal, as Canada's major industrial centre, had a high proportion of low-paid industrial workers who lived in rented quarters close to their work. According to Armstrong and Nelles, this 'differential level of social dependence on street railways' may explain 'the heightened civic interest in the street railway in Toronto.'[7]

Other factors joined high fares to ensure that horse-drawn streetcars failed to become true mass transport. Animal power was both slow and limited. In downtown areas, numerous patrons and frequent stops made walking almost as fast. Further delays were created when an additional team had to be hitched up to climb steep hills. The Canadian climate worked against efficient year-round operation. In Montreal, for example, rails became useless on snow-covered streets, and cars had to be replaced by sleighs. In early spring, streets were so muddy that the company had to revert to the omnibus. Acquiring and maintaining three types of vehicles proved costly and inefficient. Animal traction imposed a heavy burden: large barns had to be erected; numerous animals, subject to injuries and frequent replacement, had to be bought, fed, and tended.[8]

Obviously, something else was needed for urban transport.

ELECTRIC TRAMWAYS

During the 1870s and 1880s, the search continued for an efficient system, free from animal traction. Cable cars, inaugurated in hilly San Francisco in 1873, offered an initial solution. Cars were attached to an endless underground cable powered by a steam-generating plant. The system spread to various American cities in the 1880s but was never adopted in Canada. Its heavy capital costs limited its profitability to the busiest central districts, and, where it went into service, it did not completely replace horse-drawn cars.[9]

Electricity, a novelty in the 1870s, would emerge as the energy source for urban mass transport. Promoters were quick to realize its potential. Devising electricity-driven streetcars nevertheless proved a difficult challenge, which attracted prominent inventors such as Edison, Henry, Daft, Van Depoele, and Sprague. From the numerous competing systems, Frank Sprague's – which featured motors mounted directly on the axles, more reliable trolleys, and improved car gearing and suspension – emerged as the most practical and set the standard. Sprague's line in Richmond, Virginia, opened in 1888 and launched the era of the electric streetcar. The new device spread like a prairie fire and, within a few years, replaced the horsecar.[10]

Like their predecessors, electric streetcars rolled on rails, but their motive power was carried through overhead wires, supported by poles, and was transmitted by a rolling trolley to motors located on the car axles. 'The basic design of the early electric cars did not differ from that of the horsecars they succeeded.'[11] Their length was similar, and both open and closed cars were used. Nevertheless, the new cars were heavier, using a larger proportion of steel. Over the years the design evolved: much longer cars were built, and the four-wheeled single driving truck at the centre of the car was replaced by twin trucks. Gradually greater comfort became possible: better seats were provided; the front, open, driver area was enclosed with panels and windows; and the stove used in winter gave way to electric heating.[12]

Canadians were quick to seize the opportunities offered by the new system. As early as 1884 Canada's first experimental electric railway appeared on the Toronto exhibition grounds. Two

TABLE 1
Canadian cities with electric tramway systems

Atlantic Provinces
Halifax, Moncton, Saint John, St John's, St Stephen, Sydney, Yarmouth

Quebec
Hull, Lévis, Montreal, Quebec, Sherbrooke, Trois-Rivières

Ontario
Belleville, Berlin (later Kitchener), Brantford, Cornwall, Fort William, Guelph, Hamilton, Kingston, London, Niagara Falls, Oshawa, Ottawa, Peterborough, Port Arthur, Sarnia, St Catharines, St Thomas, Sault Ste Marie, Sudbury, Toronto, Waterloo, Welland, Windsor

West
Brandon, Calgary, Edmonton, Lethbridge, Moose Jaw, Nelson, Regina, Saskatoon, Vancouver (including North Vancouver and New Westminster), Victoria, Winnipeg

SOURCE: John F. Due *The Intercity Electric Railway Industry in Canada* (Toronto 1966) 5

years later an electric public transit system was inaugurated in Windsor, Ontario, and, in 1887, St Catharines followed the lead. Victoria and Vancouver electrified mass transportation in 1890; Ottawa followed the next year and Toronto and Montreal in 1892.[13] In all, 46 Canadian cities and suburbs adopted the electric streetcar (Table 1).

Rapid technological change is often accompanied by controversy and uncertainty. The heavy capital investment required for the transition from horse-drawn to electric streetcars generated bitter discussions about financing, feasibility, and timing. In the Montreal Street Railway, 'several Directors supported by many of the shareholders declared that the thing was impossible and would ruin the Company, and some of the Directors even went to the length of resigning rather than countenance such a project'[14] – but resistance was futile. Financier Louis-Joseph Forget replaced

Jesse Joseph as president and, with a new board, energetically set about implementing and financing electrification. In the process, Forget created one of the major public utlities traded on the stock exchange.

In other places conversion permitted city councils dissatisfied with poor service to start afresh. Such was the case in Ottawa, Toronto, and Winnipeg.[15] In many growing western cities, where size had earlier militated against full-scale public transit, urban mass transport started with electric traction. Edmonton, for example, inaugurated its system only in 1908, long after electric tramways had become a fact of life throughout North America.[16] Similar situations prevailed in Calgary, Regina, and Saskatoon.

Electric tramways were an immediate success and attracted many more patrons than horsecars. The Montreal company carried 11 million passengers in 1892, 60 million in 1904, and 107 million in 1914. The number of riders as a proportion of the labour force rose from only 10.6 per cent in 1892 to 40.6 per cent in 1901 and 63.1 per cent 10 years later. Equivalent figures for Toronto were 25.7 per cent, 52.5 per cent, and 83.9 per cent.[17]

Many factors contributed to the sharp rise in popularity. With its higher speed, the tramway offered an alternative to walking; geographical expansion of cities separated home and work-place and made walking impracticable. Higher salaries and reduced rush-hour rates made fares more affordable. Rapid urban growth created a greater pool of potential riders, as thousands of new city-dwellers arrived every year from farms or from overseas.

Between 1891 and 1921, the Canadian urban population rose from 1.5 million to 4.3 million (47.4 per cent of the total population). The trend was even more accentuated in Quebec, Ontario, and

When the sun's heat caused improperly laid rails to expand, they kinked, as with this freshly laid track on King Edward Street in Vancouver. (Henry Ewert)

British Columbia. In 1921, the largest city, Montreal, boasted 618,506 inhabitants (689,753 with the suburbs), whereas Toronto had 521,893. Much of this growth took place in unurbanized areas within or outside existing city limits, speeding up one of the most important phases of suburban development in Canadian history. Electric tramways were key participants in the transformation of urban space.

By the early 20th century, a variety of factors combined to make suburban expansion an unprecedented, country-wide phenomenon, no longer limited to large cities. The urgent need to provide

Transportation modes in 1914: bicycle, horse-drawn wagon, automobile, and streetcar. Jasper Avenue, Edmonton (GAC NC6-804)

Shortly after electric streetcars were introduced, open cars formerly drawn by horses were used as trailers for extra passengers on flat routes: Ste Catherine Street, Montreal, 1894. (NPA 111,370 Misc II)

The patented pay-as-you-enter (PAYE) system originated in Montreal and revolutionized streetcar design and operation. (MUCTC)

housing for a rapidly increasing population was directed beyond the city by a new breed of community planners. Turning away from congested and unhealthy downtown areas, they celebrated the advantages of the individual suburban family home, surrounded by lawns and trees, which provided a country environment in an urban context without the evils of the city. Suburbs were thus developed largely to segregate the residential environment from the work-place.

There was, however, more to the sub-urban movement. Many rapidly expanding large-scale enterprises began looking for huge tracts of land on which to build new factories. Available land on the outskirts of the city led to another type of suburb: the industrial town, with a predominantly working-class population. This phenomenon was of particular significance in Montreal, where places like St-Henri, Ste-Cunégonde, and Maisonneuve all experienced very substantial development.

Suburbanization was also fuelled by a very active real estate development in-

Streetcars still had two-man crews – conductor and motorman; passengers paid on entering at the rear, which was enlarged. (CTA 9.2.3.G no. 836)

dustry. Numerous developers promised a quick fortune to investors and a home in a pleasant environment to city-dwellers. Land promotion escalated into frenzied speculation during the decade preceding the First World War. The land boom eventually collapsed in 1913, but it left a strong imprint on urban space.[18]

The new suburb's needs for adequate and reliable public transport explain the links that often united developers and transit owners. In new communities, residents and local authorities pressed soon for convenient service. Some tramway companies were ready to build ahead of development, hoping that patrons would soon follow. Others considered the dangers of overextending lines that would generate sufficient revenues only in the long term and adopted more cautious policies. In general, Canadian

tramway companies were not involved in the market as developers or real estate speculators.

Electric traction allowed tramway operators to cover their base territory more systematically and also to extend lines into surrounding municipalities. In some instances, distinct enterprises were created to serve distant suburbs. Such was the case with the Montreal Park and Island Railway, active in the western and northern suburban areas of Montreal, and the Montreal Island Belt Line Railway (later Montreal Terminal Railway), in the east end. Their lines crossed sparsely populated rural areas and linked outlying villages with the city. In order to attract patrons, both enterprises built amusement parks, popular with city-dwellers in summer. Excursions and leisure activities came to

Easier access: a summer-equipped radial railway car in Peterborough, Ontario. Before the PAYE system, passengers could step on the running board and enter directly. (NA PA 148504)

represent a significant component of their business.

In addition to the purely suburban lines, some 25 inter-city electric railway companies operated public transit systems in Canada. In 1916, a peak year, these companies had 825 mi (1,327 km) of line in service. Many were of the radial-railway type, linking a major city to outlying comunities but carrying also suburban customers. Some, like the Toronto and York Radial and the Toronto Suburban, served primarily suburban areas. Others had many suburban customers along their inter-city line. Good transportation facilities stimulated the growth of suburban communities around railway stations. Inter-city electric railway companies actually carried a small portion – less than 5 per cent in the peak year of 1920 – of the combined ridership of urban, suburban, and inter-

city enterprises; three-quarters of their passengers were travelling on partly suburban lines. In some places, large railway companies offered suburban passenger service on their main lines.[19]

The electric tramway that shaped suburban development was also instrumental in the reorganization of downtown areas. The older housing stock left by the middle classes fleeing the city was recycled to accommodate the poorer working class and immigrants. Eventually, some of these districts became slums, a process which persuaded remaining traditional residents to move to the suburbs. But the complete transformation of central business districts (CBDs) was even more striking. Most tramway lines radiated from the core, to which they took large daily loads of employees to work in the expanding administrative, legal, and business offices of the CBD,

Special equipment for harsh Canadian winters: storm windows about to be put on, Montreal Tramways Youville Shop, 1912 (MUCTC)

where numerous tall buildings began their dramatic transformation of the urban landscape. Some manufacturing activities, especially garment and printing shops, remained central, adding to the pressure for replacement of housing by large commercial buildings. The CBD also became a large emporium, with numerous large retail stores lined up on a major street, Ste Catherine in Montreal, Yonge in Toronto. Tramways brought customers from all over city and suburbs.

Electric tramways simultaneously dispersed population and concentrated economic activity. The resultant increasing downtown street congestion then accelerated the demise of the tramway on behalf of the automobile. But in 1901,

when the federal government began collecting statistics on electric tramways and railways, urban mass transport was thriving and growing. Total trackage in Canada was only 553 mi (890 km) in 1901; it doubled in a decade and reached a maximum of 1,729 mi (2,782 km) in 1923–4. At the beginning of the period, 2,155 cars were in service; by 1920 there were 5,240 cars, most longer and seating more passengers than their predecessors. The number of riders exploded; during the first decade it tripled from 121 to 361 million, and it went to 805 million in 1920. Temporarily reduced by the recession of the early 1920s, the figures rose to a high of 833 million in 1929, before plunging in the Depression.[20]

In the early decades of the century, expanding tramway companies had an impact on rolling stock manufacturers. Since a significant proportion of the tramway technology used in Canada originated in the United States, many American streetcar builders sold equipment to Canadian transit companies. J.G. Brill and Co., of Philadelphia, was among the major suppliers. Canadian manufacturers nevertheless became key participants in the industry. The Ottawa Car Co. and Canadian Car and Foundry emerged as the most important, but some street railway companies were also involved in production of rolling stock. Montreal Street Railway, Toronto Railway, and Winnipeg Electric Railway all had extensive shops which could build streetcars or buy unequipped cars and adapt the structures to their specific needs.[21]

Adaptation of foreign inventions is an important part of any industrial nation's history, and in Canada coping with winter conditions provided a major challenge to public transport. Electric streetcars were soon expected to operate year-round. Some contracts with cities called for companies to clear snow from the streets. In Montreal, for example, abundant snowfall necessitated numerous special measures. Every winter all passenger cars had to be equipped with double windows – a total of 25,000 windows during peak years – a defroster for the driver's front window, and a pair of scrapers at the front of the car that could be lowered on to the rails. Many cars also trailed a scarifier to clear the centre of the tracks. For major snow removal, special service cars – called sweepers – featured double rotating brushes in the front and ploughs on the side. On suburban routes, cars were equipped with v-shaped ploughs or rotary ploughs to cut across large accumu-

Double truck sweepers, 1912, manufactured by the Ottawa Car Co. Canadian street railways were world pioneers in running on snow-covered tracks. Storms were rated by severity and routes cleared on a priority basis. (MUCTC)

lations of drifting snow. Similar equipment was used in Winnipeg, another city plagued with heavy snowstorms, and elsewhere in Canada.[22]

Another example of Canadian adaptability was the introduction, in 1905, of the 'Pay-as-you-enter' or PAYE system, patented in Canada and the United States by Duncan McDonald, superintendent of the Montreal Street Railway. This system, soon adopted by many North American transit companies, necessitated a distinct car design, with a longer rear entrance and platform where the conductor would stay, rather than circulating among the passengers. It contributed also to greater speed in the movement of cars and reduced the risk of accidents. While PAYE modified the conductor's task, it still relied on two men, a driver and a conductor, to operate each car. The next step, one-man operation, appeared in Canada during the First World War and gradually spread as cars were redesigned to allow entrance and payment at the front.[23]

St Lawrence and Ste Catherine, Montreal, 1893: the planning, engineering, and complexity of a well-developed urban streetcar network (NPA 102021-II)

One-man operation reduced operating expenses, even if a small bonus was given to the driver as compensation for the added responsibilities. Across Canada, management grew increasingly concerned about rising labour costs, as the wage portion of gross income rose from 30 per cent during the first decade of the century to 50 per cent after the war. The total nation-wide staff of 5,493 reported in 1901 more than doubled to 11,390 in a decade and continued to rise until the war, when it dropped significantly. The upward trend resumed after 1918, reaching 17,341 in 1920, and fluctuated slightly thereafter, with a peak of 18,801 in 1929. The high turnover rates in easily learned, low-paying jobs such as conductor and driver meant that tramways provided employment for more people than these figures suggest.[24]

Despite management's strict financial controls, working conditions improved somewhat between 1900 and 1930, primarily as a result of unionization under the Amalgamated Association of Street and Electric Railway Employees. In various cities, numerous strikes often degenerated into violent clashes and rioting. From 1901 to 1930, a total of 41 strikes affected street railways, and 371,247 man-days were lost; 21 strikes and 329,889 lost man-days occurred from 1916 to 1921, as workers struggled successfully to cope with rapid inflation.[25] But the numerous strikes inconvenienced customers and provoked negative reactions, which were instrumental in the move toward regulation of public utilities.

Except in a few prairie cities, most Canadian urban mass transport began as a private undertaking. The type of ownership found in early omnibus and horsecar systems continued with electric tramways. Unavoidably, however, public bodies were involved, as companies sought charters and rights of way on public domain, and public ownership became a bitterly contested issue.

Public bodies such as town councils or provincial legislatures granted private enterprises a fixed-term franchise, or right to operate, in return for a promise to perform as specified in matters such as routes covered, service schedule and frequency, maintenance obligations, fares, and grant payments to the city. The terms of the contract were so important that negotiations between shrewd businessmen and numerous local politicians often led to heated discussions, harsh bargaining, mounting pressures, even bribery.

Private entrepreneurs pursued two main objectives. First, they sought complete control of the market by fighting competition and trying to extract exclusive rights. Second, they attempted to maximize profits by focusing on revenue-generating activities and strict control of expenses. The drive to maximize profits, or sometimes just to survive, often led to loose interpretation or even flagrant violation of contract terms.

The drive for profitability became more critical with the advent of the tramway, because companies had to support growing capital expenses for construction of extended rail lines and acquisition of equipment. These were financed through the floating of share and bond issues on which dividends and interest had to be paid. Experienced financiers became involved in the operation and were quick to seize the rewards of overcapitalization, which justified generating higher profits. Thus transportation enterprises became not only public utilities but also private financial ventures.

In many instances, transit enterprises were closely related to, and sometimes, as in Victoria and Vancouver, fully integrated with, electric power companies. Such a link was quite natural, especially in the early years, when tramway operations represented a major share of the power market. With the growth of industrial and residential electricity consumption, tramways became a relatively less important market. At the same time, combined power and transit companies became more critical of the lower profit margins being generated by the transit component.

While capitalists insisted on profitability, customers emphasized better service. Citizens kept asking for changes such as line extensions, longer schedules, shorter intervals between cars, and low fares, which operators said could not be met without compensating gains in other areas. A clash was inevitable.[26]

The widespread battle between private and public interests reached an unequalled climax in Toronto. Tensions dated back to the horsecar era, when service was so bad that when the franchise expired in 1891 the city took over the operation for a few months. Electrification was the key to better service, but civic officials were unwilling to assume the cost. After considerable debate, a 30-year franchise was granted to the Toronto Railway Co., a new enterprise controlled by financier and railway promoter William Mackenzie. During its first years of operation, rising patronage paid for electrification and line extensions. Later, continuing urban growth

Convenient suburban living was made possible by road and streetcar extensions such as this, being given a concrete base in Edmonton in 1913. (GAC NA 1328-64600)

brought problems when the company rejected all requests for extended trackage, especially in the suburbs and newly annexed areas of the city. Toronto Railway concentrated on the highly profitable lines of the core city, within the city limits of 1891. These lines soon became congested and insufficient to fulfil the needs of citizens. In 1904, Mackenzie took control of the independent suburban companies, but he refused to merge these with the core operations, thus compelling commuters to pay a double fare.

Despite a number of attempts, city council could not persuade the company to alter its policy. Pressure from civic reformers mounted, and relations between council and company became acrimonious. Between 1911 and 1915 the city built a few lines, operated by a new public body, the Toronto Civic Railway, to serve areas neglected by the Toronto Railway, but this move was not sufficient to solve the problems. Mackenzie

offered, in 1913, to sell its property to the city, but the offer was never accepted. In 1918, a disenchanted and angry electorate voted by an 11-to-1 margin in favour of take-over by the municipality at the end of the franchise. In 1921, the Toronto Transportation Commission (TTC) took charge of the tramways and embarked on a huge program of overdue expansion and modernization.[27]

Montreal Street Railway officials, headed by Louis-Joseph Forget, adopted a different course, largely because they lacked their Toronto counterpart's exclusive franchise and had to be more responsive to the public lest competitors move in. They were hard bargainers who fought regularly with city councillors; they turned down many requests for service improvements and line extensions but would make trade-offs for further concessions. In a city where civic reform was indentified with west-end anglophone businessmen, they were able to rely upon a body of devoted aldermen, especially among the franco-phones representing the working-class wards, for whom street railways, public works, and politics were closely inter-mingled. They also relied successfully on a provincial government devoted to the interests of the big corporations. In the suburbs, the company cautiously extended its lines to selected towns in exchange for long and favourable fran-chises, but in most of the area it tolerated the existence of two suburban compa-nies which it eventually acquired and operated as subsidiaries. Campaigns for public ownership, especially in 1904 and 1905, were easily dismissed.

In 1910, the company was bought out by a new syndicate headed by E.A. Robert, who reorganized it in 1911 as the Montreal Tramways Co. By that time relations with the city had turned sour. Civic officials complained about insuffi-cient service and entered into negotia-tions for a renewed franchise. The failure to reach agreement prompted provincial intervention in 1916. A commission was created to draft a new contract for a period of 36 years. Acting on its recom-mendations, the Quebec legislature ad-opted a service-at-cost contract, a new feature at the time, with periodic adjust-ments of fares supervised by a Montreal Tramways Commission. Public trans-portation was thus removed from the responsibility of city council and main-tained in private hands, with a measure of public control.[28] That episode was an example of growing encroachments on municipal autonomy which have charac-terized provincial-municipal relations in Canada throughout the century.[29]

British Columbia experienced a dis-tinct and, indeed, unique situation. There the utilities market was dominat-ed by a single enterprise producing and distributing gas and electricity and pro-viding streetcar services. This was also the case in other Canadian cities, but the British Columbia Electric Railway was servicing not only Vancouver but also the surrounding area and Victoria. Con-trolled from abroad by a British invest-ment firm, the company was able to secure a new franchise from Vancouver in 1901. Like the Montreal company, it adopted a policy of hard bargaining with municipal council over line extensions, rather than the Toronto Railway style of entrenched resistance, and secured sub-urban franchises in order to protect its monopoly and prevent a municipal take-over. But tramway operations were less profitable in Vancouver than in the east-ern cities and were subsidized by profits from gas and electricity. The company began asking for a rate increase in 1916 and finally obtained it in 1922, escaping in the process the kind of public control being established in other provinces.[30]

In the prairies, Calgary, Edmonton, Regina, and Saskatoon launched tram-way services later and started with mu-nicipally owned operations. In Winni-peg, however, the company, controlled since 1892 by William Mackenzie and after 1919 by local interests, remained in private hands.[31] In New Brunswick, the Saint John Railway Co. was bought in 1894 by a syndicate of CPR-linked finan-ciers in Montreal and Saint John and sold in 1917 to a subsidiary of the New Brunswick Power Co.[32] In Halifax tram-way operations also remained in private hands but were submitted to the control of the Public Utilities Commission in 1914.[33]

The nation-wide pre-war outcry for better service and greater public regula-tion led to a variety of solutions. In some cities ratepayers chose public owner-ship, but private capital usually survived and remained in control, even if under the aegis of provincially appointed boards of regulation. After the war, both types of ownership faced similar prob-lems: rising labour and capital costs and

Specially equipped sprinkler cars helped keep city streets clean. In downtown Edmonton, during the First World War, an Electric Radial Railway Co. car turns from 101 Street onto Jasper Avenue. (GAC NA 1328-64341)

staggering ridership had reduced profitability. Expenses consumed 60 per cent of receipts at the turn of the century, and 81 per cent by 1921. Fare increases granted in many places lowered the figure to around 70 per cent by 1929, but the expansion years were clearly over. The emergence of the automobile signalled the end of the golden age of the tramway. There were still some good years to come, especially with the temporary revival of the tramway during the Second World War, but another era had already begun.

THE IMPACT OF AUTOMOBILES

The popularity of the automobile threatened tramway operations, favoured the shift to the bus, and in the long run transformed public mass transport. The automobile was not only another mode of transportation, it represented an alternative way of life. Whereas mass transit was a public and collective solution, the automobile was private and individual. It offered a flexible schedule, a choice of routes, and higher speed. When they could afford it, most citizens chose the private car without hesitation.

The shift was slow, extending over decades. It was even slower in Canada than in the United States, owing to differences in prices and incomes. In 1920 there were only 408,790 registed motor vehicles in Canada, 62 per cent of which were passenger automobiles; by 1930 these figures had climbed to 1.2 million and 86 per cent. Depression and war slowed the rise, but between 1945 and 1960 the number rose sharply, from 1.5 million to 5.3 million, and more moderately thereafter, to 11.3 million in 1975.[34]

Even if only a minority of Canadian families owned a car during the 1920s, the phenomenon encroached on tramway ridership, although it is not possible to measure the effect. Despite population growth, the 1929 peak of 833 million riders was not much higher than the 1920 figure of 805 million.[35] In addition, for a few years, many streetcar operators had to face the competition of privately owned jitney cars, which appeared during the war. 'Jitneys were motor vehicles rebuilt with a larger body so that they could carry up to about ten people. They operated along street car routes picking up fare-paying passengers as they went.'[36] Tramway enterprises, especially in the west, were thus deprived of significant revenues and fought fiercely to have jitneys banned from their routes. By the early 1920s government intervention had removed the threat.

Tramways were at a disadvantage vis-à-vis automobiles. Fixed to the rails, they lacked the flexibility to go around obstacles or nuisances. This proved a growing handicap, as they had to share streets with a greater number of private cars. Downtown traffic congestion slowed tramways, thus adding to operating costs and making trams less attractive for short distances.[37]

Motor vehicles were not only competition but an alternative to the tramway. Buses offered flexibility that streetcars lacked and did not require heavy investments in rails and wires. Canadian enterprises were slow to adopt the new vehicle. Only 27 were in service in 1922. In Halifax, Hamilton, Montreal, Ottawa, and Toronto, operators still relied heavily on tramways and added significantly to trackage through the 1920s. Buses were used initially as feeders for rail lines or as replacements when road works were blocking the way. Gradually they began to serve lightly travelled routes in outlying areas. All-bus operations began earlier in smaller cities; in larger centres the volume of passengers justified maintaining the tramways. In 1936 streetcars still outnumbered buses by 6 to 1.[38]

The Second World War gave tramways a new lease on life, when private automobile use was curtailed and wartime employment beefed up demand for transportation services. Total transit company ridership fell to 585 million during the worst depression year and then rose to pass the 1-billion mark in 1943 and achieve a peak of 1.345 billion in 1946. Operators stretched equipment to the limit and even reverted to older mothballed cars while adding new buses wherever possible. The demise of the overworked tramways rapidly followed the return of peace as they were replaced by buses. By 1950 buses and trolley-buses outnumbered tramways, and all the major cities, with the notable exception of Toronto, abandoned streetcar service during that decade: Winnipeg in 1954, Vancouver in 1955, Montreal and Ottawa in 1959.[39]

The electrically driven trolley-bus offered another alternative to the tramway. It arrived in Canada during the 1920s but did not gain popularity before the war. During the 1950s slightly more than a thousand of these vehicles were used in various Canadian cities, but their number declined in the second half of the 1960s.[40] The quieter trolley-bus had no obnoxious fumes and was more pleasant to ride in than the gasoline-driven bus, but overhead lines made it less flexible and ill adapted for rapidly expanding suburban areas.

The automobile gave rise to a new wave of suburban expansion from after the war until the 1980s. The urbanized area of major metropolitan centres extended over huge territories, and population figures reached a new magnitude. Metropolitan Montreal passed the 1-million mark in 1931 and then took only three decades to add a second million. In 1976, its population stood at 2.8 million. Most of this growth occurred in the suburbs, and the population of the city began to decline in 1966. Metropolitan Toronto grew at a slightly higher rate

Toronto's excellent public transit system co-ordinates subways, streetcars, and buses: a bus and streetcar at the Jane-Bloor transfer station in 1937. (NA PA-54634)

and surpassed Montreal in 1976. Rapid growth was not limited to these two cities. In fact, since the end of the war, medium-sized metropolitan areas have experienced faster growth than the major centres. In the 1970s the level of urbanization in Canada reached a plateau, as many core cities lost inhabitants and numerous city-dwellers fled to outlying rural areas.[41]

The impact of transportation on the post-war suburban movement was very different from that of the early part of the century. New suburbanites no longer needed to wait for transit line extensions before moving. Private-car-oriented communities replaced turn-of-the-century streetcar suburbs. Impatient drivers of the rising number of vehicles forced governments to build new freeways in order to speed up the longer journey to work. The freeways then stimulated further suburban development and, over the years, became so congested that they operated as urban boulevards.[42]

Public transit services still met a need in the new automobile-oriented communities. The bus was particularly fitted for rapid adaptation to the ever-changing frontier of urban settlement. A host of private inter-city bus companies began servicing outlying suburbs and linking them with the core. Over the years, the inter-city lines became more and more suburban, as had the inter-city railway earlier in the century. Useful as they were, they did not provide an integrated and reliable service. Core-city transit enterprises also expanded their lines to some of the new suburbs. But greater dispersion and lower densities made transit systems less economical to operate. New solutions had to be found for

Subway disruption: Toronto's Front Street between Union Station and the Royal York Hotel, 1950. Extensive systems of underground pipes and cables added to the expense and complications. (NA PA-111572)

such a massive transformation of the urban environment.

RAPID TRANSIT

As with the first decades of the century, later suburban expansion was accompanied by complete transformation of CDBS. An economy more and more devoted to service activities had a seemingly insatiable appetite for office space. Older buildings were demolished to make space for more and taller skyscrapers. More employees were working in CBDS, but escalating parking costs and street congestion prevented most of them from driving to work. Transit companies found themselves in a difficult position. Expanded facilities were required, but only for a couple of hours in the morning and late afternoon, five days a week, while at other times demand was static or declining.[43]

Major Canadian cities implemented a variety of rapid transit systems. In Toronto and Montreal, the size of the city and the density of the inner areas led to construction of subways. In 1946, Torontonians authorized by referendum the building of a subway. Work began three years later, and the first line, which ran along Yonge Street for 4.6 mi (7.4 km) from Union Station to Eglinton Avenue, was opened in 1954. Later extensions brought the total trackage to 35.4 mi (56.9 km) in 1980. The system was then

Montreal's rubber-tired métro is one of the world's most modern subway systems. Moving sidewalks (shown here under construction in the Beaudry station, December 1966) facilitate passenger movement. (Daggett/Montreal Star Collection/NA PA-166780)

carrying 834,000 passengers on average business days over two main routes: a v-shaped north-south line and a crossing east-west line, with a total of 59 stations. Although some tunnelling was needed, most construction was cut-and-cover or open-cut. The cars rolled on steel wheels.[44]

The Montreal métro was different. Its cars were narrower and rolled on rubber tires, allowing better traction on steep grades and providing a quieter ride. The Drapeau administration chose the French technology then being implemented in the Paris métro. Because of the rocky nature of Montreal's geology, construction underground was generally of the tunnel type. The decision to build the subway was taken in 1961, and official inauguration took place in 1966.

Three lines were then available: north-south, east-west, and under the St Lawrence, linking the city to St Helen's Island and the south shore. The total length was 15.5 mi (25 km), with 26 stations. Further extensions were started in the early 1970s; at the end of construction, in 1988, a new east-west line had been added and the total length was 38.5 mi (62 km), with 65 stations.[45]

Building subways was a costly proposition, which only Toronto and Montreal could afford. They greatly increased carrying capacity without disrupting the urban texture of central areas, but they were economical only in the most densely populated sectors and did not solve all the problems linked to suburban sprawl. Montreal and Toronto had to organize extensive networks of urban and suburban bus lines as feeders.

Other measures had to be taken to address the needs of suburban populations. Surface rail transport offered alternative solutions and was given a new lease on life. In the Toronto area, the government of Ontario created GO Transit to operate regional transportation services. A first commuter line was inaugurated in 1967 on 42.3 mi (68 km) of existing railway lines and rights of way between Oakville and Pickering. During the following decades, the network grew to 211.3 mi (340 km) plus bus feeder lines.[46] In Montreal the integration of two Canadian National suburban lines with the metropolitan transportation network was less successful, because of the weaker pressure for improved facilities in the areas serviced by these lines.

Light Rapid Transit (LRT) lines in Edmonton and Calgary represented another solution to urban and suburban transportation problems. Opened in 1978, Edmonton's 4.5-mi (7.2-km) system featured electric rail cars rolling in a 1-mi (1.6-km) subway section under the CBD and emerging on a surface exclusive

A Montreal métro car in a specially designed car wash, 1976; a cleaning and maintenance program helps protect heavy transit investments. (Juster/Montreal Star Collection/ NA PA-166784)

right of way. It was able to carry 5,000 to 6,000 passengers per hour. Patronage was from the start beyond all expectations, proof that many suburbanites were willing to leave their cars at home when efficient and speedy transit facilities were provided.[47] Toronto also built an LRT, the 4.4-mi-long (7 km) Scarborough LRT line, opened in 1985.[48]

Vancouver went a step further with the Sky Train. Inaugurated for Expo '86, the 13.3-mi (21.4-km) line links Vancouver's waterfront to Burnaby and New Westminster. It was built partly underground (1.2 mi [2 km] downtown) and at grade (3.7 mi [6 km]) but mostly elevated at a height of 19.7 to 26.2 ft (6 to 8 m) above the ground. Fully automated and computer directed, the aluminum and fibreglass cars are able to carry 20,000 passengers per hour.[49]

The development of these various rapid transit systems gave a strong impetus to Canada's transportation equipment

The Montreal métro: tunnelling in 1973 through two miles of dense bedrock for the six-station Verdun extension. The tunnel looks like a modern mine. (Leishman/NA PA-167073)

The double-decker GO (Government of Ontario) commuter train: an alternative to single-passenger use of increasingly crowded expressways. The commuter bus is more flexible in routing than trains but can get tied up in traffic. (OMT 25167-8)

industry. GO Transit bought numerous double-decker cars for its suburban lines. The building of Montreal's métro facilitated the transfer of French technology to Canada and contributed to the emergence of Bombardier as a major supplier of urban rolling stock. The Ontario-sponsored Urban Transportation Development Corporation (UTDC), now owned by Lavalin Inc., developed new streetcars for Toronto and the LRT systems and vehicles used in Scarborough and Vancouver.[50]

The opening of subways and other rapid transit systems boosted ridership figures, which had been declining from the Canadian high of 1.345 billion in 1946. In 1954, when the Toronto subway was inaugurated, they rose from 1.077 to 1.264 billion, but they continued to decline thereafter and fell under the 1-billion mark in the early 1960s. In 1966, Montreal's métro helped bring it back over that line; further developments in rapid transit and the energy crisis led to increased patronage in the 1970s.[51]

In addition to costly rapid transit systems, available only in larger metropolitan areas, other, simpler solutions to street congestion at rush hours were adopted in many cities. These included express bus lines, exclusive corridors for buses on major streets and bridges, and car pooling policies.

THE GOVERNANCE OF MODERN MASS TRANSPORTATION

The introduction of new systems did not solve all the problems associated with overexpansion of urban areas and competition from the private car. Soon after the war, transit systems faced a serious financial crisis. Purchase of expensive modern equipment, declining ridership, and operation of longer, lightly travelled lines, especially after peak hours, dramatically changed the profitability of the enterprises. Expenses consumed 69 per cent of receipts in 1944, rose rapidly to 99 per cent in 1948, and thereafter remained dangerously close to 100 per cent.[52]

The prospect of shrinking profits or growing deficits paved the way for public take-over of the private companies still operating in some major cities. The principle of public ownership no longer raised the bitter disputes that it inspired early in the century. In 1951 the Quebec government set up the Montreal Transportation Commission (MTC), which was to acquire Montreal Tramways, Canada's largest private system. A similar situation occurred in Winnipeg, where the Greater Winnipeg Transit Commission took over the system in 1953. In Vancouver and Victoria, public operation began in 1961.[53]

Most public or private networks were servicing only the core area and, in a few cases, some older suburbs. The problem of providing services in the numerous suburban towns that had mushroomed all around metropolitan areas was left unresolved, and many small-scale entrepreneurs stepped in to fill the gap. For example, in the late 1960s, 10 private bus companies operated regular transit lines in Quebec City and vicinity, and 15 others serviced regional routes, some in suburban areas.[54]

Passengers on suburban lines were denied free transfers to the city system.

Moreover, they endured poor service, particularly irregular schedules on often overworked, unreliable equipment. The proliferation of small independent enterprises could not meet the needs of the growing number of suburbanites. In addition, special services were often tendered by distinct companies. Some dealt with charter bus services; others provided school children with transportation, as larger, centralized schools brought this once primarily rural phenomenon to urban and suburban areas.

The need to regulate and co-ordinate all these operations became more evident.[55] Groups began to advocate better integration of services and a degree of regional planning. Such concern was not limited to transportation problems; it touched on other services, such as education, police, and, more generally, urban administration. Provincial legislatures had to step in and create various regional bodies. Within that context, reform of transit services often went hand in hand with reorganization of municipal structures.

An early example is Toronto, where a metropolitan municipality was created in 1953 and vested with responsibility for regional services, including public transit. The old TTC was replaced by a new Toronto Transit Commission (also TTC), and its area of operation was multiplied by seven. The new body acquired four private bus companies which operated in the suburbs and offered improved and co-ordinated service. At first, fare zones were established; they were abolished in 1973, when a system-wide single fare was established. A second public body, GO Transit, was created by the province in 1967 to manage regional transportation services.[56]

Winnipeg and its suburbs pooled their resources in 1953 to create the Greater Winnipeg Transit Commission, which bought and operated a formerly private company. In Vancouver and Victoria areas, some regional co-ordination already existed because of the long-standing unique situation of the privately owned British Columbia Electric Co., which became a crown corporation in 1961. In 1978 a new public body, BC Transit, was created to plan and manage public transit all over the province. In Vancouver, its territory extended over 386 sq mi (1,000 sq km), and it provided, in addition to ground transportation, passenger ferry services.[57]

In Montreal, creation of a regional co-ordinating body, the Montreal Urban Community, at the end of 1969, permitted replacement of MTC by the Montreal Urban Community Transit Commission, which gradually extended its authority over all the municipalities of the Island of Montreal. Two other transit commissions were later created for outlying suburbs: for the large suburban town of Laval and the North Shore and for the South Shore area. In metropolitan Quebec, two distinct public transit corporations were also created, one in 1969, for the Quebec Urban Community, the other in 1978, for the South Shore, which encompassed Lévis and vicinity.[58] The provincial government established similar public bodies in other large cities.

Canada's major metropolitan centres emerged from the 1970s with improved transit services, managed by regional public bodies which could provide integrated transportation facilities to core city-dwellers and suburbanites and plan for long-term developments. Smaller cities did not always receive the same degree of attention from governments, and their citizens had to live with a lower level of service.

By the 1970s, provincial governments were playing a much larger role in provision of urban mass transport than in preceding eras. They created new orga-

nizations and shouldered much of the financial burden from ailing systems. Operating costs had climbed so high that they could not be covered entirely by fares. Governments came to realize that these were essential social services and had to be supported by the whole society. They devised programs to provide a large share of necessary capital in addition to an annual operating subsidy. Municipal or regional administrations also had to help pay for these investments and expenditures, in order to leave affordable fares and prevent further loss of patronage. Arrangements varied over time and among provinces, according to local conditions.[59]

State intervention involved a process of policy-making. By spending lavishly on road and freeway construction after 1945, provincial governments had clearly favoured the automobile and fuelled suburban expansion. Realizing the high costs of extensive suburbanization, they reversed their strategy in the 1970s and 1980s and supported better public transportation. Instrumental in this reorientation were active citizens committees and reform groups, which strongly advocated high priority for public transit and pushed for better services while resisting fare increases. But the rising costs of the systems sparked some resistance from authorities, especially local politicians, who had to pay the bills with unpopular higher taxes. Again the old opposition between better services and lower costs became the focus of endless debates. This time it was not primarily a matter of public v. private operation. The Canadian welfare state, of which subsidized public transit had become a constituent part, was at stake. The debate occupied centrestage in the mid-1980s. Its outcome will have a major effect on the way urban mass transport will be provided at the turn of the next century.

CONCLUSION

Public transportation in Canadian cities has come a long way from the days of the horse-drawn omnibuses and early streetcars. The development of mass transportation has been a major component of Canadian urbanization since the mid-19th century. Implementation of each successive type of system helped shape urban form and addressed urban needs. Thoughout, Canadians invented or adapted the appropriate technology. As with other areas of public works, decisions involved economic, social, and political issues, as well as engineering challenges. They often raised hotly disputed debates over the respective roles of public and private enterprise, of individual and collective choices, of planning and laissez-faire. Thus urban mass transportation is much more than a purely local matter; it is, indeed, a significant and revealing component of Canadian history.

NOTES

1 On the US experience, see Ellis L. Armstrong, Suellen M. Hoy, and Michael C. Robinson eds *History of Public Works in the United States: 1776–1976* (Chicago 1976) 161–86.

2 The expression was used by Gilbert Stelter in 'The Historian's Approach to Canada's Urban Past' *Histoire sociale/Social History* 7:13 (May 1974) 5.

3 *Transit in Toronto: The Story of Public Transportation in Toronto* (Toronto 1984) 1; Edwin C. Guillet *The Story of Canadian Roads* (Toronto 1967) 79; Frank Navin and John Morrall 'History of Transit' in Richard M. Soberman and Heather A. Hazard eds *Canadian Transit Handbook* (Toronto 1980) 23–6

4 On the history of Canadian roads and streets, see Guillet's informative study, *The Story of Canadian Roads*.

5 'A Brief History of the Montreal Street Railway Company from 1861 to 1910' *Annual Report of the Montreal Street Railway Company for the Fiscal Year Ended 30th September 1910* 31

6 'A Brief History' 27; Richard M. Binns *Montreal's Electric Streetcars: An Illustrated History of the Tramway Era: 1892 to 1959* (Montreal 1973) 9

7 Christopher Armstrong and H.V. Nelles *Monopoly's Moment: The Organization and Regulation of Canadian Utilities* (Philadelphia 1986) 52–3

8 Binns *Montreal's Electric Streetcars* 9; Edgar Andrew Collard *Call Back Yesterdays* (Don Mills 1965) 211–12

9 Robinson 'Urban Mass Transportation' 165–7

10 Ibid 167–9; John F. Due *The Intercity Electric Railway Industry in Canada* (Toronto 1966) 3–4

11 Binns *Montreal's Electric Streetcars* 15

12 Ibid passim

13 Ibid 9; Due *The Intercity Electric Railway Industry* 3–5

14 'A Brief History' 32

15 Armstrong and Nelles *Monopoly's Moment* 85–9

16 Colin K. Hatcher and Tom Schwarzkopf *Edmonton's Electric Transit: The Story of Edmonton's Streetcars and Trolley Buses* (Toronto 1983) 7–11

17 'A Brief History' 42; Armstrong and Nelles *Monopoly's Moment* 133

18 On suburban development in the early 20th century, see Paul-André Linteau *The Promoters' City: Building the Industrial Town of Maisonneuve 1883–1918* (Toronto 1985); Jean-Pierre Collin 'La cité sur mesure: spécialisation sociale de l'espace et autonomie municipale dans la banlieue montréalaise, 1875–1920' *Urban History Review/Revue d'histoire urbaine (UHR/RHU)* 13:1 (June 1984) 19–34; Walter Van Nus 'The Role of Suburban Government in the City Building Process: The Case of Notre-Dame-de-

Grâces, Québec, 1876–1910' *UHR/ RHU* 13:2 (Oct 1984) 91–103; John C. Weaver 'From Land Assembly to Social Maturity: The Suburban Life of Westdale (Hamilton) Ontario, 1911–1951' *Histoire Sociale/Social History* 11:22 (Nov 1978) 411–40.

19 Due *The Intercity* 118

20 *Canada Yearbooks*

21 Binns *Montreal's Electric Streetcars*; John E. Baker *Winnipeg's Electric Transit: The Story of Winnipeg's Streetcars and Trolley Busses* (Toronto 1982); Colin K. Hatcher *Saskatchewan's Pioneer Streetcars: The Story of the Regina Municipal Railway* (Montreal 1971); Hatcher and Schwarzkopf *Edmonton's Electric Transit*; Fred Angus *Loyalist City Streetcars: The Story of Street Railway Transit in Saint John, New Brunswick* (Toronto 1979)

22 Binns *Montreal's Electric Streetcars* 131–7; Baker *Winnipeg's Electric Transit* 52–3, 180–1

23 Binns *Montreal's Electric Streetcars* 44–7 and 75–80

24 *Canada Yearbook* various years; Armstrong and Nelles *Monopoly's Moment* 225, 239

25 Numerous studies have been conducted on various local street railway strikes; a general account may be found in Armstrong and Nelles *Monopoly's Moment* 213–47.

26 On the franchise system and relations between town councils and private companies, see ibid passim; Linteau *The Promoters' City* chap 3 and 5; Patricia Roy 'The Fine Arts of Lobbying and Persuading: The Case of the B.C. Electric Railway, 1897–1917' in David S. Macmillan ed *Canadian Business History: Selected Studies, 1497–1971* (Toronto 1972) 239–54.

27 Michael J. Doucet 'Mass Transit and the Failure of Private Ownership: The Case of Toronto in the Early Twentieth Century' *UHR/RHU* 3-77 (Feb 1978) 3–33; Armstrong and Nelles *Monopoly's Moment* passim

28 Linteau *The Promoters' City* chap 3 and 5; Christopher Armstrong and H.V. Nelles 'Suburban Street Railway Strategies in Montreal, Toronto, and Vancouver, 1896–1930' in G.A. Stelter and A.F.J. Artibise eds *Power and Place: Canadian Urban Development in the North American Context* (Vancouver 1986) 187–218; Armstrong and Nelles *Monopoly's Moment* 204–5, 249–54

29 On the decline of municipal autonomy see Warren Magnusson 'Introduction: The Development of Canadian Urban Government' in Warren Magnusson and Andrew Sancton eds *City Politics in Canada* (Toronto 1983) 3–57, and John Taylor 'Urban Autonomy in Canada: Its Evolution and Decline' in G.A. Stelter and A.F.J. Artibise eds *The Canadian City: Essays in Urban and Social History* (Ottawa 1984) 478–500.

30 Armstrong and Nelles *Monopoly's Moment* 96–100, 120, 133–4, 153, 158, 207–10, 254–62; Roy 'The Fine Arts'

31 Armstrong and Nelles *Monopoly's Moment* 94–6, 262–4

32 Angus *Loyalist City Streetcars* 24, 45

33 Armstrong and Nelles *Monopoly's Moment* 197

34 *Historical Statistics of Canada* (Ottawa 1983) series T147–8

35 *Canada Yearbooks*; Norman D. Wilson 'Some Problems of Urban Transportation' in H.A. Innis ed *Essays in Transportation in Honour of W.T. Jackman* (Toronto 1941) 91–7

36 Hatcher and Schwarzkopf *Edmonton's Electric Transit* 82; see also Wilson 'Some Problems' 90–1 and Roy 'The Fine Arts' 246–9.

37 Donald F. Davis 'Mass Transit and Private Ownership: An Alternative Perspective on the Case of Toronto' *UHR/RHU* 3-78 (Feb 1979) 79

38 Ibid 66–8; *Canada Yearbooks*; Binns *Montreal's Electric Streetcars* 89

39 *Canada Yearbooks*; Davis 'Mass Transit' 69–72; Binns *Montreal's Electric Street-*

cars 91, 100–1; Navin and Morrall 'History of Transit' 24–5

40 *Canada Yearbooks*; Navin and Morrall 'History of Transit' 33

41 L.O. Stone *Urban Development in Canada: An Introduction to the Demographic Aspects* (Ottawa 1967); Statistics Canada *Urban Growth in Canada* (Ottawa 1984)

42 Francine Dumont and Pierre Labonté *Urbanisation et réseau de transport de la région montréalaise (1945–1975)* (Quebec 1977); Jean Pierre Collin *Le développement résidentiel suburbain et l'exploitation de la ville centrale* (Montreal 1981)

43 On rush hours, see Mark W. Frankena *Urban Transportation Economics: Theory and Canadian Policy* (Toronto 1979) 3–7.

44 *Transit in Toronto* 10–17

45 *Le métro de Montréal* (Montreal 1983)

46 *Transit in Toronto* 32

47 Hatcher and Schwarzkopf *Edmonton's Electric Transit* 135–44

48 *Transit in Toronto* 14

49 *Vancouver Regional Rapid Transit: The System for Greater Vancouver* (Vancouver 1985)

50 *Transit in Toronto* 14–32; I.A. Litvak and C.J. Maule *The Light-Rapid Comfortable (LRC) Train and the Intermediate Capacity Transit System (ICTS)* (Toronto 1982)

51 *Canada Yearbooks*; Navin and Morrall 'History of Transit' 35–40

52 *Canada Yearbooks*; Navin and Morrall 'History of Transit' 42–5; Frankena *Urban Transportation Economics* 4–7

53 Harold Kaplan *Reform, Planning, and City Politics: Montreal, Winnipeg, Toronto* (Toronto 1982) 396; Baker *Winnipeg's Electric Transit* 101

54 Dominique Bédard 'La problématique du transport en commun dans la zone métroplitaine de Québec' (unpublished ms, Université Laval, 1986), 38–40

55 See, for example, Canadian Federation of Mayors and Municipalities *First Canadian Urban Transportation Conference* 4 vol (Toronto 1969).

56 *Transit in Toronto* 8–9

57 Baker *Winnipeg's Electric Transit* 101

58 Andrew Sancton *Governing the Island of Montreal: Language Differences and Metropolitan Politics* (Berkeley 1985) 117–18, 128–9; Bédard 'La problématique' 41; Jean-Pierre Collin *Développement urbain et coût des services publics régionaux* (Montreal 1982) 91–2

59 For an overview of provincial subsidy policies in the 1970s, see Frankena *Urban Transportation Economics* 62–4; see also Collin *Développement urbain* 87–100.

CHRISTOPHER ANDREAE

Railways

Canada is perhaps the only country in the world to have an almost equal mix of state and private ownership in railways. The United States is the only major country to rely almost exclusively on private rail ownership, although Japan is selling its state-owned lines back into private hands. Most of the other railways in the world are state-owned. Canadian ownership patterns and railway history reflect a variety of influences, including geography, economic conditions, and national aspirations.

Railways are a part of Canada's essential public works infrastructure and cannot be judged solely on narrow economic grounds. A vast country with a limited population, Canada has long faced the problem of moving relatively small volumes of freight over long distances. There were also other needs, and so all levels of government promoted and encouraged railways as engines of change to promote settlement, foster economic development, and encourage political unification. Public support for state ownership of rail lines fit in with a Canadian pattern of public works development of transportation facilities as a means of overcoming Canada's limited private capital resources. Nonetheless government dominance emerged only gradually from 11 per cent government ownership in 1867.

Today there are about 30 railway companies in Canada, the result of the consolidation of hundreds of small lines. Railways are found in all ten provinces and the Mackenzie District of the Northwest Territories. But most of the total of main and yard trackage of 96,020.5 km (59,666 mi) existing in 1983 was completed by four organizations and their predecessors. Three were private – Canadian Pacific (CP), Grand Trunk, and Canadian Northern – and one was state-owned – Canadian Government Railways, also known as the Intercolonial. CP remains a private company, but the other three were amalgamated in 1923 and have been operated since by the federal government as Canadian National Railways (CN). CP and CN dominate Canadian rail traffic and operate the only transcontinental lines, but railways on a smaller scale also exhibit the same combination of private and public lines. The Quebec, North Shore and Labrador and the Algoma Central are large, privately owned regional railways, while the Ontario Northland and British Columbia Railways are provincially owned.

The history of Canadian railways begins with the emergence of the modern (19th-century) railway as a public development. Canada had three periods of massive railway construction between 1850 and the First World War – and a

Great Western Railway, Paris Junction (now Paris), Ontario, 1860. Broad-gauge lines were converted to standard gauge 1870–3. (AO Acc 4137-43)

decidedly different situation after 1918, with competition from trucks and cars. Over the years railways had to face changing patterns in freight and passenger traffic. By their very nature, railways were large-scale undertakings, with particular financial and regulatory needs and phases, as well as the continuing need for improvements – or betterments, as they are often called in railway circles.

EMERGENCE AS COMMON CARRIERS

Before railways, people and freight went on foot, by wagon or sled, or by ships. Water provided the cheapest transportation, and Canada's excellent inland waterways became vital commercial corridors. But water transport was slow and ill suited to move goods and people over vast distances, and the wide variety of ships, barges, and scows could not be used on frozen lakes and rivers. Road traffic was expensive, slow, seasonal, and restricted primarily to local traffic. Good roads were expensive to build, exceedingly rough when dry, and impassable quagmires when wet. Not surprisingly, much overland travel was undertaken in winter by sleigh, when frozen roads provided a hard, smooth riding surface. Clearly there was a need in Canada for economical, year-round transport that was met by neither roads nor waterways.

The idea of a railway originated in the mines of Europe during the Middle Ages. By the late 18th century, wood rail tramways with wagons hauled by man or horse were common in coal-mining districts of Britain. From this humble beginning evolved the 'modern' railways of the early 19th century.

Three important features separated 19th-century railways from their 18th-century predecessors: access, locomotion, and scale. First, the modern railway was a common carrier, hauling passengers and freight for the paying public rather than hauling goods of the railway's owner, such as a mine. Second, railways depended on mechanical or steam power rather than animal power. Third, the scale was unprecedented: 19th-century railways were hundreds of kilometres long and branched out into extensive networks serving a wide area, whereas coal trams were rarely more than a few kilometres long.

The Stockton and Darlington Railway, the first short, steam-powered passenger and freight railway, opened in England in 1825. Five years later the 51.5-km (32-mi) Liverpool and Manchester Railway demonstrated the viability of what was then considered a long railway. These developments were closely watched in Canada and the United States. In the United States, the first 22 km (13 mi) of the Baltimore and Ohio opened in 1830. Ten years later the country had 4,827.9 km (3,000 mi) of track in operation, and by 1850 the 14,483.7 km (9,000 mi) of us track had far surpassed Britain's 10,782.3 km (6,700 mi).[1]

Even though several railways were incorporated in Canada during the 1830s, not one was built. During the 1850s railways would be built over the routes of the St. Andrews & Quebec Railway, incorporated 1835, and the London and Gore, incorporated 1834, but under different names.[2] Desire abounded, but Canada lacked the population, commerce, and financial resources to construct and operate profitable railways. Ambitious intercolonial and inter-city

railway schemes of the 1830s were shunted aside by economic depression and armed rebellion in Upper and Lower Canada.[3]

Canadian railways started very modestly, with private financing. Near Montreal, the 25.6-km (16.5-mi) Champlain and St. Lawrence Railway opened in 1836 as a portage route linking Montreal with the Hudson River. A number of local lines were built to haul coal from Nova Scotia mines to harbour, and in 1850 British North America boasted 106.2 km (66 mi) of track.

The Durham Report, which followed the 1837 rebellions, led to the union of Upper and Lower Canada into the Province of Canada. Although union did not immediately stimulate railway construction, the larger colony could draw on greater capital resources to finance major public works projects, including canals and railways.[4]

The 1837 depression played its course by the early 1840s, but financial insecurity lingered and continued to discourage railway construction. British trade preferences favouring colonial goods were repealed during the 1840s, and yet another major depression began in 1847.[5] Despite the gloomy financial situation, the colonies continued to grow. In Upper Canada, population more than doubled from 432,000 in 1840 to 952,000 10 years later. Lower Canada increased in the same period from 716,000 to 890,000. Between 1840 and 1851 New Brunswick grew from 156,000 to 193,000, and Nova Scotia's 1825 population of 104,000 had climbed to 277,100 in 1851.[6]

Railways were not the only proved technology, and the Province of Canada chose to invest heavily in another: canals. During the 1840s canals were constructed along the St Lawrence River, and major improvements were made to the Welland Canal between lakes Erie and Ontario. Considerable sums were expended, but canals alone could not meet transportation needs. No single date marks the beginning of the railway era in Canada, but by 1850 the momentum for construction was unstoppable and 3,218.6 km (2,000 mi) of track would be laid in the next 10 years.

CONSTRUCTION: THREE ERAS

Railway-building did not proceed evenly, nor has it ended, but one may identify three major construction eras: the 1850s; 1870–90; and 1895–1917. These periods reflected economic prosperity and increasing population and settlement. Construction since the end of the First World War has been more modest and localized than the earlier nation-wide 'booms.'

The 1850s
Increased railway activity in the 1850s started Canada's enduring and 'constant ebb and flow of opinion on the relative merits of government and private ownership.'[7] Should railways be a public service, like roads, for the common good of people, or should private companies attempt to make a profit? Britain and the United States in the 19th century generally opted for private control, but Canada was forced to rely on both private and public ownership.

Governments of the capital-starved colonies had an easier task than entrepreneurs in raising funds. Politicians also saw railways as more than simple business ventures. The principal railways were promoted as instruments of colonial, or national, development. Governments had built roads and canals at public expense, and railways seemed a logical next step in public works to benefit the entire nation.

The first halting experiments in government railways began in the late 1840s. Canada, New Brunswick, and Nova Scotia all wanted a government-owned 'Intercolonial' railway to link the three colonies. Some people thought that private financing would be impossible and that in any case private railway ownership would be impolitic. Others favoured government ownership on principle.[8] The 'Intercolonial' scheme collapsed in 1852, when Britain refused financial support.

The Province of Canada, with some success, then switched to private ownership, with government financial assistance. Nova Scotia swung back and forth, but tended to favour public ownership. New Brunswick adopted private construction, but in 1856 it decided on government ownership when private owners were unable to complete the railway.[9]

The longest line built during the first era was the 1,564.2-km (972-mi) privately owned Grand Trunk Railway. Only three other railways had over 160 km (100 mi) of track in 1860. In Ontario the Great Western Railway had 555.2 km (345 mi), while the Buffalo and Lake Huron operated 274.3 km (162 mi) of track. New Brunswick owned the only other long railway, the 173.8-km (108-mi) European & North American.[10]

Originally, the Grand Trunk was perceived as a link in the 'Intercolonial.' It became a trunk line after the Intercolonial failed, and when completed in 1859 it extended from Detroit, Michigan, via Toronto and Montreal, to the Atlantic Ocean and Portland, Maine. Although an immense company for the era, it was never particularly profitable. As early as 1867 it was hoping that the railway might be acquired by the government – an event that did not occur for another 50 years.[11]

Building an arch culvert over the Black River, Nova Scotia, in 1871 on the Intercolonial Railway, which was built to fulfil one of the conditions of Confederation. (NA PA-21995)

The first era of railway construction ground to a halt by 1860. The depression that started in 1857 halted investments, and with many communities served by, or near, railways, only further settlement would justify new construction.

1870–90

During the second construction era, the Intercolonial was completed to link the Maritimes with Ontario and Quebec, individual rail lines were amalgamated into large networks, and, in the 1880s, the country was linked with a transcontinental railway.

Like the more famous Canadian Pacific project a few years later, a railway between the Maritime colonies and Quebec had been a condition of Confederation. In 1867 the two colonial lines in Nova Scotia and New Brunswick were transferred to the new federal government to become the Intercolonial. By 1879 these lines had been extended to create a mainline stretching from Halifax to Lévis, opposite Quebec City.

The route of the Intercolonial reflected the tension that had grown between Canada and the United States during the American Civil War and the subsequent

Ice prevented ferry crossings, so the Montreal Ice Railway offered service, using rails on timber cribs. It ran 30 January to 30 March 1880, and again in 1881 and 1882. (NPA 1143 View)

This complex array of switches and tracks at the yards in Summerside, PEI, accommodates trains of different gauges. (CNR 54067-1)

Fenian Raids on Canada. Instead of traversing populous southern New Brunswick, it crossed the lightly populated north shore in order to maximize its distance from the United States and make it more defensible in time of war.

During the 1870s and 1880s, the eastern network, in Ontario, Quebec, and the Maritime provinces, was largely completed. Individual lines grew gradually into an important transportation network, with lightly travelled branch lines feeding traffic into heavily used mainlines. More lines would be constructed later but would add to capacity rather than serve new territory. Trackage grew from 4,211.5 km (2,617 mi) in 1870 to 22,536.6 km (14,004 mi) in 1890.

The step from company networks to truly national service could occur only if rail cars were interchangeable from line to line. This meant, for example, that couplers had to be the same height and brakes compatible. Perhaps most obvious of all, the rail gauge had to be the same. The issue of rail gauges typifies the problem of standardization that companies had to deal with before the full benefits of a national network could be achieved.

During the 1850s, major Canadian railways had a wide-track gauge of 1.68 m (5 ft 6 in), while most American railways were using 'standard' gauge, 1.43 m (4 ft 8.5 in). Canadian lines converted to standard in the 1870s.[12] As if the lesson of broad gauges had not been learned, lower initial cost encouraged a brief proliferation of narrow-gauge railways – 0.91 m (3 ft) or 1.07 m (3 ft 6 in) – during the 1870s.[13] Interchangeability was more important than initial cost savings, and by the late 1880s most narrow-gauge lines were converted to standard.

Construction of the Canadian Pacific Railway stands out as another great achievement of the second railway era.

The promise of a line from Ontario to the Pacific Ocean helped entice British Columbia into Confederation in 1871. Originally conceived as a government-owned railway, it was completed in 1885 by a private company which had received government assistance.

In order to feed traffic onto its transcontinental line, CP began to create an eastern network in direct competition with the Grand Trunk. During the 1880s the companies acquired many short independent lines in Ontario and Quebec as they tried to consolidate their territory.

1895–1917

About 1902 Cornelius Van Horne, chairman of CP, noted: 'Canada has been adding sides to her hopper for a long time, but neglected to enlarge the spout.'[14] The hopper was the prairies, the country's granary; wheat production had soared from 55.6 million bushels in 1901 to 231.7 million in 1914 and exports had grown even faster, from 27 per cent of the total grown in 1901 to 59 per cent in 1914.[15] Wheat needed more transportation facilities – improvements to the 'spout.'

Wheat precipitated the third railway era, with its remarkable expansion in the railway network, mostly in western Canada, to meet the needs of prairie farmers. Canada had 26,854.4 km (16,687 mi) of track in 1897; in 1917 it had 57 per cent more – 61,747.2 km (38,369 mi) – mostly new branch lines, but also two new transcontinentals.

Until the early 20th century, only CP linked western Canada with the east. Western farmers were becoming increasingly unhappy with its traffic monopoly and inadequate capacity between Winnipeg and the Lakehead on Lake Superior. Canada's other major railway, the Grand Trunk, was frustrated at being denied access to the lucrative western traffic. Quite understandably, the federal gov-

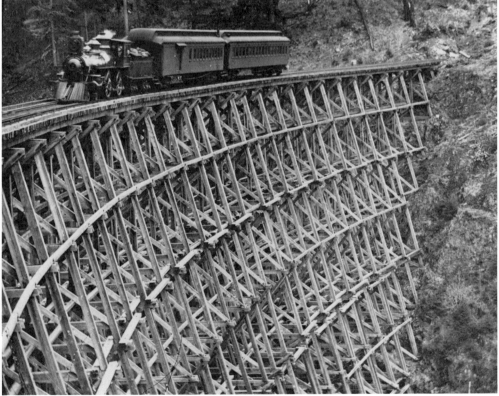

Timber structures – such as the CPR's Revelstoke Bridge and the Esquimalt and Nanaimo Railways' Niagara Canyon Trestle Bridge, both in British Columbia – saved cash-starved early Canadian railways a lot of money in heavily timbered areas. (NA PA-25048, PABC HP65794)

ernment wanted a second, competing transcontinental line, but there were major problems. Politics ruled out the cheapest solution: avoiding the expensive but unremunerative construction through northern Ontario by entering the Canadian prairies via Chicago. The government had to have a Canadian route. A compromise was reached. The Grand Trunk created a subsidiary, the Grand Trunk Pacific, to construct a system between Winnipeg and the Pacific Ocean. The federal government agreed to build the unprofitable eastern section, the National Transcontinental Railway, from the Maritimes to Winnipeg, and lease it to the Grand Trunk Pacific.

The Grand Trunk Pacific mainline, from Winnipeg through Edmonton to Prince Rupert on the Pacific Ocean, was completed in 1914, and the National Transcontinental in 1915. By then economic conditions were far different than when the lines were first proposed 15 years earlier. The Grand Trunk Pacific was effectively bankrupt and could not lease the National Transcontinental. These problems prompted creation of the Canadian National Railways.

The economic euphoria of the early 20th century produced not one but two transcontinental lines. The second company, the Canadian Northern Railway, was organized in 1899 and within three years had a mainline stretching from the Lakehead to Edmonton. Less than 15 years later, the company's rails stretched from Vancouver to Montreal. The Canadian Northern, like the Grand Trunk, had grown rapidly in an era of prosperity. And, like the Grand Trunk Pacific, it was finished just as Canada's prosperity ended and the First World War began.

To keep pace with competitors, CP increased its trackage from 11,265.1 km (7,000 mi) to 20,787.3 km (12,917 mi)

between 1899 and 1916. Further mileage was created by several regional systems. Some provincial government lines were constructed to stimulate growth. Construction began on the Pacific Great Eastern, today the British Columbia Railway, through the centre of British Columbia. The company was acquired by the province in 1918, when only a short, isolated section had been completed. Alberta in 1920 acquired a bankrupt line north of Edmonton and later built or acquired additional lines which it reorganized in 1929 into the Northern Alberta Railways, which in 1981 became part of CN. The Temiskaming and Northern Ontario, today the Ontario Northland, was created in 1902 by the Ontario government to promote northern settlement.

Newfoundland commenced a narrow-gauge railway in 1884. The track was never converted to standard gauge because the system is isolated from the mainland network. When Newfoundland became Canada's tenth province in 1949, the island railway was taken over by CN. Today the 965.6-km (600-mi) line is the longest narrow-gauge system in North America.[16]

Private lines were also built. In Yukon the narrow-gauge White Pass & Yukon was opened in 1900 between Skagway, Alaska, on the Pacific Ocean and Whitehorse. In Ontario, the Algoma Central Railway opened in 1911 between iron mines on Lake Superior and steel mills at Sault Ste Marie. In 1913 it achieved its present length of 515 km (320 mi).

American companies were attracted into Canada. The New York Central operated several subsidiaries in Ontario; the most important ran across southwestern Ontario between Windsor and Niagara Falls to provide a short line between Chicago and New York City. In Manitoba the Great Northern constructed a modest network around Winnipeg.

The company also extended lines into mining districts of southern British Columbia.

EXPANSION AFTER 1918

The First World War was a watershed for the railway industry. Excess trackage threatened the economic stability of some of the largest companies. Although overcapacity was obvious at the end of the war, it was less apparent that the railways' monopoly was soon to be challenged, by highway traffic.

By 1914 Canada's rail mileage contained tremendous excess capacity. The Canadian Northern and Grand Trunk Pacific mainlines virtually duplicated each other's service in the west. The lack of traffic was exacerbated by economic strains caused by the war. Staff and materials were unavailable, and maintenance of track suffered. In 1917 financial collapse of the two lines was imminent.

Politicians in general preferred private ownership with government regulation, but the Canadian Northern could not survive the austerity of the war years. In November 1917 control passed to the federal government to prevent bankruptcy, and operations were combined with those of the Canadian Government Railways. In 1918 'Canadian National Railways' was first used to describe all of the government-owned and -operated railways.

The Grand Trunk's timing for completing its transcontinental line could not have been more unfortunate. In 1919 the Grand Trunk Pacific was declared insolvent, and control was transferred to the Canadian government. The parent Grand Trunk was dragged down financially by the debacle and, in 1923, was also acquired by the Canadian government and became part of the Canadian National.

Thus in 1923 the structure of Canada's modern rail system was established. The private CP operated 23,495.8 km (14,600 mi) of track, the public CN 35,082.7 km (21,800 mi). Together these companies operated about 70 per cent of rail mileage in Canada. The 1920s saw completion of branch line projects interrupted by the war, and all major settled areas had some level of service.

Depression and motor vehicles would soon make major and irrevocable changes in Canada's railways. In the late 1920s highways began to challenge railway branch lines. At the end of 1929, North America plunged into a severe economic depression. Rail traffic fell with terrifying speed. In 1928 the industry carried 141.2 million tons of freight; in 1933 the tonnage had fallen in half, to 63.6 million tons, and in the 1930s major rail abandonments began. Whole districts were confronted with the loss of rail service. No federal regulations governed abandonments until 1933, when an amendment was made to the Railway Act. Until then railways could more or less remove lines as they pleased; with the amendment, railways had to justify abandonment.[17]

Lightly used branch lines and those that relied on passenger traffic were affected first. CN also abandoned much of the duplicate trackage acquired from its predecessors.

The rise of highway traffic made branch lines something of an enigma to the railways. In the prosperous era of railway monopoly, branch lines could pay for themselves, but despite their significant capital and operating costs they generated little traffic. In 1932, as highway competition was becoming serious, it was estimated that 42 per cent of Canadian rail mileage carried less than 5 per cent of rail traffic. Conversely, mainlines accounted for 10 per cent of mileage and carried 50 per cent of rail traffic.[18] Many agricultural branch lines justified abandonment because motor vehicles provided better local service. But other lines had to be maintained because they acted as distributors for mainline traffic. Economic conditions slowly improved during the late 1930s, and the Second World War brought the much-needed boost in railway traffic. Freight more than doubled, from 84.7 million tons in 1938 to 177.4 million tons in 1944.

Post-1945 construction focused on access to resources; extensive abandonments almost equalled new track in length. CN constructed several hundred kilometres of resource lines in northern Quebec, Manitoba, and Alberta during the 1950s and 1960s, while the British Columbia Railway completed about 1,126.5 km (700 mi) of new construction. The Quebec, North Shore and Labrador Railway was completed, from Sept Îles on the Gulf of St Lawrence 573.0 km (356 mi) northward to serve a massive iron deposit at Schefferville. The line was completed in 1954, followed by a 67.6-km (42-mi) branch in 1960 to a second mine site. The 310-km (193-mi) Cartier Railway reached an iron-mining development in 1960 and was subsequently extended another 262.3 km (163 mi) to a second deposit in 1972.

Canadian companies have always operated substantial rail mileage in the United States, some of which forms vital links in Canadian systems. The CP mainline extends through Maine as a short-cut to the ocean terminal of Saint John, New Brunswick. CN operates a similar short-cut across Minnesota. Most lines are, however, penetrations into American markets. From southern Ontario the CN subsidiary Grand Trunk Western extends westward to Chicago – an important source of railway traffic. The Soo Line, a CP subsidiary, owns considerable mileage in the US Midwest. Both CN and CP have added to their American systems in the 1980s.

COMPETITION FOR FREIGHT

Whether public or private, Canadian railways have historically provided two principal services: passenger and freight transport. At times they have also operated inland and ocean shipping, express business, hotels, real estate, mining, forestry, and telecommunications, but rail transport – particularly freight – has always been the core service.

Railways have passed through three phases of competition. The earliest lines competed with well-established water systems, but railways then began to compete primarily with one another. Since the 1930s, they have had competition from new transport modes, particularly highway and air traffic, while continuing to compete among themselves.

Water Transport

Nineteenth-century railway transportation was fast, relatively unaffected by seasons, and, though more expensive than water, far cheaper than road. The cost differential in 1914 is illustrated by the distance one ton of freight could travel for one dollar: by ship, 828.8 km (515 mi); by railway, 209.2 km (130 mi); by horse and wagon, 6.4 km (4 mi).[19]

In general, hauling freight by road was uneconomical but in one exceptional case railway rates were so high that in 1899 merchants instituted a 64.4-km (40-mi) wagon service between Toronto and Hamilton.[20] This reversal of cost advantage remained the exception until the advent of the automobile in the early 20th century.

Railways have always faced tough competition from water transport in parts of Canada. Three years after the Grand Trunk completed its 531.1-km (330-mi) line between Montreal and To-

Where bridges are impractical, car barges or self-powered ferries allow transport of cargo in railway cars. Here the passenger ferry ss *Slocan* pushes a car barge at New Denver, BC. (PABC 53413)

ronto in 1856, shipping one ton of freight between the two cities cost $2 or $3 by steamer or $3.50 by rail.[21] Over time, the advantages of speed and an expanded network led much of the traffic to shift from water to rail. Nevertheless, for some bulk commodities on some routes, waterways retained an advantage that persists to this day.

Other Railways

Until the development of highway traffic, railways competed primarily with each other. Companies pushed branch lines into territory served by competitors, obtained trackage rights to pick up freight on other companies' tracks, reduced rates, improved service, and built wasteful duplicate track to serve the same communities.

The often wasteful competition between CP and the newly formed CN could be supported during periods of prosperity and high traffic, but the combination of the Depression and highway competition drastically reduced traffic for both major railways. As a result, a federal royal commission was established in 1931 to examine the railway situation in Canada. Its recommendations led to the Canadian National–Canadian Pacific Railway Act of 1933. Its intent was new: to produce savings in the industry through co-operation between the companies. Duplicate lines were abandoned, trackage rights granted, passenger train services pooled, and other joint projects undertaken, but the economies of co-operation were far less than anticipated.[22] The situation was very complex, but the relative decrease in road transportation costs brought about by significant technological improvements in both motor vehicles and roads, as well as changing societal and individual expectations and preferences, was causing trouble for railways.

Other Modes

Limited use of trucks began in urban areas about the turn of the century. Toronto merchants, for example, experimented with electric trucks in the 1890s. Some writers have suggested that the motor truck began to become common in urban areas just before the First World War. Appropriate truck designs were certainly available by 1920. But until the 1920s few vehicles ventured beyond city limits – roads were too poor for commercial traffic.[23] Such trucking offered little competition to rail services.

Rural trucking to carry produce from farm to railhead began to appear in the 1920s. But poor roads in western Canada and the cautious nature of farmers retarded its adoption. In Saskatchewan, for example, haulage from farm to railhead by motor truck began in earnest in the late 1920s.[24] Once motor vehicles proved their value, railway branch lines were vulnerable to road competition.

The federal and provincial governments began to construct all-weather roads in the 1920s. 'Good' roads implied not only well built but also kept clear of snow, so that reliable year-round service could be offered. By the mid-1920s only Ontario provided a few hundred kilometres of ploughed winter roads. In the rest of Canada, large-scale year-round service was not available until the 1930s.

Inexorably the economic range of highway freight increased. Each increase in distance meant a corresponding decrease in rail monopoly. In Ontario in the early 1920s the economic limit to inter-city trucks was about 60 to 75 mi (96.6 to 121 km). By the early 1930s the radius had increased to 130 mi (209.2 km). In 1937, 'advisedly or not,' routes of 400 mi (643.7 km) were in regular operation.[25]

Highway transport offered solutions to problems that had aggravated shippers throughout the railway era. Obviously, trucks had the advantage of door-to-door service. Railways were not quick to follow suit; CP, for example, did not begin a pick-up service until 1934.[26] Railway freight had to be handled several times between shipper and receiver and required robust packaging. Truck freight required less handling and consequently cheaper packaging.

Truckers, unlike railways, were largely unregulated until after the Second World War and could charge what they wanted to underbid railways and each other.[27] Trucks' operating characteristics helped produce lower freight rates. Unlike railways, they did not own and maintain the expensive roadbed, and they had lower terminal costs because they did not require yards and stations.

Canada's first mass railway strike, in August 1950, illustrated just how much the role of railways had changed. Predictions of immediate economic disaster and paralysis did not materialize, and in nine days an end was legislated.

By the 1970s a rough equilibrium was established between road and rail traffic, in which each mode carried the most appropriate types of freight.[28] Railways continue to be an important and innovative part of Canada's transportation networks. Dieselization has reduced costs, and new types of cars are integrating rail and truck services to offer users the best of each mode. Most successful have been trailer-on-flat-car (TOFC), container-on-flat-car (COFC), and unit trains. TOFC and COFC services, known as intermodal freight, combine line-haul economics of railways with delivery features of trucks.[29]

Increased intermodal freight has reduced the need for costly branch lines and sidings. Containers and trailers are hauled by rail between major terminals and then distributed by road. Branch lines and sidings will not entirely disappear. Those industries that require great tonnages of commodities, such as steel mills, grain elevators, and thermal electric generating stations, still need rail connections.

COMPETITION FOR PASSENGERS

The social importance of and public good provided by passenger service have been immense. Prior to the automobile and, later, inter-city buses the train was the only practical means of long-distance travel. Few trains were glamorous inter-city expresses, but the quality of passenger travel reflected a company's ability to haul freight, and railway executives knew that potential shippers had to ride passenger trains.

Railway passenger traffic has always been much smaller than freight. In 1875 passenger traffic accounted for 33 per cent of gross earnings, and by 1900 the figure had dropped to 26 per cent. When ridership peaked, at 51 million passengers in 1920, it contributed only 21 per cent of gross earnings. However, the relative decline in passenger revenue to 1920 was due to rapid increase in freight rather than the unimportance of passengers.

Electric street and interurban railways were one of the few sectors of the industry that depended almost entirely on passenger traffic. These lines operated from the 1890s until the 1940s. Collectively their mileage was very small, but they carried significant volumes of passengers.

Interurban railways provided a distinctive type of operation, consisting of high-speed, self-propelled cars operating between urban areas. Large systems developed around Toronto, Hamilton, and Vancouver. In Ontario electric interurbans were promoted by Ontario Hydro just before and after the First World War. Ontario Hydro proposed an extensive high-speed system linking communities in southern Ontario from Windsor to Toronto. Only a few short sections were built, because the growing popularity of automobiles killed off interurban traffic. Some lines were later converted for freight.[30]

Once automobiles became common, rail passenger traffic began to tumble. After the 1920 peak, ridership began a steady decline until the Second World War. Automobile registration increased from a negligible 115,600 vehicles in 1917 to 1,187,300 in 1929. The Depression provided further evidence that the automobile was now an essential transportation mode. Rail ridership fell by half during the Depression and remained flat until the war. Auto registrations dipped by 10 per cent at the worst of the Depression but rebounded to 1929 levels by 1937.[31]

While automobiles took the lion's share of rail passenger traffic, inter-city buses took a further toll. The first common carrier bus licence in Ontario was issued in 1923. Inter-city bus routes appear to have become sizeable passenger carriers by 1930 and by 1937 were carrying 12 million people.[32]

Traffic demands of the Second World War created a temporary increase in rail passengers, but after the war the relentless decline recommenced. From 40.9 million passengers in 1947 the figure declined to a low of 18.8 million in 1961. In 1960 passenger traffic accounted for only 6 per cent of gross railway earnings.[33] Since then it has stabilized at around 20 to 24 million per year – much of this commuter rail traffic.

Passenger service became such a burden to the railways that the federal government created Via Rail in 1977. This crown corporation acquired the inter-city passenger services of CN and CP. Because of low ridership, a financial crisis faces VIA Rail, and neither the solution to this problem nor the future of this agency is clear.[34] Railways are an important answer to the commuter traffic problem in major centres such as Montreal and Toronto. The largest commuter railway, GO Transit, is owned by the Ontario government. Equipment is owned by GO Transit, and running rights are negotiated over CP and CN tracks. From its modest beginnings, with 96.6 km (60 mi) of track, GO Transit has grown to over 321.9 km (200 mi) of track and, in 1983, it carried 14.1 million passengers.[35]

FINANCE AND IMPROVEMENT

Financing Construction
Canadian railways were built through a combination of public and private investment. In 1975, for example, railways had a total capitalization of $318.6 million, which consisted of $180.9 million share capital, $72.9 million bonded debt, $45.5 million of federal and provincial aid, and $3.8 million of municipal aid. Thus about 15 per cent was made up of government assistance. One source has estimated that 25 per cent of construction costs was financed by government funding.[36]

Federal and provincial governments aided railway construction and, where necessary, built and operated lines, but there was no federal policy until 1874, when Ottawa introduced a system of cash subsidies, which was followed in 1884 with a land grant policy.[37]

Financial guarantees were among the oldest forms of construction assistance. A government would agree to guarantee the interest on debt, usually bonds, incurred by construction, thus facilitating the raising of money by private companies. Directly or indirectly the British government assisted the colonies in constructing public works on many occasions during the 19th century, prior to Confederation. The Province of Canada's most ambitious assistance program was the Guarantee Act, 1849, which guaranteed the interest on bonds of certain important railway proposals.[38]

Government guarantees seem to have been unpopular until the 1890s, when they were revived to foster railway development in western Canada. In 1890 the BC government guaranteed the interest on some bonds; Manitoba followed suit between 1900 and 1910. During the last major era of railway construction, government assistance was limited largely to guarantees of bond interest.[39]

Land grants, a significant form of government aid in the 1880s and 1890s, did not drain cash from the treasury. Several precedents existed. In 1826, the Welland Canal Co. received 13,000 acres (5,261 ha) in aid of canal construction.[40] A clearly defined land grant might be offered by a government prior to any demonstration of commercial interest. Thus, for example, in 1850 New Brunswick tried to encourage rail construction by making available both cash grants and a land grant of 10 mi (16 km) on either side of a proposed line. Quebec, too, provided land grants in the early 1850s as a stimulus for railway development.[41] Land grants were not, however, substantial in the first railway era, in the 1850s.

Federal policy was established in 1884 and remained in effect for 10 years. Earlier land grants, such as the 25-million-acre (10.1-million-ha) grant to CP in 1881, were negotiated on an individual basis. The first grant under the new federal policy consisted of 6,400 acres (2,590 ha) per mile (1.6 km) to the Hudson Bay Railway. Almost all subsequent grants were awarded in western Canada, reflecting extensive construction – and the absence of public land in eastern Canada. By 1906 an estimated 13 million ha (32 million acres) had been granted to railways.[42]

Cash-short railways often found it difficult to convert land grants into money. The Quebec government in the 1870s had offered land grants to encourage railways, but companies found the land difficult to sell. Later, some issued land grant bonds against the security of their lands, thereby obtaining money quickly but selecting and selling the land at their leisure.[43] Federal and provincial land grant policies, however, were not always successful.[44]

Cash subsidies formed still another means of government assistance. A precedent was provided by a British grant toward construction of the Lachine Canal in the 1820s.[45] Ontario was one of the earliest provinces to create a cash or grant subsidy policy. Commencing in 1871, it made $2,000 to $4,000 per mile (1.6 km) available to railway construction. In 1874 the federal government adjusted the amount to $3,000 per mile, on the assumption that the 100 tons of steel necessary for that much track cost $32 per ton. By 1897 the policy was fixed that railways costing more than $15,000 per mile were eligible for $6,400. As with land grants, cash grants were sometimes established before any company had expressed interest in a particular route.[46]

Government loans were occasionally used. The Grand Trunk line east of Quebec was to be financed, in part, by a loan of £3,000 per mile (1.6 km). The Grand Trunk and the Quebec, Montreal, Ottawa and Occidental received the only significant loans to railways.[47] However, during the 1850s, many municipalities in Canada West (Ontario) purchased railway stocks and bonds and made loans to the companies by means of the Municipal Loan Fund, hoping thereby to attract railways and prosperity.[48] Most of these towns and cities became saddled with excessive debt.

Other government aid took more modest forms. The federal government allowed construction materials for CP to enter the country without duties.[49] The need to assist construction ended, with construction itself, during the First World War.

Regulation

When railways first appeared, governments assumed that competition would regulate the cost and quality of service. Consequently, during the first decades of growth, railways operated in an almost unregulated environment. The nature of railway construction ensured that, except near cities, most areas received the service of only one railway. This was hardly an environment to encourage inter-rail competition. Modest, largely ineffectual government regulations began to appear in the 1850s. As the need for controls became apparent, further regulations were imposed until, by the early 20th century, the industry was highly controlled.

In 1851 the Province of Canada established a Board of Railway Commissioners to oversee construction of the Grand Trunk. The first Canadian legislation to safeguard the public interest, the Accidents on Railways Act, was passed in 1857; many accidents were due to poor operating procedures or faulty construction.[50] Rails frequently broke, boilers exploded occasionally, and primitive communications made train control difficult. Not all the problems associated with employees and technology could be regulated. Improvements in safety came about with new inventions and the evolution of professional, trained staff.

In 1867 all former colonial railways were transferred to the new federal Department of Public Works. In 1868 the first Railway Act was passed and the Railway Committee of the Privy Council established, to function in a judicial role. Until 1900 it was the only method of contesting railway services and rates. It never functioned well because of its dual political and administrative role. Committee members often lacked the technical expertise to carry out their tasks and heard very few cases.[51]

Continued railway expansion led to creation of the federal Department of Railways and Canals in 1879, to assume the railway and canal obligations of Public Works. Initially the new department operated the Intercolonial and Prince Edward Island railways; later the National Transcontinental and the Hudson Bay were added.[52]

In 1904 the Board of Railway Commissioners was created and took over the role of the Railway Committee and all judicial components of Railways and Canals. In 1936 the department was reorganized as the Department of Transport, to recognize the growing importance of highway and air transport. In 1970 it became the Ministry of Transport, which reports to Parliament on behalf of CN and the Canadian Transport Commission.

Prior to 1904 there had been no general regulations governing railway rates. The Railway Committee offered only limited control over rates. Given the importance of freight and passenger rates in developing or hindering traffic, this situation was unacceptable. Acts of incorporation provided for regulation, but government exercised little control.[53]

When the federal government began to grant construction subsidies, it some-times took this opportunity to control specific railway freight rates. The most famous was the Crow's Nest Pass Agreement, established in 1897. In return for federal aid to construct a line in southern British Columbia, CP agreed to fixed rates in perpetuity on grain moving from western Canada. Later these rates were applied to the other transcontinental lines.[54] By the time the Crow Rates were abolished in 1983, the cost of moving grain was far greater than the revenue from the statutory rate.

The absence of rate regulation was similar to that in the United States, where agitation gave rise to the Interstate Commerce Commission in 1887. Development of a similar body in Canada proceeded more slowly. The idea of a railway commission was studied in 1899, but legislation was not passed until 1903, and the Board of Railway Commissioners came into effect in 1904, with responsibility for administration of the Railway Act.[55]

The board had complete powers over location, construction, and other physical elements of the line and rights of way and came to regulate safety equipment and train operations. For example, it could regulate train speed within urban areas. In 1909 a Grade Crossing Fund was established to help communities remove dangerous level crossings. But the board's most important work was regulation of traffic and tariffs. In 1938 its name was changed to the Board of Transport Commissioners, which in 1967 became the Canadian Transport Commission.[56]

Several provinces established commissions to regulate provincial railways. At various times, Quebec, Ontario, and British Columbia had such bodies.[57]

Rate regulation has now proceeded full circle. Since the 1970s transportation companies – rail, road, air, and water – have encouraged deregulation. Ship-

The steep grade on the CPR line at Kicking Horse Pass in 1907; three locomotives do work easily done by one on level or gently undulating track. (CP 17757)

pers no longer need the protection of government rate control – competition among different transport modes effectively prevents monopoly pricing. In 1980 the Staggers Act deregulated US railways and accelerated the need for changes in Canada. American railways could now provide cheaper service than Canadian companies for much traffic. Since much of Canada's economic activity takes place close to the border, shippers have only a short haul southward to connect with American railways, where freight can be shipped cheaply east or west to re-enter Canada near its destination. Deregulation of Canadian railways occurred in 1988. The Canadian Transport Commission was disbanded; rate control was taken over by the National Transportation Agency.

Continuing Improvements
Given the challenges of financing, North American railway lines often had to build very economically and upgrade later. These betterments increased train speeds and reduced operating expenses.

Initial construction was sometimes characterized by wooden bridges, light rails, and scant ballast. Although often crude by European standards, tracks were 'quite on a par with their ability to earn money.'[58] Perhaps 19th-century North American construction appeared unsophisticated, but it was the only way vast mileages could have been built.

During much of the 19th century betterments were relatively small. The track was adequate for the traffic. But beginning in the late 1890s and continuing until the First World War most railways undertook massive betterment programs. Stations were rebuilt, heavier rails laid, and gentle grades and curves engineered into rights of way. Much of the double-tracking of the Canadian Pacific and Grand Trunk mainlines was undertaken at this time. In British Columbia, CP completed major tunnels through Rogers Pass and Kicking Horse Pass to reduce grades and effect operating economies.

The betterments of the early 20th century were adequate for the next half-century; no work could be done during the two wars, and there was no money – or traffic – for improvements in the 1930s. During the 1960s and 1970s a second betterment phase occurred, as traffic finally filled up excess track capacity. Western Canada, in particular, saw tremendous growth in the movement of bulk commodities. Both CP and CN had double-tracked extensive mileage in the west. But the most spectacular improvement has been the construction of a new CP tunnel through Rogers Pass. When completed at the end of 1988, the 14.0-km (8.7-mi) tunnel and 19.3 km (12 mi) of new approach track were to be the longest rail tunnel in North America. They will provide a second track through the most difficult area of operation on CP's transcontinental mainline.[59]

Betterments were also undertaken in terminals. New designs in freight yards illustrate ways to increase capacity. Economic freight operations require sufficient yard trackage to store and service cars and to sort, assemble, and break up trains. A modern freight yard contains kilometres of track, spread over many hectares. Early railways had very limited yard facilities, and congestion was often a problem. Large freight yards began to appear only at the end of the last century.

Freight-sorting or classification yards can be divided into two types: flat and hump yards. The choice of design depends on the type of switching. Flat yards constitute the majority of yards and range from a few tracks up to 20 or more.

In flat-yard switching, a locomotive pushes a string of cars onto the appropriate yard track. In busy yards, greater capacity came with the pole yard: by means of a long pole, the locomotive pushed individual cars until sufficient momentum was achieved for the car to roll onto the right track. This system avoided the necessity of pushing the whole train. A capacity of 100 cars per engine-hour was possible.[60] There are no pole yards in Canada today – they were replaced by hump yards.

The introduction of hump, or gravity, yards in the late 19th century in the United States nearly doubled yard capacity. A train was pushed over a low hump at the yard entrance, and cars rolled under their own momentum onto the right track. Brakemen rode down on each car, applying the brake manually when the proper location was reached. Before the early 1890s, hump yards used hand-thrown switches, requiring additional manpower – power switches were not invented until 1891. Despite these limitations, a capacity of 200 cars per engine-hour could be achieved. The first major hump yard in Canada appears to have been CP's at Fort William, built in 1911. It replaced a pole yard completed in 1905. CP's North Transcona yard at Winnipeg, completed in 1915, was another early hump yard.[61]

Hump yards have seen many subsequent refinements. Car retarders, which automatically stop freight cars at the desired place after they roll down a hump, were invented in 1924. CP took the lead in modernizing freight yards when in 1950 it opened Montreal's St Luc yard – the first hump yard in Canada equipped with car retarders. It opened a new freight yard in Toronto in 1964

To avoid fumes, electrification has been used in tunnels and mines and on commuter lines: CNR station, Montreal. (CNR 43600)

An oil tanker train at Nisku, Alberta, 1947; steam locomotives and grain elevators are two important symbols in Canadian history. (PAA P1444)

and rebuilt and expanded the Alyth yard in Calgary. During the early 1960s, CN completed four major new hump yards, in Moncton, Montreal, Toronto, and Winnipeg. Each was immense – the Toronto yard covers 404.7 ha (1,000 acres).[62]

Smoke abatement projects were yet another early-20th-century terminal improvement. Locomotive smoke was a hazard in terminal areas and tunnels. Coal smoke was toxic to train crews and obscured visibility of signals and track. The toxicity of smoke was driven home when a crew was asphyxiated after a train broke down in a tunnel under the St Clair River at Sarnia, Ontario. In 1908 the Grand Trunk electrified operations

through the tunnel to prevent recurrence of such a disaster. The Michigan Central did not wait for a similar accident and used electric operations in its tunnel under the Detroit River at Windsor from its opening in 1910.[63]

Electrification of a terminal occurred only in Montreal. The Canadian Northern began in 1918, when a tunnel under the city was electrified. CN later extended electrification to all its routes converging on Central Station. In 1922 the Montreal Harbour Board electrified its harbour trackage.[64]

With the advent of less smoky diesel locomotives in the 1950s, most tunnel and terminal electrification was taken out. Diesels replaced electric operation

Conventional motor vehicles modified to run on rails were relatively common in areas that lacked roads. This City of Winnipeg Hydro Railbus, c. 1930, served Pointe du Bois, Slave Falls, and Lac du Bonnet. (NA PA-141066)

under the Detroit River in 1953 and under the St Clair in 1958. The Montreal Harbour Board had stopped electric operation in 1942. Most of the electrification into Central Station in Montreal was removed in the 1950s and 1960s. Today, only one line into the station, under Mount Royal, is operated by electric locomotives.

Instead of building more tracks, railways could obtain additional track capacity by using faster-accelerating, electric locomotives, but unlike in the United States, mainline electrification attracted little attention in Canada. Diesels ended any interest in the process. But experimentation with electric traction did not stop. In 1963 the Iron Ore Co. of Canada completed an 11.7-km (7.3-mi) electric railway in northern Quebec, which carries heavy iron ore trains from a mine to a mill. The operation is unique in being entirely automatic. In the early 1970s, CP studied the feasibility of electrifying 1,368 km (850 mi) of mainline through the BC mountains. In the end, it decided that diesel operation would be less expensive.[65]

No further developments in electric traction occurred until 1984, when the

British Columbia Railway completed the first electric mainline in Canada. A 124-km (77-mi) line constructed to serve a northern coal mine required two long tunnels. Studies indicated that electric operation would be cheaper than building ventilation systems into the tunnels for diesel operation.[66]

Early-20th-century betterments were undertaken to upgrade earlier track and facilities. Recent improvements were necessary to provide greater carrying capacity. Future betterments will be necessary when existing track capacity is no longer adequate.

CONCLUSION

The railway industry, though substantially different from what it was 80 years ago, is still very important. As the country and its needs change, new lines are built, others abandoned or discontinued. But even abandonment provides a public works challenge and an opportunity to have that same land serve the public good in different ways. Abandoned routes offer possible pipeline, hydro, and other utility corridors. Others may become much-needed linear recreational parks.

Shifts in transportation modes are not new. The railway in its time had displaced the supremacy of water transport in Canada. Yet, at a reduced level, water transport was able to exploit market niches in bulk commodities and remains an important carrier of certain commodities. This same development has happened to railways.

Far more than waterways, railways were once used to foster national and regional development. This tradition dates back to the Intercolonial scheme of the 1840s, which antedates the first era of rail construction. Historically the business and political needs of railways have coexisted. Because of their national role,

The GO system regularly uses double-decker cars, like these in downtown Toronto.
(OMT 23070-5)

Canadian railways have survived re-markably intact into the 1980s. Even though business conditions might have forced them to adopt new practices, the federal government supported the in-dustry on political grounds.

When railways were first constructed, they offered a panacea to transportation woes in Canada. A combination of geog-raphy, politics, and economics moulded them into an essential public service far beyond simple business requirements. Today this national role is being chal-lenged. Legislation now before Parlia-ment would make railways more com-petitive, against both American railways and other modes of transportation. But, even so, the national interest dictates a continuing role for the federal govern-ment, which has a major interest in the country's rail system. Canada's railways are in transition, but their future is assured.

NOTES

1 J.M. Trout and E. Trout *The Railways of Canada for 1870–1871* (Toronto 1871, re-print 1970) 44–5; John F. Stover *American Railroads* (Chicago 1961) 14–15
2 Trout *Railways* 54–6, 87
3 W.T. Easterbrook and Hugh Aitken *Canadian Economic History* (Toronto 1956, reprint 1970) 285
4 Ibid 288; G.R. Stevens *Canadian National Railways* I (Toronto 1960) 52
5 Easterbrook and Aitken *Economic History* 293
6 Ibid 380, 396
7 S.J. McLean 'National Highways Over-

land' *Canada and Its Provinces* x (Toronto 1914) 467

8 Ibid 380, 396

9 Ibid 381–2, 388–9, 396, 407; W.L. Morton *The Kingdom of Canada* (Toronto 1963, reprint 1972) 290

10 M.L. Bladen 'Construction of Railways in Canada' *Contributions to Canadian Economics* (Toronto 1932) 43–107

11 McLean 'National Highways' 426

12 Bruce Sinclair 'Canadian Technology: British Traditions and American Influence' *Technology & Culture* 20: 1 (Jan 1979) 108–23

13 Omer S.A. Lavallée *Narrow Gauge Railways of Canada* (Montreal 1972)

14 Robert M. Hamilton *The Dictionary of Canadian Quotations and Phrases* (Toronto 1979) 225

15 M.C. Urquhart *Historical Statistics* (Toronto 1956) 14, 363

16 Lavallée *Narrow Gauge Railways* 30–4

17 Archibald W. Currie *Canadian Transportation Economics* (Toronto 1967, reprint 1976) 339

18 Canada, Royal Commission *Report of the Royal Commission to Inquire Into Railways and Transportation in Canada, 1931–1932* (Ottawa 1932) 32

19 Ontario Public Roads and Highways Commission *Report of the Public Roads and Highways Commission of Ontario* 1914, 37

20 Ontario Royal Commission *Report of the Royal Commission on Transportation* 1938, 61

21 McLean 'National Highways' 413

22 Currie *Canadian Transportation* 418–23; Dominion Bureau of Statistics, *Canada Year Book*, 1933, 648–9

23 G.P. de T. Glazebrook *A History of Transportation in Canada* II (Toronto 1936, reprint 1964) 247; John de Bondt *Canada on Wheels* (Ottawa 1970) 16; Ontario Trucking Association (OTA) *Golden Years of Trucking* (Rexdale 1977) 4, 7; see also traffic statistics in: Ontario Highways Commission *Highways Commission* 87–99.

24 Canada Department of Railways and Canals *The Canadian Highway and Its Development* Bulletin No. 7 (1925) 19; G.T. Bloomfield 'I Can See a Car in That Crop: Motorization in Saskatchewan 1906–1934' *Saskatchewan History* 37 (winter 1984) 11

25 Urquhart *Historical Statistics* 64; Canadian Automotive Chamber of Commerce *Highway Motor Transportation: Its Place in the Canadian Transportation System* by M.J. Patton (Toronto 1932) 13; D.W. Carr & Associates 'Truck-Rail Competition in Canada' in Canada, Royal Commission *Royal Commission on Transportation* III 1962 12

26 W. Kaye Lamb *History of the Canadian Pacific Railway* (New York 1977) 381

27 Ibid 380–2; OTA *Golden Years of Trucking* 72

28 Ken Romain 'Trends May Moderate Transport Growth' *Globe and Mail* 30 Nov 1981

29 Ken Romain 'Trailer, Container Piggybacking May Restore Rail's Marketing Edge' *Globe and Mail* 30 Nov 1981; 'CN Rail Refines its Intermodal Strategy' *Railway Age* (June 1985) 59–61; 'How Containerization Affects Shipping Industry' *Financial Post* 7 Nov 1980; Gus Welty 'TOFC/COFC Terminal: Key to Service and Growth' *Railway Age* (26 May 1969) 21–4

30 John F. Due *The Intercity Electric Railway Industry in Canada* (Toronto 1966)

31 *Canada Year Book, 1933* 676. Ridership may have been higher during the war, but statistics are grouped with bus lines.

32 Ontario *Royal Commission, 1938* 64, 66; J.C. Lessard 'Transportation in Canada' Appendix to *Royal Commission on Canada's Economic Prospects* (1956) 15; *Canada Year Book, 1980–81* 578–9

33 Urquhart *Historical Statistics* 535

34 Sheldon E. Gordon 'Is VIA on the Wrong Track? Or Is It Really the Solution to Canada's Passenger Rail Woes?' *Financial Post Magazine* (Nov 1979) 39–42; 'What a Way to Run a Railroad' *Globe and*

Mail – Report on Business Magazine (June 1987) 60–4; Statistics Canada *Railway Transport in Canada – General Statistics* Cat. 52–215 (1983)

35 Ibid 381–2

36 McLean 'National Highways' 469

37 Ibid 443–5, 468

38 Ibid 378–84

39 McLean 'National Highways' 469; R.E. Gosnell 'Public Administration [British Columbia]' *Canada and Its Provinces* xxii (Toronto 1914) 364–6; Chester Martin 'Political History of Manitoba, 1870–1912' *Canada and Its Provinces* xix (Toronto 1914) 132

40 Hugh G.J. Aitken *The Welland Canal Company* (Cambridge, Mass. 1954) 78

41 McLean 'National Highways' 382

42 Ibid 444–5; O.D. Skelton 'General Economic History, 1867–1912' *Canada and Its Provinces* ix (Toronto 1914) 197–8

43 A.D. DeCelles 'Quebec under Confederation, 1867–1913' *Canada and Its Provinces* xv (Toronto 1914) 167–215; J.W. DaFoe 'Economic History of the Prairie Provinces, 1870–1913' *Canada and Its Provinces* xx (Toronto 1914) 301

44 DaFoe 'History of Prairie Provinces' 314

45 Aitken *Welland Canal* 83

46 McLean 'National Highways' 408, 427, 443–4, 468

47 Lamb *Canadian Pacific Railway* 110–1; Canada, Department of Railways and Canals *Railway Statistics*, 1915 table 5

48 McLean 'National Highways' 397–8

49 Harold A. Innis *A History of the Canadian Pacific Railway* (Toronto 1923, reprint 1971) 99, 114

50 Public Archives of Canada *Records of the Canadian Transport Commission* (RG 46) General Inventory Series, 1984, 1

51 Ibid; W.T. Jackman *Economic Principles of Transportation* (Toronto 1935) 646–7; Canada, Department of Transport *A Statutory History of the Steam and Electric Railways of Canada, 1836–1937* (Ottawa 1938) 689

52 Public Archives of Canada *Records of the Department of Railways and Canals* (RG 43) General Inventory Series, 1986

53 McLean 'National Highways' 469–70

54 Ibid 468

55 Jackman *Economic Principles* 646–9, 470–2

56 Ibid 653–6; Currie *Canadian Transportation* 384–8, 394, 441

57 Thomas Mulvey 'The Provincial Executive Organization [Ontario]' *Canada and Its Provinces* xvii (Toronto 1914) 236–7; K.W. McKay 'Municipal History, 1867–1913 [Ontario]' *Canada and Its Provinces* xviii Toronto 1914) 482–4; E.T.D. Chambers 'The Government of Quebec' *Canada and Its Provinces* xv (Toronto 1914) 221

58 Marshall M. Kirkman *Science of Railways: Financing, Building and Maintaining* ii New York 1896) 138–40, 66–7

59 Alan Brown 'CPR Tackling Rogers Pass … Again!' *Canadian Geographic* 103:4 (1983) 39–40

60 Canadian National Railways, Office of Chief of Transportation *Elements of Yard Design and Yard Operation* for CNR use (Montreal 1931)

61 Union Switch & Signal Co. *Freight Classification Yards, Design and Operation* for internal use (New York 1939); 'Canadian Pacific Clearing Yard at North Transcona, Manitoba' *Canadian Railway & Marine World* (Jan 1913) 1–4; 'Fort William Yard, Canadian Pacific Railway' *Canadian Railway & Marine World* (1911) 1019; (1926) 630–2

62 *Canadian Transportation* Dec 1960, Aug 1964, July 1965

63 William D. Middleton *When the Steam Railroads Electrified* (Milwaukee 1974) 434–5

64 Ibid 435

65 Ibid 410, 435

66 'B.C. Rail Electrification Tied to Hydro Pledge' *Globe and Mail* 29 Aug 1985; Frank Shaffer 'BCR's New Coal Line: On Time, on Budget' *Modern Railroads* (July 1983) 32–72

ROBERT PASSFIELD

Waterways

From the beginnings of settlement, the use and improvement of natural waterways have facilitated the penetration of trade and agriculture into the continental interior and the subsequent development of Canada. Commercial and military waterways development has followed a remarkably consistent pattern, focusing on the St Lawrence River and the new water transportation networks that developed during the fur trade era.

The nineteenth century saw two eras of canal-building, 1815–33 and 1873–99; the twentieth century, the extraordinary engineering feats of the Fourth Welland Canal (1913–32) and the St Lawrence Seaway (1954–9). In a sparsely populated country, where difficult topography and harsh environment made construction expensive, these, like most Canadian waterways improvements, were public works or had heavy public financial assistance.

During the French regime (1608–1760), permanent settlement was confined to areas readily accessible from the sea: the lower St Lawrence and its tributaries and scattered pockets around coastal harbours in the Maritimes. But fur trade posts were established as far west as Fort Rouge (1734), at the junction of the Red and Assiniboine rivers, with military posts at key interior positions. To communicate with the interior

posts, portages were cleared around waterfalls and rapids to link rivers and lakes navigable by canoe. Two principal water routes were developed inland from Montreal: the upper St Lawrence–Great Lakes system and the Ottawa River–Lake Nipissing–Georgian Bay–upper Great Lakes route, crossing over the 'Grand Portage' from Lake Superior to the Red River, which flows northward in the Hudson Bay watershed.

Despite numerous arduous portages, natural waterways met the needs of fur trade and military supply. There was little incentive for the imperial power to undertake costly canal works through a wilderness area.[1]

Under British rule, the St Lawrence route was improved to serve the growing population of new settlements established in the interior. The British army's Corps of Royal Engineers, under Capt. William Twiss, constructed the St Lawrence military canals (1779–83). These consisted of four short lateral canals at rapids above Montreal: a 900-ft-long (274 m) canal with three locks, at Coteau-du-Lac, and shorter canals at Split Rock, Trou du Moulin (a walled canal cut), and Faucille (or Cascades) rapids. Day labourers and Loyalist soldiers worked on the project, with Cornish miners handling rock excavation. Five rubble masonry locks, 6 ft (1.8 m) wide by some 40

The *Arthur*, a sailing vessel from Toronto, accompanied in 1904 by a tug in a Welland Canal lock, near the top of the Niagara escarpment. Later locks would be far larger than these modest sizes. (AO Acc 4137-43)

ft (12 m) long, with 30 in (0.8 m) of water on the sills, were built by military artisans of the Royal Staff Corps. These were the first canal locks built in North America.[2]

BUILDING CANALS (1815–53)

For almost four decades, 1815–53, the British North American colonies experienced a canal-building age, as the British military, the governments of Upper and Lower Canada, and various private interests embarked on major canal construction. Two distinct construction strategies evolved: one military, the other commercial.

After the War of 1812, military strategists urged abandoning the exposed upper St Lawrence navigation in favour of developing an interior canals system. It required a canal to pass the Lachine Rapids at Montreal, three short canals at rapids on the Ottawa, and a canal via the Rideau and Cataraqui rivers to connect the Ottawa with Kingston on Lake Ontario.

Colonial commercial interests wanted to canalize the entire St Lawrence and extend the system beyond Lake Ontario with a canal at Niagara Falls. The spectre of the projected American Erie Canal (constructed 1817–25) capturing interior trade spurred governments to construct canals to improve and extend the St Lawrence system. The planned Ottawa-Rideau military canals system was considered too circuitous to compete with the Erie.[3]

The Lachine Canal (1821–5) was a component of both the provincial (commercial) and military canal systems. To construct it, Lower Canada engaged a British canal engineer, Thomas Burnett, and let the excavation and masonry work on contract. Seven cut-stone masonry locks, 20 ft (6.1 m) by 108 ft (33 m), provided 45 ft (13.8 m) of lockage on an 8.5-mi-long (13.7 km) canal, at a cost of £109,600.[4]

The Ottawa-Rideau military canals were built between 1819 and 1834. On the Ottawa River, the British Army's Royal Staff Corps, under Capt. Henry Du Vernet, constructed lateral canals to pass the rapids upstream at Carillon, Chute à Blondeau, and Grenville. The canals were excavated through solid bedrock to a 5 ft (1.5 m) navigable depth. The 6-mi-long (9.6 km) Grenville Canal (1819–29) was built by artisans of the Royal Staff Corps, and the other canals by civilian contractors (1829–34). Over 8 mi (12.9 km) of canals were built, with eleven locks providing 60 ft (18.2 m) of lockage at a cost of £312,000. The first three Grenville locks were on the Lachine Canal scale, and the remaining locks, 33 ft (10.0 m) by 134 ft (40.8 m), matched the new Rideau Canal.[5]

The Rideau Canal (1826–32) was built on the contract system under Lt.-Col. John By, Corps of Royal Engineers, in just six years at a cost of £822,800 ($3,656,870). Eighteen river dams and 23 waste weirs were erected on a 123-mi (198 km) slackwater system, with 47 cut-stone masonry locks providing 444 ft (135.3 m) of lockage. Several stupendous dams were built, including 9 arched stone masonry structures – the first major masonry dams in North America. Several were of a unique arched keywork masonry construction.

In building keywork masonry, as introduced by Cornish masons, rough blocks of quarried stone were set in vertical courses and pinning stones driven into the vertical and horizontal joints to form a solid unit of masonry. A thick clay puddle core wall against the upstream face of the arch rendered the dam impermeable to water. At Jones' Falls, the Royal Engineers built an arch dam of cut-stone masonry, 62 ft (18.9 m) high and 350 ft (106.6 m) long on its crest, with

The Long Island Locks, Rideau Canal. In a slackwater system a high dam – here a 9.4-m (31-ft) keywork masonry structure – floods the river to the base of the next dam upstream, locks rise to the high-water level, and ships pass up to the next dam and set of locks. Excess water flows through a waste weir not shown in this photo. (NPS)

a 250-ft (76.2-m) radius of curvature. It was the first true arch dam, as well as the highest dam to that date, in North America.

The Rideau Canal was the world's first canal designed to accommodate steamboats. The large 33-by-134-ft (10-by-40.0-m) locks far exceeded the scale of the 15-by-90-ft (4.8-by-27.4-m) Erie Canal locks and the standard 7.5-by-70-ft (2.4-by-21.3-m) 'narrow lock' on inland barge canals in Britain.[6]

Upper Canada acquired three commercial canals between 1823 and 1837. On Lake Ontario, the province constructed the Burlington Bay Canal (1823–

32). Excavated through a sandbar, the half-mile-long (0.8 km) canal cut, 120 ft (36.6 m) wide by 13 ft (4.0 m) deep, enabled lake vessels to reach Hamilton on Burlington Bay. Navigation was extended inland 3 mi (4.8 km) to Dundas, when a private company, with provincial financial assistance, dredged the Desjardins Canal (1826–37).[7]

The Welland Canal (1824–33) was built to bypass Niagara Falls and the Niagara River Rapids, through which the waters of Lake Erie fell 326 ft (99.4 m) into Lake Ontario. The 28-mi-long (45.1 km) canal, from Port Dalhousie on Lake Ontario to Port Colborne on Lake Erie, had 40 timber locks a minimum of 110 ft (33.5 m) by 22 ft (6.7 m), with 8 ft (2.4 m) of water on the sills. It was built by a joint stock company, with provincial support, and two American engineers from the Erie Canal – Nathan Roberts and Alfred Barrett – superintended the project. The canal cost £407,855, with government loans and stock purchases totalling £288,000. Heavy debts and high maintenance costs on the timber locks left the company dependent on government support.[8]

By the 1830s, two distinct approaches to canal construction were evident in North America. In the British method, durability was sought, with heavy cutstone masonry locks constructed on a large scale to meet future transportation needs. This required large initial outlays of capital and highly skilled tradesmen, but maintenance costs were comparatively low. The American approach used building materials and skills readily at hand to construct crude, but efficient timber or rubble masonry locks no larger than immediately required. Initial capital and labour costs were greatly reduced, but maintenance costs were high. In the Canadas, the British approach was confined to government-funded projects.

In the Canadas, enthusiasm for canal projects continued unabated during the 1830s. In Lower Canada, contracts were let for construction of a 12-mi (19.2-km) canal, the Chambly, to pass the Chambly Rapids on the Richelieu River. Upper Canada excavated the lake-level Long Point Canal (1834) across the Long Point peninsula to facilitate Lake Erie's coasting trade and constructed a lock at Bobcaygeon (1833) as a prelude to canalizing the Trent River.[9]

Trade boomed on waterways, with rapidly growing square timber and Upper Canadian wheat exports to Britain, heavy British immigration, and lumber shipments to American markets. Lumber was shipped in schooners across the lakes and by barge along the Richelieu, with a portage at the Chambly Rapids, and beyond on the Champlain Canal to New York.

Great Lakes–St Lawrence trade centred on Montreal and followed a triangular pattern. Barges were towed by steamers, via the Ottawa and Rideau canals, to Kingston, carrying immigrants and merchandise, and were shot down through the St Lawrence River rapids and the Lachine Canal, laden with wheat, flour, and potash, back to Montreal. The inadequacies of St Lawrence navigation, however, remained a critical concern. With the opening of the Erie Canal in 1825, New York had supplanted Montreal as the commercial entrepôt for the new American west developing in Ohio, Indiana, and Illinois. Moreover, almost 85 per cent of the wheat passing through the Welland Canal – over 264,900 bu annually – went to the Erie Canal at Oswego for export.[10]

To recapture this lost trade, the Canadas planned to canalize the St Lawrence at an estimated cost of £585,782. But construction proceeded slowly, as both provinces struggled with a heavy public debt incurred in canal-building. Lower

St Gabriel north lock, Lachine Canal, 1910; the Glenora Mills were one of many industries attracted by power and transportation. Excess water drove turbines and later electric generators for local needs. (NA PA-110110)

Canada abandoned the Chambly Canal project, and bankruptcy threatened Upper Canada, as interest on the public debt absorbed nearly the whole provincial revenue. With the onset of a worldwide economic depression in 1837, and abortive political rebellions in December 1837, work on the Trent and St Lawrence canals came to a halt.[11]

In the early 1840s, Canada developed a new organization for public works. In an effort to restore political stability and foster economic development, the British government gave the Canadas an interest guarantee for a £1.5-million loan and united Upper and Lower Canada to form the Province of Canada in 1841. A Board of Works was established in Au-gust 1841 to build public works based on waterways improvements. The board replaced the former system of appointing government commissioners to oversee particular projects.

The board was responsible for canal construction and maintenance, lighthouses and navigational aids, harbour and river improvements, public buildings, timber slides and booms, and several roads considered of provincial importance. It was based on a similar body established by the Lower Canadian government in June 1839, the first board of works in British North America.

In 1841, the government of the Canadian province appropriated the sum of £1,659,682 for a five-year program of public works, involving canal construction, timber slides, lighthouse and harbour works on lakes Erie and Ontario, and provincial road improvements. In June 1846, a Department of Public Works was established, and subsequently canal construction accounted for 75 per cent of all public works expenditures.[12]

The 1840s and early 1850s saw a canal-building boom in Canada. On the St Lawrence, the Cornwall Canal was completed (1842–3) with seven locks providing 48 ft (14.6 m) of lockage, and the old St Lawrence military canals were replaced by the Beauharnois Canal (1842–5) on the opposite, or south shore. Nine locks provided 82.5 ft (25.1 m) of lockage. The Lachine Canal was enlarged (1843–8), and, on the upper St Lawrence, the three short Williamsburg Canals were built (1844–8): the Farran's Point, the Rapide Plat, and the Galops.

The new St Lawrence navigation cost $5,665,000 and consisted of over 43 mi (69.2 km) of canals and 27 locks, providing 206 ft (62.8 m) of lockage. All locks were of heavy cut-stone masonry, 200 ft (61.0 m) by 45 ft (13.7 m) with 9 ft (2.7 m) of water on the sills – the largest canal locks in North America, perhaps in the world.

Work on the (enlarged) Second Welland Canal was completed 1842–50. It had 27 cut-stone masonry locks, 150 ft (45.7 m) by 26.5 ft (8.1 m), with 9 ft (2.7 m) of water on the sills to accommodate large lake schooners, deepened to 10 ft (3.0 m) throughout 1851–3.

The opening of the Burlington Bay Canal in 1832 had transformed Hamilton into a major commercial centre, serving a vast agricultural hinterland, and the canal cut was enlarged 1843–50.[13] On the Richelieu River, the Chambly Canal was completed 1840–2 with 9 cut-stone masonry locks, 118 ft (36.0 m) by 23 ft (7.0 m), with 7 ft (2.1 m) of water on the Sills. Downstream, the St Ours Canal was

constructed, with a single masonry lock, 200 ft (61.0 m) by 45 ft (13.7 m). The two canals enabled lumber barges to pass fully laden from the St Lawrence to Lake Champlain.[14]

At the confluence of the Ottawa and St Lawrence rivers, the Ste Anne's Canal (1840–3) was built to improve the Ottawa-Rideau military canals system, which dominated the import trade of the Canadian interior until completion of the St Lawrence canals system. It had a single cut-stone masonry lock, 190 ft (57.9 m) by 45 ft (13.7 m), on a 6-ft (1.8-m) depth of navigation.

The Trent waterway lakes navigations were extended 1843–8 with single masonry locks, 134 ft (40.8 m) by 33 ft (10.1 m), at Witla's Rapids (Scott's Mills), Crook's Rapids (Hastings), and Chisholm's Rapids (Glen Ross). They remained unique in being landlocked.[15]

As the network of interconnected canals was constructed in the decades after the War of 1812, wheat production and flour milling boomed along the navigable waterways, accounting for 75 per cent of the exports forwarded to eastern markets from new urban commercial centres west of the Trent River. East of the Trent, waterways improvements also fostered a commercial economy. But except in Montreal, this was sustained primarily by the timber and lumber trades.[16]

The new Welland–St Lawrence canals system was far superior to the Erie barge canal, with fewer and larger locks on a deeper navigation. Freight could move from Chicago to New York at $5.56 a ton but after 1848 reached Montreal at less than $4.77 a ton. Montreal, however, was unable to match New York as an ocean port. New York was on the ocean, open year round, serving a populous area with balanced inbound and outbound cargoes yielding low ocean shipping rates. Montreal, in contrast,

For safety and security, mitre gates must point toward the higher water. Tides cause variations in level, and therefore tidal canals require two sets of gates, pointing in opposite directions. The St Peter's canal system, connecting Cape Breton's Bras D'Or Lakes estuary with the Atlantic, has tidal locks. (CPS)

was an inland port, ice-bound five months of the year, with ships often arriving in ballast. Thus ocean shipping costs were comparatively high from Montreal. Overall freight costs on the popular Chicago–Erie Canal–New York–Liverpool route were $10.56 a ton, as opposed to $13.77 via the Canadian canals and Montreal.[17] Hence, New York continued to control the burgeoning grain trade of the American Midwest.

The new canals, however, were by no means a failure. The St Lawrence canals opened up a major domestic market for Upper Canadian wheat and flour in the urban centres of Lower Canada and the Maritimes. By cutting transport costs in

half, the canals also enabled Canadian wheat and flour exported via Montreal to continue to compete in British markets following the mid-century loss of the colonial preferences.[18] Moreover, the threat posed by construction of the St Lawrence canals moved the Americans to grant bonding privileges to Canadian shipping on the Erie Canal.

THE MARITIMES

In the Maritime provinces, with ready access to the sea, waterways improvements focused on navigational aids. The French erected the first lighthouse, a 70-ft (21.3 m) stone masonry, on Cape

Canada's first lighthouse, built at Louisbourg, Cape Breton Island, in 1734; from colour wash drawings, Bibliothèque nationale, Paris (NA C-15674)

Breton Island at Louisbourg in 1731–4. The light was an open flame, with a number of wicks set in a pan of oil. Under British rule, early lighthouses were erected at Halifax harbour on Sambro Island (1758–60); at Saint John, New Brunswick, on Partridge Island (1791); on McNutt Island near Shelburne, Nova Scotia (1788–91); at the entrance to the Bay of Fundy on Brier Island (1809); and at Fort Amherst (1811–13) overlooking St John's harbour.[19]

To avoid a hazardous coastal voyage, Halifax merchants formed the Shubenacadie Canal Co. to connect Halifax harbour with the Bay of Fundy along a chain of interior lakes and the Shubenacadie River, which all but bisected Nova Scotia. With financial support from the legislature, work commenced in 1826. Over 300 men were employed, including 44 stone masons brought out from Scotland to construct masonry locks of cut granite, 87 ft (26.5 m) by 22.5 ft (6.9 m), on a 9-ft-deep (2.7 m) navigation. As of November 1831, with funds exhausted and over £68,000 spent in constructing 13 of a planned 18 locks, the project was abandoned.[20]

Discouraged, Nova Scotia and New Brunswick redoubled efforts to aid coastal shipping. Principal lighthouses were erected in the Bay of Fundy on Seal Island (1830), Gannet Rock and Point Lepeau (1831), and Machias Seal Island (1832). They had octagonal timber-frame towers, with sloping sides, and a catoptric (mirror or reflector) light apparatus with a sperm oil reservoir.

To safeguard transatlantic shipping, imperial and provincial authorities combined to erect lighthouses: in Cabot Strait, off Nova Scotia, on Scatarie Island and St Paul Island (1839); and in Newfoundland at Cape Spear (1836), Harbour Grace Island (1837), and Cape Bonavista (1843) – the first public works erected by the provincial legislature. In Prince Edward Island, a 60-ft (18.3-m) circular brick tower was erected at Charlottetown harbour on Point Prim in 1846.[21]

IMPROVEMENTS (1841–67)

Timber slides were designed to facilitate the descent of squared timber past rapids and waterfalls. Two types were constructed: the single-stick slide (or flume), for passing timber piece by piece; and the crib slide, designed to pass the 25-ft-wide (7.7 m) cribs, formed of squared timber framed together with dowels and traverses, which were the basic unit of the large river rafts floated down to Quebec for export.

The timber crib slide, a Canadian invention, was built of cribwork forming a long channel, 26 ft (7.9 m) wide, through which water flowed in passing over an inclined plane. The slides were built adjacent to rapids and waterfalls, with the length and slope gradient of the inclined plane conforming to the fall in the river.

The world's first crib slide was built in 1829 at Bytown (Ottawa) to pass the Chaudière Falls, and the first public slides were constructed by the Canadian Board of Works in 1843. Thereafter government crib slides, flumes, and booms were constructed along the Ottawa River system and the Trent, as well as on the St Maurice and Saguenay. By 1867, government expenditures in constructing timber slides and booms since 1841 totalled over $1 million, reflecting the economic importance of the timber trade in a period when but $500,000 was spent on road building.[22]

At mid-century, saw mills proliferated on the Ottawa River. Vast quantities of lumber were barged to the New York market via a new canal system. It linked the Ottawa military canals (the Grenville, Chute à Blondeau, and Carillon),

The first Great Lakes lighthouse, built at the mouth of the Niagara River in 1804 and lit by
Argand lamps or tallow candles with reflectors. From an early-19th-century line engraving
(NA C-41730)

the Ste Anne's, the Lachine, and the St
Ours and Chambly on the Richelieu,
with the American Champlain Canal–
Hudson River system. This new network soon ranked second only to the
Welland–St Lawrence in commercial
importance.[23]

In the Maritimes, the timber trade was
focused in New Brunswick on the Mir-
amichi, St John, and Restigouche rivers.
Most major New Brunswick rivers were
navigable well into the interior, negating
any need for timber slides. A number of
flumes, however, were constructed to
carry single sticks past waterfalls on the
St Croix River, where sawmilling had a
boom in the 1830s and 1840s.[24]

Everywhere, improvements in waterways transport fostered rapid economic
development during the 1830s and
1840s, and by the 1850s, manufacturing
industries were being established to take
advantage of the hydraulic power furnished by canals.[25]

During the canal-building era, the
need for navigational aids proliferated.
In Upper Canada prior to 1841, navigational aids were erected and maintained
by a Board of Commissioners appointed
by the legislature, as in the Maritimes. In
Lower Canada, the legislature established Trinity houses on the British model: at Quebec (1804), for the lower St
Lawrence; and at Montreal (1832), for
the upper. The earliest lighthouses were
erected on Lake Ontario at Mississauga
Point (1804), on the Niagara River portage to Lake Erie, and at Gibraltar Point
(1808), on Toronto Island; and in the
mouth of the St Lawrence River on
Green Island (1809). These stone masonry towers ranged from 40 ft (12.2 m) to 90
ft (27.4 m) in height.

After 1841, the Board of Works assumed responsibility for navigational
aids and harbour improvements and the
direction of the two Trinity houses.
Many buoys, beacons, and harbour piers

and lights were erected on Canadian canals and navigable waterways. Lighthouse construction was concentrated on the St Lawrence River and the Gulf of St Lawrence, with the establishment of transatlantic steamship lines. In Newfoundland, the imperial government built landfall lighthouses at Cape Pine (1851), Cape Race (1856), and Cape St Mary's (1860). British North America's first dioptric (see-through) light, employing glass lenses and prisms to obtain a far brighter and more efficient light, was introduced in 1852 on the refitted Fort Amherst lighthouse.

Unlike Britain and the United States, Canadian authorities did not convert all lighthouses to the dioptric system. Rather a new fuel was introduced. In 1846, kerosene or coal oil had been distilled by Dr Abraham Gesner, a Nova Scotian geologist, and experimented with in a harbour lighthouse at Maugher's Beach, Halifax. Kerosene proved the cheapest fuel and produced an excellent light, bright and steady. In 1865, it was adopted for use in all Canadian catoptric lighthouses. A few major landfall and headland lighthouses were converted to the dioptric system, but otherwise catoptric lighthouses were built and/or maintained in both Canada and the Maritimes.

In 1860, the world's first steam fog whistle was installed at the Partridge Island lighthouse at Saint John. It was invented by Robert Foulis, a New Brunswick civil engineer. Steam fog whistles were quickly adopted elsewhere and continued in service throughout the 19th century.[26]

By 1867, the Canadian government alone was maintaining 120 lighthouses and had spent $1,002,780 on lighthouse construction and maintenance since 1841. In the same period, $1,707,724 was spent on harbours, piers, and dredging, and $2,202,025 on building and main-

taining timber slides. Canal building cost $11,158,219;[27] by its completion in 1853, government attention turned to railways to strengthen and extend the commercial system based on water-borne trade.

At mid-century, the British North American provinces entered a golden age of prosperity, as the price of export commodities more than doubled. This prosperity in turn generated a railway construction boom, as the various governments sought the trade of the continental interior.[28] The newly completed canals system required little attention. In 1854, a contract was let for a 2.5-mi (4.0-km) Chats Canal at the Chats Rapids on the upper Ottawa River. Two years later, with almost $483,000 spent in excavating hard igneous rock, the project was abandoned.[29]

On the lower Ottawa, the military canals at Grenville, Chute à Blondeau, and Carillon were transferred by Britain to the government of Canada in 1856, along with the Rideau Canal (and the old, defunct St Lawrence military canals). Responsibility for the canals, hitherto exercised by the Corps of Royal Engineers under the British Army Ordnance Department, was assumed by the Department of Public Works.[30]

In Nova Scotia, after a hiatus of 22 years, a private company completed the Shubenacadie Canal (1854–61). It was built on a reduced scale as a barge canal, with rubble masonry and timber locks, 66 ft (20.1 m) by 17 ft (5.2 m). Only nine locks were required, with inclined marine railways built on two steep ascents: the Porto Bello incline, with a 35-ft (10.7-m) rise; and the Dartmouth incline, overcoming a 55-ft (16.8-m) rise. Cradle cars drew barges up the incline rails by means of a wire cable and drum worked by a 'Scotch' turbine using the head of water at the top of the incline.

The canal failed to establish Halifax as the entrepôt for the Bay of Fundy trade.

The introduction of coastal steamers and erection of lighthouses deprived the canal of its projected advantage – a safe waterway, free of the fog hazards, wind, and tide delays that had plagued sailing vessels.[31]

In 1854, the long-contemplated St Peter's Canal was undertaken by Nova Scotia to enable schooners to pass through Cape Breton Island, thereby avoiding a hazardous coastal voyage. The canal, to provide a southern outlet for the interior Bras d'Or Lakes, required an excavation up to 50 ft (15.2 m) deep across the half-mile-wide (0.8 km) Isthmus of St Peter's and a single tidal lock. Construction languished, however, as government monies were committed to railway construction.[32]

In Canada, by 1860, railways paralleled most navigable waterways. In less than a decade, over $100 million had been spent on railway construction, heavily subsidized with government grants and loans. But trunk railways did not capture the wheat trade of the American Midwest for the St Lawrence commercial system, owing to parallel construction of American railway systems westward from New York. Trunk railways, however, did tie Canadian feeder railways into the St Lawrence system, thereby meeting the challenge posed by American railways reaching out to Canadian border points.

In contrast to the American experience, railways did not supersede canals in Canada at mid-century. Where parallel systems existed, railways were unable to compete directly with canals for bulk freight traffic – the wheat, flour, and lumber staples of the export trade. The major Canadian canals were but short links in major lake and river navigations. On these long-distance, open-water navigations, bulk freight could be forwarded cheaply.[33]

After failure to capture the Midwest trade, attention shifted by the late 1850s to the Hudson's Bay Company lands west of Lake Superior. If the prairies could be settled and developed into one of the world's major grain-producing areas, it would ensure full use of a transportation system second to none. Deeply burdened with debt, however, neither private railway companies nor the Canadian government could undertake a major rail or water extension of the transportation system. Only through confederation of the British North American provinces could westward expansion proceed.

On 1 July 1867 the Province of Canada was divided into two provinces, Ontario and Quebec, and united with Nova Scotia and New Brunswick in the new Dominion of Canada. Thereafter, a new Department of Public Works assumed responsibility for canals, lighthouses and navigational aids, timber slides, federal public buildings, roads of a national character, and government railway holdings. Public works of a purely local nature rested with the provincial governments. Strengthened by political consolidation, the new federal government looked toward westward expansion and the development of transportation links to the 'new West.'[34]

THE 'NEW WEST'

After the 1821 merger of the North West Co. with the Hudson's Bay Co., the far-flung western fur trade posts were supplied from Hudson Bay, via the Hayes and/or Nelson rivers to Lake Winnipeg, and beyond on the three major river systems flowing into that lake: the Winnipeg River–Rainy Lake (southwest); the Red River–Assiniboine River (south/southwest); and the South and North Saskatchewan River (westward). To the north, the fur trade system extended from the Saskatchewan River across several short portages and intermediate rivers onto the Athabasca–Mackenzie River system, flowing into the Arctic Ocean and beyond on tributary rivers across a short portage onto the Yukon River system.[35]

In effect, an integrated waterways transportation system extended across western Canada: on the 414,000-sq-mi (1,072,256-sq-km) Nelson–Winnipeg–Red–Saskatchewan drainage system, which discharges into Hudson Bay; the 696,700-sq-mi (1,804,446-sq-km) Athabasca–Peace–Mackenzie watershed of the Arctic Ocean; and, beyond, onto the 324,000-sq-mi (839,156-sq-km) (125,000 sq mi [323,748 sq km] in Canada) Yukon drainage area, discharging into the Bering Sea. Canoes were supplemented on the rough river stretches by bateaux or York boats – 30-to-40-ft-long (9.1 to 12.2 m) keelboats. At major portages, the Hudson's Bay Co. constructed rollerways for transporting the heavy boats.[36]

Transportation had remained unchanged until 1859, when the introduction of sternwheel steamers on the Red River brought a new orientation. Brigades of ox-carts proceeded northward from St Paul, on the upper Mississippi River, to connect with Red River steamers running between Georgetown, Minnesota, and Fort Garry (Winnipeg). The trade of the Hudson's Bay Co. and the expanding Red River settlement turned southward. The developing trade of the Northwest might well be carried to seaboard by American transportation.[37]

In response, the new Dominion purchased the Hudson's Bay Co. lands for £300,000 in March 1869, created the new province of Manitoba in 1870, and undertook to open Canadian transportation to the Red River. Built 1868–71, the Dawson Route consisted of a 450-mi (724-km) wagon road/waterway with portages linking navigable stretches along the Rainy Lake–Rainy River–Lake of the Woods navigation. It immediately proved incapable of competing with the American route, improved in 1871 by a railway connecting Duluth, on Lake Superior, with Georgetown.[38]

On British Columbia entering Confederation in July 1871, the Canadian government agreed to build a transcontinental railway. Henceforth, western transportation needs would be met by railway construction rather than waterways improvements. In the interim, steamers proliferated on the western rivers, bringing in immigrants, merchandise, and flour and exporting furs, buffalo robes, and, commencing in 1876, wheat. Prairie steamboats, however, were but temporary expedients, superseded by the transcontinental railway.[39]

The Department of Public Works did improve the Red River at the St Andrew's Rapids. The St Andrew's Canal (1903–10) was built with a single concrete lock, 215 ft (65.5 m) by 46 ft (14.0 m), and 9 ft (2.7 m) of water on the sills, adjacent to a movable steel curtain dam.[40]

In Yukon, waterways continued to play a vital transportation role after the mid-19th century, despite the decline of the fur trade. Introduction of the steamboat, however, reoriented transportation. During the Klondike Gold Rush of 1898, a fleet of sternwheelers and barges was placed on the upper Yukon River to form a link with the White Pass and Yukon Route Railway (built 1898–1900) between the port of Skagway, Alaska, and Whitehorse.[41]

On the Pacific slope, two major rivers (the Columbia and the Fraser) and their tributaries had initially provided transportation in the interior for the canoe brigades of the fur trade. River transport, however, had to be supplemented, and was finally superseded, by overland transport.

As early as 1805, the North West Co. had penetrated overland through mountain passes to establish posts on the upper Fraser and along the Columbia River system. By 1813, trade with the new interior posts was reoriented toward the Pacific. Canoe brigades from tidewater at Fort George (formerly Astoria) served the entire Columbia system, with a pack-horse brigade trail branching northward, bypassing the turbulent waters in the lower Fraser canyons, to the foot of navigation on the upper Fraser watershed. Furs were transported to China for sale, and, following merger with the Hudson's Bay Company, supplies were brought by sea from London.[42]

Ultimately, waterways transport was replaced by the Canadian Pacific Railway, built up through the Fraser canyons 1881–5. One canal, however, was undertaken by a private company with government support. The Baillie-Groham Canal (1887–9) was built to link the meandering upper reaches of the Kootenay and Columbia steamboat navigations across a mile-wide (1.6 km) flats. The canal had a single timber lock, 30 ft (9.1 m) by 100 ft (30.4 m), on a 4-ft-deep (1.2 m) channel, but failed to generate any traffic.[43]

BUILDING CANALS (1873–99)

East of Lake Superior, the new Dominion entered a second canal-building era soon after Confederation. Cheap transportation to seaboard was essential if the prairies were to be settled and developed as a major wheat-growing area. On the Great Lakes, bulk freight could be transported at one-tenth to one-eighth the cost by rail.[44]

The transcontinental railway was the key to western settlement, but enlargement and extension of the canal system were no less critical. The government undertook to enlarge the Welland and the six St Lawrence canals, and to construct a Canadian canal at Sault Ste Marie, to enable large lake freighters to pass from the Lakehead to Montreal without transshipping cargoes. Barge canals along the Ottawa and Richelieu rivers were also to be enlarged.[45] The onset of a severe world-wide depression in 1873, however, brought retrenchment and piecemeal canal construction.

On the upper Ottawa River, lumber transport was improved with the Culbute Canal (1873–6) at the Calumet Rapids. Two combined locks, 200 ft (61.0 m) by 45 ft (13.8 m), opened a 77-mi (123.9-km) interior river navigation. The St Peter's Canal, completed 1867–9 with a single tidal lock 122 ft (37.2 m) by 26 ft (8.0 m), was enlarged (1875–80) with a lock 200 ft (61.0 m) by 48 ft (14.7 m). In the west the Fort Frances Canal, with a single lock 200 ft (61.0 m) by 36 ft (11.0 m), was undertaken (1875–9) to eliminate a portage on the Dawson Route but was abandoned when it was all but completed.[46]

With increasing prosperity, in 1878 a new Conservative government came to power committed to a 'National Policy' of economic development: settlement of the prairies through immigration; development of prairie lands as a major wheat-exporting region; fostering of industrialization through tariff protection for nascent industries; and construction of a transcontinental railway and enlarged canal system, to carry Canadian manufactured goods to prairie farmers and prairie wheat to world markets. In 1879, a Department of Railways and Canals was formed to push canal enlargement. The Department of Public Works remained responsible for timber slides, harbour and river improvements, and public buildings.[47]

The Second Carillon Canal was built (1873–82) with two locks and a semicircular timber crib dam 1,200 ft (365.8 m) long and 24 ft (7.3 m) high, across the Ottawa River. The submerged Carillon dam flooded out the Chute à Blondeau Canal. The Grenville Canal was also enlarged (1871–84), as was the Ste Anne's (1879–83). All the locks were of cut-stone masonry, 200 ft (61.0 m) by 45 ft (13.8 m), with 9 ft (2.7 m) of water on the sills. They served a heavy barge traffic as sawn lumber shipments from the Ottawa Valley increased to an all-time record 550,472 tons in 1889.[48]

The Rideau Canal had proved adequate for the timber/lumber trade and freight traffic after Confederation. But the derelict Tay Canal branch, built 1831–4 by a private company along the Tay River to Perth, was rebuilt. The second Tay Canal (1883–91) had two masonry locks 134 ft (40.9 m) by 33 ft (10.0 m), on an altered alignment directly overland from Rideau Lake to the upper Tay River. It generated little traffic.[49]

On the Richelieu River, the Chambly Canal locks were rebuilt piecemeal (1880–95) on the original scale. Shipping on the Richelieu canals peaked in 1912 at 618,415 tons of freight, principally Canadian lumber and pulpwood to the United States and Pennsylvania coal to Montreal.[50]

At Niagara, the Second Welland Canal had become a bottleneck in the grain export trade as early as 1860. Deep-draught vessels had to be 'lightened,' through transshipping part of their cargo into rail cars, before entering the canal. The Third Welland Canal was constructed (1873–83), with stone masonry locks 270 ft (82.3 m) by 45 ft (13.8 m) and 12 ft (3.7 m) of water on the sills, and deepened (1883–7) to 14 ft (4.3 m) throughout.

On the St Lawrence, the Lachine Canal (1873–84) and the Cornwall Canal (1884–95) were enlarged, with locks 270

ft (82.3 m) by 45 ft (13.8 m) with 14 ft (4.3 m) of water on the sills. The three Williamsburg Canals were similarly enlarged (1891–9), and the Beauharnois was replaced with a new canal on the north shore. The 14-mi (22.5-km) Soulanges Canal (1891–9) had five locks and 82.5 ft (25.1 m) of lockage.

On Lake Ontario, a 5-mi (8.0 km) canal, 80 ft (24.4 m) wide and 12 ft (3.7 m) deep, was excavated across the Isthmus of Murray. The Murray Canal (1882–9) enabled coasting schooners to avoid a long voyage around the Prince Edward County peninsula.[51]

The mile-long (1.6 km) Sault Ste Marie Ship Canal was constructed (1889–95) with a single flotilla lock, 900 ft (274.3 m) by 60 ft (18.3 m), and a 20-ft (6.1 m) navigation. The Canadian canal enabled large upper lakes freighters to double their tonnage capacity in carrying iron ore and wheat eastward to Lake Erie ports and coal westward to the Midwest. The Sault Ste Marie Ship Canal was the world's first electrically powered lock, as well as the first North American canal totally illuminated with electric lighting. An emergency swing bridge dam protected the canal. It could be swung across the canal, enabling wickets to be swung down, gradually closing off any torrent of water flowing from Lake Superior.[52]

The enlarged canals system, with 74 mi (119.1 km) of canal and 48 locks providing 553 ft (168.6 m) of lockage between Montreal and Lake Superior, opened a 1,200-mi (1,931.2-km) inland ship route to vessels of 14-ft (4.3-m) draught. Almost $53 million was spent enlarging and extending the national canals system after Confederation, including work on the Trent.[53]

The Ontario government had extended the Trent waterways in constructing locks at Young's Point and Rosedale (1868–72), and subsequently the federal

Operation of Chambly Canal locks, 5 September 1911. The barges, heavily laden with pulpwood or firewood, suggest the economic importance of canals. The Chambly was one of the few Canadian canals built with a tow-path for horses to pull barges or ships. The horse barn is visible in the upper photo. (NA PA 85695 and C-60786)

When a ship crashed through the Sault Ste Marie Canal locks in 1909, the surge of water ripped the gates off. The emergency swing bridge in the background was therefore installed, and from it wickets and shutters could be dropped to cut off the flow of water gradually. (NA PA-146241)

government undertook to open a 250-mi (402.3-km) barge route from Georgian Bay through to Lake Ontario. The Trent-Severn Waterway, with locks, 134 ft (40.9 m) by 33 ft (10.0 m), was intended to augment western grain transport.[54] Two major innovations were made: the introduction of structural concrete into Canadian canal construction, commencing with the first mass concrete lock completed near Peterborough in 1896; and the building of North America's two first, and only, hydraulic lift locks.

The Peterborough Hydraulic Lift Lock (1896–1904) had a lift of 65 ft (19.8 m), 30 per cent higher than any previous hydraulic lift. The large lock chambers, 140 ft (42.7 m) by 33 ft (10.0 m), with an 8-ft (2.4-m) depth of water, placed an unprecedented 1,800-ton load on each of the 7.5-ft-diameter (2.6-m) rams operating under a pressure of 600 psi. The

Kirkfield Hydraulic Lift Lock (1900–7) had a 49-ft (15.0-m) lift. Both hydraulic lift locks remain in operation today.[55]

Long before its completion in 1920, the Trent-Severn Waterway appeared destined to serve only local traffic. The opening of the ship canals system had cut shipping costs from the Lakehead through the Great Lakes from 29 cents to as low as 3 cents a bushel. Attention turned to providing an even larger ship canal system through to seaboard at Montreal.[56] By the 1930s, pleasure craft outnumbered commercial vessels 5 to 1 on the Trent-Severn system.[57]

THE MARITIMES

In the Maritimes, a private company tried but failed to complete the Chignecto Ship Railway (1888–91), across the

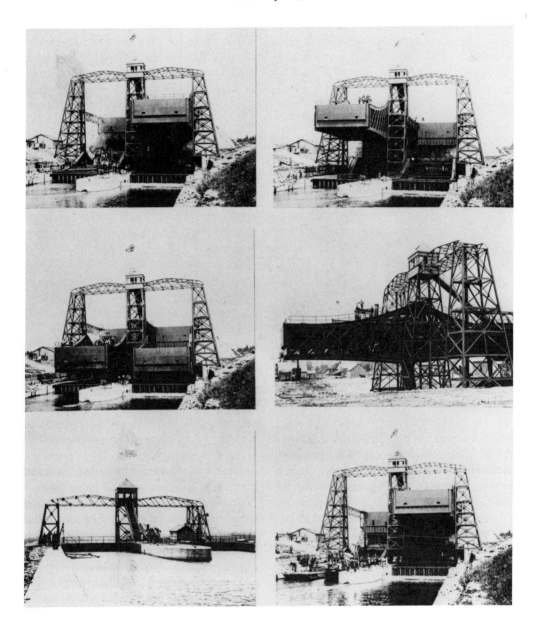

Hydraulic Lift Lock at Kirkfield, Ontario, second in size only to that in nearby Peterborough. As one counter-balanced chamber rises, the other falls from upper- to lower-water level. (NA PA-29203)

The Peterborough Hydraulic Lift Lock, the largest of its type in the world and, when built, the world's largest massed – or unreinforced – concrete structure. The design used less water and less space than conventional mitre-gate locks. (NA PA-43492)

17-mi-wide (27.4 km) Isthmus of Chignecto, owing to financial difficulties. It was intended to portage coasting trade vessels of 1,000 tons burthen between the Gulf of St Lawrence and the Bay of Fundy, saving a 500-mi (804.6-km) voyage around Nova Scotia.[58] The coasting trade was facilitated, however, through enlarging the St Peter's Canal (1911–17) with a new concrete lock, 300 ft (91.4 m) by 48 ft (14.6 m).

More recently, a ship canal was built to maintain navigation through the Straits of Canso on construction of the Canso Causeway, connecting Cape Breton Island with the Nova Scotia mainland. The ¾-mi-long (1.2 km) Canso Canal was built (1953–5) with a single tidal lock, 820 ft (250 m) by 80 ft (24.4 m), with 32 ft (9.8 m) of water on the sills. It was a commercial success, carrying over 2 million tons a year by 1972.[59]

LIGHTHOUSES

After Confederation, the need for additional lighthouses became acute. A new Department of Marine and Fisheries was established in 1870 with responsibility for navigational aids. Only major lighthouse construction remained with the Department of Public Works.

A major program of construction was undertaken on the Straits of Belle Isle in the Gulf of St Lawrence, in Georgian Bay, in Lake Superior (for the first time), and, after 1875, on the Pacific coast, where previously only three major lights had existed: Fisgard Island lighthouse (1860), at Esquimalt Harbour; Race Rocks lighthouse (1860), on the Juan de Fuca Straits; and a lightship in the Fraser River estuary. Most of the new lighthouses were of timber frame construction, with catoptric lights fuelled by

The diaphone fog alarm at Fame Point, Quebec, 1910; it could be heard for many kilometres. The air compressor was powered by a steam-engine. (NA PA-148189)

kerosene. Main headland towers were often of masonry construction, with either dioptric lenses or revolving catoptric lights.

By 1914 Canada had over 1,460 lighthouses, triple the number at Confederation, and over 100 were equipped with fog alarms. Moreover, efforts continued to improve navigation aids with establishment of the Lighthouse Board of Canada (1904) and a Dominion Lighthouse Depot (1903), at Prescott, Ontario, to manufacture and experiment with illuminants, burners, lanterns, and lenses.

Acetylene replaced kerosene in the St Lawrence River lights after experiments at the Father Point Lighthouse in 1902. Acetylene was found to double the range of reflector-type lamps and yield a fivefold increase in candlepower. As early as 1895, an electric light was installed in the Reed Point Lighthouse, New Brunswick. Electrification, however, proceeded systematically only after 1945. Commencing in 1954, mercury vapour lamps were introduced. They provided light of a high intensity and longer life and were used after 1960 with simple plastic 'bulldog' lenses.

Major advances, stemming from Canadian inventions, were made in improving fog alarms. By 1904, the department undertook to replace steam fog

Point Abino lighthouse, Lake Erie, 1928. With its classical detailing and elegant touches, such as the balustrade around the light, it looks like an Italian Renaissance villa. (NA PA-148015)

alarms with a compressed air horn, the diaphone apparatus, developed by J.P. Northey of Toronto. Since 1965, however, another compressed air horn of Canadian invention, the 'Airchine' fog alarm, has provided a much more economical installation of comparable range, using an electrically powered air compressor.[60]

TWENTIETH-CENTURY EXPANSION

During the twentieth century Canada has undertaken two of the most ambitious waterways projects in the world: the Fourth Welland Canal (1913–32) and the St Lawrence Seaway (1954–9). Despite heavy expenditures on improvements, the ship canals system had become inadequate for the booming grain export trade. By 1913, over 130 million bu of grain were shipped eastward each fall from the Lakehead, but the newly enlarged St Lawrence canals handled only 11.5 million bu. The bulk of the Canadian grain harvest was carried on 625-ft (190.5-m) upper lakes ore freighters to Georgian Bay ports, for transport by rail to Montreal; to the American Lake Erie ports, for carriage by rail to major American seaboard ports; or to Buffalo, for export via the Erie Canal. The 255-by-43-ft (77.7-by-13.1-m) Welland Canal freighters could carry only 70,000 bu of grain on a 14-ft (4.3-m) draught to Montreal, but the 625-by-60-ft (190.5-by-18.3-m) vessels could carry almost 300,000 bu on 20-ft (7.0-m) draught, offsetting heavier costs for partial reliance on rail transport.[61]

To capture the burgeoning Canadian grain trade, further enlargement of the Welland–St Lawrence system was required. The Fourth Welland Canal was built (1913–32) on a straightened alignment from Port Colborne to a new harbour, Port Weller, on Lake Ontario at a cost of $130 million. Seven reinforced concrete locks, 829 ft (252.7 m) by 80 ft (24.4 m), with 46.5-ft (14.2-m) lifts, were built, with three locks twinned. The new 30-ft (9.1 m) deep canal reduced passage from 15 to 5 hours.[62]

Over 100 million bu of grain passed through the new Welland Canal each year, with Canada emerging as the world's leading wheat exporter. Through 150 years of development, and $340 million spent on improvements – canals, harbours, and lighthouses – the competitive position of Canadian ports had been maintained and enhanced.[63] The 14-ft (4.3-m) draught of the St Lawrence ship canals, however, remained a bottleneck in the shipping system.

During the Depression, only one canal project was undertaken. The St Ours was enlarged (1930–3), with a 339-by-45-ft (103.3-by-13.7-m) lock to match the scale of the Champlain Canal in New York. A planned enlargement of the Chambly Canal was suspended indefinitely during the Second World War.[64]

The 30.4-m (100-ft) reinforced-concrete lighthouse at Estevan Point, BC, completed in 1910, is an octagonal structure with eight flying buttresses. All building materials had to be hauled from the landing place to the construction site on a specially built 3.6-km (2.25-mi) trolley track. (NA PA-149680)

Flight Locks at Thorold, Ontario – the most dramatic site on the Welland Canal and a major tourist attraction. Three twinned locks allow parallel passage through approximately 42 m (140 ft), almost the height of the escarpment. (St Lawrence Seaway Authority)

Strong lake winds at the base of the Flight Locks often cause ships to turn, and great skill is required to take large ships through the canal, which links Lakes Erie and Ontario. (St Lawrence Seaway Authority)

In 1952, the Canadian government established the St Lawrence Seaway Authority to construct an all-Canadian seaway. Two years later, the United States agreed to participate. The St Lawrence Seaway was constructed (1954–9) on the same scale as the Fourth Welland Canal, with seven locks, 800 ft (243.8 m) by 80 ft (24.4 m) having 30 ft (9.1 m) of water on the sills. The locks, five in Canada and two in the United States, provided 226 ft (68.9 m) of lockage on a 27-ft-deep (8.2 m) waterway between Prescott and Montreal.

Construction focused on three areas of the St Lawrence River: the International Section, to overcome the series of rapids formerly bypassed by the Galops, Rapide Plate, Farran's Point, and Cornwall canals; the Soulanges section, to replace the Soulanges Canal in overcoming the rapids between Lake St Francis and Lake St Louis; and the Lachine section, superseding the Lachine Canal at the Lachine Rapids above Montreal. Each country paid for the canal works within its borders, at a total cost of $330 million for Canada and $130 million for the United States; $650 million was spent on power development.

On completion, the Seaway ranked as one of the great ship canal systems in the world and in its combined aspects – water control, navigation facilities, and power development – embodied a truly monumental feat of engineering and construction, completed in less than five years. With its opening in 1959, traffic on the St Lawrence soared from an average of 11 million tons a year during the 1950s to 57 million tons in 1973. Eastward-moving grain accounted for almost half the tonnage; Labrador iron ore moving westward, a quarter.[65] The new Seaway enabled the largest upper lakes freighters, carrying 300,000 bu of wheat, to proceed directly to Montreal. Overall, 80 per cent of Seaway tonnage was carried

The Prince Shoal (or Haut-fond Prince) lighthouse, Saguenay and St Lawrence rivers, completed 1964. Designed to withstand and deflect ice floes from any direction, it rests on a massive pier anchored by several thousand tons of rocks and cement and metal pilings driven 10 m (32.8 ft) into the river bed. (NA C-21637)

in lake vessels, and 19 per cent in ocean freighters.[66]

CANALS AND GOVERNMENT

As of the 1960s, only the ship canals of the Great Lakes–St Lawrence Seaway system, and the Canso Canal, continued to carry a large tonnage of freight. Elsewhere, commercial traffic almost disappeared on Canadian inland navigations.[67] Many secondary barge canals, however, were maintained in operation for recreational purposes by the federal Department of Transport, which superseded the Department of Railways and Canals in 1936.

With recreational boating increasing dramatically during the 1960s, a $12-million program was undertaken to modernize the Trent-Severn Waterway.

On the Ottawa, a new Carillon Lock, 188 ft (57.3 m) by 45 ft (13.7 m) with a 65-ft (19.8-m) lift, was constructed to maintain the navigation where a Hydro Québec power dam (1959–62) flooded out the former Carillon and Grenville canals.[68]

In 1972, a number of government canals were transferred to the Parks Canada branch, Department of Indian Affairs and Northern Development. Included were the Rideau Canal and its Tay Canal branch; the Trent-Severn Waterway and adjacent Murray Canal; the Chambly and St Ours canals on the Richelieu River; the new Carillon Canal Lock and Ste Anne's Canal on the Ottawa River; and the St Peter's Canal in Nova Scotia. Thereafter, these canals were operated under a new mandate, with emphasis on historic preservation and interpretation, natural environment protection, and recreational development. In 1978 the Lachine Canal, and a year later the Sault Ste Marie Ship Canal, were similarly transferred to Parks Canada (now the Canadian Parks Service).

Today, except for the abandoned St Lawrence ship canals, most of Canada's improved inland waterways remain in operation. The major role played by government in constructing canals, inland harbours, timber slides, lighthouses, and various navigational aids, as well as in enlarging and preserving the inland navigations, attests to the critical importance of waterways to Canadian development. Expansion of trade and settlement inland depended almost totally on waterways transport during the first canal-building age (1815–53), and navigable waterways remained central to national transportation long after the arrival of the railway.

After Confederation, improvement of waterways transport remained a major component of public works. Extensive canal enlargement inaugurated a second canal-building age (1873–99) and culminated in the prodigious efforts and expenditures involved in constructing the Fourth Welland Canal (1913–32) and the St Lawrence Seaway (1954–9). The secondary barge canals are no longer commercially viable, but these public works now constitute a major component of the National Historic Parks and Sites system. As such, they are being commemorated, preserved, and maintained in operation for the benefit and enjoyment of future generations.

NOTES

1 G.P. de T. Glazebrook *A History of Transportation in Canada* I (Toronto 1964) 10–32

2 John C. Kendall 'The Construction and Maintenance of Coteau du Lac: The First Lock Canal in North America' *Journal of Transport History* 1 (Feb 1971) 39–50

3 G.M. Craig *Upper Canada: The Formative Years* (Toronto 1968) 46–52, 124–50

4 Lt.-Col. Phillpotts, RE 'Report on the Canal Navigation of the Canadas' *Papers on Subjects Connected with the Duties of the Corps of Royal Engineers* (London 1842) 169–70

5 Robert F. Legget *Ottawa Waterway: Gateway to a Continent* (Toronto 1975) 139–44 and Normand Lafrenière *The Ottawa River Canal System* (Ottawa 1984) 23–33

6 Robert W. Passfield *Building the Rideau Canal: A Pictorial History* (Toronto 1982) 18–19, 138–9, and Robert F. Legget 'The Jones Falls Dam on the Rideau Canal, Ontario, Canada' *The Newcomen Society, Transactions* 31 (1957–9) 205–18. See also R.F. Legget *Rideau Waterway* (Toronto 1955).

7 Robert F. Legget *Canals of Canada* (Vancouver 1976) 112–13 and Adam Shortt and Arthur G. Doughty eds 'Shipping and Canals' *Canada and Its Provinces* x

(Edinburgh 1913) 522

8 Hugh G.J. Aitken *The Welland Canal Company* (Cambridge, Mass 1954) 46–69 and Phillpotts 'Report' 145–50. See also John N. Jackson and Fred A. Addis *The Welland Canals: A Comprehensive Guide* (St Catharines 1982).

9 John P. Heisler *The Canals of Canada* Canadian Historic Sites, Occasional Papers in Archaeology and History, No. 8 (Ottawa 1973) 81, 104–6, and Alex McCall 'Normandale and the Van Normans' *Ontario History* 20 (1923) 95

10 Heisler *The Canals of Canada* 41–55 and Phillpotts 'Report' 140–71

11 Heisler *The Canals of Canada* 91–4, 105–6

12 Douglas Owram *Building for Canadians: A History of the Department of Public Works, 1840–1960* (Ottawa 1979) 7–22 and J.E. Hodgetts *Pioneer Public Service: An Administrative History of the United Canadas, 1841–1867* (Toronto 1955) 176–84

13 Heisler *The Canals of Canada* 92–7

14 P.-André Sévigny *Trade and Navigation on the Chambly Canal: An Historical Overview* (Ottawa 1983) 27–47

15 Heisler *The Canals of Canada* 99–107 and Howard Pammett 'The Steamboat Era on the Trent-Otonabee Waterway, 1830–1950' *Ontario History* 41 (June 1964) 73–5

16 John McCallum *Unequal Beginnings: Agriculture and Economic Development in Quebec and Ontario until 1870* (Toronto 1980) 54–84

17 William L. Marr and Donald G. Paterson *Canada: An Economic History* (Toronto 1980) 315–16 and Heisler *The Canals of Canada* 114–16

18 McCallum *Unequal Beginnings* 16–18, 71–7, and T.C. Keefer 'On the Canals of Canada' *Proceedings and Transactions of the Royal Society of Canada* 11 (1893) 48

19 Edward F. Bush *The Canadian Lighthouse* Canadian Historic Sites, Occasional Papers in Archaeology and History, No. 9 (Ottawa 1974) 11, 34–45, and Judith Tulloch 'Nineteenth Century Lighthouse

Technology' in R.A. Jarrell and A.E. Roos *Critical Issues in the History of Canadian Science, Technology and Medicine* (Ottawa 1981) 47–52

20 R.W. Passfield 'The Shubenacadie Canal' Historic Sites and Monuments Board of Canada, Agenda Papers 1979–80, unpublished report, Parks Canada, Ottawa, 1979, 59–64

21 Bush *The Canadian Lighthouse* 11–55 and Tulloch 'Nineteenth Century Lighthouse Technology' 48–9

22 T.C. Keefer 'President's Address' *Transactions of the Canadian Society of Civil Engineers* 2 (1888) 24–7 and Sandra J. Gillis *The Timber Trade in the Ottawa Valley, 1806–1854* Parks Canada, Manuscript Report Series, No. 153 (Ottawa 1975) 104, 257–91

23 A.R.M. Lower *The North American Assault on the Canadian Forest: A History of the Lumber Trade between Canada and the United States* (Toronto 1938) 109–11, 140

24 Graeme Wynn *Timber Colony: A Historical Geography of Early Nineteenth Century New Brunswick* (Toronto 1981) 33–110

25 Larry McNally 'The Relationship between Transportation and Water Power on the Lachine Canal in the Nineteenth Century' in R.A. Jarrell and A.E. Roos eds *Critical Issues in the History of Canadian Science, Technology and Medicine* (Ottawa 1981) and McCallum *Unequal Beginnings* 84

26 Bush *The Canadian Lighthouse* 16–74; Tulloch 'Lighthouse Technology' 48–52; and T.E. Appleton *Usque ad Mare: A History of the Canadian Coast Guard and Marine Service* (London 1968) 107, 113

27 Canada *Sessional Papers* 8 Vol 1–5, 1867–8, 98–9, Appendix No. 1, 3–5, and Appendix No. 17, 157

28 Marr and Paterson *Canada: An Economic History* 140–3

29 Heisler *The Canals of Canada* 107–9, 121

30 George Raudzens *The British Ordnance Department and Canada's Canals, 1815–1855* (Waterloo 1979) 115–46

31 Passfield 'The Shubenacadie Canal' 64–76

32 Heisler *The Canals of Canada* 129

33 McCallum *Unequal Beginnings* 99 and W.T. Easterbrook and Hugh G.J. Aitken *Canadian Economic History* (Toronto 1956) 300–18

34 Owram *Building for Canadians* 66, 89–103

35 Eric W. Morse *Fur Trade Canoe Routes of Canada/Then and Now* (Ottawa 1969) 18–39, 87–100

36 Glazebrook *History of Transportation in Canada* 26–30

37 A.A. den Otter 'Transportation and Transformation: The Hudson's Bay Company, 1857–1885' *Great Plains Quarterly* (summer 1983) 172–8

38 Owram *Building for Canadians* 104–11

39 On the prairie steamboat navigations, see den Otter 'Transportation and Transformation' 172–8; Marion H. Herriot 'Steamboat Transportation on the Red River' *Minnesota History* 21 (Sept 1940) 245–71; and Bruce Peel 'Steamboats on the Saskatchewan' *Alberta Historical Review* 16:2 (summer 1968) 11–21.

40 Legget *Canals of Canada* 106 and A.H. Harkness 'Design and Construction of the Dam at St. Andrew's Rapids, Manitoba' *The Canadian Engineer, An Engineering Weekly*, Toronto, 20 (26 Jan 1911) 201–9

41 Gordon Bennett *Yukon Transportation: A History* Canadian Historic Sites, Occasional Papers in Archaeology and History, No. 19 (Ottawa 1978) 17–62

42 Carol MacLeod *The Fur Trade on the Southern Pacific Slope, 1779–1858* Manuscript Report Series, No. 163 (Ottawa 1975) 72–183, and David Smyth 'Hudson's Bay Company Brigade Trail (Hope to Kamloops) and the Dewdney Trail' unpublished report, Historic Sites and Monuments Board of Canada, Agenda Papers, 1985-39, 301–10

43 R.W. Malcolmson 'The Baillie-Groham Canal, B.C.' unpublished report, Historic Sites and Monuments Board of Canada, Agenda Papers, 1964-8, 37–9

44 R.W. Passfield *The Sault Ste. Marie Ship Canal, 1889–1985: Essays in Canal Building Technology* Microfiche Report Series, No. 297 (Ottawa 1986) 4

45 Owram *Building for Canadians* 113–24 and Keefer 'On the Canals of Canada' 29–31

46 Heisler *Canals of Canada* 30, 129

47 Owram *Building for Canadians* 136–9

48 Lafrenière *The Ottawa River Canal System* 42–58 and Ernest Marceau 'The Carillon Canal, Dam and Slide' *Transactions of the Canadian Society of Civil Engineers* Paper No. 153 (Oct 1900) 102–16

49 See Larry Turner *The Second Tay Canal in the Rideau Corridor, 1880–1940* Microfiche Report Series, No. 295 (Ottawa 1986) and H.R. Morgan 'The First Tay Canal: An Abortive Upper Canadian Transportation Enterprise of a Century Ago' *Ontario History* 29 (1933) 103–6.

50 Sévigny *Trade and Navigation* 51–64

51 Heisler *The Canals of Canada* 115–16, 132–6

52 See Passfield *The Sault Ste. Marie Ship Canal* and Brian S. Osborne and Donald Swainson *The Sault Ste. Marie Canal: A Chapter in the History of Great Lakes Transport* (Ottawa 1986).

53 E.L. Corthell 'An Enlarged Water-way between the Great Lakes and the Atlantic Seaboard' *Transactions of the Canadian Society of Civil Engineers* Paper No. 48 (12 Feb 1890) 46–7

54 John Witham 'Building Trent-Severn: A Summary' *Kawartha Heritage, Proceedings of the Kawartha Conference* (Peterborough 1981) 32–33

55 R.W. Passfield 'The Peterborough Lift Lock, Peterborough, Ontario' unpublished report, Historic Sites and Monuments Board of Canada, Agenda Papers, 1979-28, 579–601. See also Jean M. Cole ed *The Peterborough Hydraulic Lift Lock* (Peterborough 1987).

56 David Battle 'Plans for a New Welland

Canal' *Canadian Engineer* (4 June 1909) 744–5

57 Pammett 'The Steamboat Era' 100

58 'The Chignecto Ship Railway' *Engineering News* (7 Sept 1889) 218–20 and John O'Rourke 'The Chignecto Ship Railway' *American Society of Civil Engineers, Transactions* 24 (Feb 1891) 13–20

59 Legget *Canals of Canada* 27–35

60 Bush *The Canadian Lighthouse* 18–29, 80–2, and Keefer 'President's Address' 27–8

61 Glazebrook *A History of Transportation* II 227–33 and 'The Canals of Canada' *Canadian Engineer* (18 June 1909)

62 Department of Railways and Canals *The Welland Ship Canal between Lake Ontario and Lake Erie, 1913–1932* (London, England 1935)

63 Passfield *The Sault Ste. Marie Ship Canal* 162

64 Sévigny *Trade and Navigation* 30

65 Legget *Canals of Canada* 183–216 and 'St. Lawrence Deep Waterway' *Encyclopedia Canadiana* IX (Toronto 1972) 170–6

66 Heisler *The Canals of Canada* 162

67 *Canada Water Year Book* 1975 (Ottawa 1975) 145–50

68 Pammett 'The Steamboat Era' 103 and Lafrenière *The Ottawa River Canal System* 53–60

A.A. DEN OTTER

Irrigation and Flood Control

In the relatively short history of irrigation and flood control in Canada, advocates of such schemes encountered considerable public resistance. Early projects were local in application and failed to gain widespread provincial or national support. Water conservation projects were usually very expensive and required extensive state assistance; voters refused to approve government aid until convinced that these works were economically useful.[1] State intervention in large development projects required a dramatic change in public attitudes. Coincidentally, then, development of water conservation was an integral part of increasing government intervention in the nation's economy and society.

IRRIGATION

Irrigation has not become a national concern because most of Canada's arable lands enjoy adequate rainfall. In 1981, only about 596,000 ha (1.47 million acres), or 1.4 per cent, of Canadian farmland was irrigated. Farmers in the Atlantic provinces used sprinkler systems on 983 ha (2,427 acres), in Quebec on 5,989 ha (14,788 acres), and in Ontario on 32,127 ha (79,326 acres). The remaining irrigation works are in western Canada – 75 per cent in southern Alberta and 19 per cent in British Columbia.[2] There, too, irrigationists use large dams and

canal systems. It was these works that faced initial public opposition.

Early government attitudes also help to explain public resistance to irrigation. In the late 19th century, the Canadian government launched an intense campaign to sell western lands to prospective settlers. Intent on making the Northwest attractive to immigrants, it denied that any but a very small segment of the prairies was unfit for settlement.[3] In 1875, geologist G.M. Dawson of the boundary survey endorsed the idea of colonizing the plains, adding only as an afterthought, 'with the exception of a limited area.'[4] Several years later, Sir Charles Tupper defended the plans of the Canadian Pacific Railway (CPR) to lay its mainline through the southern and driest part of the plains. 'We believe we have there [on the prairies],' he boasted, 'the garden of the world.'[5] And Deputy Minister of the Interior A.M. Burgess warned his officials to 'deal gently with the question' of irrigation because 'at this stage of the history of the country, much harm would result from any public discussion which would seem to indicate that any considerable proportion of the land is unfit for cultivation except by the aid of irrigation.'[6]

Government opposition to irrigation lessened in the early 1890s when it granted generous land subsidies to railway companies. The Alberta Railway

The federal government and Alberta's two major railway companies worked together to irrigate large tracts of semi-arid land. The headgates shown here released water from Reservoir No. 1 of the Western Irrigation Block. (NA PA-11682)

and Coal Co. (AR&CCO), for example, earned 440,000 ha (1.09 million acres) in the heart of ranching country as a subsidy for building railways eastward from Lethbridge to the Canadian Pacific mainline and southward to Montana. The company sold nearly 4,000 ha (9,876 acres) near the present town of Cardston to Charles Ora Card, a charismatic Mormon leader, who intended to settle a number of Mormon families in southern Alberta. Card had extensive irrigation experience in Utah, and he proposed an irrigation scheme for the AR&CCO's lands. The plan was premature and initially failed to attract financial backers, but it laid the foundation for irrigation of

Alberta's semi-arid lands.[7]

One of Card's strongest supporters was the AR&CCO's land commissioner, Charles A. Magrath, an aggressive executive and prominent territorial politician. This champion of irrigation shared with many Canadians a vision of reconstructing the western wilderness into a productive, civilized society.[8] His argument was simple. 'The lands are valueless in their present condition,' Magrath declared, but 'by assisting irrigation the balance of [these] lands will be so enhanced in value that one acre will bring as much as five acres and ten acres in other districts where irrigation is not absolutely required.'[9]

Cognizant of local economic benefits, the territorial press, particularly the *Lethbridge News*, joined the cause and insisted that the federal government, as the largest landowner in the territories, should assume the cost of initial surveys and water measurements – an expensive but necessary step to prevent a costly and inefficient conglomeration of haphazardly built irrigation ditches. The government should assist private firms to build the works so essential to settlement. 'Railway after railway may be built through a section of the country until it is covered with a network of iron rails,' the *News* asserted, 'but the country will never be a paying speculation until there is agricultural production.'[10] By the mid-1890s, therefore, many influential residents believed that only irrigation could realize the economic value of southwestern lands.

Natural elements soon assisted local pressure groups. A prolonged drought began in the southwest in the late 1880s and lingered into the early 1890s, creating the nagging fear that perhaps aridity was the prevailing feature. Angry farmers blamed the CPR and the Canadian government for leading them to the western prairies, and they agitated for relief. In this climate of opinion, the persistent arguments of Magrath and the southern Alberta press began to take effect. So did rumours that Montana was planning to divert part of the St Mary River for an irrigation scheme of its own, thus threatening the Canadian project.[11]

The Canadian government began to see irrigation in southern Alberta in a new light, partly because of the CPR's reluctance to accept semi-arid lands west of Medicine Hat. Suitable land elsewhere in the territories was scarce, and so CPR President William Van Horne reluctantly accepted the argument that an irrigation project on the Bow River could make these lands useful and valuable.[12] Van Horne insisted that only after the government granted these lands as a large single block would the CPR 'take the chance of them being hereafter made available for settlement and cultivation by some comprehensive system of irrigation.'[13]

The work of William Pearce, government agent in the Northwest, also forced the government to reassess its anti-irrigation stand. Since 1885, Pearce's reports to the Department of the Interior had urged the federal government to remedy the irregularity of rainfall on the southwestern prairies by encouraging extensive irrigation projects and by preserving scarce water resources with careful regulation. Through his close contacts with American and other irrigation associations and publications, this surveyor learned that only large-scale projects used water and soil efficiently.[14]

By 1894, the government had accepted the need for orderly development of irrigation on the western fringe of the prairies. At this time, A.M. Burgess recommended that the government support the CPR irrigation scheme because 'the growing of cereals could only be rendered safe and sure by the application of an extensive and scientifically planned system of irrigation.'[15] After consultations with western Canadian, American, and other irrigation experts, the government passed the North West Irrigation Act in July 1894, making itself the sole owner of all the western interior waters and providing for their controlled development.[16] In the summer of 1895, C.J. Dennis, chief inspector of surveys and an active supporter of irrigation, launched a comprehensive survey of southern Alberta rivers 'so that an intelligent control might be exercised in the application of the available water supply for the reclamation of unproductive areas.'[17] After several expeditions, Dennis determined that irrigation was possible at several locations across the south-western plains, including the St Mary and Bow rivers. The government allowed the AR&CCO to consolidate most of its holdings into a large block south of Lethbridge.[18]

Government studies and concessions did not spur immediate completion of the large-scale irrigation projects on the Bow and the St Mary. Although a feasibility study concluded that the Bow could irrigate about 2 million acres (0.81 million ha) of farmland, the CPR's directors refused to approve the project.[19] With a federal election near, the CPR, as well as the AR&CCO, decided to delay implementation of any extensive irrigation works. The long-lived Conservative government still emphatically refused financial assistance as long as humid lands were available elsewhere on the prairies.[20] Local promoters recognized the need for irrigation, but more cautious central Canadian and foreign investors waited for sufficient government incentives.

In the mid-1890s a complex series of events brought a dramatic change in the economic background to western settlement. Spectacular gold discoveries in South Africa helped to stem the decline in world wheat prices and generated a great feeling of optimism. US homestead lands ran out, and settlers looked to the Canadian Northwest, where introduction of dry-farming and hardier wheat strains made agriculture more profitable than ever before. Improvements in overseas wheat shipping technology, such as grain elevators, railways, and large grain ships, turned the prairies into one of the world's great granaries. The new economic buoyancy and the federal government's revamped immigration program attracted hundreds of thousands of American, British, and European immigrants to western Canada every year.[21] As the trickle of settlers swelled into a flood,

western Canadian development once again interested foreign financiers and irrigation in southern Alberta became an attractive investment.

The projects also profited from political change. In 1896, Wilfrid Laurier's Liberals replaced the beleaguered Conservatives, and a new perception of the far western prairies gained prominence. Liberal politicians, with their natural inclination for decentralization and the welfare of the farmer, eventually adopted the settlers' commitment to turning semi-arid rangelands into cultivated fields. Frank Oliver, gadfly member of Parliament (MP) from Alberta, editor of the *Edmonton Bulletin*, and avowed champion of western settlement, ceaselessly attacked southern Alberta's large grazing leases as detrimental to settlement and advocated irrigation. 'This government must facilitate irrigation in every possible way,' Oliver lectured Laurier, but particularly with low land prices and lenient regulations.[22] Always concerned with small operators, Oliver argued that it was 'for the benefit of the Country that Irrigation should be entered into as largely as possible by all classes of settlers.'[23]

Oliver found a sympathetic listener in the new minister of the interior, Clifford Sifton, from Manitoba. A fervent advocate of progress and efficiency, Sifton viewed prairie colonization in business terms as a problem to be solved with proper marketing techniques: in his opinion, Canada's lands needed to be sold through aggressive advertising in Europe, Britain, and the United States.[24] Less opposed to ranchers than Oliver, Sifton favoured farmers as the most productive users of land, and, unlike his predecessors, he had no qualms about adverse publicity emanating from the demands of irrigationists. He actively supported their cause. In 1897, after only one meeting with Magrath, Sifton prom-

Steam and animals often worked side by side, as in this irrigation project near Vernon, BC, in the 1920s. (NA C-23381)

ised to refund all the survey fees the AR&CCO had paid on its land grant.[25]

While not large, the subsidy coincided with the rise of new markets for southern Alberta crops. Extension of the CPR through the Crow's Nest Pass, in 1897, provided access to the coal and metal deposits of the Crow's Nest and Kootenay regions, creating new towns and expanding markets. Simultaneously, the Klondike gold rush stimulated the western economy and promised even more consumers. The prospect of a nearby market and the flood of immigrants onto the plains greatly enhanced the value of the AR&CCO and the CPR's rangelands, particularly if irrigated.[26]

Backed by the optimistic reassessment of the economic potential of the Northwest, the AR&CCO hammered out an agreement with the Mormon church to supply the labour for canal construction in exchange for land. On 26 August 1898, Charles Ora Card ploughed the first furrow for the ditch. The plan called for the canal to be dug from the St Mary, at a point close to the US border, to angle northeastward and pass near the present-day towns of Magrath and Stirling and terminate near Lethbridge. A long canal was necessary because the St Mary flowed nearly 100 metres (330 ft) below the lands to be irrigated. To spare the cost of pumping stations, the company placed the water intake at an upstream site that lay above the lands to be watered. It was a considerable undertaking, as no steam shovels or dredges were used. During the fall and winter, 30 to 40 teams of horses excavated the heavy cuts, and in the spring another 200 teams joined them. They had to move over a million cu m (1.3 million cu yd) of dirt and use over a million board feet of lumber for the sluiceways, gates, and several buildings. Ironically, heavy rains saturated the area for two successive seasons and so hampered the work that the ditches were not finished until late in the summer of 1900. By then, the workers had excavated 185 km (115 mi) of canals, including a 51-km (31.7-mi) branch to Lethbridge and a 35-km (21.8-mi) extension to Stirling.[27]

Completion of the St Mary scheme, and the rush of settlers into the western plains, spurred the CPR to reconsider the Bow River project. Unwilling to pioneer in massive, expensive irrigation, the CPR, which had awaited the outcome of the AR&CCO's plan, contributed $100,000 to the venture, expecting the investment to be returned in increased rail traffic.[28] The AR&CCO also proved willing to accept a solid block of land east of Calgary as part of its subsidy. By 1914 an army of steam shovels, graders, trains, and horse-drawn wagons had completed about 2,600 km (1,616 mi) of canals and laterals. Company engineers concluded that the elevation of the central section was too high for economical irrigation and commenced work on the eastern section, an engineering challenge that dwarfed the earlier Lethbridge and western schemes. The Bassano Dam, a 210-m-long (689 ft) earthen embankment and a 216-m (621-ft) concrete dam, raised the Bow 13.8 m (45.3 ft) and permitted diversion of water into an irrigation canal. Completed in 1914, the Bassano and the large viaduct at Brooks made the CPR's eastern irrigation works one of the world's foremost systems. The CPR had spent more than $18 million to adapt its semi-arid lands to intensive cultivation.[29]

The two railway companies built efficient irrigation systems to attract settlers and create traffic. As Galt explained

quite simply, 'We had expended large sums [on the coal mines and railways] and we were compelled to go ahead and protect what we had already invested.'[30]

Irrigation simply as land speculation proved unprofitable. A case in point was the Southern Alberta Land Co., a flashy combination of land speculators, politicians, and Canadian and British financiers, which built a large irrigation system southeast of Calgary. Shady real estate transactions, questionable charter transfers, and watered stock placed a heavy drain on the company, while faulty designs and shoddy construction required extensive rebuilding.[31] By 1914, after the company's land prices had soared to $41 per acre, well beyond the region's average, it and affiliated firms were bankrupt. Without the backing of large and diversified corporations, irrigation was not profitable in southern Alberta.

The St Mary and Bow irrigation projects also faced serious difficulties. Their completion coincided with the rapid spread of dryland farming. Developed on the American great plains, this technology used deep ploughing, subsurface packing, repeated cultivation, and special machinery to preserve the soil's moisture during droughts. Like a religious-revival movement, dryland cultivation swept across the American plains and into western Canada, becoming a potent competitor for irrigation, a more expensive and difficult technology. Coupled to rising wheat prices, growing markets, and a succession of wet seasons, the dryland gospel attracted thousands of settlers to southern Alberta.[32]

To counter the popularity of dryfarming, the two railway companies encouraged cultivation of high-value, specialty crops such as alfalfa and sugar beets and built experimental farms to demonstrate irrigation techniques and

A soil-saving dam across a gully, probably in Alberta, in the 1940s. It consists of rocks between two rows of poplar logs. Water would pond behind the dam and flow out slowly after depositing much of its silt load. (NA PA-166862)

A simple irrigation turnout controls water flowing from an irrigation channel into smaller field ditches: Agricultural Research Station, Swift Current, Saskatchewan, 1946. (NA PA-166856)

Near the badlands: a simple soil-saving dam built in a gully on the Dominion Range Experimental Station, Manyberries, Alberta. Slowing water flow would conserve eroded soil. (NA PA-166861)

new crops. The model farm at Lethbridge devised the technique of inoculating Alberta fields with soil containing the nitrogen-fixing bacteria essential to healthy alfalfa crops.[33] The renamed Alberta Railway and Irrigation Co., with generous government assistance, also expanded and improved its canal system to twice its former capacity.[34] Despite these measures, high land and water costs left most irrigation farms barely able to compete with traditional dryland settlements.

At the outbreak of the First World War, the provincial government began to assist communities in organizing and managing irrigation districts. In 1917, it passed the Irrigation Districts Act, which encompassed all irrigation schemes and brought considerable expansion, such as the Lethbridge extension to Taber in 1920. In 1921, construction began on the Lethbridge Northern District, which diverted water from the Oldman River to

The creation of an irrigation reservoir often involved excavation of a deepened storage area and erection of a dam: Jensen Dam site, St Mary's Irrigation Project, near Lethbridge, Alberta, 1946. (NA PA-166860)

irrigate almost 40,000 ha (100,000 acres). For the first time in southern Alberta, workers employed power equipment, such as draglines, steam-shovels, and gasoline ditching machines, to construct irrigation projects.[35]

Meanwhile, the periodic return of drought in the first decades of the 20th century wreaked havoc among dry farmers on the southern prairies. Hot, searing winds crumbled the pulverized mulch of summer-fallowed land to dust and carried it away in dark clouds. At first, the euphoria of rising wheat prices, insatiable markets, and bumper crops quickly erased fears, but in the following decades, repeated droughts, always ac-companied by high winds and ravenous grasshoppers, drove thousands of home-steaders from their land.[36] While dry-land farming made Canada the leader in wheat production, it also brought heart-ache to thousands.

The crisis caused by the combination of devastating drought and economic depression in the 1930s forced the feder-al government to act. In 1935, it estab-lished the Prairie Farm Rehabilitation Administration (PFRA) to combat the rav-ages of prairie drought. With painstak-ing effort, the administration rejuvenat-ed prairie soil and revitalized dryland farming.[37] The PFRA also provided tech-nical and financial assistance to individ-

Diversion tunnel and flume, St Mary's Irrigation Project, 1954. Such projects allowed agricultural diversification and a sounder economic base. (NA Lowell/PA-166858)

ual and community water storage projects but initially did little to expand the existing irrigation systems in Alberta, which by then served 1.2 million ha (3 million acres). Later, the PFRA became involved in other large-scale water development and conservation programs, such as the South Saskatchewan River Irrigation Project, which included the world's largest earth-fill dam, the James G. Gardiner, on Lake Diefenbaker. In the 1940s, the CPR surrendered its projects to co-operatives, which finally made them financially successful.[38] Subsequent developments in irrigation were limited primarily to sprinkling systems rather than new large-scale ditch and flooding techniques. Some significant

engineering projects were undertaken to reduce water loss in ditches and make more effective use of available water. In 1981, southern Albertans employed sprinklers to water 287,118 ha (709,000 acres), comprising 65 per cent of sprinkler irrigation in Canada.[39]

In British Columbia, irrigation developed differently than on the prairies. The province lacked the co-ordinating drive of large companies, backed by a powerful federal government. Most irrigation occurred in the dry belt valley of the Okanagan and nearby Kamloops. With the late-19th-century growth of interior mining towns and coastal cities, fruit farming spread rapidly southward from the northern end of the Okanagan valley. The BC government encouraged the change from the traditional ranching economy because it wanted to reduce the province's dependence on American imports. But it failed to regulate the expansion of irrigation.[40] Without a comprehensive water policy, a conglomeration of small companies built an inefficient network of irrigation canals during the fruit boom in the first decade of the 20th century – a costly and wasteful use of scarce water resources.[41]

The rapidly developing fruit industry, dependent upon inefficient water suppliers, pressed the provincial government to establish a universal irrigation policy and build a comprehensive, integrated canal system. The government resisted the lobby as long as it could, but finally, in 1907, it established a royal commission chaired by Fred J. Fulton of Kamloops. Fulton used the commission's recommendations to draft the British Columbia Water Act of 1909. Like Alberta, British Columbia created irrigation districts and accepted responsibility

Spillway, St Mary's Irrigation Project, 1954 (NA Lowell/PA-166851)

The irrigation flume over the Deadman River at Savona, BC, 1927, reminiscent of the flumes built for mining (NA PA-20288)

Sprinklers in Kamloops, BC, in 1954: one method for final placement of irrigation water (NA Lowell/PA-166859)

During the Depression, Prairie Farm Rehabilitation Act (PFRA) workers dug water-saving dugouts such as this one, near Swift Current, Saskatchewan, photographed in 1946. (NA PA-166852)

for assisting irrigation projects, but it refused to undertake its own schemes.[42] In any case, the act came too late to organize irrigation in the Okanagan, and by 1914 the fruit growers were in financial trouble. Having bought expensive irrigated lands, they suffered a debt crisis when the immigration boom collapsed. Moreover, several irrigation companies went bankrupt, leaving the fruit growers with cheaply built, deteriorating wooden irrigation structures and no water. The chaotic irrigation system contributed to the collapse of the fruit boom during the war. After 1920, the province advanced money to irrigation districts to buy out the companies. It also became directly involved in a modest endeavour in the southern Okanagan. As the fruit industry gradually recovered, the irrigation works were modernized; nevertheless, most irrigation districts suffered from heavy debt loads, especially burdensome during the Depression. In the 1960s, under the Agricultural Rehabilitation and Development Act, the federal government helped finance the latest modernization of Okanagan irrigation; underground pressurized pipelines and sprinklers largely replaced the old open ditches and wooden flumes.[43]

British Columbia's reluctance to guide and assist the initial development of irrigation in its dry belt valleys prevented the emergence of integrated, efficient large-scale projects. This occurred despite the precedent set in Alberta, where the federal government drafted comprehensive irrigation legislation and then assisted two large land and railway companies to convert their land subsidies from natural grasslands into irrigated, cultivated fields. In both regions, the objective for irrigation was relatively narrow – enhancement of economic returns and competition with nearby regions. In both cases, the public initially resisted public spending on projects designed to promote only one area, but eventually proponents convinced governments to act. By the 1930s, when state intervention in economic development was quite acceptable, channelling of funds into narrowly defined projects also became prevalent. This new perspective, which assisted western farmers to manage irrigation districts, also profoundly changed public attitudes toward flood control.

FLOOD CONTROL

Canada's first experience with floods came early in its history, but the experience was no harbinger for future action. In the late 17th century, Acadian settlers moved onto the marshes of the Rivière au Dauphin and the headlands of the Bay of Fundy. They constructed ingenious dike systems with one-way valves, called clapets, which drained the land at low tide and prevented flooding at high tide. The reclaimed land, which was very fertile, became the basis for prosperous agricultural communities, successful because the Acadians understood the obvious regularity of Fundy high tides and designed flood control measures accordingly.[44]

Everywhere else, Canadians encountered sporadic flooding, which was much more difficult to control. Common particularly in spring, floods occur everywhere in Canada. If snowfall has been heavy and spring late, then warm and wet, and if rains beat on frozen ground, rivers cannot contain the sudden onrush of meltwater. Jammed with ice, they overflow, often causing considerable damage. At other times, violent electrical storms or hurricanes dump tons of water on the earth, causing rapid and localized flooding.[45] Fortunately, most floods are relatively minor and cause only slight damage. Others, like

Cities built on flood plains or on the banks of rivers experienced frequent flooding. Ice jams were a major cause of flooding in Montreal. (NA c-65447)

the 1954 flood in Toronto, are serious disasters, with devastating results, including loss of life.

Canadians have done little to prevent floods. In fact, they deliberately built many of their cities, railways, and highways in broad and attractive fertile river valleys, where flood damage is inevitable. After a brief flurry of post-flood debate, people forgot disasters until the next serious inundation.[46] Municipalities had few resources and discovered that other communities regarded floods as local events and were reluctant to invest in broad measures encompassing an entire watershed. Some hazards became unacceptable, however, and local leaders, working together, pressed provincial and federal governments to assume responsibility for flood control. Provincial and federal assistance to flood-control schemes, as in irrigation projects, required profound transformations in public attitudes, often precipitated by costly disasters. In the 1950s a series of unusually severe floods forced

A flood in a city could affect a wide area. Here the Grand Trunk Railway Yard has flooded in Montreal, delaying service. (NA C-1161)

senior governments to intervene in local flood problems. After a century of ignoring similar disasters, provincial and federal administrators began to view floods as more than local problems to be solved by municipal governments; they accepted responsibility for financing a major portion of projects on watersheds such as the Fraser, Red, Thames, Grand, and Don rivers.

Flood-Plain Settlement

The proclivity of humans to build in flood plains and their reluctance to provide comprehensive prevention measures are illustrated clearly in the case of the Lower Fraser River basin, perhaps Canada's most flood-prone valley. Individual farmers protected their properties with local, uncoordinated dikes as early as the 1860s. At the turn of the century, after a disastrous flood, the provincial government started to provide technical and financial assistance, but it never furnished sufficient financial support to permit flood districts to construct and maintain a sound system of dikes and other flood-control measures. In May 1948, a devastating flood tore out the weakest dikes and inundated valuable farmlands, homes, and factories, causing millions of dollars in damage. For 30 days, Vancouver lost all surface communication with the mainland.

The 1948 flood prompted a flurry of government activity. With provincial and federal financial assistance, the Fraser Valley Dyking Board rebuilt, extended, and improved some of the dikes, but it did not create a totally integrated

When a flood threatened to destroy the bridge over the North Saskatchewan River in Edmonton, an empty freight train was pulled onto the bridge to help weigh it down. (NA PA-117997)

The main casualty of the flooding of this portion of low-lying South Edmonton in June 1915 was a lumber yard. (NA PA 117995)

system. However, it proposed some grand schemes, but the traditional bias of engineers toward solutions involving construction and toward technical feasibility rather than overall economic and social factors lessened the desire for comprehensive solutions, and occupation of the flood plain continued unabated.[47]

Another classic example of flood-plain settlement is the Red River valley, with its inevitable floods. Draining over 117,000 sq km (45,000 sq mi), the Red crosses the flat bed of an ancient glacial lake, with a very gradual slope. The shallow channel meanders slowly northward, crinkling snakelike across the landscape. Oral tradition recounts an enormous flood in 1776, which created a giant lake south of the junction of the Red and Assiniboine rivers. Despite its size, the 1776 flood presented no great hazard, primarily because there were no permanent settlements in the valley.

Once people settled in the Red River valley, floods began to cause damage and became natural hazards. The first recorded flood, in 1826, set the pattern. An extremely cold winter with unusually heavy snowfalls followed a wet autumn. A late spring suddenly broke the river ice on 5 May, sweeping before it many of the settlement's houses, buildings, fences, and livestock. The flood crested on 22 May and then subsided quickly. Warm summer weather permitted the colonists to rebuild quickly and harvest an adequate crop. Within a year, conditions were back to normal, and the calamity was forgotten until 1852, when another flood inundated the valley. It was less severe than the first and did not last as long, but property damage and dislocation were worse, because the settlement had grown considerably since 1826. Weather patterns were similar, although the water rose more slowly this time and gave ample warning for people to remove their possessions to high

ground. Only a few houses were swept away, the colony recovered quickly, and the flood soon receded from memory. In 1861, the valley experienced another flood. Although circumstances were similar, the crest was considerably lower than previous times and property damage was relatively light. Nevertheless, settlers along the valley above Upper Fort Garry were driven from their homes.[48]

The three recorded floods set a pattern. They all occurred after rainy autumns followed by extremely cold and snowy winters and late, warm, wet springs. Except in 1826, the floods rose gradually and gave residents ample warning. As a result, while loss of life was rare, property damage was widespread and costly, particularly for the poor, who traditionally clustered in the most flood-prone areas. Significantly, the settlement recovered far more quickly than anyone ever anticipated; consequently, the floods became immediate disasters rather than long-term impediments to development.[49] In 1881, for example, the CPR ignored the advice of its chief engineer, Sandford Fleming, who carefully documented flood risks at Winnipeg and recommended a more northerly route, through dry Selkirk. The company, instead, accepted the bonuses offered by Winnipeg's importunate town council and drew the mainline southward near the flood-prone junction of the Red and Assiniboine. As a result, a large city mushroomed on a well-known flood plain.[50]

The apparent lowering of flood levels throughout the years gave residents a false sense of security, as expressed by the Nor-Wester in 1861: 'We do not think that the country below Fort Garry will ever be flooded again, for experience shows clearly that each successive flood has indicated far less depth on the plains than its predecessors – a fact fully ac-

High water and ice toppled a wooden CPR bridge in Saskatoon. (NA PA-37828)

The sign 'Automobiles Left Here At Owners Risk ' takes on new meaning in this Belleville, Ontario, garage. (NA PA-57741)

counted for by the rapid widening of the river channel. There may be the same volume of water in each flood or very nearly so and the ever increasing width of the river will explain the disparity of depth in the main land.'[51] Although frequent, all subsequent floods were relatively minor and appeared to vindicate this view; therefore, little was done about protecting valley residents from another inevitable serious inundation.[52] Successive city councils lacked funds to construct elaborate works, and the province did not think it politic to spend tax revenues on what seemed to be a merely local problem.

Toward Long-Term Solutions

Government apathy in Red River was for a long time mirrored in Ontario. London, for example, experienced frequent and tragic flooding from the Thames River and its tributaries before effective control measures were put in place. Typically, rapid growth in the mid-19th century, caused in part by expansion of railways, saw construction of residences, bridges, and dams on cheap, conveniently located flood-plain land. These structures often accentuated flooding, as they impeded the flow of water and collapsed. Although floods were frequent up to the early 1880s, they were minor and damage was low because the population was small. People discussed protective measures but did nothing, because they perceived floods as capricious but natural events about which they could do little.[53]

In July 1883, an early summer electrical storm during an unusually wet season swept a flash flood through London West, killing 17 people and causing heavy property damage. But willingness to spend money on control measures decreased as time passed, and London built only minimal protective structures. It erected a dike and breakwater in 1885 and extended, heightened, and reinforced them at the turn of the century. Although it was clearly on a flood plain, real estate development continued unchecked behind a defensive wall sufficient only for frequent minor floods. The constantly increasing flood damage potential became painfully evident in 1937, when the breakwater could not contain the worst-ever recorded flood in southwestern Ontario. Heavy rains in April filled the river, and water spilled over

the breakwater, inundating at least 1,000 homes, forcing the evacuation of 6,000 people, and causing millions of dollars in property damage.[54]

The flood of 1937, which affected districts never before afflicted, including some affluent areas, increased calls for drastic preventive measures. Traditional suggestions, ranging from demands for reforestation to dam and reservoir construction, resurfaced, but so did the first call for total river-basin flood-control measures. Increasingly, as well, discussions looked to provincial and federal governments for assistance. The timing for such aid was premature, as the waning depression spilled into wartime. People continued to see floods as local problems and natural acts to which they adjusted and from which they recovered on their own. City councils did very little and paid virtually no compensation to flood victims. As floods receded from public memory, people again lost interest in controls. The 1937 flood therefore spelled no great change in policy, led to no widespread action, and only laid the foundation for future measures, with the conclusion that flood protection required the co-operation of all river valley municipalities plus massive provincial and federal assistance.[55]

This new attitude owed much to developments in neighbouring Grand River valley, where local communities took initiatives to counter periodic floods. A flood in 1912 had impelled formation of the Grand River Valley Boards of Trade, with the mandate to represent the interests of various communities within the watershed. The unified boards of trade lobbied the provincial government to conduct several flood surveys of the valley, the last one under the Grand River Conservation Act of 1932. But concrete action awaited the extensive damage caused by the major flood in 1937. The Ontario government rewrote the Grand River Conservation Act in 1938, included within its jurisdiction major communities such as Brantford, Galt, Kitchener, and Waterloo, and established the principle that 75 per cent of construction funding be shared equally by the senior levels of government and the remaining 25 per cent be raised by municipalities. This formula became the basis for completing the Shand Dam in 1942 as the first defence against flooding on the Grand.[56]

The Grand River campaign demonstrated clearly that public attitudes had changed dramatically. The combination of increased government intervention during the Depression and American and European examples helped Canadians accept senior government financing of large-scale river-control projects. Remedies were clearly beyond the means of municipalities, and the new philosophy expected provincial and federal governments to protect citizens living in flood plains and to compensate them for their losses. Only a massive infusion of capital could stimulate the co-operation of all municipalities within a river valley.

The new attitude allowed the expenditure of senior-level funds on projects, but initiative remained with local authorities. The provinces, which possessed sole jurisdiction over rivers, did no more than regulate flood-control measures and promise possible financial help if necessary. In 1946, for example, the Ontario legislature passed the Ontario Conservation Act, providing for formation of conservation authorities. While the act stated that flood-control measures must be broad and encompass entire river basins, it left initiative with municipalities. Unfortunately, as the Grand River experience had demonstrated, changing attitudes were not enough to prompt large expenditures; only a calamity could produce concerted activity.

In the case of the Thames valley a potential disaster, looming late in March 1947, spurred local administrations to work together to end the flood menace. A succession of thaws and heavy rains, interspersed with a blizzard, drove the Thames to within a few feet of the West London breakwater. When the water threatened to rise even further, a thousand residents fled their homes. Fortunately, the swirling waters only trickled across the lowest sections of the dike and then receded without causing any significant damage. The near miss had a lasting impact, however, and the *London Free Press* noted: 'There has been ten years of delay and we are not prepared to blame anyone. It is difficult to secure cooperation of municipalities and particularly of rural municipalities. But this second disaster should surely bring action so that ten years from now we will not confess nothing has been done.'[57]

The 1947 scare confirmed that Thames River floods were not aberrations; it showed that numerous meetings, conferences, and surveys had produced few results; and it renewed interest in local measures. The crisis led to establishment, in August 1947, of the Upper Thames Valley Conservation Authority, comprising cities, towns, villages, and townships in the upper Thames watershed. With the assistance of provincial and federal funds, the conservation authority completed the Fanshawe Dam just north of London in 1952 and established the limits of the flood plain in which there should be no further construction. The authority also co-operated with provincial parks and the London Planning Board to build other, minor structures and several parks in order to establish a modern system of flood control and recreation areas.[58]

Unified Action

If residents along the Thames needed only a potential disaster to remind them of the inevitability of serious flooding, the citizens of Winnipeg still required a full-scale calamity before they took action. Disaster struck in 1950. The previous fall was wet, while the winter was extremely cold, with heavy snowfalls, particularly toward its end. April 1950 witnessed record snowfalls, and May experienced heavy rains. The US Corps of Engineers had been taking moisture content surveys of snow on the American end of the Red River valley since a serious flood two years before. The Corps and the US Weather Bureau, which issued flood forecasts, warned Winnipeg's city engineer, W.D. Hurst, on 11 April that a flood was imminent.

Unfortunately, Canada did not have a similar service, and local authorities could not accurately predict flood levels; they could only rely on American warnings. Moreover, the Winnipeg city council had failed to implement a 1948 report from its engineers calling for an expenditure of $1.2 million on dikes and flood walls.[59] All that the city could do in May 1950, when flood waters reached Winnipeg, was reinforce existing dikes with rocks and millions of sandbags. On 5 May, two dikes collapsed and large parts of the city were inundated. The Canadian army took over relief operations, including a giant airlift with 35 aircraft, and supervised the evacuation of over 100,000 people. On 13 May, flood waters crested at 3.75 m (12.3 ft) above flood stage, forming a giant lake 121 km (75.2 mi) long and 40 km (24.9 mi) wide, flooding 10,500 homes, and closing 50 schools. The waters did not begin to recede until the end of the month, when the massive clean-up commenced.[60]

The magnitude of the flood required a massive restoration effort. Extensive news coverage prompted an outpouring of humanitarian aid, channelled through the Red Cross and the Manitoba Relief Fund. These two organizations provided flood victims with the basic necessities of life and replaced some of the possessions they had lost. After considerable wrangling, the provincial and federal governments, using the precedent set in the Fraser River flood, shared the cost of rehabilitating damaged properties. Although the federal government bore the bulk of the financial burden, the province assumed leadership in relief and reconstruction.[61]

The high cost of relief, cleaning, and rehabilitation and the unnecessary risk to human life forced Manitoba to consider preventive measures. The government set up a flood forecast committee, which placed numerous gauges along the rivers and measured snow moisture content. Since floods on the Red and Assiniboine are caused by spring run-off, the committee could predict floods with reasonable accuracy. The Greater Winnipeg Dyking Board and the city council also enlarged the system of dikes and pumping stations. The revamped control measures could handle river levels as high as those of 1950 and protected the city in the floods of 1956 and 1960. Yet city officials were very concerned because unexpectedly favourable weather conditions reduced the severity of the 1956 flood; none were confident that the dikes would have held without the change in weather.

Clearly, more permanent measures were needed. The federal government's Red River Basin Investigation report, issued in 1953, had discussed several physical flood-protection possibilities and their likely benefits. This federal report became the basis of Manitoba's 1956 Royal Commission on Flood Cost-Benefit, which found that the 1950 flood was the most costly on record primarily because of heavy industrial and residential development. It recommended construction of a 48-km (30-mi) floodway around the east side of Winnipeg, a dam

The flood of 1950 was Winnipeg's most dramatic to that date. A century earlier engineers had advised against building a town at that site. The flood finally convinced the city to protect itself. (PAM Floods 1950 10-1)

and storage reservoir on the Assiniboine near the Saskatchewan border, partial diversion of the Assiniboine at Portage la Prairie into Lake Manitoba, as well as several smaller dams and dikes. Although the remedy was drastic and costly, the commissioners argued that total expenditures would not be much greater than the $22.5 million in damages caused by the 1950 flood.[62] Although not innovative, the proposals were comprehensive and sound from an engineering point of view.[63] The scheme did not offer any solutions for upstream flooding in rural areas, however, and the provincial government, elected primarily from rural constituencies, lacked the political confidence to finance a project of benefit

to only one city. Not until the early 1960s did Duff Roblin's Conservative government launch a vigorous campaign to complete the floodway.[64]

In October 1962, one of the largest excavation jobs in Canadian history commenced, exceeding the Canadian portion of the St Lawrence Seaway or half of the Panama Canal. A mammoth project, the Red River floodway forms a 48-km (30-mi) semicircle east of Winnipeg, varying in depth from 7.2 m (23.6 ft) to 20.1 m (66 ft) and with a ground-level width of 210 m (689 ft) to 300 m (984 ft). It required the removal of 75 million m³ (98 million yd³) of Red River valley gumbo and earth. Trapezoidal in shape, the sides are sloped gently to lessen erosion

The Red River Floodway, completed in 1968, cost $63.2 million. During peak spring flooding, the Red River divides between its natural channel and the man-made diversion (upper part of photo). (W. Newton, P ENG, MWRB)

of the fragile gumbo and are grassed to prevent deterioration and enhance appearance. Floodway completion required rerouting two major trunk highways, building seven railway and six highway bridges and two aqueducts, and accommodating six hydro transmission lines and one oil and one gas pipeline. To minimize disruption of rail, road, and telephone communications and distribution of utilities, planners developed a complex construction schedule. The entire project cost $63.2 million, to which the governments of Canada and Manitoba contributed about $37 million and $26 million respectively.[65]

The floodway begins as a simple cut in the east bank of the river. Nearby, an elaborate control structure, consisting of concrete abutments on both sides of the river and a central pier supporting two 10.5-by-33.9-m (34.5-by-111-ft) gates submerged in 1.8 m (5.9 ft) of water, stretches across the river. When a flood threatens, the gates are raised and the water is forced into the floodway. Adjacent to the inlet structure are two dikes, one 10 km (6.2 mi) long on the east side running parallel to the floodway, the other reaching westward 34 km (21.1 mi) onto higher ground. Since the floodway drops more slowly than the river, an outlet structure, consisting of a concrete spillway and stilling basin, reduces the energy of flood water as it drops 4 m (13 ft) into the Red River, preventing scouring and erosion.[66]

The Red River floodway, virtually

completed in 1968, and the accompanying dam and diversion canal on the Assiniboine have protected Winnipeg on several occasions. While the upper river valley still floods regularly, inundating thousands of hectares of farm lands and small communities, the metropolis is reasonably safe. Provincial and federal authorities accomplished a major objective – protection of a densely populated and industrialized urban area. Yet, as elsewhere, government officials did not move until a major disaster forced concrete action.

The familiar pattern of frantic – and multi-level – activity after disaster replayed itself in the Toronto area. In October 1954, Hurricane Hazel swept across Lake Ontario and blasted the Toronto metropolitan area before heading inland. Swollen by an abnormally wet autumn, the Don and Humber rivers could not cope with the 20 cm (7.9 in) of rain that fell in 48 hours. The hurricane and subsequent flood cost 81 lives and $20 million in property damage. In response, the federal government appointed a Commission on Hurricane Damage, which did little, while the Ontario government established the Flood Homes and Building Assistance Board, assessed damage, paid compensation, and bought up some properties in the flood plain. Beginning in 1958, the three levels of government spent about $13 million on several small dams and reservoirs on the Don River. The primary benefit of the system was additional recreational facilities, but it promised the metropolitan area some protection from future flooding.[67]

The 1980s
The projects on the Fraser, Red, Thames, Grand, and Don rivers represent the major flood-control works in Canada. More recently, governments have concentrated on much smaller projects. In May 1981, for example, Environment Canada and Newfoundland's Department of Environment signed the Canada-Newfoundland Flood Damage Reduction Agreement, which provides financial assistance to flood-protection schemes. It also officially designates qualified communities as flood-risk areas. One such community, Rushoon on the Burin peninsula, is threatened periodically by rafting river ice. In 1986, Rushoon received $100,000 to put higher foundations under five houses and raise the height of a retaining wall. A flood-risk map, published under the agreement, helps municipal authorities to develop by-laws and policies. Perhaps most significantly, private developments built in the flood-risk area after publication of the map will not be eligible for flood disaster assistance. Similar restrictions now exist on other Canadian flood plains. Although the program aims at small projects, it touches at the root cause of flood damage – settlement of flood plains. The program also reflects the extent to which senior governments have assumed responsibility for flood protection.[68]

Government funding has not ended flood damage in Canada, however, and every spring and summer rivers overflow their banks. In 1985 the Exploits, in 1986 the North Saskatchewan, in 1987 the St John rampaged through their valleys, driving hundreds from their homes and causing massive property damage. Seemingly capricious, floods continue to strike at random all across the nation. Yet flood victims immediately rebuild, and, confident that disaster will not strike again, they quickly forget the calamity. The eagerness to settle flood plains, therefore, is the most important cause of flood damage. People insist on occupying flood-risk areas. In Calgary, for example, urban developers have built the downtown core on the

Bow River flood plain, hoping that upstream dams and reservoirs, dikes, and
cribbing will protect their real estate.
This protection, however, is only limited, and the likelihood of major damage
sometime in the future is large.[69] Even
the most elaborate flood-control structures establish a false sense of security,
as technology can fail in face of the
awesome and unpredictable force of ice,
rain, and water. Thus, as long as people
insist on developing flood-risk areas,
they periodically must suffer the cost of
flood damage.

Modern technology has lessened the
risk of settling flood-prone areas, just as
it has increased the possibility of culti-
vating arid lands. In both flood control
and irrigation, humans employ costly
technological structures to defy natural
processes; they changed the ecology for
economic objectives. Modern technology has permitted the frugal use of valuable space, but its potential fallibility
must not be forgotten.

NOTES

1 K. Smith and G.A. Tobin *Human Adjustment to the Flood Hazard* (London
1979) 1–2

2 Canada, Statistics Canada *1981 Census of
Canada* Agriculture, Table 20-1

3 A.A. den Otter 'Adapting the Environment: Ranching, Irrigation, and Dry
Land Farming in Southern Alberta, 1880–
1914' *Great Plains Quarterly* 6 (Summer
1986) 171–89

4 George M. Dawson *Report on the Geology
and Resources of the Region in the Vicinity of the Forty-Ninth Parallel* (Montreal
1875) 299

5 Canada, House of Commons *Debates* 10
May 1879

6 University of Alberta Archives (UAA) Box
8, No. 3-35, Burgess to Pearce, 21 Jan
1891

7 National Archives of Canada (NA), Ca-

nadian Transport Commission, Vols
853, 857, and 995; A. James Hudson
Charles Ora Card, Pioneer and Colonizer
(Cardston, Alberta 1963); and A.A. den
Otter *Civilizing the West: The Galts and
the Development of Western Canada* (Edmonton 1982) 204–14

8 C.A. Magrath *The Galts, Father and Son:
Pioneers in the Development of Southern
Alberta* (Lethbridge 1936)

9 NA, Magrath Papers, Vol. 10, File 51,
Magrath to Daly, 4 Feb 1893

10 *Lethbridge News* 8 June 1892

11 NA, Magrath Papers, Vol. 10, File 51,
'Notes on the Earlier Efforts to Bring
about Irrigation in Southern Alberta'

12 NA, Canadian Pacific Railway Papers,
Van Horne Letterbook 47, Van Horne
to Pearce, 27 Aug 1894

13 Glenbow-Alberta Institute (GAI), Lawrence Burns 'The Canadian Pacific Railway Company's Irrigation Blocks, 1894–
1943' Part I, Glenbow Foundation Research Project, History of the Canadian
West, History of Agriculture, Aug
1959 (Burns, CPR Irrigation Block), Van
Horne to Daly, 15 Feb 1894

14 E. Alyn Mitchner 'William Pearce and
Federal Government Activity in Western Canada, 1882–1904' PHD thesis, University of Alberta

15 GAI, Burns, CPR Irrigation Block, Burgess
and Pearce to Daly, 25 Jan 1894

16 UAA, Pearce Papers, Box 71, No. 22-83,
Pearce to Magrath, 23 Nov 1893

17 Canada, Department of the Interior *Annual Report 1895* III 35

18 Canada, Order-in-Council, 18 Jan 1896

19 GAI, Burns, CPR Irrigation Block, Pearce
to Van Horne, 20 Aug 1894; NA, Canadian Pacific Railway, Van Horne Letterbook 49, Van Horne to Pearce, 1
July 1895

20 Memorandum by Daly, 16 Nov 1895
(misdated 1885), attached to Canada,
Order-in-Council, 18 Jan 1896

21 K.N. Norrie 'The Rate of Settlement of
the Canadian Prairies, 1870–1911'

Journal of Economic History 35 (June 1978) 410–27

22 NA, Laurier Papers, Vol. 20, Oliver to Laurier, 17 Sept 1896

23 NA, Sifton Papers, Vol. 50, Oliver to Sifton, 26 May 1898

24 D.J. Hall 'Clifford Sifton: Immigration and Settlement Policy, 1896–1905' in H. Palmer ed *The Settlement of the West* (Calgary 1977) 60–85

25 NA, Magrath Papers, Vol. 10, File 51 'Memorandum: The Beginning of Irrigation in a Large Way in Southern Alberta' April 1942

26 See interview with Elliott Galt, *Manitoba Free Press* 9 Sept 1904.

27 GAI, North Western Coal & Navigation Co. Papers, Galt to Sifton, 15 Dec 1897; NA, Magrath Papers, Vol. 10, File 51, Magrath to Sifton, 8 Nov 1897; Canada, Order-in-Council, 6 Jan 1898; Lethbridge Public Library, Sam G. Porter and Charles Riley 'A Brief History of the Development of Irrigation in the Lethbridge District' (1925); Melvin S. Tagg 'A History of the Church of the Latter Day Saints in Canada, 1830–1953' PHD thesis, Brigham Young University, 1963; GAI, Charles Riley 'A Scrapbook Compiled in the Office of the Alberta Railway and Irrigation Company, 1896–1956'

28 UAA, Pearce Paper, 9/2/7/3-11, Van Horne to Pearce, 26 Dec 1897; NA, CPR Records, Shaughnessy to Galt, 5 Jan 1898

29 GAI, Robert S. Stockton 'History of the Western Irrigation District up to 1922'; Bassano *Best in the West by a Damsite, 1900–1940* (Bassano, Alberta 1974) 198–217; 'Canadian Pacific Railway Company, Report' (Calgary 1959); GAI, Eric J. Gormley 'Canadian Pacific Railway and Irrigation in Southern Alberta, 1880–1920' (June 1982)

30 NA, Galt Papers, Vol. 8, 'Transcribed Interview of Galt in Sifton's Office' 16 May 1904

31 Keith A. Stotyn 'The Bow River Irriga-

tion Project, 1906–1950' MA thesis, University of Alberta, 1982

32 Paul Leonard Voisey 'Forging the Western Tradition: Pioneer Approaches to Settlement and Agriculture in Southern Alberta Communities' PHD thesis, University of Toronto, 1982

33 Canada North-West Irrigation Company *Irrigated Lands in Southern Alberta* (Winnipeg 1900) and *The Colorado of Canada: Irrigated Lands, Southern Alberta* (1900) are two examples of advertising pamphlets; see also Porter and Raley 'Development of Irrigation' 26 and GAI, W.L. Jacobson 'Biographical Sketch of William Harmon Fairfield (1874–1961)' in 'History of Irrigation in Western Canada, History of Agriculture' 1–8; and Alex Johnston 'Early Agriculture and the Dominion Experimental Station, Lethbridge' paper presented to Historical Society of Alberta, 1973.

34 GAI, Documents Relating to the Alberta Railway and Irrigation Company, 1902–1919, Copy of data from the files of the Department of Lands and Mines, Keys to AR&ICO, 7 March 1908

35 H.G. Cochrane 'Irrigation in Alberta' *Alberta Historical Review* 16 (spring 1968) 5–13

36 David C. Jones ' "It's All Lies They Tell You": Immigrants, Hosts, and the CPR' in Hugh A. Dempsey ed *The CPR West: The Iron Road and the Making of a Nation* (Vancouver 1984); James H. Gray *The Winter Years: The Depression on the Prairies* (Toronto 1966)

37 James Gray *Men against the Desert* (Saskatoon 1967)

38 A. Mitchner 'The Bow River Scheme: CPR's Irrigation Block' in Dempsey *The CPR West*

39 Statistics Canada *1981 Census of Canada* Agriculture, Table 20-1

40 Margaret Ormsby 'The History of Agriculture in British Columbia' *Scientific Agriculture* 20 (Sept 1939) 61–72

41 Lawrence B. Lee 'American Influences in

the Development of Irrigation in British Columbia' in Richard A. Preston ed *The Influence of the United States on Canadian Development: Eleven Case Studies* (Durham, NC 1972)

42 Lawrence B. Lee 'Dominion Ditches and British Columbia Canals: A History of the Western Canadian Irrigation Association' *Journal of the West* 7:1 (1968) 31–40

43 Arthur W. Gray 'The Story of Irrigation – Lifeblood of the Okanagan Valley's Economy' *Thirty-Second Report of the Okanagan Historical Society* (1968) 69–80

44 R. Cole Harris ed *Historical Atlas of Canada I: From the Beginning to 1800* (Toronto 1987) Plate 29

45 Roy Ward *Floods: A Geographical Perspective* (New York 1978)

46 I. Burton 'Flood-Damage Reduction in Canada' in J.R. Nelson and M.J. Chambers eds *Water: Selected Readings* (Toronto 1969)

47 W.R. Derrick Sewell *Water Management and Floods in the Fraser River Basin* Department of Geography, University of Chicago, Research Paper No. 100 (1965)

48 J.M. Bumsted 'Flood Warnings' *The Beaver* 66 (April-May 1986) 47–54

49 Ibid 54

50 Alan Artibise *Winnipeg: A Social History of Urban Growth, 1874–1914* (Montreal 1975) 64–73

51 *Nor-Wester* 1 May or 1 June 1861, cited in Bumsted 'Flood Warnings'

52 W.D. Hurst 'The Red River Flood of 1950' Historical and Scientific Society of Manitoba *Papers* Series 3 No. 12 (1957) 55–84

53 Christopher Lawrence Hives 'Flooding and Flood Control: Local Attitudes in London, Ontario: 1790–1952' MA thesis, University of Western Ontario, 1981, 16–58

54 Ibid 67–120

55 Christopher L. Hives 'The Effect of the 1937 Flood on Public Policy: A Case Study of London, Ontario, and the Thames Valley' *Ontario History* 78 (March 1986) 25–48

56 Arthur Herbert Richardson *Conservation by the People: The History of the Conservation Movement in Ontario* (Toronto 1974) 30–1; Kenneth Hewitt and Ian Burton *The Hazardousness of a Place: A Regional Ecology of Damaging Events* (Toronto 1971)

57 *London Free Press* 7 April 1947, cited in Hives 'The 1937 Flood'

58 Hives 'Flood Control' 154–8

59 Hurst 'Flood of 1950' 67–9

60 Ibid 70–8

61 J.M. Bumsted 'Developing a Canadian Disaster Relief Policy: The 1950 Manitoba Flood' *Canadian Historical Review* 68 (Sept 1987) 347–74

62 J.A. Griffiths 'The Red River Floodway' *Canadian Geographical Journal* 70 (Feb 1965) 38–49

63 Ward *Floods* 144–63

64 W.L. Morton *Manitoba: A History* (Toronto 1967) 482–9

65 Manitoba, Department of Agriculture and Conservation, Water Control and Conservation Branch *The Red River Floodway: The Story of One of Canada's Biggest Excavation Projects* (Winnipeg 1963)

66 Ibid

67 Burton 'Flood-Damage Reduction'

68 *Evening Telegram* (St John's) Mar 1988

69 Burton 'Flood Damage Reduction' 92–5

ARNOLD ROOS

Electricity

The history of the electrical power industry in Canada is not one story but many, with each province and territory providing its own mix of politics, economics, geography, and technology. Although each area drew from a common technology, there was considerable variation in organization and political involvement; one of the main choices was between private enterprise and publicly owned utility. If there is a common thread, it is that each province pursued its own course.[1]

To understand Canadian public works – electric power or any other – is to come to grips with change: in demand, administrative structure, and technology. Demand for electric power in the early 20th century and the available technology allowed development of many isolated electric generating plants, whether thermal or hydro. The capitalist outlook of the time meant that this technology would be undertaken by private business or – where this type of development was not forthcoming, or appeared to be lacking in some respect – by municipal governments. Because of the technology, the utilities that did grow up evolved quickly into monopolies. As demand grew, and technology evolved, economies of scale forced system integration over ever-increasing geographical areas, with concomitant expansion of monopolies. As cheap and reliable power underlies a province's well-being, and as the rights of private utilities to profit could not be disputed, government regulation became inevitable. Depending on such factors as political will, population density, and vested interests, intervention or regulation came at different times and in different ways.[2]

Just as technology would interact with political decisions, so too would natural resources and geography play their parts. Thus, for example, Alberta, with its large fossil fuel supplies, would construct thermal plants, even though it also has good water-power potential. In 1955, however, water power supplied approximately 90 per cent of Canadian electric power needs. The 10 per cent supplied by thermal generation was concentrated in Nova Scotia, Saskatchewan, and Alberta. By 1980, Ontario's reliance on hydroelectric power was less dramatic but significant nonetheless: 90 per cent reliance in 1955 had dropped to 63 per cent by 1975 and 57.3 per cent by 1983. A number of factors are responsible for these shifts – most important, changing technology, which did not force change but presented new options.

CHANGING TECHNOLOGY

The second half of the 19th century saw the transformation of electricity from scientific curiosity to usable technology.

The Daniel Johnson Dam, completed in 1971 as part of Hydro Québec's ongoing development of the province's hydroelectric potential. It is the world's largest arch and buttress dam: 214 m (702 ft) high and 1,314 m (4,311 ft) long. (HQ 76-7641)

Numerous historians have recounted the electrical contributions of Michael Faraday, H.C. Oersted, W. Siemens, and Thomas Edison,[3] as well as the parallel work in turbines of B. Fourneyron, J.B. Francis, L.A. Pelton, and C.A. Parsons.[4] But for our purposes, the most important feature is the potential these developments created. By the 1880s the electrical industry had created a viable energy source, but it was not without its limitations.

The largest single use for this new source was for traction motors on street railways, as reflected in the names of many early electric power companies across Canada: the St John's Street Railway Co. (1900) in Newfoundland, the Halifax Electric Railway Co. (1896), the Quebec Railway, Light and Power Co. (1899), Montreal Light, Heat and Power Consolidated (1901), Hamilton Cataract Power Light and Traction Co. (1898), the Winnipeg Electric Street Railway Co. (1892), and the National Electric Tramway and Lighting Co. (1888), in British Columbia. The new technology was not cheap, and such companies faced heavy start-up investment costs, which they often sought to alleviate by finding other markets for excess electric capacity. Municipal street lighting offered one such market, and many private producers of electric power tried, often successfully,

Precise and elaborate concrete work: the water deflector at Ontario Hydro's Queenston site, 1921 (NA PA-84664)

Harnessing the enormous power potential in Canadian rivers: construction in 1926 of the Shawinigan Power plant, St Narcisse Falls, Batiscan River, Quebec (NA PA-20217)

to win contracts to light city streets either by arc or by incandescent lamps. In some cases this aroused considerable controversy and resentment from either gas companies, the traditional suppliers of street lighting, or citizens and municipal officials, unsatisfied with cost and/or reliability of service. Many early power companies were notorious for their excessively high rates.

Early generators of electrical power could not transmit direct current (dc) over large distances. This limited potential customers and increased investment costs per household, which had to be regained by high energy prices and in turn increased customer dissatisfaction.

Lack of private investment capital or consumer dissatisfaction led to early entry into the power field by some municipalities. When Saskatchewan became a province in 1905, all generating systems were municipally owned. Other early entrants in the west included Edmonton (1903), Winnipeg (1906), and Calgary (1909).

Development of the step-up and step-down transformer and a workable alternating current (ac) motor gave electric power usage an enormous boost. These essential elements in an emerging ac system opened the door for longer transmission distances and partial abandonment of the dc system, which had such limited transmission potential at the time. Later dc would emerge as a key element in very-high-voltage long-distance transmission. The longer transmission distances of ac removed dependence on power generated nearby and opened the way for larger generating stations, supplying distant markets.

As is often the case in the emergence of a new technological system, numerous factors were involved. The ac power industry required major improvements in turbines, generators, bearings, transformers, and insulators, as both generated power and voltage increased. As an example, early transmission lines borrowed pin insulators from telegraph technology but even with increased size and improvements in design reached a limit at 88,000 volts. Introduction of the suspension disc insulator in 1907 and improvements of it in the following decade meant that insulators would not be a critical factor in transmission voltages for a number of decades. As early as 1910, Ontario and Quebec were using disc insulators and had constructed 110,000-volt lines.[5]

The new technology put many early, small, local-market stations at a disadvantage. The ever-widening range of uses in homes, commerce, and industry – as well as public works applications such as pumping water – put an ever higher premium on reliable service and freedom from breakdowns. One road to reducing power outages was to integrate a number of stations into one larger system, so that failure to generate from one source could be compensated for by power from another. If a diversified system served customers with peak uses at different times, it could sell more power, operate closer to maximum potential more of the time, and reduce the unit cost of electricity through diversifying the load.

Even though some early practices

might seem to us rather crude, the generation and transmission of electricity have always depended on research and on skilled technical and engineering personnel. Continuing developments meant that officials in public utilities and private industry had to have and call on ever-increasing levels of engineering, technological, and scientific expertise. Electrical utilities became increasingly dependent on sophisticated research and highly skilled personnel, a trend best illustrated by the massive research and development programs undertaken to generate electricity from nuclear power. Numerous government agencies or departments and private companies played essential roles, including Atomic Energy of Canada Ltd, Ontario Hydro, and the National Research Council of Canada.[6] Although deployed in three provinces, the CANDU reactor is a major player only in Ontario.

With the growing importance of electricity as a basic need for commerce, industry, and domestic life, and the apparent economies offered by large-scale integrated systems which demanded very heavy investments, there came the need for fundamental choices. The choices were not new, merely the guise in which they appeared. Were essential services or utilities to be provided by private or public bodies? How and to what extent were they to be regulated?

GEOGRAPHIC REGIONS

Although municipalities or provinces could choose from a number of types and levels of technology, as well as administrative and ownership structures, there was little they could do about basic geography, topography, and resource bases.[7] There are six physiographic regions in Canada: the Appalachian and Acadian region in the east, the St Lawrence Lowlands, the Canadian –

Ruins at Pinawa, Manitoba, attract industrial archaeologists examining earlier and smaller-scale hydroelectric development in Canada. (PAM)

A sense of scale: penstock sections about to be installed at Queenston, Ontario, in September 1921. Some projects were so massive that few people could imagine their size. (NA PA-84667)

or Precambrian – Shield, the Hudson Bay Lowland and Arctic Archipelago, the Interior Plains, and the Cordillera in the west. The Canadian Shield offered the greatest potential for hydroelectric development, but the others had resources, and water was not the only key to electric power.

The Appalachian and Acadian region covers the Maritimes and the land south of the St Lawrence. It is hilly country, at times mountainous; its generally short, steep river systems offer good hydroelectric potential. Hydroelectric sites have been created on a number of these rivers, including the St John in New Brunswick; the Mersey, Black, and East in Nova Scotia; and the Exploits, Mobile, and Corner Brook in Newfoundland.

Proceeding westward one encounters in the south the St Lawrence Lowlands, stretching from Quebec City to Lake Huron, and within it three mighty rivers – the St Lawrence, Ottawa, and Niagara – that played crucial roles in early Canadian hydroelectric development. In the north, however, in the Shield, one finds the vast reserves of water power that became so important in Ontario, Quebec, and, to a lesser extent, Manitoba. Rivers such as the Abitibi, Albany, Bersimis, Churchill, Manicouagan, Mattagami, Nelson, Outardes, Saguenay, St Maurice, and Winnipeg contributed heavily to industrial and urban growth as well as to mining and resource development.

Further west the rivers in the interior plain did not lend themselves to hydroelectricity. Fortunately much of the region is underlain by coal, oil, and gas, all useful in thermal electric generation. Lying primarily within British Columbia is the Cordilleran region, three mountain chains divided by two valleys. Some of the rivers, such as the Columbia, Fraser, Kootenay, and Thompson, quite long and with lakes forming natural reservoirs, are similar to those of the Canadian Shield. Closer to the coast, short, rapid descents lead rivers such as the Bridge, Campbell, and Lillouet directly into the Pacific. Together, these two types of rivers have allowed British Columbia to rely on water power as the mainstay of its electricity.

We have looked at the technological and geographical frameworks within which electricity has developed in Canada. Now we can take a closer look at the main lines of development and characteristic features in specific provinces, starting with the largest producers, Quebec and Ontario.

QUEBEC

Hydroelectric power plays a preeminent role in Quebec: it is a major export, a major employer, an engine of economic growth, and, in 1983, source of 91.6 per cent of the province's power needs. The provincial agency Hydro Québec is a world leader in electrical technology and engineering, but it is also a relative newcomer, for much of the province's history has been dominated by private control of hydroelectric power.[8]

In major centres, early street lighting demands had been met by private companies, such as the Montreal Gas Co. (1837) and the Quebec Gas Co. (1848), which quite understandably opposed the new source of power and forced the new electric companies to concentrate initially on the business and domestic electric markets. Once established, these private companies then lobbied for tendering of street lighting contracts and soon put gas on the defensive. In Montreal the Royal Electric Co. soon dominated street lighting and merged in 1901 with the Montreal Gas Co. and two other electric companies to form Montreal Light, Heat and Power Consolidated.

Loggers wanted unobstructed rivers, but electric power required dams. Log chutes met both needs: Lièvre River, Buckingham, Quebec, before 1920. (NA PA-110883)

Similar developments in Quebec City led to creation of the Quebec Railway, Light, Heat and Power Co., later Quebec Power. By 1940 five major power companies supplied 90 per cent of the province's needs: Shawinigan Water and Power (1898), Montreal Light, Heat and Power (1901), Southern Canada Power (1916), Saguenay Power (1924), and Gatineau Power (1926).

Private utilities in Quebec took three paths. The first is exemplified by Montreal Light, Heat and Power, which was primarily a retailer of power. It built or acquired plants mainly to maintain its monopoly within its market area. The second is that taken by such companies as Gatineau Power and Beauharnois Light, Heat and Power Co., formed to produce power and sell most of it in blocks to other power companies: Beauharnois sold to Ontario Hydro and to Montreal Light, Heat and Power. The third is exemplified by Shawinigan Water and Power. The 42.7-m (140-ft) Shawinigan Falls on the St Maurice River had attracted a group of investors who wanted to use it to power energy-intensive industries, which then became the basis for industrial growth. Metallurgical,

Hydroelectric development by Shawinigan Water and Power Co. (shown 1919) provided the base for electrochemical and metallurgical industries. (NA NFB/PA-164739)

chemical, and pulp and paper companies were the principal customers. But Shawinigan Water and Power also sent power to Montreal as early as 1903 and continued to diversify its load and increase its customer base by supplying a growing number of residential users. As part of this process, it acquired a number of small, uneconomical companies, some private and some public, which had served municipal markets.

Shawinigan Water and Power's acquisition of small companies was part of a widespread pattern in Quebec: mixed private and municipal ownership. The Denis report noted that 20 of the 119 power plants in Quebec in 1918 were owned and operated by municipalities. In 1940, five private companies supplied 90 per cent of the power. However, there was public input which aimed at orderly growth, fairness, and proper use of water-power resources.

The Commission for the Management of Running Waters in Quebec (the Quebec Streams Commission) was created on 4 June 1910 to obtain and provide hydrological data on rivers in Quebec and recommend construction of dams for water storage and regulation of water flow. It was most active prior to 1925, and the LaLoutre and Gouin dams on the St Maurice are two important examples of its work. Without these storage and control dams annual fluctuations in water flow would have been too extreme for the continuous, uninterrupted water-supply needed for economical

Loading an atomic reactor core on a barge for delivery to Hydro Québec's Gentilly 2 power station, near Trois-Rivières, November 1976 (NA John Daggett/Montreal Star/PA-166926)

hydroelectric production. By the time the Quebec Streams Commission was abolished in 1955, it operated 25 reservoirs and had helped develop the Au Sable, Chicoutimi, Gatineau, Lièvre, Métis, St Francis, and St Maurice rivers.

Notwithstanding technical advances and wider service, there was increasing consumer dissatisfaction. Residential rates were almost invariably higher than in neighbouring Ontario, where Ontario Hydro, a public utility, was the major supplier. During the 1930s the growing clamour for public power forced the provincial government to set up a commission to look into nationalization. Several new organizations that resulted neither met the province's needs nor satisfied critics. In 1944 the Quebec Hydro-Electric Commission (Hydro Québec),

similar to Ontario Hydro, was created. It was to supply power to municipalities and commercial enterprises at the lowest possible rate and to generate, transmit, and distribute electricity throughout the province.

Once established, Hydro Québec acquired its own physical plants and developed its technical capabilities. Like earlier private companies, Hydro Québec grew by taking over existing facilities and creating new ones. It acquired Montreal Light, Heat and Power, Montreal Island Power Co., and Beauharnois Light, Heat and Power. It then expanded the Beauharnois power station from 500,000 to 1,424,000 hp. By 1953 it developed two power plants on the Bersimis River from which it transmitted power at 315 kv. By the late 1950s it had again expanded Beauharnois and started the Carillon development on the Ottawa River.

In 1960 Jean Lesage's new Liberal government granted Hydro Québec rights to all ungranted rivers, marking the beginning of a period of consolidation. The growing capacity was plagued by unintegrated electrical regions, with uneven rates. Integration led to stormy debate and the 1963 decision to nationalize existing utilities. Hydro Québec quickly acquired the shares and debts of most privately owned suppliers, and 8 companies and 45 local co-operatives disappeared. Along with consolidation came creation of new facilities through construction of the Manic Outardes generating station and participation in the development of the Churchill Falls site in Labrador.

The 1970s and 1980s may be seen as a period of rationalization and maturity. The James Bay project, which had started amid such controversy, added to installed capacity, and in 1978 Hydro Québec was reorganized under a board of directors. In terms of scope, research, size of projects, and transmission voltage, Hydro Québec was moving into world leadership, and Hydro Québec International was established to export this expertise. What had been created in 1944 from a proliferation of private companies had, by 1984, become one of the 10 largest public utilities in North America.[9]

ONTARIO

Unlike its neighbour Quebec, most of Ontario's 20th-century electrical history is dominated by a publicly owned utility.[10] But in both provinces the earliest steps were taken by private companies. The Ottawa and Hull Power Manufacturing Co. developed Chaudière Falls, located between the two cities. But most good sites were not close to major industrial centres, and much early development centred on small thermal electric generating stations.

However, with the potential created by long-distance ac transmission, southern cities looked to suitable, relatively remote hydro sites. The first of these sites was DeCew Falls, where the Hamilton-based Cataract Power Co. generated power and transmitted it 56.3 km (35 mi) to Hamilton. This first use of the Niagara River's electric potential produced power dramatically cheaper than locally generated thermal power.

As long-distance transmission capability improved, various southern communities began to regard Niagara Falls as the key to escaping from inadequate or overly expensive electric power. The power at Niagara Falls had early fallen into the hands of two American firms supplying the US market and a Canadian outfit, the Electrical Development Co. The latter was tied in with street railway operation in Toronto and had opened its Niagara Falls plant in 1906 to supply the Toronto market, 144.8 km (90 mi) distant. The reputation and past performance of the parties connected with Electrical Development suggested that electricity would be sold at the highest price the market would bear. Many municipalities and boards of trade in southern Ontario felt that cheap power, from the one good site available to them with existing technology, was essential if they were to compete with neighbouring US cities or other Canadian centres with cheaper power. The driving force for public control came from key people in Brantford, Guelph, Ingersoll, London, Stratford, Toronto, and Woodstock who saw transmission from Niagara Falls as essential to economic growth – even to survival of their businesses – as well as the comfort and convenience of their citizens.

Continuous, well-orchestrated, and well-informed pressure from municipalities and industry eventually forced Ontario to incorporate the Hydro Electric Power Commission of Ontario (5 July 1905). Adam Beck, the focus and driving force behind the legislation, became first chairman. Ontario Hydro was given legal authority to control the rates charged for electricity and the right to generate and distribute electrical energy. As wholesaler of power to municipalities under contract, it controlled the rates they charged. The province was responsible for funding Ontario Hydro, and any money forwarded to the latter was to be repaid with interest.

The organization of Ontario Hydro represented a very radical and equally controversial approach to supplying electric power. It remained to be seen whether municipalities would actually buy energy from this new public utility. Support was overwhelming. In 1907, many local referendums were held, and by the summer 16 municipalities had signed with Ontario Hydro. Ontario Hydro then had to supply electric power. It started by purchasing power from the Ontario Hydro Co. at Niagara Falls but constructed its own high-voltage transmission line to send power to these communities at 110,000 volts. In 1910 London became the first city to receive Ontario Hydro power; by the end of 1911, 15 cities and towns had joined the grid. As a result of low prices and vigorous campaigning to explain and extol the virtues of electric power, Ontario Hydro was supplying 550 communities by 1930.

Ontario Hydro very quickly moved away from relying on power bought from others and, through construction and purchase, built its own generating network. In 1913 it started construction of its first generating station, at Wasdell Falls on the Severn River, and in 1914 it bought the Big Chute generating station from the Simcoe Light and Power Co. In 1915 it completed the Eugenia Falls generating station on the Beaver River, and three years later it started the Cameron Falls station on the Nipigon River. While these actions helped it meet customer needs – and clearly indicated that it was not simply 'Southern' Ontario Hydro – the big and essential site remained Niagara Falls.

Consolidation and construction at Niagara Falls would make Ontario Hydro the province's leading force in the generation and distribution of electricity. The rapidly growing demand for power, especially during the war, made it clear that Ontario Hydro would need to build its own generating capability at Niagara Falls and that it could eventually use all the power that the falls could produce; but first it would have to purchase generating rights and sites from others. In 1917 construction work started on the Queenston-Chippawa generating station and Ontario Hydro purchased the Ontario Power Co.'s installation and began to enlarge its capacity by 25 per cent.

Ontario Hydro still needed more water allotment for generation plans at Queenston and began negotiations to buy it from the Electrical Development Co. In one large and complicated deal, Ontario Hydro and the city of Toronto paid $32,734,000 for the Electrical Development Co., Toronto Power Co., Toronto and Niagara Power Co., Toronto Electric Co., Metropolitan Railway, Toronto and York Radial Co., and the Schomberg and Aurora Railway. This purchase represented a major development in publicly owned transportation as well as electric power.

As if to symbolize the rapid development and importance of publicly owned hydroelectric facilities, Ontario Hydro on 28 December 1921 turned over the

Ontario's Hydro Electric Power Commission (Ontario Hydro) used publicity vehicles. The first Hydro Circus, started in 1912, consisted of a tandem horse-drawn wagon and a three-ton electric-power Gram truck. Two identical circuses visited rural communities and fairs in southwestern Ontario. Beginning in 1939 the Rural Electrification Coach toured the province with home and farm appliances. (OHA HP664, OHA HP663)

first unit of the world's largest generating station, at Niagara Falls. In the following year, it made operational four of the station's five initial turbines, to a combined capacity of 240,000 hp. This station, later named the Sir Adam Beck Generating Station No. 1, had been expanded to 10 units by 1930.[11] Construction of Sir Adam Beck No. 2 after the Second World War brought total developed power at this site to 2,030,000 hp.

Throughout this period of rapid expansion and consolidation, Ontario Hydro also worked toward its goal of cheap power and between 1913 and 1923 led Canada in reducing domestic power rates – crucial to Ontario's industrial growth. Small towns and rural areas had long supported Ontario Hydro, and they were not forgotten. As early as 1912 the Hydro Circus started its tours to familiarize people with electricity's potential for everyday chores. Lower customer density in rural areas meant higher installation costs, but in 1921, as part of a drive to increase rural electrification, Ontario Hydro started paying half the cost of primary and secondary distribution lines to serve rural customers. Similar programs by other Canadian utilities revolutionized farm life.

Despite massive expansion, Ontario Hydro needed more power. By the early 1920s, the most accessible sites had been developed, and demand was continuing to grow. Two options remained. Ontario Hydro had either to develop thermal power or to import electricity from Quebec, which had an abundance of unused hydro capacity and undeveloped water power. Ontario Hydro chose the latter route, and a series of agreements in the 1920s and 1930s helped reduce supply problems. Several diversion projects increased usable water flow, and Ontario Hydro built new facilities, such as those in the north at Twin Falls, in 1921, and Abitibi Canyon, 1933–42. Private devel-

opment continued, particularly in the north, where resource-based companies, such as Inco, Spruce Falls Pulp and Paper, and Abitibi Pulp and Paper, built their own generating facilities, largely to serve their own needs.

During the Second World War, domestic production of war materiel was absolutely crucial to the Allied effort. The massive industrial effort strained generating capability across the country. Demand growth continued after the war, and from 1947 to 1949 Ontario Hydro instituted rotating blackouts until new projects came onstream. It complemented continuing development of hydroelectric sites with fossil-fuel-fired thermal plants, such as the coal facilities in Lambton, Nanticoke, Toronto, and Windsor and the oil-fired plant at Lennox.

Additional input came from nuclear-powered thermal generating plants. Ontario Hydro, like Hydro Québec and Manitoba Hydro, has become a major producer of advanced technological knowledge as well as a consumer. Hiroshima and Nagasaki had demonstrated one use of the nuclear technology that had grown so much during the war. But there were other potential applications. Ontario Hydro, Atomic Energy of Canada Limited, and Canadian General Electric constructed a Nuclear Power Demonstration Plant at Rolphton to produce 20 megawatts of power when it opened in 1962. The resultant reactor system has proved successful in Ontario, New Brunswick, and abroad, and the world's largest nuclear thermal-electric station is currently under construction at Darlington, Ontario.

The Ontario Hydro Electric Power Commission was born out of a clearly stated public desire, but not without controversy. Public-ownership does not eliminate such controversy. Meeting energy needs requires huge investments

Workmen installing 4.6-m-diameter (15 ft) steel penstock at Ontario Hydro's Aguasabon Power Development, Terrace Bay, July 1948 (NA Wilfred Doucette/NFB/PA-167006)

Power-house (in background) and 72-m (235-ft) surge tank, Terrace Bay, July 1948
(NA Wilfred Doucette/NFB/PA-167004)

The world's largest nuclear generating facility: Ontario Hydro's immense and complex Darlington Nuclear Station on Lake Ontario, 1983 (OHA DAR 2555)

and selecting from various options. With long, ever-increasing lead times, some decisions have to be made with less than perfect knowledge. For example, load growth depends on many factors beyond control or accurate prediction. There will be uncertainties and debate. One can expect only that a public utility will be run conscientiously, with the needs of communities as a whole in mind. For that one can find adequate evidence in Ontario Hydro's history.

MANITOBA

Manitoba exhibited the same early desire to embrace the new electrical technology that one finds in other parts of Canada.[12] In 1882 Winnipeg streets were lit by the arc lights of the Manitoba Electric Gas and Light Co. Other firms followed suit, and one, the Winnipeg Electric Railway Co., dominated, through a process of expansion and acquisition. As frequently happened, there was dissatisfaction with a private monopoly – it charged 20 cents per kilowatt hour (kwh), and later 10 cents – and in 1906 ratepayers voted overwhelmingly for establishment of the municipally owned Winnipeg Hydro-Electric System, which lived up to its promise of electric power at $3\frac{1}{3}$ cents per kwh, with a 10 per cent discount for prompt payment. This it achieved

Generators in the Slave Falls Development, Winnipeg River, opened in 1931 by municipally owned Winnipeg Hydro-Electric (NA PA-41484)

through building its own generating site at Pointe du Bois on the Winnipeg River and transmitting power 124 km (77 mi) to Winnipeg.

Pointe du Bois was later updated, but in order to guarantee supply for essential services, the system brought into service the steam-turbine-powered Amy Street plant in 1924, an important venture in co-generation and municipal ownership. For reasons of economy, the new plant was combined with a district or central steam-heating system for Winnipeg's commercial core. In order to minimize consumption of coal for generating steam heat, electric boilers were installed to generate steam from Pointe du Bois's off-peak electrical output, otherwise unused. In 1931 the Winnipeg Hydro-Electric System opened a new generating station at Slave Falls, considerably smaller than the Seven Sisters station opened by the privately owned North-West Power Co., which was a subsidiary

Power-house and dam of the Seven Sisters Power Development on the Winnipeg River, opened 1931. The owner, North-West Power, was a subsidiary of Winnipeg Electric. (NA NFB/PA-164738)

of Winnipeg Electric. There was discontent over a public utility paying a private company for power, but private and public utilities commonly coexisted. In 1931 control of water power passed from the federal government to the province, and a series of steps started that would alter the face of Manitoba power.

The transfer of jurisdiction led to the province's creation in 1931 of the Manitoba Power Board – in effect, an extension of the Manitoba Power Commission, established in 1919 – to provide electricity to consumers. By 1933 electricity was being provided to 65 communities (and by 1947 to 157), and there existed a 10-year plan for rural electrification.

Pressures created by the expanding government system and growing rural needs pointed to an integrated province-wide system. In 1953, two years after the opening of a major generating station at Pine Falls, the Manitoba Hydro Electric Board, created in 1949 to develop and generate electric power, purchased Winnipeg Electric, in order to gain control of its generating and transmission systems. In 1955 Winnipeg Hydro agreed to serve customers within the city, with other areas being given to the Manitoba Power Commission, and both utilities arranged to buy electricity from the Manitoba Hydro Electric Board at cost. The final step in rationalization took place in 1961, with merging of the Manitoba Power Commission and the Manitoba Hydro Electric Board to form Manitoba Hydro, with province-wide jurisdiction.

Creation of Manitoba Hydro opened the way for further expansion of generating facilities and long-distance transmission capability. Manitoba had long dreamed of bringing Nelson River power to the southern part of the province, but the distances, in excess of 800 km

(500 mi), were too great for the conventional ac transmission systems which decades earlier had proved the key to long-distance transmission. However, significant advances with mercury arc valves and subsequently solid state thyristor devices led to vastly increased dc capability, permitting use of power from Nelson River sites at Kettle Rapids, Long Spruce, and Limestone, which is currently under construction. The Nelson plants highlight Manitoba Hydro's leadership in high-voltage dc (HVDC) transmission.

SASKATCHEWAN AND ALBERTA

The neighbouring provinces of Saskatchewan and Alberta are studies in the early and ongoing importance of thermal electric generation, but their histories reflect their widely divergent political ideologies.[13]

Electric light made its first appearance in Saskatoon in 1890 with a steam-engine-powered generator. Moose Jaw and Prince Albert followed suit in the same year. Each of these was a private venture, and as electricity grew from novelty to necessity, there was corresponding irritation over price and quality of service. As a result, by 1905, each city had bought out its private power concerns. This trend was followed by 20 other centres prior to the First World War, and by 1929, 119 utilities served approximately 20 per cent of the population.

A low-density, largely rural province militated against an integrated, low-cost service to a majority of the population, but attempts were made as early as 1912 to form an integrated power system. In 1926 the Saskatchewan Power Resources Commission called for formation of a government-regulated system with its main plant on the Estevan coalfield, and in 1929 the Saskatchewan Power Com-

The Rehabilitation Centre in Edmonton prepared returning veterans for work in public works and construction. Here a student linesman is learning how to install a transformer on a line pole (March 1946). (NA J.F. Mailer/NFB/PA-167007)

mission was formed. This was not, however, the beginning of an extensive, integrated system. The three major cities took different stands: Saskatoon joined the scheme, Regina expanded its municipally owned plant, and Moose Jaw sold its generating plant to a private company. Some municipalities feared loss of their own electric systems – an important source of revenue.

The significance of the transition from municipal to provincial power was illustrated by a story out of Humboldt on 24 September 1931. During the previous week McNab Flour Mills had 'changed from steam to electrical power.' The manager had started negotiations for electric power in 1918, 'but during the years the plant was operated by the town it was not possible to secure power at a price that would make the change a practical one from the standpoint of cost … Since the plant was taken over by the Saskatchewan Power Commission, however, the cost of production of power has been considerably reduced, and a rate satisfactory to both the Commission and the McNab Flour Mills Limited has been agreed upon.'[14]

The beginning of the end for municipal control came in 1944 with the election of the Co-operative Commonwealth Federation (CCF), which had included in its platform formation of a province-wide public utility. Following the Second World War, the Saskatchwewan Power Commission started to expand its facilities through the purchase of Dominion Electric Power, Prairie Power, and the Saskatchewan holdings of Canadian Utilities Ltd. In 1949 the commission was given wider powers and renamed the Saskatchewan Power Corp. The Rural Electrification Act, 1949, was to provide for electricity for the many farms and hamlets ignored by the municipal systems and placed heavy demands on the new corporation. By 1960, half the population of the province had electricity. The buyout of municipal systems continued, and in 1964 Regina's, the last major holdout, was purchased.

Saskatchewan has high-grade lignite, oil, and gas, and most power needs were supplied by thermal generating stations such as Boundary Dam, near Estevan, and the Queen Elizabeth Plant, near Saskatoon. The coal at Estevan has a very low sulphur content and is strip-mined relatively close to the surface, at depths ranging from 15 to 35 m (49 to 115 ft). This coal will probably be used in the proposed Shand Power Station, southeast of Estevan. Hydroelectric power has been developed at sites such as Island Falls, where Churchill River Power Co. built a generating station in 1929–30,

primarily to supply the Flin Flon mine in Manitoba. During the 1960s, major sites were developed at Squaw Rapids and Coteau Creek; though small in comparison to thermal sites, they were nonetheless important.

Alberta has approximately 87 per cent of Canadian coal reserves, as well as vast oil and gas reserves.[15] Thermal energy has dominated electric development. Most of Alberta's significant hydro sources are distant from population centres. The pattern of ownership is markedly different from Saskatchewan's; private ownership is the norm. Approximately 50 per cent of electric capacity is held by Calgary Power Ltd, controlled by Royal Securities in Montreal. There are also other large private companies. The largest public utility is Edmonton Power. Following the normal Canadian pattern, Edmonton Power traces its roots back to a private company, Electric Light and Power, which in 1891 installed a steam generator on the banks of the North Saskatchewan. Set up primarily to provide street lighting and some home service, it was purchased by the city in 1902 and almost immediately expanded. The plant was located on a flood plain, and the city wisely moved it to Rossdale. Expansion and new construction have kept pace with continuing growth of demand.

In Alberta's mixed private-public utility system for electric power, there is integration and co-operation. During the 1920s the provincial government looked into acquisition of private companies and creation of a linked or integrated system but found projected costs prohibitive. Nonetheless, there was some interconnection between various utilities, and in 1972 the new Electrical Utility Planning Council formalized the practice. The cases of Alberta and Saskatchewan illustrate how similar results have been achieved through separate paths.

'Class portrait': workmen in typical pose with scroll tube at hydroelectric site, Powell River, BC (NA PA-41085)

BRITISH COLUMBIA

As with Quebec, British Columbia until mid-century relied almost exclusively on private utilities to produce electrical power.[16] When the B.C. Hydro and Power Commission (B.C. Hydro) was created in March 1962, its major component was the British Columbia Electric Railway Co. (BCER), which traced its origins back to the 19th century. Robert Burns McMiking introduced electric lighting to British Columbia with the arc lights he installed in Victoria in 1883. Other companies followed in his wake, and in 1897 BCER absorbed two of them, Victoria Electric Railway and Lighting and Consolidated Railway. By this time the first hydroelectric plant had appeared in Brit-

ish Columbia, at Sandow on Vancouver Island, and others quickly followed. Through its subsidiary, Vancouver Power, BCER moved to the mainland, and in 1905 the first Coquitlam-Buntzen plant came into being. This started a period of continuing growth and impressive technical achievement, which continued until BCER and subsidiaries became part of B.C. Hydro in 1962.

During early hydroelectric development, government was simply a regulatory agency. Although a Public Utilities Commission was created in 1939, formation of a public utility appears to have started in 1943, when the government formed a Rural Electrification Committee. Two years later the B.C. Power Commission was charged with unifying the province's electric systems.

Between 1945 and 1962, the two major players were the B.C. Power Commission and BCER. The former engaged in acquisition and new construction, and the latter continued construction. Both introduced large-scale thermal generating stations. Some private resource industries produced their own power, the most famous installation being the one at Kemano-Kitimat, by Alcan Smelters and Chemicals in 1954.

In the 1960s the Columbia River Treaty and Peace River developments began a new era of large, public-utility projects. Although terrain and economic bases will continue to make British Columbia distinctive, ownership is now like that found in most other areas of Canada.

THE ATLANTIC PROVINCES

The patterns of development in the Atlantic provinces have some similarities to other sections of the country.[17] Prince Edward Island, even more than Alberta, relies on private-utility-generated thermal power. Like the rest of Canada, electric generation dates back to the 19th century: in 1886 Maritime Electric Co. Ltd. erected its first thermal generating plant, in Prince Edward Island. With fewer people than many Canadian cities, the island's electric power needs are not massive, but recent growing demand has led to interconnection with the grid of the New Brunswick Electric Power Commission.

Newfoundland, part of the Appalachian highlands, also started early and had close ties between lighting and electric traction. Electric generation started when the St. John's Electric Light Co. completed a small thermal plant in St John's. Later the St. John's Street Railway Co. built Newfoundland's first hydroelectric generating station, at Petty Harbour. The companies combined in

1920 as St. John's Light and Power, which in 1924 became Newfoundland Light and Power. Other small companies grew to meet local or regional needs, but major early actors were pulp and paper companies, such as Abitibi Price and Bowater, which by 1948 produced 93 per cent of the island's electrical energy.

Major changes followed Newfoundland's entry into Confederation in 1949. The Newfoundland Power Commission, established in 1954, challenged the dominance of private utilities and power companies. It was to supply isolated areas, promote rural electrification, and provide power at low rates to industries and at a uniform rate to private utilities already in operation. The resultant network, except that section held by Bowater, amalgamated in 1966 as the Newfoundland and Labrador Power Commission. As in other provinces, the new commission increased service and embarked on expansion. The Baie d'Espoir site more than doubled the island's hydroelectric generating capacity.

Even more massive development took place in the mainland portion of the province, in Labrador, on the rugged Canadian Shield. The Churchill River offered enormous potential, but at great expense. The British Newfoundland Corp. (Brinco) and the provincial utilities of Quebec and Newfoundland combined as the Churchill Falls (Labrador) Corp. to take on the challenge. When completed in 1972, the hydroelectric power station was the largest of its kind in the world, and in 1983 it was the source of over 75 per cent of provincial capacity.

Electrification in New Brunswick also started in the 19th century, with a series of steam plants, the first being built in 1884 by the Saint John Electric Light Co. Hydroelectric development began early in the 20th century, with the St. George

A 1964 artist's sketch of proposed Mactacquac power development on the St John River, 22 km (14 mi) north of Fredericton, now an essential source of power for New Brunswick (NA Montreal Star/PA-166925)

plant on the Magaguadavic River, built in 1903 by St. George Pulp and Paper. There followed the usual period of expansion, with combined private and public ownership and dissatisfaction over uneven access and often unreasonable rates. Public power supporters provided constant reminders of the wonders wrought by the Ontario Hydro Electric Power Commission, and in 1920 the New Brunswick Electric Power Commission came into being. The commission immediately began to construct a distribution network covering the southern part of the province and power plants to feed the system. In 1922 it built a hydro plant at Musquash, followed nine years later by a steam plant at Newcastle Creek. In order to meet customer demand it also bought power from private concerns and by 1927 was drawing 30 per cent of its needs from these sources.

Clearly the province needed a co-ordinated, planned, province-wide sys-

tem to unify the many isolated units. Long-term development of the St John River was started at Grand Falls in 1928 by the Saint John River Power Co., a subsidiary of International Paper. This process continued until six generating units were installed at Mactaquac between 1968 and 1980.

The New Brunswick Electric Power Commission also grew through purchase of private utilities, but by the 1970s there were few left to acquire, the most economical sites had been developed or were planned for, and the only clearly viable option was thermal electric power. By 1977 hydroelectric power accounted for only 27 per cent of the provincial supply, with fossil-fuel thermal units providing the rest. In 1983 New Brunswick joined the exclusive nuclear club of Quebec and Ontario with the commissioning of the CANDU generating plant at Point Lepreau.

Nova Scotia would also explore non-traditional means of generating electric

Power developments led to prosperity for manufacturers: a generator under construction in the 1920s at the Canadian General Electric plant in Toronto. (NA C-36957)

power. The Halifax Electric Light Co., formed by Halifax Gas Light and Water, supplied the city's first electricity in 1884. It later merged with the Halifax Electric Railway: the new firm introduced streetcars in 1896 and formed the basis of the Nova Scotia Light and Power Co. in 1928. Nova Scotia did not plan a few giant projects; numerous steep, short rivers were more suited to small and moderate-sized hydroelectric stations, up to 9,000 kw. By 1983, 34 stations had total installed capacity of 366,402 kw. One station alone, Wreck Cove, on the Cheticamp River, completed in 1978, provided 200,000 kw.

Small sites and the large power needs of the pulp and paper industry ensured early development by private and public ownership. The Nova Scotia Power Commission, created in 1919, began building in the 1920s and by 1932 was operating 11 stations, which accounted for a little over half of the province's capacity. In 1972 the commission combined with the privately owned Nova Scotia Light and Power as the Nova Scotia Power Corp., a public utility.

As with New Brunswick and Ontario, Nova Scotia saw the proportion of hydroelectric power drop dramatically, from 65 per cent in 1934 to 47.8 per cent in 1952 and 16.7 per cent in 1983. More recently thermal electric generation has faced serious problems. In the years following the Second World War, Nova

Scotia, along with many other regions, turned to cheap oil from the Middle East for thermal electric power. Costs soared when OPEC ended the era of cheap oil. Once again coal became attractive, and in Cape Breton, where it is abundant, the provincial utility constructed a coal-fired 150-megawatt generator, since expanded to quadruple output.

Most recent planning has centred on the extremely high tides of the Minas Basin. Electric power generation from tidal power has become a reality in North America with the work of the Nova Scotia Tidal Power Corp. Tidal power has an uncertain future, but it symbolizes the continuing search for public power in Canada: the creative use and adaptation of new technology under a variety of circumstances to produce reliable, reasonably priced power.

CONCLUSION

The evolution of Canada's electric utilities is not one story but several. The provinces have jurisdiction over property, and hence the power industry could not be regulated on a national level. Each province reacted distinctively to a technology that demanded the creation of a monopoly. Such monopolies had their own view of the rights of private property and fostered opposition, based on real and imagined grievances. Regulatory commissions – often termed public utilities commissions (PUCs) – could often reconcile producers and consumers, but BC power interests managed to prevent formation of one, and Ontario created a public utility.

As systems grew and provincial and interprovincial integration became a necessity, in order to achieve maximum efficiency through diversification of load and supply, regulation became more important. The distinction between private and public utilities became rather blurred, as in Alberta. Some provinces felt that the only path to rationalization was through creation of a public utility. Manitoba set up a public utility in line with the political ideas of its CCF government and to foster rural electrification. Political factors also played a major part in the creation and eventual dominance of Hydro Québec. Canada today has a pluralistic approach, from the dominan-the public electric utilities, in provinces such as Ontario and Quebec; through mixed private and public utilities, as in Alberta and Newfoundland; to the dominance of a private utility, in Prince Edward Island.[18]

NOTES

1 A number of works deal with this subject in more detail than this brief overview: Institute of Electrical and Electronic Engineers Inc. (IEEE), Canadian Region *Electricity – The Magic Medium* (Thornhill, Ont. 1985); C. Armstrong and H.V. Nelles *Monopoly's Moment: The Organization and Regulation of Canadian Utilities, 1830–1930* (Philadelphia 1986); Pauline Chung 'A Comparative Study of Electrical Production in Canada,' MA thesis, University of Ottawa, 1972; E. Bush 'A History of Hydro-Electric Development in Canada' unpublished report, Parks, Environment Canada, Ottawa, 1986. For a historical study that looks at the industry city by city see Leo G. Denis *Electric Generation and Distribution in Canada* (Ottawa: Commission of Conservation 1918).

2 For the driving forces behind system growth in the electrical power industry see Thomas Hughes *Networks of Power* (Baltimore 1983). For the Canadian context see Armstrong and Nelles *Monopoly's Moment.*

3 A number of historical works deal with

the evolution of electrical engineering. See, for example, W.J. King *The Development of Electrical Technology in the 19th Century: The Early Arc Light and Generator* United States National Museum Bulletin 228 (Washington 1962); H.I. Sharlin *The Making of the Electrical Age: From the Telegraph to Automation* (London 1964); E. Whittaker *A History of the Theories of Aether and Electricity* (New York 1960).

4 For the history of the turbine see L.C. Hunter *Waterpower in the Century of the Steam Engine* (Charlottesville 1960).

5 The development of electric power distribution has received little historical research. See, however, A.E. Roos *Technological Consideration in Historic Hydro-Electric Site* Selection (Ottawa 1988) for 1880–1950. For the development of the CANDU reactor see note 6, below.

6 For the nuclear power industry in Canada, see Wilfrid Eggleston *Canada's Nuclear Story* (Toronto 1965) and Gordon H.E. Sims *A History of the Atomic Energy Control Board* (Ottawa 1981).

7 Aside from the works produced by the Commission of Conservation, such as Denis *Electric Generation* and A.V. White *Water Powers of Canada* (Ottawa 1911), there are more recent works, such as Canada, Department of Northern Affairs and National Resources, Water Powers Branch *Water Powers of Canada* (Ottawa 1958).

8 The main monographs for Quebec are John D. Dales *Hydro-electricity and Industrial Development, Quebec 1898–1940* (Cambridge, Mass. 1957) and André Bolduc et al *Québec: un siècle d'électricité* (Montreal 1979, 1984).

9 Hydro Québec is analysing its historic resources and has finished a number of site studies.

10 The central position of Ontario Hydro in the evolution of public works in Canada has attracted the attention of a number of historians. In addition to sources cited in note 1, see, for example, H.V.

Nelles *The Politics of Development* (Toronto 1977), Meril Denison *The People's Power: The History of the Ontario Hydro* (Toronto 1960), and Paul McKay *Electric Empire* (Toronto 1983).

11 Robert Blake Belfield 'The Niagara Frontier: The Evolution of Electrical Power Systems in New York and Ontario: 1880–1935' PHD thesis, University of Pennsylvania, 1981. For the relation between boundary waters, such as the Niagara River, and hydroelectric development, see L.M. Bloomfield and Gerald F. Fitzpatrick *Boundary Water Problems of Canada and the United States* (Toronto 1958).

12 For Manitoba, see the brochure *Manitoba Hydro: A History of Hydroelectric Power in Manitoba* (Winnipeg n.d.) and Irene M. Spry 'Water Power' in *Encyclopedia Canadiana* x (1977), as well as works cited in note 1.

13 See Clinton O. White *Power for a Province: A History of Saskatchewan Power* (Regina 1976) and Lois Carol Volk 'The Social Effects of Rural Electrification in Saskatchewan' MA thesis, University of Regina, 1980.

14 Don Telfer ed *The Best of Humboldt* (Humboldt, Sask. 1982) 582

15 A comprehensive history of electric power in Saskatchewan has yet to be written. In addition to works cited in note 1, see Canadian Manufacturer's Association *Industrial Canada* (Toronto 1900–30) and Queen's/King's Printer *Canada Year Book* (Ottawa 1905–77).

16 For an introduction to the history of electric power in British Columbia, see B.C. Hydro's brochure *B.C. Hydro Facts* and works cited in notes 1 and 15.

17 See Armstrong and Nelles *Monopoly's Moment*, Chung 'Comparative Study,' Denis *Electric Generation*, IEEE Canada *Electricity*, and Spry 'Water Power.'

18 For a good analysis of the growth of utilities monopolies and reactions toward them see Armstrong and Nelles *Monopoly's Moment*.

LETTY ANDERSON

Water-Supply

From earliest times, and until relatively recently, inadequate supply of clean water has constrained urban size. In any community, there is a population maximum at which ground water and wells, for instance, will support the population without becoming too polluted. When urban settlements reach and surpass this size, different water-supply technology is needed. Simple transportation of water from a pure and protected source will overcome this initial constraint. This is what the first water-supply systems did.

In North America, water provision was a municipal (as opposed to regional or provincial) undertaking and therefore depended partly on the level and effectiveness of municipal organization. The private sector, and private capital, played an important intermediate role in the early stages of water provision, although community growth and extension of water systems usually required capital outlays that could be accomplished only by governments. Typically, systems were eventually purchased by municipalities when public pressure necessitated expansions that private companies were unwilling or unable to undertake. Most North American systems built before 1920 were constructed by private companies, then expanded by municipalities after public take-over.

The growth of Canadian cities is mirrored by water system development.

Cities in eastern British North America, relatively small at the end of the War of 1812, became sizeable by mid-century and grew rapidly after the Irish migration of the 1840s and early 1850s. By 1850, in round numbers, Halifax had reached 21,000, Saint John 23,000, Quebec City 45,000, and Montreal 78,000. Toronto was a city of 31,000. Western cities developed with the opening of the railroad and experienced major expansion after 1900. Urban size was the major impetus in demand for pure water, and by 1850 most of these cities had done something about water-supply.[1]

THE DEMAND FOR WATER

The simple act of turning on the household water tap activates a complex chain of events. Water in volume adequate to meet the needs of a community is first collected, stored, and transported to a distributing reservoir or main pumping station. There, it enters a distribution network consisting of mains, smaller pipes, treatment plants, and pumping stations. From water mains laid along street patterns lateral lines connect to fire hydrants; service lines connect to household taps.

Prior to having a water-supply system, urban dwellers would supply their water needs by means of a well in a private backyard or on a public street

Water delivery by dog cart, Atlin, BC, before pipes supplied individual households (NA PA-32367)

corner or by hauling water from a nearby pond, river, or creek, depending on the nature of local sources. The rich could buy spring water from private sellers who sold buckets or jugs from water carts. The advantages of tap water are obvious: a 2-gallon (9-l) bucket of water weighs about 16 lb (7.3 kg). As a community grew, many households were no longer near the supply of clean water, and the source itself was increasingly in danger of being polluted. The enthusiasm with which communities greeted the first water-supply systems is apparent from newspaper reports of civic celebrations and from rhapsodic editorials. The easing of domestic chores was not the sole reason for delight: often local water sources had become seriously polluted and tasted foul.

Aside from population size, two other major sources of water demand were fire protection and preservation of health. Some historians argue that fear of fire usually motivated the water decision; public health concerns arose much later

– as Artibise documents for Winnipeg. Many North American cities built initial supply systems that piped water into the centre of town expressly for fire purposes; construction of the rest of the system followed later, as finances permitted.[2]

The role of the fire insurance industry was important, providing a financial incentive that became well known. In 1888, a member of the American Waterworks Association reported that towns with waterworks could expect a 20 to 50 per cent rate reduction for fire insurance. By 1900, members of the waterworks industry claimed that cumulative savings on fire losses would pay for a water-supply system within five years.[3] Paralleling the rising influence of the fire insurance industry was increasing demand from health and medical professionals for pure water. The connection between pure water and public health, while not proved until the discovery of bacteria in the 1880s and the subsequent development of bacteriology, was sus-

In 1912 city dignitaries in St Boniface, Manitoba, showed how to open a water reservoir that would provide a cleaner and more reliable water-supply. (MA Foote Collection 2375)

pected as early as the 1790s. The miasmatic theory of disease, which prevailed in North America until about the 1850s, attributed diseases to filthy urban conditions. (Miasma is the poisonous atmosphere that can arise from swamps, marshes, urban gutters, or streets.) The prevention of disease required urban cleanliness, and that required water.[4]

When the miasmatic theory was eventually challenged by the contagion theory, water purity became a more important issue. Contagion theory had existed, side by side with miasma, but began to gain ascendancy in the 1850s after the English physician Dr John Snow demonstrated the connection between cholera and the sources of drinking water in

All that remains of the Customs House in Saint John after the Great Fire of 1877. The water in the nearby harbour must have added to the sense of helplessness. Disease, industrial needs, and periodic conflagrations gave many Canadian cities a war-torn look and prompted investment in modern water-supply systems. (NA PA-103066)

New Westminster, BC, had its great fire in 1898. (NA PPA-53002)

Ottawa and Hull were lumber towns, ideal sites for major conflagrations; a fire in 1900 destroyed numerous buildings, including McKay's Mill in Hull. (NA C-2989)

The fire that swept Trois-Rivières in 1908 reduced much of the town to rubble. (NA PA-29274)

London's 1854 epidemic.[5] Institutional pressure for improved water-supply came via government. In Canada, government involvement in health issues began with creation of provincial boards of health in Ontario in 1882 and Quebec and New Brunswick in 1887. Initially, their powers were advisory. But by 1895 the boards of health in Ontario and Quebec required that plans for water supplies and sewer systems be submitted for approval, and in 1908 sanitary engineering divisions were created within these boards, in order to secure better control of newly constructed works and to upgrade older ones.[6]

Formation of boards of health in Canada's two most populous provinces coincided with development of financial incentives from the fire insurance industry for a larger quantity of water, delivered under pressure. But while organized institutional pressure for water systems became well developed in the 1880s, a large number of systems antedated this.

GROWTH OF WATER SYSTEMS

By 1850, only three water-supply systems existed in British North America. Three more were built in the 1850s. One more had appeared by 1870. Growth began in the 1870s, when 23 systems were built. Seventy-five additional systems were built in the 1880s, and 130 in the 1890s. By 1900, 235 systems existed in Canada.[7]

As Table 1 indicates, water-supply construction in the 20th century was brisk up to 1940, particularly in the 1920s. The construction activity reflected in Table 1 took place against a backdrop of improving technology, improving municipal organization, and decreasing cost of construction. These factors made water-supply systems much more accessible to smaller towns. At the same time, the urban population was increasing,

TABLE 1
Waterworks plants in Canada 1850–1940

Year	Number of systems in operation	Increase over preceding decade
1850	3	–
1860	6	3
1870	7	1
1880	30	23
1890	105	75
1900	235	130
1910	419	184
1920	518	99
1930	1,182	664
1940	1,275	93

SOURCE: A.E. Berry "Developments in Canadian Waterworks Practice 1850–1904' *Water and Sewage* (Dec 1940) 10

and many places reached a size at which building a water-supply system became necessary.

Saint John, New Brunswick, is credited with having constructed the first system, in 1837, although some Quebec sources dispute this contention: Montreal had a partial system under private ownership from 1801. Toronto's dates from 1841, Halifax's from 1848. The waterworks of Kingston, Ontario, date from 1850, and Quebec City's from 1854. Montreal's is dated at 1857, completion of the first comprehensive municipal system. The single addition during the 1860s was in Hamilton, Ontario, in 1863. The dearth of construction during the 1860s probably reflects the difficulty in importing pipes, particularly of cast iron, during the American Civil War.[8]

Many early attempts at water provision began with private companies, which typically did not feel obligated to supply the entire population. Additionally, technological and financial obstacles led to a series of discrete steps, periodic minor additions to or major revisions of the system, in response to growing demand. Characteristically, demand grew faster than supply. It is

Thomas Coltrin Keefer, a leading hydraulic engineer, designed the Hamilton Pumping Station, opened 1863. Such facilities were built in response to growing demands for disease-free domestic water as well as water for industry, commerce, and fire fighting. (NA)

Victorian belief in machines: engines of the Hamilton Pumping Station; *Canadian Illustrated News* (Hamilton), 26 September 1863 (NA)

illustrative to consider early attempts in Montreal and Saint John and, for contrast, Quebec City.

In 1801, Montreal's first water company was formed under the name Proprietors of the Montreal Water Works; the principal shareholder was Joseph Frobisher, a retired fur trader and former partner of Simon McTavish. The company's charter, granted by the government of Lower Canada, gave it the exclusive right to pipe in water for a term of 50 years. This first system was simple: water was brought from springs at the back of Mount Royal, in wooden pipes laid for miles around the southwest slopes, taking the water to two cisterns downtown. The pipes frequently leaked, the supply of water was highly uncertain, and the company's reputation suffered. It was a very unsuccessful enterprise: 'The

wooden pipes frequently burst and so, finally, did the company.'[9] The franchise was sold in 1816 to a new firm, which abandoned the original scheme and instead established a steam-pumping plant to pump water from the St Lawrence through 4-in (10.2-cm) cast-iron pipes to wooden cisterns downtown. In the early 1820s, the company changed hands, and the system was again extended. Rapid city growth had necessitated a larger supply. In 1845, the city purchased the system and immediately extended it, adding more cast-iron pipe and constructing a reservoir on St Louis Square.

The pattern of marginal additions to a probably overworked system was broken when, in 1852, two fires levelled more than one thousand buildings, including much of the waterworks. Thomas C. Keefer was commissioned to advise the city on new waterworks. He proposed construction of a 4¾-mi-long (7.64-km) canal extending from 1½ mi (2.4 km) above the Lachine Rapids on the St Lawrence to a wheel-house at the lower end of the rapids. The wheel-house pumps were hydraulic, powered by the water in the canal. Water was pumped into a reservoir on the mountain, the site of the later McTavish Reservoir.

The new works, completed in 1856, were not without problems. Ice, which slowed the flow of water in the canal, reduced the power of the hydraulic pump. Auxiliary steam pumps were installed in 1868. The system was expanded early in the 20th century, primarily through enlargement of the aqueduct. [10]

Saint John is on the Bay of Fundy at the mouth of the St John River. The city has two separate water-supply systems, one for each side of the river and harbour. The eastern side is the city proper. The city's water-supply history is not unlike Montreal's. The earliest attempt was private: in 1820, a Saint John water-supply company was formed with $10,000 capital, to develop a system using Lily Lake as the source. Before construction began, it became evident that $10,000 would not be sufficient for completion, and so the company set up instead a banking and money-lending business.

A second water-supply company was organized in 1836. On the advice of American engineer Col. George Baldwin, a project was begun to transport water from Lily Lake to the city. This first system, completed in 1838, was minimal. Water was carried from Lily Lake through a wooden duct to a steam pumping station, then pumped through a 10-in (25.4-cm) cast-iron main to a reservoir. From there, a 12-in (30.5-cm) cast-iron pipe ran to a fire hydrant at Market Square. Supply was intermit-

tent. Water in the distributing reservoir was doled out once daily to consumers between 6 and 8 a.m. The customer had to draw enough supply during these two hours to last for the balance of the day. If a fire broke out, no water was available at any hydrant until the water was let down from the reservoir and the mains were filled.

Around 1850 additional water-supply was obtained from Little River, 5 mi (8 km) distant, which was dammed and connected to the city system. After construction of the Little River supply, the distributing reservoir was fed by gravity, but in cold weather pressure was insufficient. This, plus the cholera epidemic of 1854, incited the citizenry to demand a better water-supply. The outcome was public control, in 1855. The system was further extended in 1857 and again in the 1880s. As of 1850, the eastern side (the city) was supplied with water from the Loch Lomond system, a chain of five lakes located 10 mi (16 km) east of the city, and conveyed by gravity. The west side was supplied with a combination of gravity and pumping from the Spruce Lake system. [11]

In both Saint John and Montreal, small systems were expanded as conditions dictated; it is difficult to say when their systems became comprehensive. Quebec City offers a counterpoint. When it first decided to install a waterworks system in 1847, it advertised for private companies but found no takers. Perhaps it was just as well. With a population of 36,000, it was authorized by the Quebec legislature to spend the money necessary to construct a system. In 1848 the city retained the noted engineer George Baldwin, who recommended a project consisting of a dam on the St Charles River, a subsiding reservoir, a cast-iron aqueduct, and a large distributing reservoir. The main pipe was to be 40,000 ft (12.192 km) long and 18 in (45.7 cm) in diameter. The capacity of the distributing reservoir was to be 10 million gallons (45.46 million l). The difference in elevation between the river and the reservoir was 115 feet (35 m), and the aqueduct was calculated to supply 3 million gallons (16.6 million l) per day. With per capita consumption estimated at 30 gallons (166 l) per day, the waterworks were intended for a capacity population of 100,000, a level that the city would supposedly reach in 30 years' time.[12]

Baldwin's plans did not exactly come to fruition. The works were not built until 1854, and both reservoirs were omitted in the final construction. The 18-in (45.7-cm) pipe was a mainstay of the system, though, and was still in use in 1925. The system performed very well, having to be extended only in response to increases in population. New mains were laid in 1884 and 1913. A special commission appointed in 1924 found that water usage was 228 gallons (1,036 l) per capita per day – seven times Baldwin's 1848 estimate[13] – but that it could be accommodated by construction of a large distributing reservoir of the type that Baldwin had envisioned 70 years earlier.[14] Quebec City's experience illustrates the value of municipal ownership and good planning.

TECHNOLOGY

The early struggles of Montreal and Saint John reflect the evolution of water-supply technology as well as of municipal organization. Although the basic principles of waterworks technology were developed in a few large cities by the 1840s, the technology was not easily transferred: every site was different. As well, some system components were still unreliable.

An unfortunate choice of material or of system design in the planning phase could lead to the recurring nightmare of high maintenance costs: pipes had to be dug up and leaks repaired, pumps replaced or augmented with duplicates in case of equipment failure. This sort of experience could lead to bankruptcy of a private company or abandonment of a project by a municipality. The history of water systems in North America is full of examples of private companies that collapsed and/or whose delivery performance worsened steadily until the franchise expired or a buyer (usually a municipality) put them out of their misery. Scores of systems were abandoned in favour of alternative, new plans.[15]

Improvement in pipes and pumps in the 19th century greatly increased performance and lowered initial and operating costs; by the turn of the century smaller towns could use the technology. The technology 'trickled down' from larger to smaller towns. Cost reductions that occurred as the market expanded facilitated diffusion by bringing system costs within reach of smaller governmental units.

The first pipes used in North America were made of wood. They leaked at the joints, necessitating heavy repair bills. Iron pipe could withstand much more water pressure than wood without leaking but was much more expensive. In places where water itself was plentiful, wood was used until late in the 19th century, because it was cheaper. When replacement became necessary, the revenue from consumers would be sufficient to pay for cast-iron pipe. Saint John installed a wood stave conduit in 1905 when a consulting engineer argued that the money saved plus interest could pay for a replacement in 20 years. In fact, with creosote treatment, the conduit lasted until 1950.[16]

Improvements in cast-iron pipe manufacture and use, however, made it the overwhelming first choice for distribution systems. A vertical cast technique

Fredericton's 1883 pumping station began to treat water in 1906. It is still in use, and some of the earlier equipment is on display. (City of Fredericton)

developed in 1846 produced greater pipe strength, uniformity, and accuracy of measurement. A coal-tar mixture that dates from 1857 prevented ferric hydroxide build-up inside pipes. When, in the 1870s, the cost of cast iron fell substantially, its ascendancy was assured. Manufacture of cast-iron pipe in Canada dates from this decade.[17]

Pumping equipment evolved rather steadily after the 1840s. In 1844, the direct steam pump appeared. This incorporated the compounding principle, which increased power. The duplex direct-acting pump, invented in 1857 by H.R. Worthington, was widely used for waterworks throughout North America because of its reliability and relatively low operating cost. By 1875, the duplex pump had superseded the Cornish engine, but experimentation in pump design and manufacture continued. The crank and flywheel pump became widely used in the 1870s; its most famous variation was the vertical triple expansion engine, developed in 1886. By 1914 the latter was the standard for larger North American systems, but its supremacy was short-lived. By 1911, water systems were switching over to a geared steam-turbine version, the centrifugal pump, with greater capacity at one-quarter the cost and one-sixth the weight. By the 1920s, the electric motor-driven centrifugal pump was making waterworks affordable for many smaller Canadian towns – probably a major reason for accelerated construction in the 1920s.[18]

System design is critical. The design must be adapted for such major factors as supply characteristics, elevation, climate, soil characteristics, frost, and population growth. The case of Quebec City and George Baldwin illustrates the advantage of good initial design and of hiring a first-rate consulting engineer – to plan, if not construct, the system. Cities and towns in Canada sought good advice, and water-supply engineers consulted quite widely throughout North America.

Expertise was fairly easily available. One of the most prominent figures was T.C. Keefer. Canadian born and educated, he has been described as a 'railway promotor, bridge designer, and McGill's first lecturer in engineering'[19] and as one of North America's foremost hydraulic engineers. Keefer drew up the plans for the new Montreal waterworks of 1862. In addition, he advised Toronto on its waterworks, and his plans were instrumental in the Toronto design of 1873. He had drawn up plans for Hamilton's waterworks in 1859, advised Halifax on its water needs in 1868, and planned the works constructed in Ottawa in 1872. The works in Peterborough, Ontario, built in 1882, were a smaller replica of Ottawa's and were also built from Keefer's plans.[20]

Along with Keefer and scores of other Canadian engineers, a number of American engineers contributed to Canadian system design. William McAlpine, whose work on the Brooklyn Dry Dock and the Erie Canal was well known, was employed as a consultant by Toronto and Montreal. He approved Keefer's plans for the Montreal works in 1853 and those of Louis Lesage for extensions in 1874.[21] E.S. Chesborough consulted on Toronto's new waterworks of 1873 and also was employed by Winnipeg in 1882, along with the famous sanitarian Alan Hazen. Hazen himself designed the first slow sand filter for Toronto in 1910. Rudolph Hering, based in New York, consulted in Toronto in 1888 and 1895

and in Winnipeg in 1897 and again in 1913 on the Shoal Lake project.[22]

The practice of hiring a consulting engineer did not always pay off, however, and American engineers did not always know best. When Vancouver wanted to lay a submerged pipe across Burrard Inlet, it hired John F. Ward, chief engineer of the waterworks in Jersey City, NJ. Ward had developed the technique for laying submerged pipes and came highly recommended. But his employment was a major disappointment: 'Ward arrived in Vancouver in the Spring of 1888. After inspecting his task, he expressed his confidence that the contract could be completed easily and quickly. ... He decided to substitute a steel wire cable for a wrought iron rod to help align the pipe. When this cable was stretched across the inlet, it became fouled on a small boulder, and all efforts to dislodge it failed. Ward then notified the company that he had been called to St. Paul, Minnesota, on urgent private business. He did not return.'[23]

SUPPLY SOURCES

The differing physical environments of cities required the expertise of the consulting engineer. Environment determined the city's water-supply strategy, which had to recognize the interdependence of water-supply and sewage disposal. One writer argues that water-supply strategy is determined primarily by a city's location with respect to the predominant water source.[24]

Cities located on large freshwater lakes have the highest degree of interdependence and the highest probability of water-supply contamination. They have no trouble with volume of water but tended to filter and chlorinate their water earlier than other centres.

Cities located on salt water usually discharge their sewage into the ocean and look inland for water sources. Contamination by the city is not a problem; in fact, if the city exerts sufficient control over the watershed area, treatment may not be necessary. But city growth usually provokes reliance on more and more distant water sources; and the long aqueducts – the Croton and the Catskill for New York, the Hetch Hetchy and Colorado River for Los Angeles – associated with some coastal cities attest to this.

River cities can be divided into two types: those on major rivers and those on minor. A major river can supply the water volume required for the city's needs; a minor river usually cannot. Major-river cities tended initially to treat the water-supply problem as simple: water was taken from upstream, sewage discharged downstream. Other cities on the river could affect raw water quality, however, and did so more frequently as cities grew. Major-river cities responded with filtration and treatment. Minor-river cities have problems not so much of water quality as of quantity. Characteristically, they use diverse water sources and may construct impounding reservoirs or dams. Water may or may not require treatment.

Salt-water Cities

Halifax and Vancouver, both salt-water cities, arrived at similar solutions for water-supply problems. The Halifax system was built by a private company in 1848 and bought by the city in 1861. In 1868, the city engaged T.C. Keefer as a consultant. By 1897, Halifax was supplied by four inland lakes, with a distribution system consisting of gravity flow through 8 mi (12.9 km) of mains. The system expanded to 77 mi (124 km) of mains by 1916, and 93 mi (150 km) by 1931, when the population reached 60,000. The gravity system lasted until 1942, when pumping became necessary to increase system pressure. The reservoir built in 1913 withstood the Halifax explosion of 1917, in which all the nearby structures were demolished, and seemed unaffected by the 1945 explosion in which the Bedford Magazine blew up. At this point, however, the water commission found that, while the reservoir had withstood explosions, it was less immune to the elements: the roof had to be replaced.[25] Because of relatively slow growth, the Halifax system has avoided severe demand pressure. In the early 1970s, the Pockwock Water System was completed. Its headworks won the Canadian Architect Yearbook Award of Excellence in 1975.[26]

Vancouver's system was built by the privately owned Vancouver Waterworks Co. in 1887–9. This involved a dam across the Capilano River and a $7\frac{3}{4}$-mi (12.5-km) transmission through riveted steel supply main and tunnel, including 1,086 ft (331 m) of submerged pipe across Burrard Inlet. The submerged pipe was the first of its kind laid in those particular water, depth, and current conditions. Over the years, the supply system has required augmentation, but expansion has been accomplished easily through extensions of the original system. The excellent, far-sighted design was accomplished by a private water company. The company laid a second main across the inlet in 1889, and the city purchased the operation in 1892. In 1908, water from the Seymour River was added to the system. When Coquitlam was amalgamated into the system in 1931, Lake Coquitlam became the third major water source for the area. These three sources supply the city now.[27]

Typically, salt-water cities have had to reach further and further inland for fresh water to accommodate population growth. The exceptional case of Vancouver seems to be the result of a happy combination of geographical advantage, foresight, and government organization,

Public fountains – such as Soldiers' Memorial Fountain erected 1903 in the Halifax Public Gardens – rely on the system that delivers water to homes, institutions, and industry. (NSM N-7414)

which has facilitated control of the watershed area. The excellent quality of the water has been a source of pride for the city. It took the full weight of federal government pressure during the Second World War to convince the city that it had to chlorinate its water. It did so very reluctantly.[28]

These two salt-water cities are notable for good water-supply solutions arrived at early. Each found a source appropriate for the city size. Although Vancouver grew much more dramatically, even it was not forced to seek supplies at long distance. The length of the transmission main – $7\frac{3}{4}$ mi (12.5 km) – is very short compared to the experience of other cities located on salt water. Victoria, for example, extended its original Elk Lake system by building a gravity supply from Sooke Lake, 38 mi (61 km) distant. Like Vancouver, Victoria as late as 1931 maintained that no purification was necessary.[29]

A Lake City
Toronto, situated on Lake Ontario, has a water-supply history typical of a great lake city: as Toronto grew, pollution, not water quantity, was the major issue. Water filtration and chlorination were resorted to very early; after 1918 all the water in the system was filtered and chlorinated.

In 1857, the city of Toronto, following years of dissatisfaction with the performance of the Toronto Gas, Light and Water Co., entertained proposals for a new system. Financial problems and difficulties in obtaining the necessary enabling legislation, however, delayed further action.[30] The city did not purchase the system until 1873, when it also undertook construction of a new system, completed in 1877. Water was piped from an infiltration basin on Toronto Island, across the island to a 36-in (91.4-cm) cast-iron pipe under the bay, to a pump-

ing station on the shore. The lakeshore system consisted of feeder and distributing mains and a reservoir, holding 33 million gallons (149.8 million l), on the north side of the city. The filtration basin had a capacity of 1 million gallons (4.54 million l) per day and was designed to be a natural filter for the water.[31]

By 1879, the basin was abandoned, because of problems associated with sand clogging the connecting channels. It was replaced in 1881 with a large wood stave pipe, the capacity of which was reached by about 1887. In the late 1880s the municipal government consulted Rudolph Hering and S.M. Gray about seeking an alternative water-supply source inland. Hering and Gray advised the city to use the Lake Ontario supply and extend the system. The extension was completed in 1889.[32]

Rapid growth of population and industry put continuing pressure on the water-supply. Interruptions in supply caused more discontent with the lake as a source, and by 1895 Lake Simcoe and Oak Ridges were again recommended as sources. James Mansergh, a consulting engineer from London, England, was called in to settle the controversy. He recommended Lake Ontario for quantity, as the water was abundant and reasonably clear. Filtration would remove impurities, and the city engineer's plan to construct a tunnel under the bay, to connect with the intake on the other side of the island, would eliminate the possibility of bay sewage contaminating the supply. This recommendation was adopted, and wood stave was replaced with steel; by 1898 a 72-in (1.8-m) steel intake extended 2,220 ft (676.7 m) from shore. The tunnel under the bay was finished in 1908.[33]

Municipal governments sometimes had to make decisions with conflicting advice from experts, and some decisions did not turn out as well as anticipated –

Filtration plant, Toronto Island, 1923. The plant drew water from Lake Ontario and passed it through sand filters whence it was pumped to reservoirs in the city. (NA PA-86370)

one of the risks in the learning process associated with developing urban public works. In Toronto, disagreement arose in 1909 when the municipal government, after much consultation about sewage disposal, adopted the recommendation of Rudolph Hering and John D. Watson: sedimentation and removal of solids, with discharge of the effluent into the lake 4½ mi (7.2 km) east of the waterworks intake, at Morley Avenue. The consultants saw no danger of pollution, since prevailing currents in the lake moved from west to east. The Board of Water Commissioners went on record opposing the plan without sterilization or other means of neutralizing the effect. Their contentions were justified; the sewage disposal works seriously polluted the raw water. They recommended a duplicate intake at Scarborough, 2 mi (3.2 km) from shore in a hundred feet (30 m) of water, 7 mi (11 km) east of the effluent discharged from the Morley Avenue Disposal Works. This extension was delayed for many years.[34]

The 1910 typhoid fever epidemic marked a turning point in water treatment in Toronto, when many residents died. Chlorination of raw water was tried for the first time, to combat the disease: it worked. By 1911, the death rate from typhoid had fallen from 44 to 22 per 100,000. In 1912, Toronto's first filtration plant was completed. The typhoid rate fell soon by half again, and steadily thereafter.[35]

The vulnerability of Toronto's drinking water to pollution is reflected in the city's leadership in filtration and purification techniques. The slow sand filter that went into operation in 1912, designed by Alan Hazen, was one of the largest plants of its type in North America, with a capacity of 40 million gallons (182 million l) per day. The system was augmented in 1918 with a second filter of the drifting sand variety, patented in England and previously installed on a small scale at Merthyr Tydfil, Wales. The

Fresh water for Winnipeg: reusable concrete forms and rail-mounted concrete mixing and placing equipment for the Shoal Lake Aqueduct (Canada Cement LaFarge Ltd)

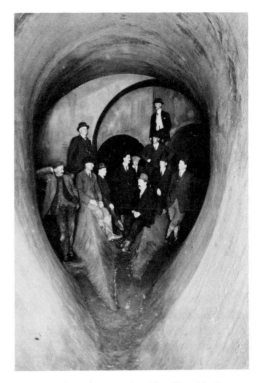

Local and professional pride: Shoal Lake Aqueduct, 1916, showing the sort of complex concrete work needed in many public works projects (PAM Foote Collection 851 N2451)

first large-scale installation, in Toronto, with a capacity of 60 million gallons (273 million l) per day, received much attention in the engineering press. The filters were washed by ejecting the filter sand from an inverted conical bottom through a small number of pipes. The sand was then carried to the top of the bed and would fall in showers or drifts. The dirty water was washed from above the beds. Drifting sand filters were never widely adopted, although Toronto's worked well enough. A rapid sand filter, with 100 million gallons (454.6 million l) per day capacity, was added in 1941, and Toronto became the only city in the world where all three types of filters coexisted in a single system.[36]

Chlorination was first practised in Canada in Toronto and Montreal in 1910. Toronto was also the first Canadian city to introduce super-chlorination, de-chlorination, and pre-chlorination. Super- and de-chlorination involved chlorinating the water and later mixing it with a chemical that bonds to the chlorine and removes it, in order to neutralize the unsavoury taste that sometimes is produced by chlorination. Pre-chlorination refers to chlorinating the

water before it is filtered and was initiated as a cost-effective measure.[37]

With creation of the metropolitan level of government in 1953, regional planning became a reality. The water system has been extended as the area has grown, and growth has been rapid. In 1958, for example, the city reported 30 major extension projects in progress.[38]

Cities on Major Rivers

Edmonton, Fredericton, Montreal, Ottawa, and Quebec City are all located on major rivers. They all can supply their water needs from the river but face different circumstances and have different histories, and their water systems have developed in different ways. For

Good-bye to privies and wells: sewer and water line construction in 1929 on Saskatoon's 4th Street, between Eastlake and Broadway (CPWA Sask Chapter)

example, Quebec City does not obtain water from the river; its main source for years has been Lake St Charles.

Montreal had an early water-supply system, but a postscript is in order here. Like Toronto, it chlorinated its water after the 1910 typhoid epidemic. Its first filtration plant, completed in 1918, had a capacity of 50 million gallons (227 million l) per day. The system assumed a regional character when, in 1927, the Montreal waterworks authority took over the Montreal Water and Power Co., which had been supplying several outlying municipalities. Since then, major extensions and improvements have been made to keep pace with demand. By 1970, the system served over 2 million people, and the filtration plant handled 350 million gallons (1,591 million l) per day.[39]

The Fredericton water system was built in 1882–3 by the city. The St John River was pumped directly into the water mains, with a broken-stone filter in the intake crib providing some natural filtration. In 1906, a mechanical rapid sand filter was added to the system, and in 1926 the system was upgraded with electric pumps. By 1931, the water was chlorinated, as well. Expansions have occurred as necessary. In 1949, the city hired James F. MacLaren Associates, Toronto, to survey the water system. The report recommended a new 2-million-gallon (9.1-million-l) reservoir, with two additional miles of supply mains. The river was to remain the source of the water. Because the city has not grown very rapidly, the water system has evolved slowly, without excess population pressure on the supply sources.[40]

Edmonton's river, the North Saskatchewan, provides a good volume of water, but, as generally in the west, there is a problem with water quality. The result has been an extraordinary level of treatment. The system was constructed around 1902; by 1913 the water was softened and filtered.

The North Saskatchewan has good volume but a problem with turbidity. Water level, hardness, and alkalinity all vary. The river is also subject to pollution from surface run-off (as in all agricultural areas). It was described in 1913 as prone to another kind of pollution as well, which became problematic when the ice broke up in April: in the winter months, the river was used as a highway.[41]

The water plant was extensively revamped in 1941, and again in 1944, at which point Edmonton boasted the largest water-softening plant in the country. The treatment continued to be comprehensive, in what is known as the largest domestic water system in northern Canada. In 1978, Edmonton's water treatment, probably the most extensive in the country, included all of the following: carbon treatment, chlorination, filtration, flocculation, fluoridation, sedimentation, sludge removal, and softening.[42]

Cities on Minor Rivers

A river is defined as minor if it does not provide enough water to supply the needs of the city. The problem may be insufficient minimum flow or water quality. Smaller cities located on these rivers typically rely on ground water; if they grow large, they usually seek surface water, often at some distance. Moose Jaw, Regina, and Winnipeg rejected the river as a source because of poor water quality as well as low volume.

Regina and Moose Jaw illustrate the water-supply problem in southern Saskatchewan. Only the north and south branches of the Saskatchewan River provide streams of any magnitude. The few lakes that exist are too high in mineral and/or saline content to use for domestic supply. This leaves ground water as the most likely supply source – a common solution in the west. But the average sub-surface water is high in calcium, magnesium, and sodium sulphate, and ground water is hard to find.

After 1935, the Prairie Farms Rehabilitation Administration did much to assist with water-supply projects in the prairies.[43] Completion of the Buffalo Pound Lake Project in 1955 marked the end of a struggle for both Moose Jaw and Regina. The South Saskatchewan had been suggested as a supply source for the two cities as early as 1910, but implementation was delayed by world wars and the Depression. Moose Jaw obtained a supply from the river in 1940 by pumping water at Riverhurst into a canal that spilled into the Caron Flats, from which the water was collected; it was then pumped to the city. This method proved costly. Regina had depended on artesian wells.

The Buffalo Pound system consists of an intake 2 mi (3.2 km) from the east end of Buffalo Pound Lake, a filtration plant 2 mi (3.2 km) south of the Lake Pumping Station, and a pipeline running 37 mi (59.5 km) to Regina. The location of the filtration plant was unusual, but the reasons given made sense. First, it was unknown at the time of construction if Moose Jaw would join the system, and the location allowed for this possibility. Second, the long pipeline was initially to be used at a flow rate well below its capacity of 20 million gallons (90.9 million l) per day. It was felt that at low volumes raw water might foul the pipe. With an estimated cost of $66 million, it was an ambitious project but offered a more or less permanent solution to the problem. A project of such magnitude involved several levels of government. The federal government guaranteed protection of the water level in Buffalo Pound Lake; the province contributed $650,000 toward the headwork.[44]

By far the most dramatic response by a relatively small river city, and Canada's most ambitious water-supply project, is Winnipeg's Shoal Lake Project. By 1906, it was clear that the old artesian-well supply was inadequate, and studies and surveys began. A report to the public utilities commission in 1912 recommended Shoal Lake as source and suggested involving adjacent municipalities. The city decided to make the project a joint one, largely because of projected expense. In 1913 the Greater Winnipeg Water District was formed, including Assinboia, Fort Garry, Kildonan, St Boniface, St Vital, and Transcona. In 1913, a three-man board of consulting engineers appointed by the Winnipeg city council reported on the feasibility and cost of obtaining water from Shoal Lake, Ontario. Rudolph Hering, Frederic P. Stearns, and James H. Fuertes recommended the Shoal Lake Project. Acceptance was immediate: the report was adopted by the water district on 6 September and by city council two days later; a popular vote approved it on 1 October. By 20 October, five field parties were making preliminary surveys.[45]

In 1915, a progress report described the system:

In brief the work may be said to include 104.2 miles [167.7 km] of railway track for construction purposes, a diversion dyke and channel, an intake, thirty-five miles [56 km] of cut-and-cover aqueduct from the intake to the site of a future reservoir south east of Transcona, 9.8 miles [15.8 km] of 60-in [1.5 m] steel pipe from the reservoir site to the Red River, a tunnel beneath the river, and 2.3 miles [3.7

km] of 48-in [1.2 m] cast iron pipe from the river to the McPhillips Street Reservoir. Advantage is taken of a gross fall of 294 feet [90 m] between Shoal Lake and Winnipeg to bring the water in by gravity. The estimated cost is $13.5 million, daily supply will be eighty-five million gallons [386 million l].[46]

The description is accurate, but it conveys little of the magnitude of the project. The engineering commission had taken the long view, that the city should use Shoal Lake for three reasons: inexhaustible supply, excellent water quality, and gravity. Later additions could and should include a storage reservoir to allow for such contingencies as aqueduct repairs and supply interruptions, a pumping station, and a second branch aqueduct.[47]

The project involved a good deal of preparation. Since Shoal Lake is a tributary of Lake of the Woods, which is crossed by the US border, and since the Ontario border passes through the intake point in Indian Bay, permission of the US and Ontario governments was necessary – and was secured by January 1914. Five parties surveyed the aqueduct line over the winter of 1913–14, and once the line was established clearing the right of way began. This was finished in June 1914. The standard width of the right of way was 300 ft (91.4 m), slightly greater where necessary.

Construction started with the telephone line, 91 mi (146 km) long, begun in May 1914 and costing about $32,500. The railway was then constructed in order to facilitate building of the aqueduct, but it has also proved essential in maintaining it. The aqueduct line had to traverse 56 mi (90 km) of virgin land; highway transportation was not feasible. Preparation for the railway required excavating and backfilling 7.5 million cu yd (5.72 million cu m) of earth and excavating 16,000 cu yd (12,000 cu m) of rock. Construction used 455,000 cu yd (347,000 cu m) of concrete, 10,000 tons of reinforcing steel, and 575,000 barrels of Portland cement.[48]

To facilitate construction, the water district decided to let the work in sections of 'moderate length' to various contractors. This encouraged participation by local contracting organizations, but it also required central organization and a system to transport workers and materials and to excavate and supply sand, gravel, and crushed stone for manufacture of concrete. This the district provided. Using two sources of sand and gravel throughout most of the construction period, it supplied a sand and gravel mixture to each work site, minimizing transportation difficulties and ensuring a uniformity of construction material. It carried out laboratory tests to determine the optimal mix of Portland cement and concrete and supplied Portland cement to the contractors. The number of camps along the line varied from 11 to 22, and the district operated 3 of its own. The maximum number of men engaged on the project was 2,500.[49]

The work was completed in the spring of 1919. Remarkably, given the scale of the operation, the total cost of construction did not exceed the estimate. This is attributed to careful allowances in the original estimate to cover anticipated difficulties with materials transportation, soil variation, drainage, and stream crossings and a contingency for elements difficult to foresee. Exceptional care in construction also kept costs down. A member of the board of consulting engineers has pointed out that an increase of one inch (2.54 cm) in thickness of aqueduct arches and inverts would have increased the project cost by about $500,000.[50]

As in the case of Vancouver, expansion of the Shoal Lake supply system has been easily accomplished over the years.

Chlorination (and ammonia chlorination) have been employed to sterilize relatively pure water, and fluoridation to prevent dental cavities. Activated carbon, along with copper sulphate, has been used intermittently to treat algae and odour in the several reservoirs. All treatments have been established with no political fallout. Three distribution reservoirs have been added over the years, as well as two new pumping stations.

THE CANADIAN CONTEXT

Canadian water-supply practice has occasionally reflected fundamental characteristics of the country itself. The influence of the railway on Canadian development, for example, is evident in the water-supply problems of places like Winnipeg or Regina, which grew rapidly on sites where transportation (especially the railway) was excellent, but local water sources were unsuitable. The Canadian National Railway paid half the construction cost for a waterworks at Jasper, Alberta, because it needed the water for its own purposes. As a result, the 600 residents of Jasper in 1925 received pure water and fire protection.

The long, undefended border with the United States has created several areas, such as Detroit-Windsor, that exist in two countries. The water system in St Stephen, New Brunswick, is integrated with that of Calais and Milltown in Maine. St Stephen was supplied originally by the Maine Water Co. When the contract expired, St Stephen agreed to buy the distributing system from Calais, and it found a new supply. The new system was described in the 1930s as having a T-connection in the piping system connected to two reservoirs, one in St Stephen and one in Calais. The latter reservoir is a fall-back for the former, and water can flow either way through the

Northern 'utilidors' protect above-ground water and sewer pipes from extreme cold and avoid costly excavation: Flin Flon, Manitoba, 1950. (William McKay, P ENG, UMA Engineering)

system. St Stephen at that time supplied water to Calais and Milltown – perhaps the only system with the source in one country and the distributing system in another.[51]

Government assistance has been creative in other ways, too, and has affected governments themselves. In most large urban areas, regional districts have been created for the purpose of water planning. In Ontario, there are regional water districts, but the provincial government has involved itself with water issues through the Ontario Water Resources Commission (OWRC), created in 1956. By 1961 its functions and powers included control of 'collection, production, treatment, storage and transmission, distribution, and use of water for public purposes.' Its approval was required for plans for all new water-supply

systems, but its involvement could also be direct: the OWRC would loan money to municipalities for waterworks, on condition that the OWRC would help build the plant and would operate it thereafter. Dr Albert Berry, who proposed creation of the OWRC and became its first manager, said: 'In this way, we are different from any Commission anywhere in the world.' By 1981, the OWRC had overseen expenditures of $4 billion on water and wastewater treatment plants across Ontario.[52]

This chapter should not end without mention of a technology problem particularly Canadian: climate. In communities inside the Arctic Circle, engineers continue to work with problems of water provision. The systems developed rely partly on heating water and partly on continuous circulation.[53]

An early attempt at this type of construction took place in Flin Flon, Manitoba, in 1933. Flin Flon is built on muskeg and rock; the frozen muskeg, described as being 'so hard that pick and shovel are virtually useless,' lies a mere 18 in (45.7 cm) below the surface of the ground. The 1933 system took the water from a nearby lake; water was pumped from the lake to a main pump-house, where it was heated by injections of steam from an adjacent boiler into the water discharged from the pump. From there, the water entered into a system of distribution pipes above the ground, protected by cedar boxing that ran the length of the line. The pipe formed a complete loop, allowing constant circulation of water; this, plus the initial heating treatment, kept the water from freezing.[54]

CONCLUSION

The comprehensive listing published by *Water and Pollution Control* in 1978–9 included 1,099 waterworks plants in Canada and indicated a wide variety of water systems. That at Beaverlodge, Alberta, provided untreated well water to 1,350 people; Montreal's served about 1.8 million.[55] Today, pure water is available to Canadians no matter where they live. Regardless of size of community, characteristics of locally available water, or problems of geography or climate, Canadians take good water for granted. The learning process that went on over the years as technology was developed and adopted was facilitated by government support at all levels. One result has been the emergence of a group of waterworks professionals who use water-supply technology and also work to advance it.

Much of the ongoing work goes unheralded. In 1974 the *Canadian Architect* magazine presented its award of excel-lence for the design of the Lorne Park water plant in Mississauga, Ontario. The judges praised the designers for their underground, unobtrusive, 'non-building,' which allowed the site to remain in its prior use as a park. The judges' remarks prompted the editor of *Water and Pollution Control* magazine to comment that it was a pity that the designers had not rather acknowledged 'the key role played by water supply and pollution control in community life by integrating the process, the plant, and the community a little more,' allowing wider understanding of how intimately we live with this essential, if mundane, part of urban life.[56]

But in water-supply – as in many aspects of public works –attention seems to be drawn only by crisis. Once water is provided to the satisfaction of the public, water-supply ceases to be an issue. If municipal water-supplies are once again under scrutiny or – as in the case of Toronto – subject to competition from sellers of bottled spring water, it is due to wider issues of pollution which the water-supply industry cannot resolve by itself. Such resolution will likely necessitate other measures, such as development of an industrial pollution strategy and better co-operation among governments and the private sector. Some of this has already come to pass.

Such precedents as exist are heartening. When the inhabitants of cities and towns first attempted to solve their water problems, eventual success depended on the assistance and co-operation of the private sector, on development and adoption of workable technology, and on a fundamental change in the way governments viewed their responsibilities in matters of public health and safety. When the next chapter in the history of Canadian public water provision is written, one hopes it will be the story of how such co-operation finally achieved effective protection of our water resources.

NOTES

1 Christopher Armstrong and H.V. Nelles *Monopoly's Moment: The Organization and Regulation of Canadian Utilities, 1830–1930* (Philadelphia 1986) 5–7
2 Ibid 20; Letty Anderson 'Hard Choices: Supplying Water to New England Towns' *Journal of Interdisciplinary History* 15 (autumn 1984) 211–34; Alan F.J. Artibise *Winnipeg: A Social History of Urban Growth 1874–1914* (Montreal 1975) passim. See also Armstrong, Hoy, and Robinson eds *History of Public Works in the United States: 1776–1976* (Chicago 1976) 217–46; Adrian C. Leiby *The Hackensack Water Company* (Bergen County [NJ] Historical Society 1969); Nelson M. Blake *Water for the Cities: A History of the Urban Water Supply Problem in the United States* (Syracuse 1956).
3 Anderson 'Hard Choices' 211–18
4 Ibid
5 Ibid
6 Théo J. Lafrenière 'Progress in Sanitation' *Engineering Journal* 20 (June 1937) 384–8
7 Albert E. Berry 'Developments in Canadian Water Works Practice' *Water and Sewage* (Dec 1940) 9–19, 42–5
8 Ibid
9 Address by Col. Wilfred Bovey 'Report of the Canadian Section of the American Water Works Association, 17th Annual Meeting' *Canadian Engineer* 72 (27 April 1937)
10 Ibid; Armstrong and Nelles *Monopoly's Moment*; John Irwin Cooper *Montreal: A Brief History* (Montreal 1969) 27; C.J. Desbaillets 'The Montreal Waterworks' *Journal of the American Water Works Association* 29 (June 1937) 774–90; Kathleen Jenkins *Montreal: Island City of the St. Lawrence* (New York 1966) 361–2; Théo J. Lafrenière 'Water Works Practice in Quebec' *Journal of the American Water Works Association* 13 (June 1925) 613–18
11 R. Fraser Armstrong 'Water Supply of the City of St. John, N.B.' *Canadian Engineer* 30 (6 April 1916) 415–16; W.R. Godfrey 'Canada's Oldest Water-Supply System' *Municipal Utilities* 88 (Nov 1950) 22–4, 32–7
12 Lafrenière 'Waterworks' 615–16
13 Ibid
14 Ibid
15 Armstrong and Nelles *Monopoly's Moment* 11; Letty Anderson 'The Diffusion of Technology in the Nineteenth-Century American City: Municipal Water Supply Investments' PHD dissertation, Northwestern University, 1980, 6–34, 113–24; for the history of water-supply development in the United States, see Blake *Water for the Cities*.
16 Anderson 'Diffusion'; Godfrey 'Canada's Oldest'
17 Anderson 'Diffusion' 6–34. An advertisement for the Gartshore-Thompson Pipe and Foundry Co. Ltd, of Hamilton, Ontario, claims that the company, established in 1870, is the 'oldest manufacturer of cast iron pipe in Canada'; *Canadian Engineer* 50 (29 March 1926) 109.
18 *The National Cyclopaedia of American Biography* 28 (New York 1926) 207; Anderson 'Diffusion' 6–34; Lafrenière 'Progress' 384; S.W. Kitson 'Waterworks Pumping 1840–1940' *Water and Sewage* (Jan 1940) 18–21, 53; (Feb 1940) 11–13, 42–5; (March 1940) 21–3, 33
19 Cooper *Montreal* 27: M.N. Baker 'Highlights Reflecting Canadian Water Works Practice' *Engineering News* 126 (5 June 1941) 77
20 *Engineering News* (9, 16 July, 10, 17 Sept 1881); *Canadian Engineer* (27 April 1937)
21 Dumas Malone ed *Dictionary of American Biography* (New York 1933) xi, 549; *Engineering News* (21 May 1881)
22 *Engineering News* (9 July 1881); Artibise *Winnipeg* 231–2; Baker 'Highlights'

77; James H. Fuertes 'The Basic Principles Used in the Designs for the New Water Supply Works of Winnipeg, Manitoba' *Journal of the American Water Works Association* 7 (Sept 1920) 693–748

23 Louis P. Cain 'Water and Sanitation Services in Vancouver: An Historical Perspective' *BC Studies* 30 (summer 1976) 30

24 Louis P. Cain 'An Economic History of Urban Location and Sanitation' *Research in Economic History* 2 (1977) 337–89

25 *Engineering News* (Sept 1881); M.N. Baker ed *The Manual of American Water Works* 1897 edition (New York 1897) 586; Leo G. Denis *Water Works and Sewerage Systems of Canada* (Ottawa 1916) 9; 'Directory of Important Waterworks Systems of Canada' *Contract Record and Engineering Review* (11 March 1931) 304; J.D. Kline 'Improvement Program for Halifax Water System' *Engineering Contract Record* 60 (June 1947) 82–90

26 *Canadian Architect* (Dec 1975–Jan 1976) 20–1, 31–3

27 Cain 'Vancouver'; Baker *Manual* 610–11; Denis, *Water Works* 132–3; 'Directory' 311; Alan Morley *Vancouver: Milltown to Metropolis* 3rd ed (Vancouver 1974) 128–9. The system is now a regional one. The Greater Vancouver Water District (GVWD) was formed in 1926, consisting of Vancouver, South Vancouver, and Point Grey. These three were joined by Burnaby in 1927, the districts of North Vancouver and West Vancouver in 1928 and 1929, and New Westminster, Richmond, Coquitlam, and Port Coquitlam in 1931. By this final date, the GVWD covered most of the populated area of the lower mainland.

28 Eric Nicol *Vancouver* (Toronto 1980) 194, 200, 238

29 Denis *Water Works* 133; 'Directory' 311

30 Armstrong and Nelles *Monopoly's Moment* 13–18; R.C. Harris 'The Toronto Waterworks System' *Journal of the American Water Works Association* 21 (Dec 1929) 1609–11

31 Harris 'Toronto Waterworks' 1609–11

32 Norman J. Howard 'Progress in Purification of the Toronto Water Supply during the Past Fifty Years' *Contract Record* 34 (9 June 1920) 540–3, 548

33 Jesse Edgar Middleton *Toronto's 100 Years* (Toronto 1934) 44

34 Howard 'Progress' 542; Harris 'Toronto Waterworks' 1612–13

35 Howard 'Progress' 543

36 F.L. Small *The Influent and the Effluent: The History of Urban Water Supply and Sanitation* (Saskatoon 1974) 235; Baker 'Highlights'

37 Discussion of paper 'Purification and Treatment' by James O. Meadows *Canadian Engineer* (9 March 1926) 45

38 *Canadian Municipal Utilities* (July 1985) 45

39 Small *Influent* 231

40 Baker *Manual* 583; Denis *Water Works* 17; 'Directory' 304; 'First Stage of Municipal Improvements Program Completed in Fredericton' *Municipal Utilities* (Aug 1953) 21–2, 49–51 33

41 'The Water Supply of Edmonton, Alberta' *Canadian Engineer* 25 (18 Sept 1913) 471–4

42 Ibid; Robert G. Watson 'Three Years' Experience with Canada's Largest Municipal Water Softening Plant' *Water and Sewage* 82 (Jan 1944) 11–13, 40–1; 'Waterworks Plant Statistics' *Water and Pollution Control* (1978/79 Directory) 36–53

43 J.G. Schaeffer 'Water Problems in Saskatchewan' *Engineering and Contract Record* 59 (Dec 1946) 297–300; L.B. Thompson 'How Municipal Water Supply Systems Are Being Developed on the Prairies' *Municipal Utilities* 92 (Oct 1954) 27, 52–5

44 A. Shattuck 'City of Regina Acquires New Water Supply from Buffalo Pound Lake' *Municipal Utilities* 92 (Oct 1954) 30, 42, 44, 46, 48; Earl G. Drake *Regina: The Queen City* (Toronto 1955) 230–1

45 Artibise *Winnipeg* 212–21; Fuertes 'Basic Principles' 695

46 'Winnipeg–Shoal Lake Aqueduct Construction: Progress on the $13,500,000 Undertaking of the GWWD – Completion of 102.4 Mile Railway – Falcon River Diversion Dyke and Channel – Review of 1914 Work and Forecast of 1915 Activities' *Canadian Engineer* 28 (29 April 1915) 495–7

47 W.G. Chase 'Construction Features of the Water Works of the Greater Winnipeg Water District' *Journal of the American Water Works Association* 7 (Nov 1920) 931–49. These latter two additions were to be constructed when average daily consumption reached 25 and 35 million gallons (114 and 159 l) per day, respectively. This was expected to happen by 1930; however, growth was slower than anticipated, and the second branch of the aqueduct was not under way until 1960. See N.S. Bubbis and R.C. Sommervile 'Aqueduct and Pumping Station for Greater Winnipeg' *Engineering Journal* (Aug 1960) 43–52.

48 Chase 'Construction' 935

49 Ibid 935–8

50 Fuertes 'Basic Principles' 746

51 A.A. Laflin 'Maritime Water Supplies' *Journal of the American Water Works Association* 30 (Jan 1938) 164–5; J.M. Wardle 'Water Works System at Jasper, Alberta' *Canadian Engineer* 50 (16 Feb 1926) 222–3

52 'One Water Agency Does Two Water Jobs' *Engineering News-Record* (5 Oct 1961) 48–52; see also 'Portrait of Dr. Albert Edward Berry – Canada's Pioneer Environmentalist' *Water and Pollution Control* (Dec 1978) 12–13 and 'An Engineering Legend Passes On' *Water and Pollution Control* (Jan-Feb 1985).

53 R.R. Foster 'Arctic Water Supply' *Water and Pollution Control* (March 1975) 24–8, 33

54 Frank E. Simmons 'Water System and Sewers at Flin Flon, Manitoba' *Canadian Engineer* (28 Feb 1933) 25–7 34

55 'Waterworks Plant Statistics' 36–53

56 'Profile: Lorne Park Water Plant' *Water and Pollution Control* (Feb 1975) 34

DOUGLAS BALDWIN

Sewerage

Sewage is a fact of life. In nomadic or lightly populated societies, prudence and natural processes can bring relative freedom from problems created by sewage. Elsewhere the growth of urban centres, with their ever-increasing population densities, make sewage control, and later treatment, a societal problem requiring concerted and unified action. Similar situations prevail in agriculture and a variety of industries where more concentrated activity – in feed lots, large steel mills, or chemical plants – and greater variety of processes and by-products require more than simple prudence and dilution.

One brief chapter cannot provide a detailed history of Canadian sewage treatment; the subject is both too vast and too complicated. However, introduction of trends, issues, explanation, reasons for action – or inaction – and examples may lead to greater appreciation of what has been achieved and what remains to be done.

THE GROWING NEED FOR SEWERS

In the first half of the 19th century, Canadian cities were health menaces. Decaying garbage, kitchen slop, and the excrement of thousands of horses, cows, and pigs filled the streets. Farmers' markets drowned in blood, animal carcasses and fish heads, rotting vegetables, and offal. Slaughter-house wastes mingled with street refuse and accumulated in the lower regions of towns to become noxious cesspools. Buildings lacked indoor plumbing. In most cities it was common to store human excrement and other wastes in pails, which were then dumped in the streets or emptied into the nearest body of water. In Montreal, for instance, the civic government in 1760 ordered residents to pile their refuse in front of their property daily. Collectors then dumped the garbage into the St Lawrence River, rather than continue the common practice of heaving the filth over the city walls.[1] An observer described York (Toronto) in the spring of 1832: 'Stagnant pools of water, green as a leek, and emitting deadly exhalations are to be met with in every corner of the town – yards and cellars send forth a stench from rotten vegetables sufficient almost of itself to produce a plague.'[2]

Most other Canadian cities were no better. Only a few wealthy neighbourhoods had sewers. At best, open drains carried away urban waste and the accompanying filth. Two sisters travelling through Montreal during the cholera epidemic in 1834 caustically noted that the ditches were receptacles 'for every abomination' that 'rendered the public thoroughfares almost impassable, and

Toronto used Lake Ontario for drinking water and for sewage outlet; at the foot of Yonge Street, 1929. (NA PA-86380)

loaded the air with intolerable effluvia, more likely to produce, than stay the course of the plague.'[3]

The first serious attempts to provide sewerage arose from successive waves of cholera in 1832, 1843, 1849, and 1854 and the typhus and typhoid epidemics in the mid-1840s. Following the 1832 cholera epidemic, for example, Montreal insisted that all citizens keep the city well drained, Haligonians vigorously debated the best means of improving drainage and sewerage, and the Toronto Board of Health recommended construction of a public sewer. After the 1854 plague, Hamilton installed several sewage drains, and Saint John, New Brunswick, appointed a water and sewerage commission board.[4] Unfortunately, once the peril receded, good intentions soon faded.

Saint John was one of the few places to construct permanent sewers. To avoid the expense that often led to the early demise of sewage schemes, city council built sewer sections gradually, wherever sufficient households agreed to pay a set fee for joining the common sewer line. Using the city's natural inclines, a gravity-operated wooden sewer system emerged in the 1830s. The entry fee, however, limited connections to wealthier areas, and even by mid-century most homes still dumped excrement into the streets.[5]

This lack of public health provisions reflected the primitive nature of urban life prior to Confederation. Dirt and foul odours were simply facts of life. As in most pioneer societies, financial constraints and rudimentary administrative systems were ill-suited to providing

Workers in the Garrison Creek storm sewer at Strachan Avenue, Toronto (CTA)

expensive public works. However, as urban populations grew, the stench and filth became almost intolerable and contaminated drinking water.

These conditions demanded the attention that only municipal incorporation could provide. The increased taxes and supervision required for such costly undertakings as sewerage and waterworks necessitated an elected body. St John's, Newfoundland, for example, sought and gained incorporation in 1888 largely for this reason.[6] Almost everywhere, city councils in their first term of office enacted laws regulating privies, pigsties, and sanitary conditions.

The prevailing theory of disease provided an additional spur to sewage construction. Mid-century physicians knew nothing about viruses or bacteria. Most believed that disease was caused by foul air, known as miasma, arising from filth,

marshes, and decomposing animal and vegetable matter. It followed from this theory that cleaning up filth and installing sanitary facilities such as drains and sewers would help prevent disease.

Improved environmental sanitation depended on trained personnel. The emergence of the sewer-gas theory of disease strengthened the perceived need for sanitary engineers. Sewer gas arose from defective closets and privy vaults, house drains, cellars, cesspools, or stagnant ditches. Most privy closets were no more than enclosed cupboards connected to a cesspool by an unventilated pipe which, under certain conditions, might reverse the flow of noxious odours. In the late 19th century, sewer gas was regarded as the source of virtually every communicable disease.

The remedy seemed to be installation of proper sanitary fixtures, supervised by sanitary engineers. Samuel Keefer's presidential address to the Canadian Society of Civil Engineers in 1889 outlined the importance and satisfaction to be derived from sanitary engineering: 'There is no branch of the engineering profession in which a man can do more good to his fellow man than in protecting and promoting the health and cities where he can apply his beneficent art to save life, and preserve the health of the living. It will be his pleasing duty to provide pure water, pure air, clean streets, and a perfect system of drainage, that shall carry off all surface water before it has time to become stagnant, and all waste from houses and yards before noxious gases are allowed to generate, and to convey the same with all possible dispatch to the proper outfall, there to be disposed of as circumstances shall dictate.'[7]

Sewers and drains were not new ideas. Engineering efforts to remove human excrement date back to about 1500 BC, but with the fall of Rome, sanitary engineering went into eclipse. Not until the mid-19th century did urban governments in Britain begin to adopt modern sewage-disposal practices.[8]

THE GROWTH OF SEWERAGE

Although British and American cities provided examples, high costs often delayed sewer construction in Canadian cities until the end of the century. The general economic downswing in the quarter-century following Confederation imposed added fiscal restraint. Despite the growing pollution of Toronto harbour, for example, ratepayers twice vetoed improved sewage facilities in the mid-1880s rather than spend $1.4 million.[9] There were also unresolved but fundamental issues, such as how the cost of services should be met: should services be provided for all or only those who could pay? Wealthier citizens in particular resisted sewage construction projects. In Saint John, for instance, the wealthy prevented construction of public sewers in the poorer districts because the well-to-do taxpayers would have to provide the funds. Civic expenditures, many asserted, should not supersede private responsibility.[10]

Prejudice reinforced the lack of funds and narrow self-interest. Such was the case at Cobalt, in northern Ontario. In 1905, this frontier silver-mining town had only one toilet per 25 residents. A visiting provincial health officer reported: 'Garbage, wash water, urine and faeces were all mixed together in frozen heaps out in the open, on top of rock practically bare in its greater area. The cold has been steady so far and all is frozen, but when the thaws come, the accumulations will all be washed into the valleys and the lake, polluting all water sources. If nothing is done ... then in all human probability there will be a severe outbreak of disease in and about the settlement.'[11] The worst conditions prevailed in the so-called foreign quarter, which housed the mine workers. Without votes or influence, this area was excluded form the town's first sewerage plan. As late as 1914, the main sewer disgorged into a nearby ditch situated just below a row of poorer-class cottages.

Nonetheless, most Canadian cities and towns constructed sewers before 1914. Doctors, civil engineers, and social reformers led the fight. They viewed sewers, water closets, and pure water as not only healthful but also as major civilizing influences. The discovery in the 1880s that many diseases were water-borne accelerated the campaign for sewerage. The 1910 standard American text on public health, *Municipal Sanitation in the United States*, by Charles V. Chapin, affirmed that 'the need for sewers has scarcely to be urged by health officers. The public so appreciates their advantages that they are usually demanded when needed.'[12] Consulting engineers trumpeted the need for sanitation as an investment in the future health of the people. Since they regarded pollution problems as environmental, the solutions were to be technological. Prominent American civil engineer George E. Waring visited several Canadian cities and advocated combined sewers. Montreal sanitary engineer R.S. Lea, who designed Vancouver's sewage system, was internationally known. North American engineers knew the latest technology through such trade journals as the *Engineering News* and the *Canadian Engineer* or professional publications such as the *Transactions of the Canadian Society of Civil Engineers*.

The increased water-supply that flowed from public waterworks promoted the need for urban sewers and drainage. Abundant water caused overflowing cesspools and surface drainage problems, as large parts of city land turned into stinking morasses. The solution once again was physical and technical: sewers and paved streets.

There were economic, as well as medical and aesthetic, reasons for good sewage systems. During the late 19th century many Canadian cities began to compete for immigrants and capital. City councils that promised free utilities, tax-free sites, and monetary gifts to attract Canadian or American manufacturing firms also wanted to boast of a good municipal health record. Aquatic life and beaches ruined by raw sewage hurt the economy.

Real estate developers and land speculators influenced city councils to build suburban sewers and thus raised their property values at taxpayers' expense. Many Montreal suburbs installed sewers well in advance of housing construction. The early history of Notre Dame de Grâces provides a typical example. It had been a farming area, but when the Montreal street railway pushed out in its direction by 1906 many landowners dreamed of riches by making the area an attractive suburb for the well-to-do. This meant providing costly modern conveniences, including sewers. The villagers first applied for a town charter to enable them to borrow the funds for public works construction, and between 1906 and 1910 the town implemented a crash program of utility installation. The town realized that the ratepayers couldn't afford a $350,000 sewerage bond, but that, too, had been planned for. In 1910 it successfully sought annexation to Montreal and distributed the debt over the entire city.[13]

The decision to construct sewers brought with it the problem of what to do with the effluent, and this often delayed progress for several years, as experts, quasi-experts, and politicians debated the merits of each scheme. The most popular choice was to dump raw sewage into the most convenient body of water. Effluent was carried away by the tide or became mixed with fresh water, where, it was argued, it would be purified by natural chemical actions.

Unfortunately, urban populations seriously overloaded these natural systems, and dumping merely transferred a serious pollution problem from the ground to the water. Sewage often washed up on populated shores, where it created tourism problems and health hazards. Hamilton, for example, hired men to cart away such deposits, and in 1887 the provincial board of health recommended that, in lieu of expensive chemical treatment, the city carry the sewage 'out to a sufficient distance from the shores to prevent the accumulation of floating matter on the latter, and into a sufficient depth of water to obtain such a dilution of the sewage as will prevent its being in

Construction of the northwest branch of the Garrison Creek sewer in Toronto. Properly made and maintained, brick sewers have a very long life, though they are no longer being built. (NA PA-55176)

Sewers that were egg-shaped in section, as here on Avenue Road in Toronto, maintained flow during low water, thereby minimizing sediment deposition, which reduced carrying capacity. The wooden form would be moved further on as the arch was completed. (NA PA-55379)

any sense a nuisance. The depth of water should be not less than 15 to 20 feet [4.6 to 6.1 m], and the distance from the shore not less than 2,000 feet [609.6 m]. Should it be found that the head of water required to keep free from deposit a pipe of this length is not available pumping would have to be resorted to.'[14] Similarly, a 1907 Halifax by-law required that every sewer 'shall discharge in Halifax Harbor below the low water mark.'

Before the First World War, few, if any, cities did more than pass their sewage through gates and strainers designed to break up the material before dumping the effluent into the water. The

Ontario Division of Sanitary Engineering investigated intermittent downward sewage filtration in 1888 and 16 years later constructed an experimental plant in Toronto to investigate sewage treatment methods. By comparison, chemical precipitation had become so popular in Britain that by 1894 as many as 500 patents had been granted for chemical precipitants.[15]

Sewage farms offered another possibility for eliminating effluents. Prior to the installation of water closets, 'nightsoil' had sometimes been sold as fertilizer. By mid-century, many people in Britain and continental Europe spread water-diluted sewage on land to maintain its level of valuable nutrients. By 1880, approximately 100 British towns had sewage farms. Canadians noticed their success, and Toronto's medical health officer argued in 1886: 'Even a new country cannot afford to systematically throw away material so necessary to maintain the soil for vegetable products. Beside [sic] there are within a short distance of Toronto waste lands which could, by the aid of this very substance, be made fertile fields.'[16]

City councils also had to decide between combining sewage and drainage systems or constructing separate sewers and whether to force owners to connect their homes with public sewers once they were completed. Initially, most cities charged for the privilege of using common sewers but did not legislate mandatory use. Later, they required that homes be connected at the owners' expense but often failed to enforce the regulations.[17]

Such were the choices that each city confronted. And although municipalities closely watched developments elsewhere, few followed the same path. Each town had its own needs, problems, resources, and desires. The struggle for sewerage in Charlottetown, Winnipeg, and Vancouver provides a better understanding of the evolution of Canadian sewers.

THE STRUGGLE FOR SEWERAGE

Charlottetown (1866–1920)
The first urgent attempt to cleanse the health facilities in Charlottetown, Prince Edward Island, had occurred in 1866, when the spring accumulation of filth and excrescences from adjoining outhouses overflowed into the streets. City council ordered medical practitioners to recommend sanitary measures for prevention of contagious disease. After considerable debate, the physicians advocated improved sanitary by-laws, formation of a scavenging company, better drainage methods, and regular privy inspections.

Two years later, during an outbreak of 'low fever,' Municipal Health Officer Dr Jenkins discovered that all the sufferers used the same well water. Ground covered with frost and snow ruled out miasmatic causes, and Jenkins told council that British researchers had linked cholera to water polluted by human excrement. He recommended that the offending well be closed and that all well water in the city be subjected to chemical analysis. According to custom, the authorities submitted the well samplings to an odour test. The results proved positive, and so identical jars filled with well water and pure spring water were weighed and compared. The well water weighed more, and so the councillors removed the offending well's pump handle – but kept it nearby in case of fire – ordered the cesspools cleaned, and instructed Jenkins to test other wells that might have been contaminated by nearby cesspools.

Once a crisis passes, memories are often short and the public purse proves difficult to open. Despite knowledge about the benefits of sewers, and notwithstanding recent British experiments linking typhoid with contaminated sewers, construction of a city sewer system was not seriously discussed in Charlottetown until the late 1880s. Instead, city council periodically, and usually in reaction to recent typhoid, cholera, or smallpox outbreaks, encouraged homeowners to use water-tight cesspools and privy boxes. Sink wells were limited to a depth of 1.2 m (4 ft), and all cesspools were to be cleaned regularly to prevent them from overflowing or backing up into floor drains. Council also instructed the city health officer to close all unsanitary private sewers. This latter duty placed the officer in a contradictory situation. If he ignored the filthy sewers, he placed citizens' health in jeopardy. If he closed them, however, the officer merely shifted the danger to the sewers' source. 'On the one hand,' Dr Richard Johnson reported in 1885, 'our civic laws very properly forbid that citizens shall keep filthy yards; they also very properly disallow the use of deep cesspools for the accumulation of sewerage; but on the other hand, they make no public provision for the construction of orderly, efficient, and permanent drains or sewers.'[18] Once again a fundamental unresolved issue arose; proper sewerage systems required concerted action, not just action by and for those who could afford to pay.

Ironically, the opponents of sewerage initiated the first serious legislative discussion of the need for better drainage. In 1884, a private bill to incorporate a waterworks company appeared before the provincial legislature. Since sewerage, unlike waterworks, was not considered a paying proposition, opponents sought to link the two measures and thus defeat the waterworks scheme. Without sewers, they claimed, the increased volume of water would combine dirt and decayed matter, become stagnant, and emit injurious exhalations into the atmosphere. Charlottetown would soon be 'floating in filth.' The great benefit of having water in a house, declared one member, 'is to wash away all filth through the sewers.'[19] This powerful argument delayed installation of a pure-water system in Charlottetown until 1888.

Pure-water advocates had argued that its implementation would greatly reduce deaths due to 'zymotic' diseases. However, early in 1889, several cases of typhoid fever appeared in the low-lying areas of town. At the end of the year, the recently instituted system of disease notification revealed that the proportion of deaths due to zymotic illnesses had increased from 20.9 per cent to 31.4 per cent.[20] These revelations sparked considerable public discussion.

Dr Johnson opened the debate. Citing several British studies, he advocated returning human waste to the soil in order to recycle its nutrients as fertilizer. He praised the economic benefits of sewage farms, extolled the wholesomeness of their produce, and pointed out that inadequate sewage systems were costly and did not save money. Based on the number of people who had contracted typhoid fever in the previous five years, he estimated that their loss of time and labour, and the cost of medicine and doctors' bills, equalled $8,000 for this disease alone, 'a sum probably twice as large as would be required for the maintenance of an effective system of sewering.'[21] This was an important point, but one frequently misunderstood or overlooked; it is all too easy to see public works expenditures simply as money spent rather than as money invested in prevention, health, and quality of life.

Two years later, city council hired Col. George E. Waring jr of Newport, Rhode Island, to examine local conditions and comment on the possibility of constructing a sewage system. Waring, described by historian S.K. Schultz as 'perhaps the most influential sanitary engineer of the late-nineteenth century,' was a flamboyant consultant, in great demand in Europe as well as in North America.[22] A brief visit convinced him that 'sewers can be constructed here more cheaply than in almost any other town that I have examined.' Although he thought that a sewage farm would benefit farm and city alike, he recommended the less expensive method of discharging sewage into the harbour during ebb tide. This plan, which included Waring's patented separate sewage systems for surface water and sewage, would cost approximately $150,000.

Charlottetown's health officer questioned Waring's plan. Dr Johnson believed that the sewage would back up, 'spoiling the now splendid advantages for bathing in the harbour and its approaches, and poisoning or frightening away the shoals of fish,' which are 'among the strongest attractions to draw summer tourists to the City.'[23]

Unfortunately, this debate had put the cart before the horse. Few people opposed the principle of sewage, provided that it was commensurate with their means. Many taxpayers, however, believed that the city's modest resources did not warrant the enormous outlay needed for a proper sewage system and were not willing to pay higher taxes. Equally important, advocates had not yet convinced the population of the necessity of sewerage. Charlottetown's physicians favourably compared mortality rates in European cities before and after the introduction of sewerage, but the termination of local mortuary statistics in 1892 prevented the city health officer from substantiating his statements that each year Charlottetown was becoming increasingly imperilled by its exposure to epidemic diseases.

Finally, in 1897, both mayoralty candidates pledged to support a sewerage system if the accompanying plebiscite returned a positive verdict. When citizens cast 1,153 of the total 1,770 ballots in favour, only the method remained to be decided. This was precisely where the matter had begun in 1890. Such slow progress may seem agonizing, but public projects depend on public opinion,

knowledge, and willingness to pay, and these do not always progress as quickly as one might wish.

In the absence of any simple, compelling incident, Charlottetown's change of heart might best be attributed to the citizens' long-term exposure to, and revulsion with, the evils of pollution. Also, most medical practitioners had come to accept the bacteriological revolution of the 1880s, which scientifically linked unsanitary water and sewage with ill-health and demonstrated the connection between germs and contagion. Continual debates in council and legislature concerning the advantages of dry-earth privies and sink wells, stricter enforcement of sanitation laws, provision of scavenger service, and the growing powers of the city sanitary officer reflected growing concern for hygiene and informed people of the perils of pollution. The annual reports and visitations of the sanitary officer, appointed in 1888, and the health officer further publicized unsanitary conditions and their inherent dangers.

The city's improving self-image also helped change attitudes. Charlottetonians enjoyed comparing their city favourably to other centres in the Maritimes. Electric lights, pure water, low crime rates, good beaches, and fine parks all marked a progressive city. Pride and economic reality helped people see that old decaying gutters and sewers, 'those relics of barbarism,' tarnished the city's wholesome image and threatened to destroy the nascent tourist industry.

In 1898 the newly created Commission of Sewers and Water Supply consulted authorities in Boston and Montreal before engaging the services of Freeman C. Coffin, a Boston civil engineer, to design and superintend a sewer system. Assisted by R.S. Lea of Montreal, Coffin's first task was to decide on the best method of sewage disposal. The sewage-farm plan received little attention. Despite favourable medical opinion, consumer resistance to sewage-grown produce stayed high in Europe. Increased knowledge of bacteriology had heightened the prejudice against sewage-farm products. Moreover, such farms grew a limited range of suitable crops. Excessively damp seasons created more sewage than most farms could use, and large amounts of land had to be left fallow to receive the winter supply. Coffin initially preferred but later rejected sewage purification methods such as downward filtration and chemical precipitation. After reviewing the scientific literature, Coffin reported that the strong harbour currents, outgoing tides, and freshwater outlets were sufficient to disperse and dilute the sewage of up to 20,000 persons. After all, he stated, sewage was simply slightly fouled water.[24]

Coffin ultimately decided to discharge the untreated sewage directly into the harbour and to construct a separate system for surface drainage. Using floats to chart the harbour's currents, the engineer determined that the best time to release sewage was during the first four hours of ebb tide: 'I am of the opinion, that with the quantity of sewage to be disposed of, for some years at least, that its dispersion and dilution, and of the oxidation of the organic matter would be so complete, that no offensive or unsanitary conditions would result from a continuous discharge, if discharged far enough beyond the end of the docks to prevent deposits in the dock and immediate vicinity.'[25] The only tarnish on these efforts was the comparatively small number of households that applied for sewerage connection. This problem would plague the city for another two decades.

City council required sewerage connections in all buildings erected after 1898, but not in existing structures. However, inertia and the 10-dollar connection fee meant that cesspools and filthy streets and cellars remained a public health menace. Universal sewage connection came about only with the replacement of Charlottetown's old, unsightly buildings. 'It is a pleasure to note how many beautiful new dwellings are taking place of old out-of-date and unsanitary buildings,' the health officer commented in 1920. 'Every new house means another sewerage system to replace that menace, the unsightly and unsanitary water closets, and it will be a great boon when this city sees the last of the ancient and obsolete system.'[26]

Confronted with complex technological issues and an expanding population, Charlottetown's city council had proceeded with cautious prudence. At each step it consulted qualified experts. When their advice differed substantially, the politicians postponed decisions until a consensus could be reached. Although council avoided seizing the initiative, it generally responded to the dictates of public opinion and was more than willing to be guided by it. Although costs and civic promotion were important considerations, the inexorable diffusion of bacteriological and technological knowledge ultimately tipped the scales in favour of a cleaner environment. As a result, less than 10 years after the first concerted public demand for better sewers had been launched, Charlottetown boasted a modern sewerage system.

Winnipeg (1880–1905)
The struggle for adequate sewerage in Winnipeg illustrates the problems sanitary reformers faced in large, heterogeneous, and class-divided urban centres.[27] Although the wealthier sections of town had installed sewers by the 1880s, few homeowners had taken advantage of them. In 1889, for example, only 10

per cent of all buildings used public sewers, and as late as 1902, only one-third were connected. Residents used outdoor box-closets or pit-closets. The former was a not-necessarily water-tight wooden box perched on the ground. Pit-closets were simply holes dug or sunk into the earth. On some streets, outdoor toilets, forming continuous lines, drained into open ditches, which soon became long latrines. This situation was aptly compared by one physician to that of European villages in the Middle Ages.

Despite complaints in the local press, by the medical profession, and by the provincial Board of Health, city council did nothing, claiming lack of funds. Yet the city spent thousands of dollars annually on advertising for immigrants and capital and on railway construction. The underlying motive for council's hesitancy apparently was the fact that the worst conditions existed in the town's North End, whose residents council considered unworthy of assistance. It would take a traumatic event to reverse this attitude.

The first step in awakening the populace to the dangers of poor sanitation was the decision to have Winnipeg's medical health officer collect detailed mortuary statistics. Prior to 1899, no statistical data existed to illustrate the growing threat of disease. The figures gathered over the following five years provided solid evidence for sanitary reform. The 1904 typhoid epidemic then gave the dramatic demonstration needed to bring about change. Prior to 1900, such outbreaks had usually been attributed to the drinking water drawn from the Red River. Since a municipal waterworks had begun operation that year, the cause had to be sought elsewhere.

The medical health officer reported that typhoid infected 1,276 people and killed 133. He blamed the situation on lack of sewer connections, and his report recommended enforced sewer connections and the abolition of box-closets. City council again ignored the deteriorating sanitary situation, but demands for action increased and the city fathers funded two external investigations – the first by a New York sanitary engineer, the second by a prominent medical authority, Dr Jordan, at the University of Chicago. Both reports attributed the typhoid epidemic to Winnipeg's poor sanitary condition and noted that the city's typhoid death rate was the highest on the continent. Dr Jordan concluded: 'It must be remembered that in sanitary matters the welfare of one section of the city is inseparably connected with that of another. The interests of the community so far as public health is concerned are not restricted by geographical or social boundaries. The presence of a large amount of infectious material from typhoid fever patients in the open privies of Wards 4 and 5 is a distinct menace to the health of the whole city, and, as recent events have shown, is likely sooner or later to involve even distant districts.'[28]

These reports finally moved council to action. The municipal health department received several new members, and a committee prepared legislation to compel sewer connections. Compulsory connection had been a contentious issue since the 1880s, as many citizens considered the practice an unwarranted imposition on private property. The danger of another typhoid epidemic, however, carried the day. In 1905, new legislation required connection to public sewers in the business section of downtown Winnipeg. If no sewers existed, pit-closets were to be cement-lined.

This by-law was ineffective. Many North End residents could not afford the required improvements, and council hesitated to prosecute. In other cases, fines were absurdly low. One landlord, found guilty of non-compliance with the sewer regulations on six separate properties, was fined only three dollars and costs.[29] Some landlords connected their properties to the sewers but did not install toilets.

Another typhoid visitation in 1905 led to more progressive legislation, which recognized that the poor needed both concessions and protection. For poorer householders the cost of sewer connections was spread out over five years, and council required apartment owners to provide at least one water closet and one sink for every 20 people. This legislation eliminated outdoor privies in Winnipeg and resulted in an enlarged health department, with an increased staff of sanitation inspectors. Winnipeg had accepted responsibility for its citizens' health. However, sewers emptied untreated effluent into the Red and Assiniboine rivers, which by 1910 had become sluggish, noxious eyesores.

Vancouver (1886–1914)
Unlike Winnipeg, Vancouver viewed public health facilities as a sign of municipal progress. Winnipeg incurred public debts through industrial bonusing and railway construction to encourage economic growth. Vancouver took another approach and improved its public health facilities to attract immigrants and capital.[30] In the 1880s, Vancouver was as filthy as most other towns of similar size. The water-supply was becoming contaminated, and outbreaks of typhoid fever and diarrhoeal diseases were common. Thus in 1886 the first city council voted $25,000 for sewerage and drainage and instructed the sanitary engineer to install a system that would keep abreast of population growth.

Vancouver's relative youth allowed it to benefit from others' mistakes. Other than the omnipresent Canadian Pacific Railway, few vested interests existed to

TABLE 1
Sewerage by-laws in Vancouver[31]

Year	Amount ($)	In favour	Opposed
1892	150,000	243	35
1899	150,000	313	117
1904	150,000	1155	162
1906	100,000	1424	197
1907	300,000	1518	76
1909	500,000	1709	268
1913	1,000,000	4093	229

oppose council's plans. The city's topography was well-suited to a gravity-flow sewer system, and the effluent could be dumped into the ocean. More important, the public clearly wanted modern health facilities and, as Table 1 indicates, was overwhelmingly in favour of paying for them.

The first sewers emptied directly into Burrard Inlet and False Creek. By 1911, sewage pollution had become so alarming that many beaches had to be closed. The municipal councils of Vancouver, Burnaby, South Vancouver, and Point Grey united to form the Burrard Peninsula Joint Sewage Committee, which hired R.S. Lea of Montreal to draft plans for a comprehensive sewerage system. Based on extensive studies of European and North American sewers, Lea's 1913 report laid the foundations for much of Vancouver's subsequent sanitary development.

To protect the beaches from pollution, and to preserve the fishing industry, Lea relocated sewer outfalls away from recreational areas and shallow harbours to locations where winds, waves, and currents could disperse and dilute urban faecal matter. Lea also recommended that the Joint Sewerage Committee construct separate sewer and drainage systems rather than the cheaper and more common combined system. He noted that, although contemporary wisdom considered separate systems a luxury, today's luxury often became tomorrow's

Fascinated onlookers at the sewer line, Bloor Street West, Toronto (NA PA-61131)

Concrete and brick sewer in Toronto during construction. The horse barely visible in the background hauled construction materials along the temporary railway track.
(NA PA-55423)

necessity. Surface water would be diverted to English Bay, False Creek, and Burnaby Lake, which were not suited for raw sewage.

In the same far-sighted vein, Lea's sewerage scheme could easily be expanded to service a community of 1.4 million people – Lea's estimate of Vancouver's 1950 population. On that perennially difficult topic of how much to invest in public works improvements, Lea wrote: 'To construct a sewer that becomes too small for the needs of a district and has to be rebuilt before the loan under which it was constructed, is repaid, is bad economics, and it is equally bad to burden the ratepayers of today with a large capital outlay on a sewer that will not be called upon to do its full duty till many years after the completion of the payment of the loan.'[32]

Finally, Lea recommended establishment of a joint supervisory board, as in Melbourne, Australia, Birmingham, England, and Boston. He pointed out that where municipal councils shared supervision effective co-ordination was often lacking. In 1914, British Columbia established the Vancouver and District Joint Sewerage and Drainage Board. This board accepted most of Lea's suggestions, which have sustained no basic change in strategy to this very day.[33]

THE EMERGENCE OF PROFESSIONALS

Sanitary Engineers (1870–1914)
As the technological expertise needed to understand sewerage problems became more specialized, decision-making gradually shifted from politicians to qualified experts. This led to the emergence of a

Storm sewer in Ottawa, July 1912. A trench was cut in bedrock and an arched concrete top added. (NA PA-42766)

new profession: municipal sanitary engineers combined the knowledge of physician, chemist, biologist, and civil engineer in one person. Some experts became consultants and offered their services from town to town. Toronto civil and sanitary engineer Willis Chipman, for example, had prepared reports on sewers in Victoria, Barrie, Brantford, Brockville, and Cornwall by 1890.

Other sanitary engineers joined the civic bureaucracy, where they supervised sewerage programs, designed local plumbing regulations, and licensed plumbers. Toronto adopted the first plumbing ordinances in Canada in 1887, and by 1914 most urban areas had enacted similar regulations, though only Alberta, New Brunswick, and Saskatchewan had provincial licensing policies. Unfortunately, the public often ignored

A city employee inspecting damage in a concrete sewer, Ottawa, 1912. Note large cracks on both top and bottom. (NA PA-42778)

most ordinances. In 1913, plumbing inspectors and master plumbers in western Canada formed an organization to create a uniform system of municipal licensing, inspection, and regulations. Establishment of the *Canadian Engineer* in 1893 reflected the growth and interest in technical matters, as did formation in 1887 of Canada's first professional engineering society, the Canadian Society of Civil Engineers.

The construction of waterworks and sewage systems not only lowered urban mortality rates but also inspired long-range planning. Sewers required the purchase of land and materials, new technologies, day-to-day administration, and contingency plans. Many urban reformers considered such matters too complex for aldermen, who spent much of their time squabbling over patronage or vying for re-election. Most cities thus established semi-autonomous sewage commissions staffed by permanent employees. These commissions formed a buffer between functioning engineers and municipal politicians. In the process, local governments lost some of their autonomy to provincial bodies. In 1895, for instance, the Ontario Provincial Board of Health required all municipalities to submit proposed sewerage plans for inspection.[34]

Dominion Health Conference (1910)
In 1910, health officers from across Canada met at the Dominion Health Conference in Ottawa. One of their chief concerns was the growing pollution of Canadian and international waterways. Lake Erie was a 'sink of corruption.' Niagara River was fouled. Even the St Lawrence River was becoming unhealthy. Riparian cities cared little about people downstream. Senator De Veber complained that the city of Ottawa emptied 'its sewage into the Ottawa River without any thought or care of the peo-

ple below, who must, of necessity, use the water for domestic purposes; but when Aylmer, a small village, talks about emptying sewage into the river, Ottawa is filled with indignation, threatens legal proceedings and offers to pay one-half of the cost of putting in a system for the purification of that sewage; but it does not care in the least for the trouble it causes to the people of Montreal. It is the Ottawa River that is causing typhoid fever in Montreal.'[35] The problem was the lack of adequate provincial and federal sanitary controls. Only Saskatchewan had sufficient powers to force its municipalities to obey provincial sanitary regulations.

The conference therefore recommended that 'the Government of the Dominion of Canada enact a law prohibiting and penalizing the deposition of raw sewage, garbage and factory wastes in the waterways of Canada and in waters tributary thereto.' The conference proposed that the federal minister of agriculture administer such an act and that the federal and provincial governments co-operate in these matters. Moreover, commissioners of public health and provincial boards of health were to be given additional powers so that no system of waterworks or common sewers could be voted on or constructed without their approval. The health officers further urged 'Provincial authorities to adopt legislation providing for the systematic supervision and inspection of all water purification and sewage disposal plants' and 'the Government of the Dominion of Canada to consider the necessity of conferring with the Government of the United States, with a view to preventing any further pollution of international waters.'[36]

Despite these sensible recommendations, very little was done, and during the first half of the 20th century, individual urban areas generally tended to

TABLE 2
Sewerage systems in Canada, 1916

Province	Sewers (no. of systems)			Sewage treatment (no. of systems)	
	Combined	Separate	Total no. of miles	Not treated	Treated
Nova Scotia	16	4	153	20	–
Prince Edward Island	–	2	28	2	–
New Brunswick	5	5	123	10	–
Quebec	60	38	829	86	12
Ontario	54	41	1,670	60	35
Manitoba	5	4	335	6	3
Saskatchewan	3	12	237	3	12
Alberta	7	7	407	8	6
British Columbia	5	11	441	9	7
Total	155	124	4,223	204	75

SOURCE: Leo G. Denis ed *Water Works and Sewerage Systems of Canada* (Ottawa: Commission of Conservation 1916) 176

TABLE 3
Typical sewage treatment results

Removal of BOD and ss	BOD		SS	
	% removed	Effluent (mg/l)	% removed	Effluent (mg/l)
Primary plant	30–40	90–150	40–60	100–150
Secondary plant	95	15	90–95	15
Tertiary plant	98	5	98	5

SOURCE: Ontario, Ministry of the Environment *Treatment Operations* (Toronto 1978)

dump their raw sewage into the nearest body of water. In 1916, for example, 29 Quebec municipalities disposed of their sewage into the St Lawrence, and 10 Ontario communities emptied raw effluent into Lake Ontario (see Table 2).

MODERN SEWAGE TREATMENT

Methods of Treatment
Increased bacteriological knowledge during the last quarter of the 19th century and better understanding of the role of micro-organisms in breaking down organic wastes hastened the adoption of sewage treatment. In Ontario, the first serious field-work into sewage disposal began at Berlin, now Kitchener, in 1902. Ten years later, population growth and urbanization and industrialization along the Great Lakes led to creation of the International Joint Commission to investigate ways of preventing pollution of Canadian-US waterways.

Sewage consists chiefly of water. The average ton contains only one pound (454 gm) of solid matter, which can be divided into such inorganic solids as sand and sticks and organic matter such as vegetables, fats, and faeces. Left untreated, the organic matter decomposes, releases offensive gases, and provides an ideal breeding ground for disease germs. The sanitary engineer uses sever-

Dumping snow down a storm sewer – not a common practice – probably in Toronto, 1929 (NA PA-89479)

al yardsticks to calculate sewage pollution levels – suspended solids (ss) and biochemical-oxygen demand (BOD) are the two most common tests. ss measures those wastes that do not sink or settle in the sewage; BOD is the amount of oxygen needed in the water to decompose organic sewage (see Table 3).

Municipal sewage is treated and disposed of in a variety of ways: primary, secondary, or tertiary treatment and lagooning. Although many centres still discharge raw sewage into nearby water bodies, most areas employ primary treatment to remove large solids. The effluent then goes through a grit chamber, where the heavy organic particles sink to the bottom. It next passes through a comminutor, which shreds the coarse sewage before the liquid enters the sedimentation tanks, where it stands for several hours to allow the solids to sink to the bottom as sludge or

be skimmed off the top. Separation may be further improved by adding such chemical coagulants as alum, ferric chloride, or lime to combine or flocculate with the impurities and sink to the bottom. The remaining sludge is buried, incinerated, or used as fertilizer, and the effluent is discharged into the nearest body of water after disinfection with chlorine. In many smaller urban areas, where the total amount of sewage is small and the receiving water body is large, this is the only treatment used.

Primary effluent, however, may contain toxic oil, scum, and impurities that require secondary treatment, which introduces air into the sewage to promote bacterial growth. The bacteria feed on the organic matter in the sewage and decompose it. The most common secondary treatment methods are trickling filters and activated sludge. Sand filters are effective, but expensive, and require

TABLE 4
Canadian sewerage works, 1950

Province	No. of sewer systems	Population served	% of total pop.	Sewage treatment plants			
				Total no. of plants	Partial treatment plants	Activated sludge plants	Trickling filter plants
Alberta	53	400,000	45.8	47	34	7	6
British Columbia	43	619,000	55.5	14	8	2	4
Manitoba	23	327,000	42.0	10	6	0	4
New Brunswick	24	149,000	28.8	1	1	0	0
Newfoundland	6	82,000	23.6	4	4	0	0
Nova Scotia	37	280,000	43.4	0	0	0	0
Ontario	212	2,800,000	63.5	176	115	45	16
Prince Edward Island	3	24,000	25.5	0	0	0	0
Quebec	240	1,700,000	43.6	64	61	1	2
Saskatchewan	26	203,000	23.6	18	5	10	3
Total	667	6,584,000	48.5	334	234	65	35

SOURCE: *Municipal Utilities* (Dec 1950)

an acre of land for every 1,000 people. Considerably cheaper, and from 90 to 95 per cent efficient, is the activated sludge process, in which air is blown into the sewage to form slimes, which attract and decompose organic matter. The resultant mass sinks to the bottom, where it is collected by mechanical means. Most secondary plants add chlorine to the effluent as a final disinfectant.

Several Ontario municipalities have recently abandoned secondary treatment plants for the more economical method of lagooning, while others have enhanced and extended secondary treatment plants. Where secondary treatment proves inadequate, tertiary treatment can reduce phosphorus levels to satisfy the Canadian-American Great Lakes Agreement.

Many less densely populated areas employ sewage lagoons or oxidation ponds 0.6 to 1.2 m (2 to 4 ft) deep. There, raw sewage is purified by the combined action of wind, temperature, sunlight, algae, and bacteria. In some areas, mechanical aeration and chemical additives further enhance purification.

Treatment (1900–50)

Adoption of sewage treatment processes came slowly in Canada. As Table 4 illustrates, in 1950, only 334 of the 667 Canadian communities with sewerage systems had treatment plants, and only 30 per cent of these went beyond primary treatment. Nova Scotia and Prince Edward Island provided no treatment facilities for raw sewage. Brantford, Ontario, was the first North American city to construct an activated sludge plant (1915), and by 1933 the province had 33 such centres. In Winnipeg, concern over rising pollution in the 1930s led to establishment of the Greater Winnipeg Sanitary District in 1935 as a government unemployment relief measure. Under the direction of W.S. Lea, a collector system and treatment plant were constructed to serve Winnipeg, St Boniface, West and East Kildonan, and St Vital.

High costs slowed adoption of treatment plants. The situation in Saskatchewan towns prior to the First World War illustrates the problem. The towns' limited tax base was exacerbated by the Canadian Pacific Railway's extensive

Storm sewers in a growing city: a 54-in (1.54-m) line being installed on Avenue B between Spadina Crescent and 19th Street in Saskatoon in 1932 (CPWA Sask Chapter)

tax-exempt land holdings. Prairie towns were as boosterist as Winnipeg, Edmonton, and Vancouver, and they borrowed heavily to provide an attractive infrastructure of sewers and waterworks. Treatment plants were simply too expensive. Then, when the inevitable occurred and raw sewage polluted the North and South Saskatchewan rivers, the prairies' major water-supply, the province enacted legislation in 1910 that gave the provincial Health Department control over municipal sewage disposal. The province hired a Toronto consulting sanitary engineer, who designed disposal works for Moose Jaw, Prince Albert, Regina, Saskatoon, Swift Current, Yorkton, and several smaller towns. These plans called for separate sewage and waste water systems, as well as primary and secondary treatment using crushed rock filters.

Apathy and hard times thwarted these good intentions. In Saskatoon, for example, outdoor privies continued to predominate in the 1920s. The privies became such a health menace that the municipal health officer tried to force householders to link up with the public sewers. But the Trades and Labour Congress accused him of discriminating against labourers and the poor, and when the courts vetoed compulsory connection in 1930, the matter was dropped.[37] Elsewhere, the Depression prevented introduction of costly public works programs. Moose Jaw, for example, defaulted on its outstanding debentures in 1937 and took 12 years to regain its credit rating.

Sewage expenditures awaited the end of the Second World War. Even then, rising construction costs persuaded smaller communities to opt for the least expensive methods, such as activated sludge compact plants and the combined clarifier-digester (clarigester). Money flowing from the discovery of oil at Leduc, Alberta, in 1947 allowed the Provincial Self-Liquidating Projects Act to provide smaller Albertan centres with low-cost financing for constructing new sewage centres. The official openings of some of these early systems were colourful affairs. The highlight of one opening, for example, was the burning of a privy on the main street.

The inexpensive and easy-to-operate Imhoff tank was popular in areas that required only primary treatment. Similarly, lower-cost rock filters, first introduced in Canadian wartime installations, found general use in secondary treatment plants. Incineration disposed of the remaining sludge, and western Canadian cities sold sludge cakes for fertilizer. In Moose Jaw, the British American Oil Co. each month purchased sewage effluent worth $500 to $700 to use as a cooling agent in its refinery. Finally, most plants used chlorination either as replacement for secondary treatment or to obtain more complete purification.[38]

In the inter-war period, Canada depended largely on American examples, research, and equipment. Civil engineers used American textbooks and relied heavily on American technical journals. US sanitary equipment manufacturers dominated the Canadian market and worked closely with Canadian sewage associations and contractors to develop better materials and processes.[39] Slowly, however, Canada began to show more interest in research. The monthly journal *Water and Sewage* broke away from the *Canadian Engineer* in 1940 to cater to this growing interest. And by the late 1940s, the Canadian Institute on Sewage and Sanitation, the Maritime Water Works Association, and the Western Canada Water and Sewage Conference promoted research and disseminated the latest technological advances. Even so, lagoons were not adopted in western Canada until North Dakota's state sanitary engineer read a paper on lagoon design and operation at the 1953 Western Canada Water and Sewage Conference in Edmonton.

Treatment (1950–80)

The most ambitious sewerage plan in the 1950s was the construction of sewage and storm drainage in Metropolitan Toronto. In 1950, Scarborough, York, Weston, Swansea, and Long Branch each had a treatment plant. East York had two plants, North York had three, and New Toronto and Mimico shared one. Toronto had two sewage plants. The activated sludge plant in the north end handled sewage from North Toronto, Leaside, and Forest Hill Village. The plant at Ashbridge's Bay had been constructed in 1913 and was designed for a flow of 150 million l (33 million gallons) daily. The population explosion in Metro Toronto after 1945, however, had overloaded practically every sewage plant, with a new plant at Ashbridge's Bay handling 363.7 million l (80 million gallons) daily. Toronto suburbs were particularly ill equipped to cope with the needed public works projects. When a subsequent government report revealed that sewage from municipalities bordering the Don and Humber rivers was polluting Lake Ontario, the provincial government decided to act on the report's recommendation that it create a single authority to co-ordinate water-supply, sewage, and drainage matters.[40] The Greater Vancouver Sewerage District and the Greater Winnipeg Sanitary District (1937–61), examples of sound regional planning, influenced Ontario.

In 1954 Toronto's newly established metropolitan system of local government facilitated extension of basic physical services to outlying townships. Instead of continuing to construct and operate a large number of small treatment plants in each area, Toronto decided that large plants discharging directly into Lake Ontario would be less expensive and more practical. In 1957, the Ontario Water Resources Commission set pollution standards and began to assist municipalities in constructing treatment works. In the mid-1960s, the federal government provided additional funding through the International Joint Commission studying pollution in the Great Lakes. Today, the province monitors all industrial and municipal discharges.

Population growth and industrialization created similar pollution problems on the West Coast. To rectify this problem, the BC government built a treatment plant in 1963 on Iona Island, at the mouth of the Fraser River, and four years later began to prohibit discharge of sewage without a permit. By 1976, several new treatment plants served almost all the lower mainland, and from 1971 the provincial government required secondary treatment of municipal sewage emptying into the Lower Fraser River. Sewage costs thus increased from $500,000 in 1956 to $10 million 20 years later.[41] According to a 1981 study by Leon Kolankiewicz, however, the Greater Vancouver Sewerage and Drainage Districts regularly exceed their BOD limits and have been among the least tractable bodies in limiting sewage pollution.[42]

After the Second World War, smaller urban areas turned to sewage lagoons and oxidation ponds as the easiest and most economical methods of treating raw sewage. By 1962, approximately 200 such installations functioned in the prairie provinces alone, and the federal Department of National Health and Welfare was conducting experiments in the Maritime provinces.[43]

When the Saskatchewan government decreed that Moose Jaw and Regina had to provide better sewage treatment, the two cities took divergent paths. Regina adopted chemical treatment to remove phosphorus from effluent. However, phosphorus, while a pollutant, is also a valuable fertilizer, and in 1982 Moose Jaw became the first large city in Canada to use lagoon effluent as a source of irrigation water. By 1987, waste water was being used to irrigate land south of Moose Jaw. Small surpluses not used for irrigation were to be disposed of in infiltration basins in the same area.[44]

Elsewhere, heated debates over the location of such treatment ponds delayed implementation for several years. Winnipeg, in 1974, adopted the first Canadian sewage treatment plant using generated oxygen to sustain bacterial growth and has continued to upgrade its facilities. Today, Winnipeg's per capita expenditure for sewerage ranks very high among Canadian cities.

The Maritimes Today

In December 1986, federal Environment Minister Tom McMillan declared the lack of sewage treatment facilities in the Maritime provinces 'shocking and nothing less than a scandal.' East of Ontario only 10 per cent of municipal liquid wastes were treated, compared to 80 per cent in the rest of Canada. In a statement undoubtedly calculated to shock as well as to inform people of the gravity of the situation, McMillan declared that the Maritimes used a system of waste water management that had not 'progressed substantially since Roman times.'[45]

This news surprised few Maritimers. Several private and government reports in the previous 20 years had revealed growing pollution problems. A 1969 background study for the Atlantic Development Board, for example, discovered that most municipalities discharged untreated sewage into the nearest water body, and in Summerside and Malpeque Bay, Prince Edward Island, pollution was curtailing recreational use and threatening to destroy oyster harvesting. In 1966 only 5.5 per cent of Maritimers were served by public sewers with treatment facilities; 42.7 per cent had public sewers but without treatment facilities.[46]

Today, most Nova Scotian municipalities, including Halifax, North Sydney, Yarmouth, and Reserve Mines, still dump raw sewage into the water. Existing treatment plants are generally simple, low-maintenance oxidation lagoons. The majority were built after 1970, usually in smaller communities. In older settlements, combined sewers often cause overloading and flooding. Piecemeal development is slowly phasing out these combined systems. Lack of money is the main problem. In many areas the bedrock is too close to the surface, and sewers would be very costly to install. Strip development and low-density residential areas add to the per person costs. Recent inter-municipal cooperation has provided a note of optimism. In 1975, the Pictou County District Planning Commission erected an activated sludge plant to serve New Glasgow, Trenton, and Stellarton. A similar project (1980) in Kings County treats sewage from Kentville, New Minas, and Coldbrook. This aerated lagoon system is one of the largest such plants in North America: each of the four cells is as wide as a football field and twice as long.[47] Further joint works are being planned. East Hants, for example, received $2 million from the federal government in 1987 to erect joint sewer and water systems for Lantz, Elmsdale, and Enfield. In New Brunswick, both Moncton and Saint John have begun multi-million-dollar sewerage collection and treatment programs.

Halifax continues to have difficulty finding economically efficient means of treating its sewage. Haligonian sewers, portions of which antedate Confederation, use the combined system. In some areas of mainland Halifax, however, only septic tanks and sanitary sewers are available, and surface run-off is carried away in open ditches, culverts, and natural water courses. In 1970, Halifax initiated a program to install interceptor sewers and a treatment plant, but these are very costly, beyond local or provincial means, and the plan had to be discontinued for lack of federal funds. Phase 1 of a harbour clean-up program costing $60 million was due to begin in 1988. In 1993, if everything proceeds on schedule, 60 per cent of Halifax's sewage will be treated before entering the harbour.[48]

The Future

The most pressing problems today include the need for more sewage treatment plants, the search for new methods to accommodate growing types and amounts of chemical wastes, and the increasing flood of urban waste water. The problem of chemical wastes is being fought at the source or by banning the use of such chemicals as DDT and PCBS. Although more advances in waste-water treatment have taken place in the last 15 years than in the previous 100, increased volumes of surface run-off water continue to overload sewerage systems and treatment plants. As a result, approximately 5 per cent of the sewage passing through Canada's treatment plants is discharged untreated.[49] Until recently, the conventional remedy dictated separate sewage systems – estimated in 1969 to cost $45 billion for the 7 million

Canadians, mostly in downtown areas, served by combined sewers.[50] This implies that surface run-off requires no treatment, but this is no longer true. Animal and avian faecal matter in particular has contributed greatly to the deterioration of the bacteriological quality of the Rideau River. Even disinfection by chlorination does not eliminate all disease-causing organisms. In addition, chlorination generates unwanted toxic by-products.[51]

If Canada is to keep pace with ever-increasing volumes of liquid wastes, it will have to devote more money and energy to research. Continued dependence on foreign technology may hinder the search for solutions to uniquely Canadian problems.[52] Needed are more research stations, such as Environment Canada's Wastewater-Technology Centre in Burlington, Ontario, and modern facilities, such as the automatic monitoring and computer control at the Ashbridge's Bay plant in Toronto. Canada has come a long way, but the solution is not yet in sight, nor will there be any simple answer.[53]

NOTES

1 Kathleen Jenkins *Montreal: Island City of the St. Lawrence* (New York 1966) 161
2 *Canadian Freeman* (17 May 1832) in C.M. Godfrey *The Cholera Epidemics in Upper Canada, 1832–1866* (Toronto 1968) 20
3 The Strickland sisters, quoted in Jenkins *Montreal* 288
4 Geoffrey Bilson *A Darkened House: Cholera in Nineteenth-Century Canada* (Toronto 1980) 72, 102, 134, 135
5 T.W. Acheson *Saint John: The Making of a Colonial Urban Community* (Toronto 1985) 204–5
6 Melvin Baker 'The Politics of Assessment: The Water Question in St. John's, 1844–1864' *Acadiensis* (autumn 1982) 71. For Toronto, see Victor L. Russell ed *Forging a Consensus: Historical Essays on Toronto* (Toronto 1984).
7 Quoted in Norman R. Ball ed *Let Us Be Honest and Modest: Technology and Society in Canadian History* (Toronto 1974) 249
8 Charles Singer et al *A History of Technology* (London 1965) chap 16
9 Heather A. MacDougall 'The Genesis of Public Health Reform in Toronto, 1869–1890' *Urban History Review* (Feb 1982) 6
10 Geoffrey Bilson 'The Cholera Epidemic in Saint John, N.B., 1854' *Acadiensis* (autumn 1974) 97
11 Ontario, Board of Health *Annual Report* (1906) 98
12 Stanley Schultz and Clay McShane 'To Engineer the Metropolis: Sewers, Sanitation, and City Planning in Late Nineteenth-Century America' *Journal of American History* (Sept 1978) 395
13 Walter Van Nus 'The Role of Suburban Government in the City-Building Process: The Case of Notre Dame de Grâces, Quebec, 1876–1910' *Urban History Review* (Oct 1984) 93–100
14 *Sixth Annual Report of the Provincial Board of Health of Ontario* (1887) lxiii
15 Singer *History* 518
16 MacDougall 'Genesis' 6
17 See, for example, James D. Davison ed *Mud Creek: The Story of Wolfville, Nova Scotia* (Wolfville 1985) 128.
18 Quoted in the *Charlottetown Daily Examiner* 5 Sept 1885
19 Prince Edward Island *Parliamentary Reporter* (1884)
20 *City of Charlottetown Annual Report* Appendix E, 70
21 Ibid (1890) 72
22 Schultz and McShane 'To Engineer' 394
23 *City of Charlottetown Annual Report* (1892)
24 Public Archives of Prince Edward Island, Minute Book, Commissioners of Sewers and Water Supply, Engineer's Report, Vol. 577, 10 Dec 1898
25 *City of Charlottetown Annual Report* (1898) Appendix E
26 Ibid (1919) 152

27 This section is taken largely from Alan F.J. Artibise *Winnipeg: A Social History of Urban Growth, 1874–1914* (Montreal 1975) chap 13.

28 Ibid 352, n 18

29 Ibid n 23

30 Margaret McAndrews 'The Best Advertisement a City Can Have: Public Health Services in Vancouver, 1886–1888' *Urban History Review* (Feb 1984)

31 Ibid 21

32 Louis P. Cain 'Water and Sanitation Services in Vancouver: An Historical Perspective' *B.C. Studies* (summer 1976) 37

33 Ibid 39

34 For an expanded discussion of this topic, see John H. Taylor 'Urban Autonomy in Canada: Its Evolution and Decline' in G.A. Stelter ed *The Canadian City: Essays in Social History* (Ottawa 1984) 478–500.

35 Commission of Conservation of Canada *Second Annual Report* (Montreal 1911)

36 Ibid 166–7

37 Don Kerr and Stan Hanson *Saskatoon: The First Half of the Century* (Edmonton 1982) 123, 277–8

38 R.A. McLellan 'Trends in Sewage Disposal' *Municipal Utilities* (Oct 1950)

39 Ibid 7

40 *Water and Sanitation* (Jan 1950) 17–21, (Aug 1950) 19–26, 36–8

41 Cain 'Water'

42 Leon Kolankiewicz 'Compliance with Pollution Control Permits in the Lower Fraser Valley, 1967–1981' *B.C. Studies* (1986–7) 44

43 *Sewerage Manual and Directory* (1962) 35

44 Letter from A.J. Schwinghamer, city engineer, Moose Jaw, 23 Jan 1987

45 Halifax *Chronicle Herald* 5 Dec 1986

46 *Water Resources of the Atlantic Provinces* Background Study No. 6 (Ottawa 1969)

47 Nova Scotia, Department of Municipal Affairs 'Provincial Sewer and Water Inventory' (Halifax 1981)

48 *Chronicle Herald* 1 May 1987

49 D.H. Waller 'Problems and Possibilities in Urban Drainage' *Canadian Journal of Civil Engineering* (1976) 394

50 Ibid 4

51 Minister of National Health and Welfare *Municipal Wastewater Disinfection in Canada: Need and Application* (Ottawa 1984)

52 J. Glynn Henry 'Recent Developments in Water Pollution Control' *Canadian Journal of Civil Engineering* (1980) 271

53 This chapter benefited from the comments of A.J. Schwinghamer, city engineer, Moose Jaw; B.W. Brunton, commissioner of works, Etobicoke; Peter E. Kessler, senior engineer, Bureau of Water Pollution Control, City and County of San Francisco; and Thomas Spira, Department of History, University of Prince Edward Island.

PHYLLIS ROSE

Solid Waste

Other fields of public works made essential contributions to the historical development and growth of the Canadian economy and society. The field of solid waste collection and disposal has developed to deal with the by-products of growth. Once, when the value of goods was measured by their longevity, solid wastes were more of a resource than a problem. Almost everything was made of natural materials, which were either recycled in one way or another or, if not, eventually returned to the land. Often the principal recycling agents were pigs and chickens. Country people and many town residents composted all the organic wastes that the pigs and chickens would not eat. With industrialization – development of a society based on mass production and mass consumption – increasing amounts of man-made materials were used. In quantity and quality these by-products of modern Canadian society posed problems of collection and disposal with which earlier Canadians did not have to deal.

Until recently, plenty of room existed on the outskirts of any village, town, or city to locate a communal dump. In such circumstances dumps created relatively little hazard or unpleasantness. Once Canada changed from its rural beginnings to a highly urbanized country, the disposal of its garbage, empty cans and bottles, wastepaper, and later plastics

became a real challenge. Collection and disposal of solid waste traditionally have been considered solely local, municipal responsibilities.

In most 19th-century cities, municipal crews picked up the waste at curbside and carted it away to the dump. Dumping refuse on open land or into water was by far the most common practice. Well into the 20th century, 'since urban methods were diverse as well as plentiful, no universally accepted methods of collection and disposal had developed. In addition to organic wastes – garbage, manure, human excrement, dead animals – there were also tons of coal and wood ashes, street sweepings, wastepaper, old shoes and other rejectments.'[1] Throughout the 19th and early 20th centuries scavengers roamed urban streets and rural areas looking for rags, bones, wastepaper, metal leavings, and any other possible valuable material and recycled them to manufacturers or middlemen. A variety of private disposal services gradually emerged in the late 19th and early 20th centuries. They have been complemented by the participation of various levels of government.

After the Second World War, closed trucks took to the streets and back alleys, replacing horse-drawn carts and open dump trucks. With the ability to compact tons of refuse in one gulp, these noisy trucks quickly became the backbone of

Port cities could use solid waste to extend harbourfronts: Toronto, 1922. (NA PA-84921)

Horse-drawn wagons taking solid waste to the Toronto waterfront, a common sight in 1915 and not regarded as at all improper (NA PA-61249)

A Toronto collector carries domestic coal ashes to his wagon in 1918. (NA PA-71001)

the collection industry. Rear-end loaders became a familiar sight and sound in residential communities as they emptied cans at curbside and carted the waste to dump and incinerator.

Municipalities began to pick up a limited number of garbage containers, perhaps two or three from each homeowner. Commercial enterprises required more service, and private contractors stepped into the gap during the 20th century. To deal with large quantities of waste, containerized collection developed in commercial and industrial markets. Front-loading trucks picked up, emptied, and compacted container loads of as much as 0.764 sq m (8 cu yd) of garbage. Another containerized system, roll-off, is used for larger volumes of industrial refuse.

Since the mid-1950s the population explosion and the proliferation of non-returnable plastic containers have led to enormous problems in waste disposal and redistribution of responsibility. Thousands of open dumps were fouling water systems; incinerators were fouling the air. Solid waste had once been a municipal concern; now provincial and federal governments began to take an active interest. Today, provincial ministries are generally responsible for a wide range of services intended to control contaminant emissions, establish environmental safeguards, manage water and waste, and develop and maintain the natural environment. Environment Canada is the key federal department responsible for environmental quality throughout the country. It administers the Environmental Contaminants Act, which is implemented through the Environmental Protection Service. Toxic substances are one of the high-priority issues for Environment Canada, which has been researching the various technologies of waste disposal. In 1969, Ontario became one of the first provinces to announce a major change in government policy regarding solid waste management. It incorporated all aspects of environmental and pollution control into the Department of Energy and Resources Management, later into the Ministry of the Environment. The legislation was considered the most advanced in the country, as it instituted environmental assessment procedures.

LANDFILL OPERATIONS

In the second half of the 20th century open dumps were being replaced by sanitary landfills. A sanitary landfill is an excavated site that uses the excavated soil to cover the waste. In general, there are three types of sanitary landfill. The first type is unrestricted in regard to material. It must be located in some spot where there is no possible chance of ground water pollution. Such a site is difficult to find and depends on thorough geological investigation. A second type is the site that can take ordinary municipal waste refuse, excluding liquid wastes from industries of most kinds. Here, too, great care must be taken to select a spot where ground water will not be contaminated. The third kind of landfill is used only for materials that will not decompose or leach. These can, supposedly, be placed almost anywhere that fill is needed, without any chance of later problems with pollution. Supposedly,

they produce no odour, no vermin, no flies. Recently, public works engineers have designed highly sophisticated sanitary landfill sites.

Most rural areas still follow the simplest methods. New Brunswick, among other provinces, has found that regular collection in rural areas represents a great challenge. Not only are hauling distances and equipment requirements substantial, but the administrative framework to organize a collection schedule is usually non-existent. Because of this and also because land-use pressures are not as great in the countryside, the traditional response has been to use small local dumps, often run on shoestring budgets. In June 1986 the Environmental Council of New Brunswick recommended to the minister of municipal affairs and environment that containers be placed in sparsely populated outlying areas, where residents could drop off their waste. The containers would be emptied regularly.

Recent legislation in many provinces governs the operation of sanitary landfill sites. In traditional dumps, solid waste is spread out in thin layers, compacted with a bulldozer, and covered with clean soil at the end of each day. When the site is filled, it can be covered with a few metres of clean soil and then used for a park or some other purpose. For sites that accept only clean landfill, designers have created spectacular spaces –for example, at Expo '67 (Montreal) and Ontario Place (Toronto). Winnipeg's Northeast Landfill will be a 162-ha (400-acre) recreational park; already the park has been named Kilcona, and a nine-hole golf course has been built on a 27-ha (67-acre) adjacent parcel.[2] Landfill sites used for playing fields, ski hills, and public enjoyment guarantee that land will remain undeveloped and under public ownership for the foreseeable future.

Garbage dump at the foot of York Street in Toronto, 1925, being levelled by men with pitch-forks (NA PA-86054)

Civic-owned abattoirs ensured proper standards and methods of slaughter. Toronto, 1924 (NA PA-86959)

As landfills began to be used to accommodate mushrooming industrial wastes, including liquid and hazardous materials, most pits were found not to be environmentally secure. Over time, regulations were developed that prescribed impermeable soil conditions and ground water well below the landfill. They specified that the ground must slope away from the landfill in all directions, so that water cannot run across its surface. A secure landfill should have an underground system to collect any leachate, pump it out, and treat it. It also became necessary to keep accurate records of what is in the landfill. Harold Crooks describes work at such a place:

The equipment operator spends his shift trying to develop the working face on an incline between twenty and thirty degrees, spreading the refuse against the slope while moving a steel-wheeled crawler dozer up and down, tearing and compacting the waste and eliminating voids. He makes passes across the slope, depressing the surface until it rebounds as much as it is pushed down. As construction of the cell progresses, the earth-moving equipment spreads and compacts cover material which has been excavated by dragline nearby and transported to the site by dump truck. At day's end, the cover is graded to prevent erosion and to keep water from ponding.[3]

Sanitary landfills have become engineering achievements requiring enormous technical expertise.

A modern, secure landfill site is usually a huge clay basin, its bottom at least 15 m (50 ft) thick and resting on solid bedrock. It is equipped with a drainage system, gas venting system, and monitoring wells for inspecting the contents. It includes a wastewater treatment plant to process any toxic leakage. Before disposal of materials, chemists analyse the industrial wastes that will be accepted for burial. Workers separate shipments on arrival to prevent contact between those that might react with one another. If wastes are liquid, they are turned into paste before being packed into drums. After burial, the wastes remain under continual surveillance.

In addition to finding and devising safe means to move and store wastes, one must also face the increasingly difficult problem of finding acceptable waste disposal sites. Three major landfills and two minor ones exist within the Greater Vancouver Region. Two of the major sites have 25-year capacity remaining. Other communities are not so fortunate. Toronto is quickly running out of capacity.

Most communities truck the waste picked up at curbside directly to the landfill. A few major cities use transfer stations, where curbside pick-up material is forwarded to the landfill in larger trucks. Collection trucks, both municipal and private, enter these plants over a weigh scale and dump their loads, under direction, onto a large flat floor. The material is crushed and pushed into a hopper, where it is compacted for the transfer trailer. A single driver can haul waste picked up by four municipal collection trucks.

The transfer station in Victoria was formerly used to put collected wastes onto a barge, which could then be towed to sea; the wastes were simply dumped in the Pacific Ocean. The station was converted to a transfer station for hauling to Victoria's sanitary landfill. Edmonton operates two transfer stations; Toronto seven.

The site of Halifax's transfer station was once a harbourside dump, which continually oozed its contents into the water. For a few years, an incinerator operated next door, but it, too, is gone. Because of the pressure of a growing city in search of land and because a good deal

Most solid waste from Metro Toronto is deposited at the Brock West Landfill Site, which is rapidly nearing capacity. (MTWD)

of the area is exposed bedrock, wastes from the city are transferred for hauling 32 km (20 mi) to a regional landfill site.[4]

The area around Drumheller, Alberta, uses a unique waste transfer system. Its central feature is an enormous stationary storage bin (35 cu m, or 46 cu yd) that can be inverted so that its contents can be dumped into an open-top, 84-cu-m (110-cu-yd) trailer. The idea was based on silage dumpers that farmers use to collect freshly cut silage from a field and then dump into trucks travelling beside the unit. A small chute is the entry point for individual bags of garbage, but larger quantities can be accommodated as well. When the container is full, a hydraulic system raises the container and inverts it over the open-top trailer. Litter screens cover the top when the trailer is loaded. At the landfill site, waste is removed by several sets of floor chains.

A similar system of bins and trailers is being used in Banff National Park. Waste is hauled out of the park to Calgary's Spy Hill Landfill, a round trip of over 410 km (250 mi). The bin sites within the park are surrounded by steel walls to keep bears out. Park employees collect waste from townsites and campgrounds in packer trucks and prepare it for delivery in large trucks to the distant Spy Hill landfill site.

Potential problems often arise in the vicinity of existing and proposed landfill sites. These areas can produce significant volumes of landfill gas, a mixture made up mostly of equal volumes of carbon dioxide and methane, an odourless, colourless gas. Explosive when it is in contact with air, the mixture can ignite. Landfill gas can migrate for considerable distances.

Winnipeg has been aware of the problem since 1974, when seven large industrial buildings were constructed on the St Boniface Landfill Site. As the site settled, large cracks appeared in the floors of these buildings, allowing landfill gas to enter. Ignition caused several small fires at these cracks. These buildings were eventually demolished or used for unoccupied cold storage only. Investigation showed that Winnipeg has at least 36 active and closed landfill sites within its boundaries, including engineering sanitary landfills, municipal garbage dumps, incinerator ash dumps, and pits filled with topsoils and vegetation. Each site presents a different potential risk only recently recognized. However, public

After the Second World War, many Canadian cities moved away from open dump-type garbage trucks to enclosed packers, such as these in Saskatoon. (CPWA Sask Chapter)

At the Scarborough Transfer Station, solid waste picked up by neighbourhood collector trucks is put on larger trucks for removal to disposal sites. (MTWD)

works officials can solve the problems or prevent use of the site.

INCINERATION

One of the first alternatives developed to the outright dumping of wastes was incineration. Small individual units were designed for use in backyards, homes, or apartment houses. While the short-term effect was to reduce the amount of solid waste for collection and disposal, small incinerators produced large amounts of fly-ash (tiny particles of unburned and partially burned material) that blow away from the fire. Faulty small-scale incinerators contributed heavily to air pollution load in Canada. In recent decades, they have been banned by many communities.

Larger municipal units were developed, which have been important alternatives to dumping. As early as 1890, when Toronto's population had grown to 160,000, officials recognized the need for an economical and sanitary method for the disposal of household waste. As a result, they built a 'garbage crematory.' With two furnaces, the plant operated for only a few years before it was itself destroyed by fire. But incineration was considered a valid method for disposing of solid wastes.

More incinerators were built, and by 1967, when Metropolitan Toronto took over disposal of all municipal refuse generated within Metro, seven incinerators were in operation. The most modern plant was built on Commissioners Street in 1955. It consisted of six circular mono-hearth furnaces and had a rated capacity of 815 tons per day. Most of Toronto's incinerators were built prior to the 1960s, before there was as much public concern and instrumentation to measure their contribution to air pollution. Only the units that underwent costly rehabilitation could expect to operate to today's

standards. Renovated in 1974, the Commissioners Street plant is the only incinerator operating in Toronto today. It was rehabilitated by installing three new rocker grate furnaces, three conditioning towers to cool the effluent gases, and three electrostatic precipitators to reduce the particulate emission to meet the provincial Air Pollution Code.

As early as 1910, a 3-ton-per-hour incinerator was built in Regina. This eventually was expanded to a 10-ton-per-hour facility, but it had to be shut down in 1981 because of the expected cost to retrofit it with air pollution control equipment. A 25-ton-per-hour pulverizer has been installed in the incinerator building to take advantage of useful waste storage, but the furnaces themselves have been dismantled.

In Montreal, a modern 1,200-ton-per-day incinerator plant was completed in 1970. This $8.8-million system is more efficient in terms of reducing the amount of pollution emitted, and more economical as well. Its waste-to-energy design produces steam by burning solid wastes. The steam is distributed along 6,096 m (20,000 ft) of pipes made of carbon steel surrounded by carbon insulation and a stainless steel jacket. The pipes distribute the steam – at a pressure of 260 psi at a temperature of 302°C (575°F) – to 17 plants, mainly along the Canadian Pacific Railway right of way, including clothing manufacturers, laundering and dry cleaning services, and an industrial plant.[5]

Prince Edward Island is also delivering steam generated from the combustion of solid wastes. In the planning stage for five years, the $10-million incinerator/steam plant went onstream in June 1983. The Charlottetown plant serves about one-third of the island's population and sells steam to a nearby hospital.[6]

Several controlled-air incinerators

Toronto's 'garbage train' on its way to the civic incinerator, 1925 (NA PA-87013)

The Commissioners Street Incinerator disposes of 3 per cent of Metro Toronto's refuse. (MTWD)

Energy from waste: Victoria Hospital, London, built its facility 1986–7, as part of a major expansion program. The hospital asked: 'Can Victoria Hospital Help Your Health By Treating Your Garbage? You Bet.' (VH)

Victoria Hospital: Trucks enter the tipping bay and dump solid waste through the doors on the right into the pit, from which it is taken by bridge crane to the feed hopper and the primary and secondary burning chambers. (VH)

process solid waste in British Columbia. At Lake Cowichan, a plant is located in an abandoned borrow pit, approximately 3 km (1.9 mi) from the village centre. There are no nearby residences. A site at Duncan, cleared from a sloping forest area with an adjacent depression, is used for residue and building waste disposal. The incinerator at Duncan's Royal Jubilee Hospital is located next to the heating plant, within the complex of hospital buildings.

The Greater Vancouver Region has approved a contract for construction of the area's first solid-waste incinerator. The plant, located in South Burnaby, was expected to begin operation in 1988. It was to cost $47.7 million, including $5 million for the most modern pollution

Victoria Hospital: Heat produced in the boiler is used both for steam heating and to power a turbine producing electric power. Operation is monitored by computers and television cameras. (VH)

control equipment, and was expected to handle about 15 per cent of the region's refuse. Energy generated by the incinerator will be sold to a nearby packaging plant. From 50 to 90 collection vehicles a day will deliver to the plant. Emission limits set for the scrubbing equipment are said to be the most stringent in North America.[7]

There remains widespread public debate over the environmental impact of garbage-burning incinerators. Concerns range from short-term fears that the ash and air emissions of incineration pose new pollution threats to long-term worries that the high cost of incineration will make other, longer-term strategies like recycling impractical.

RECYCLING

Historically, the only alternatives for disposing of solid wastes have been to dump and to burn; the resulting by-products have polluted land, air, and water. As incinerators spew unacceptable levels of toxins into the air and as sanitary landfill sites are filling up, many people regard recycling as the solution to the solid waste problem. This concept dates back to the rag and bone collectors. Many Canadian municipalities work with local organizations to promote awareness of the idea that individual citizens, private companies, and public agencies can no longer produce large amounts of solid wastes without regard for their environmental and economic costs. Recycling programs attempt to reduce at the source the amount of waste generated, for example, by using refillable pop bottles instead of throwaway cans. One of the oldest forms of waste recycling is the reprocessing of wastepaper. For many years, wastepaper was collected by the Boy Scouts and the Salvation Army. As their efforts faded, residents were served by public works depart-

ments. In many urban areas, since 1974, bundled newspapers have been collected curbside weekly or bi-weekly by municipal crews or authorized private contractors.

Communities are now paying attention to recycling other materials. Many municipalities now collect glass containers and metal cans from large bins placed in parking lots of shopping centres and recreation centres. Other programs are also in operation, such as leaf composting, white goods recovery, oil recycling, handling of hazardous waste from private households, and waste paper recovery from municipal offices. Some public works officials think that 'operating a recycling program has taught us that only convenient uncomplicated methods will win public support.'[8] A certain amount of preparation is required before residents set out recyclables. Newspapers must be tied with string; glass and metal containers should be rinsed. While not elaborate, these processes require an effort beyond that of simply discarding the material.

More and more communities have made this effort. In 1977, a private contractor in Kitchener, Ontario, asked residents to bundle newspapers and place them next to other waste on normal collection days. The contractor's packer trucks were fitted with racks on one side so that newspapers and other waste could be collected simultaneously. At first, less than 1 per cent of the population co-operated, but a promotional campaign increased interest. A conservation handbook was prepared, featuring articles like 'The Art of Discriminating Shopping' and 'Compost – Gold in Your Garbage.' Some homes received blue 'We Recycle' boxes to hold glass bottles and metal cans with bundled newspapers set on top. The blue boxes were designed to make collection more convenient for both residents and collection staff. They also serve as a constant reminder to participate. As a result of the efforts, participation levels increased to 70 to 80 per cent, indicating that the public is attuned to environmental concerns and is ready to help. Kitchener now recovers two-thirds of its newspaper, one-third of its glass, and one-quarter of its metal cans. Based on the success of the program, Ontario has developed a program that offers funds to all municipalities in support of the start-up cost and the first five years of operating costs of a community recycling program. Ottawa, Gloucester, Nepean, and Mississauga are among those communities that have started the program.

Perhaps an indication of a future trend, the township of South-West Oxford (population 8,400) was the first municipality in Ontario to require recycling. If recyclable glass, newspaper, and metal containers have not been separated, household garbage is not collected, and a large orange sticker is applied to the garbage bag or bin. To date, only one other Canadian municipality, Saanich, on Vancouver Island, has a similar mandatory recycling program.

Some recycling efforts have gone beyond individual municipalities. In Churchill, Manitoba, 3,500 tons of scrap metal, which had been dumped haphazardly over a long period and mixed with demolition rubble, gravel, and other non-recyclable materials, were moved to recycling centres in southern Manitoba. This complex project required varied input from federal, provincial, and municipal agencies, as well as the private sector. It was necessary to arrange financing, then a favourable transportation rate from Canadian National Railways. Agencies that had contributed scrap metal to the dump were expected to help financially. The metal included heavy-gauge water pipe, culverts, beams, radio towers, grain-screening cylinders, boilers, buses, metal drums, several transformers, and other consumer and industrial products.[9] Approximately 3,000 metal drums and three transformers were assessed and declared safe for travelling by Environment Canada and the Manitoba Environment and Workplace Safety and Health staff. The decision allowed the railway to carry the metal. The end use of this site will be typical: 'After further cleanup and disposal of non-recyclable materials, maybe we'll make a park out of it or a golf course.'[10]

Recycling solid wastes has become a business as well as a civic responsibility. Private companies now hold contracts with many municipalities for separate curbside recycling collections. Industries historically have been held responsible for collecting waste that they produce, and there, too, private contractors fill the gap. They also serve large installations and entertainment facilities, so that front-end packers haul from the Parliament Buildings, army barracks, and professional ball parks.

A company established five years ago by two engineering professors at the University of New Brunswick handles recyclying in Fredericton. The company reorganized and expanded local collection, sorting, sensification, and marketing of householder-segregated materials – newsprint, fine and corrugated paper, glass, plastics, ferrous substances, and aluminum. Next on Fredericton's agenda is a demonstration composting project. Large, private waste-management firms are developing resource-recovery plants for a number of Canadian municipalities.

HAZARDOUS WASTES

In recent years, the management of hazardous solid wastes has been a focus of discussion and research in Canada.

Quebec, Ontario, Alberta, and British Columbia every year produce about three million tons of hazardous, potentially toxic wastes.[11] But until the 1970s, the dumping of hazardous wastes was not understood to be a special environmental problem. Before that time government agencies in Canada were not required to monitor where toxic wastes were dumped. In 1971 the Waste Management Branch of Ontario's Ministry of the Environment organized a meeting of about 200 government and industry representatives to discuss problems created by industrial refuse. At that time it was assumed that about half of the province's annual output ended up in landfills. The ministry decided to fund a treatment plant in an industrialized part of southern Ontario. A parcel of land was bought in Mississauga and a long lease awarded to Canadian Industries Ltd to operate a major incineration facility. Dwindling support caused the plant to close in 1978.

A provincial crown agency, the Ontario Waste Management Corporation (OWMC), was created in November 1980. Its mandate is to implement a province-wide, long-term program aimed not only at treating and storing wastes but also at assisting in reducing and recycling them. OWMC conducts studies to identify the type, location, and quantity of waste generated, assess available treatment technology, and identify opportunities for encouraging reduction and recycling of wastes.

An environmentally and socially acceptable site operates in Alberta as a fully integrated facility, the Alberta Special Waste Treatment Centre, at Swan Hills. Municipal and industrial waste management programs operate throughout the province, and the centre provides the ultimate repository for organic and inorganic wastes for which there is no other disposal, exchange, or recycling option.

The hazardous waste section occupies 9.3 ha (23 acres) of the 130-ha (320-acre) tract.

The centre has a variety of facilities: administration and laboratory buildings, a weigh scale, crane and containerized unloading, physical/chemical treatment plant for inorganic wastes, incineration plant for organic wastes, tank farm and drum storage area, deep well for clean run-off and process water, landfill cells for dry treatment residues, water retention ponds for site run-off, and a transformer treatment area. The centre processes 20,000 tons of waste annually, of which approximately 75 per cent is organic. It recently acquired a hazardous waste shredder, which takes contaminated 205-l (45-gallon) drums, along with liquids, solids, and sludges, and reduces them to fist-sized pieces in seconds for easier handling, storage, and/or incineration.

Some hazardous wastes can be recycled, but until recently industry has not bothered to recover materials or energy from its hazardous wastes. So long as fresh raw materials and fuels were relatively inexpensive, industry found it easier and cheaper simply to dispose of the waste and buy new materials. As the costs of energy, raw materials, and waste disposal continue to rise, industry has found it more economical to recover and recycle the waste produced.

Another approach to recycling has recently developed, involving the transfer of one company's waste to another company that can use it. The wastes most likely to be transferred are concentrated acids, bases, solvents, oils, other flammable wastes to be burned as fuels, surplus chemicals, and wastes with high concentrations of recoverable metals. In order to be cost effective, the locations of buyer and seller must be convenient. The Canadian Waste Material Exchange reported that in 1986 it added 126 new listings, to bring the total to over 2,500. It recorded 21 new exchanges, which added 10,000 tons per year. The replacement value of the new exchanges was $1.4 million, bringing the total over the nine years of operations to $10.4 million.

One successful reuse of a waste material involves pickle acid, a waste liquid from steel processing. The pickle acid is transferred to a power plant that generates electricity with geothermal steam. As the steam comes out of the earth, it contains small amounts of hydrogen sulphide. After the steam has been used to generate electricity, it is treated with pickle acid. The iron sulphate in the pickle acid reacts with the hydrogen sulphide to form a sludge of iron sulphide and sulphur. This sludge is a valuable addition to some soils.

Another alternative for hazardous waste disposal is incineration. Pesticides and PCBs can be totally destroyed by burning at high temperatures. Complicated and expensive equipment is available to prevent toxic fumes from escaping up the smokestack. Chlorinated organic materials can be incinerated in a cost-effective manner by using them as fuel in manufacturing cement. Cement, made by burning a mixture of lime and clay, requires large amounts of energy. Tests have shown that chlorinated organic wastes could replace as much as 20 per cent of the regular fuel and be burned away completely.

The Canada Cement Lafarge plant in Woodstock, Ontario, recently burned more than 1.14 million l (250,000 gallons) of selected waste solvents as kiln fuel in a successful test. The Ontario Ministry of the Environment issued a special temporary permit for the incineration, which was monitored by the Ontario Research Foundation. Materials included solvents from the automotive paint, ink and printing, cosmetics, and photographic industries. All solvents were carefully screened for PCBs, and only small quantities of benzene, sulphur, and nitrogen were permitted. Materials were burned at temperatures as high as 2940°F (1600°C). Smokestack emissions were observed and compared with emissions from conventional fuel. Researchers found no significant chemical increases and no adverse effects on the company's cement products.[12]

Chemical and biological processes have been developed that can treat hazardous wastes. Bacteria can destroy some organic chemicals using trickling filters. Wastewater passes through a bed of stones or synthetic materials covered by a film of bacteria. As the water trickles downward, biodegradable materials are destroyed by the bacteria. Composting is a tried and true method for degrading organic waste with bacteria.

Because the construction of new treatment facilities is very expensive, smaller communities have sought other options in dealing with hazardous wastes. In New Brunswick, the quantity of toxic material produced annually is not great enough to warrant construction of an expensive destruction facility similar to those existing or being built in Ontario and Quebec. So New Brunswick has arranged to ship its hazardous waste out of the province.

This option, for other reasons, also appeals to larger metropolitan areas. Metropolitan Toronto Chairman Dennis Flynn has suggested shipping waste to northern Ontario by train and burying it in abandoned mine sites. He said that the mines are made of impervious rock that would stop the leakage of toxins into the environment, and the province could charge municipalities a fee for the waste disposal. This idea parallels a suggestion made by Ross L. Clark, commissioner of works for Metropolitan Toronto in the 1960s, to bale Metro Toronto's solid waste and ship it by rail to disposal sites hundreds of kilometres north.

New technologies for disposal of hazardous waste are appearing frequently: deep well injection, new methods of burial in secure landfills, and burning wastes on ships at sea. Ocean incineration more than a hundred miles (161 km) offshore, using closed barges to transfer refuse, is a possible option for large maritime communities. But some wastes cannot be recycled or effectively treated. In such cases, hazardous material must be separated from the non-hazardous part at the site where it is produced. Hazardous components have to be concentrated, using a solidification process. This step reduces the costs of handling, transporting, and eventual disposal. A secure landfill site for toxic materials differs from a traditional landfill where household trash is buried. Specifications call for a filled secure landfill pit to be capped with a layer of impermeable clay or a synthetic material or both. Water from monitoring wells located in and around the pit should be analysed to detect leaks.

ADVOCACY GROUPS

While the idea of environmental concern is not new, the issues have evolved over time. In the 19th century, smell, aesthetics, and growing rodent populations were primary worries in small towns near sites to which growing cities transported their wastes. Later, the recognized connection between waste and disease increased anxiety. Today, such concerns are expressed by organized environmental groups like Pollution Probe, the Canadian Environmental Law Association, and the Friends of the Earth.

Many local groups organize for the purpose within an area. In the Region of Durham, east of Toronto, residents have formed PACT – Pickering Ajax Citizens Together – to fight a plan for a new sanitary landfill site in their area. Durham since 1970 and the Region of York, north of Toronto, since 1983 have had agreements with Metropolitan Toronto for joint use of landfill sites. Unimpressed by warnings that space is running out, still they do not want a dump in their backyard. Who does? Since the 'not in my backyard' syndrome is widespread, 'waste disposal is becoming a world problem of gigantic proportions that unites municipalities.'[13]

Public participation has become a prerequisite for managing solid waste. Despite occasional hostility, there are important examples of effective co-operation. The lower BC mainland is a regional community with a population of about one and a half million people. In October 1983, the community decided to develop a co-operative solid waste management plant. One feature of the Lower Mainland Refuse Project was its prominent 'public interface' program. Solid waste management had been a volatile public issue for a decade, with various attempts to locate facilities in several different suburban municipalities. This time representatives of some 20 key public and special interest groups were invited to participate early in the process, and eventually more than 4,000 citizens became involved. Most residents favoured waste reduction, separation of refuse at source, and increased public education. They urged that the volume of refuse buried in landfills be reduced. And they were willing to contribute financially and through individual recycling efforts to achieve a more environmentally sound waste management program.

Seven workshops were held to share technical information with a core group of about 20 interest group leaders, in part to gain feedback from the participants.

Five issues of a four-page newsletter were distributed, with articles expressing various points of view, including both positive and negative reaction. Two conferences were held to review the draft recommendation with more than 500 representatives. This comprehensive and systematic program of public information and consultation accounted for more than half of the project's budget. The final report of the project manager supported a major program of incineration, with the objective of ending the landfilling of raw waste within 10 years.[14]

Over the relatively short history of solid waste disposal, no major new methods have replaced the sanitary landfill site and the incinerator. Each of the major newly developed technologies – composting, refuse-derived fuel, and resource recovery – enjoyed a brief period in the limelight, but most have failed to realize fully the performance claimed for them. Plants have been closed, or continue to run with drastically reduced operation levels, and many major corporations have withdrawn from the field. Many primitive methods, especially open dumping, are still common in some communities. Periodically, new variations on these familiar themes have appeared, mostly in recycling activities, such as shredding or magnetic separation of components.

The change in composition of municipal waste during the past 30 years has come about because of the continent-wide increase in production and prompt discard after use of plastics, bottles, and paper. Primitive people, in caves or tribal communities, had problems with solid wastes. Every once in a while they needed to collect a few bones, skins, entrails, broken tools, and shattered pottery and carry them off a distance and deposit them on the ground – an unsophisticated but immediate solution,

which created a repository for future archaeologists.

Today, with a vastly increased population crowded into urban centres and producing waste in growing varieties and amounts, modern Canadian society has to resolve the dilemma. As public works officials dealt with the early-20th-century problems of dirt and disease, there is every reason to believe that specialists and the general public will cope with the solid waste problems of the century's later decades.

NOTES

1 Martin V. Melosi *Garbage in the Cities* (College Station, Texas 1981) 40
2 *Civic Public Works* 35 (June 1983) SG2
3 Harold Crooks *Dirty Business* (Toronto 1983) 23
4 R.C. MacKenzie 'Halifax Sets Landfill Trend in Nova Scotia' *Civic Public Works* 36 (June 1984) 22
5 Eileen Goodman 'Montreal Converts Its Garbage into Steam' *Civic Public Works* 35 (June 1983) 22
6 'P.E.I. Plant Proves an Alternative to Landfill' *Civic Public Works* 35 (Aug 1983) 16
7 'GVRD Approves New Garbage Incinerator' *Civic Public Works* 37 (June 1985) 11
8 Steve Gyorffy 'Pilot Recycling Program Goes City-wide' *APWA Reporter* (Jan 1988) 20
9 'Scrap Metal Site' *Civic Public Works* 39 (Aug 1987) 19
10 Ibid
11 Crooks *Dirty Business* 84
12 'Cement Plant Tries Wastes as Kiln Fuel' *Civic Public Works* 37 (March 1985) 28
13 Derwyn Shea *Globe and Mail* 20 Jan 1988, 12
14 Desmond M. Connor and Ann C. Svendsen 'Involving the Public in Solid Waste Management Planning' *Civic Public Works* 39 (July 1987) 64–9

MARK FRAM and JEAN SIMONTON

Public Buildings

Public buildings can be as interesting for their architecture as for their engineering. Public building involves both process and product, and in what follows there is at least as much emphasis on the process as on its products. As products, public buildings vary wildly in type, scale, history, and importance. There is in Canada an almost limitless range of public functions, most of which require permanent accommodation.

Public buildings comprise all properties that are not houses or places of private commerce. The core group consists of post offices, legislatures, court houses, town halls, and the associated structures that were and are built for public service and access by one or another level of government.

Spending public money for capital facilities inevitably requires some formal bureaucratic process. Canadian jurisdictions needing many facilities, notably the federal and provincial governments, tended quite early to establish departments of public works to oversee their property portfolios. Initially, this work was the responsibility of a chief engineer, but a parallel position of chief architect soon appeared to deal with many types of public building within the larger mandate of public works. Smaller jurisdictions, such as counties and municipalities, where major building activi-

ties were undertaken less frequently, often created special building committees for specific projects, such as municipal halls.

Public building design was often an overt political decision. Public buildings have always symbolized the role of government in society and how that government wishes to be perceived by current and future populations. Sometimes the intent was to create an imposing government presence conveying strength and stability and setting high standards of architectural design and technical competence; at other times, the purpose was to provide moderate and economical structures blending into the architectural fabric of the community. Beyond appearances often lay the intention to stimulate the economic activity of the private sector or to encourage private investment.

Confederation in 1867 rationalized and formalized much of British North America's ongoing public building activity and instigated a flurry of construction of new federal facilities, most notably of post offices, custom houses, and inland revenue offices. The British North America Act of 1867 set out responsibilities for the provinces (such as judicial administration, education, and health) and the federal government (for example, immigration, customs, postal service, and

Library of Parliament, Ottawa, during construction, 1860s. It was a thoroughly modern building, with the first iron-framed roof in Canada and double windows to help keep out the cold. Still in use, it survived the 1916 fire that destroyed the rest of the Centre Block. (NA C-80781)

defence). In line with these duties existing public buildings were transferred to the provinces or retained by the central government.

Each level of government (and its agencies) has built a range of facilities in line with its legal responsibilities. The government of Canada has designed and erected its own Parliament Buildings and departmental buildings; post offices, customs houses, and national revenue offices; immigration buildings and quarantine stations; armouries, drill halls, and prisons; and observatories, national parks, and experimental farms. Each province has built legislative and departmental buildings; court houses, registry offices, and jails; hospitals and asylums; universities, technical colleges, and schools; and provincial parks. Municipalities have built town halls, markets, fire halls, police stations, libraries, schools, and public recreation facilities.

Architectural expression in Canada has been shaped externally by the colonial legacy and by powerful influences from the United States. Canadian public buildings have borrowed from British and American precedents. This national expression was further influenced by the country's unique political organization. Strong regional identities in Canada

Registry Office, L'Assomption, Quebec. A single-function building: secure storage for property registration records (ŇA PA-36748)

Near Kemptville, Ontario: a typical rural one-room schoolhouse (OMCC)

Ontario Psychiatric Hospital, St Thomas, Ontario. Such institutions appeared in response to widening demand for social services. (Mark Fram)

Bonsecours Market, Montreal, symbolizes city's ambition to be gateway to the North American interior. (NA C5017)

militated against a centralized model of public design. Provincial legislatures provide the best collective illustration of this phenomenon. Each is a distinctive local expression that fuses in its own way British, provincial, and American state models.[1] Municipal building tended to reflect architectural fashions of the day.

THREE BUILDING TYPES

At initial glance, there appears an almost endless variety of approaches to the design of public building. But we can gain insights into the building process at all levels of government and the problems and forms of many other public buildings through examination of three general types: post offices, a federal responsibility since Confederation; district/county court houses, built by the colonies and later by provincial governments,[2] with local involvement; and town halls, always a purely municipal responsibility.[3]

Post Offices

The Post Office became one of the major clients of the federal Department of Public Works after 1867, and post offices reflected most strongly the presence of the federal government in 19th-century Canada. Between 1881 and 1896, the government constructed 78 post offices.

Post Office, Markham, Ontario. By the 1960s, the federal government sought low visibility. (Mark Fram)

As these buildings frequently contained facilities for other federal offices, such as customs and inland revenue, they were often substantial structures, regarded as important public landmarks in their communities.

Surviving post offices from this era represent a large part of the work undertaken by the Department of Public Works.[4] They reveal much about the operation of this department and its approach to the design of a large number of facilities with specific and often similar functional requirements. Of particular interest was the development of the standard plan, periodically updated and modified, which addressed the functional similarities of post offices. A standard plan was a possibility only when Public Works became responsible for the construction of a large number of similar facilities.[5]

Since Confederation, post offices have reflected in their design much of the federal government's feeling about public architecture at any given time. In the 1880s, they were used to create an imposing government presence across the country. But by the 1960s, the physical visibility of the federal government had a low priority, and many of the older post offices were replaced by small facilities deliberately located off the main street.

Richmond County Court House, Arichat, Nova Scotia, attests to stature and solidity of colonial justice. (C.A. Hale, CIHB)

Standard plan for Saskatchewan court houses, 1920s, used in Assiniboia, Gravelbourg, Melfort, Shaunavon, and Wynyard (CIHB)

Court Houses

The oldest surviving court houses in Canada date from the British colonial period – only with the arrival of the British system was there a need for a specialized building for judicial purposes. County court houses such as those at Picton, Ontario (1832–41), Gagetown, New Brunswick (1836–7), and Arichat, Nova Scotia (1846–7), attest to the stature and solidity of the judicial function in the colonies.

Unlike post offices, court houses involved various levels of government – though provinces took over financial responsibility as they entered Confederation – and thus reflect the full range of the public building process. Some embodied the central federal agency, with its standard plans, such as the territorial district court houses in Wynyard, Shaunavon, Gravelbourg, Melfort, and Assiniboia in what are now the prairie provinces. However, there was the variety and eclecticism of the efforts of individual building committees, such as Ontario's district/county court houses – for instance, in London (Scottish Gothic), Perth (Greek Revival), and Brampton (orientally tinged Gothic/Classical).

The special value of court houses as a building type is tied to their visual importance, often emphasized by architects. Frequently, these buildings were centrally located, carefully designed to stand out from other forms of public building nearby, and widely regarded as landmark structures. As a type, court

Middlesex County Court House, London, Ontario. Individual building committees produced variety and eclecticism. (CIHB)

houses comprise a well-documented set of architecturally and historically significant buildings.

Town Halls

The variety of Canadian town-hall construction mirrored the variety of municipal scale, ambition, and wealth. Town halls are closely linked to communities and reveal much about local character and a municipality's perception of itself. Some, such as those at Pontiac, Quebec, Bath, Ontario, and Mortlach, Saskatchewan, offered no more than a room for local council meetings and tended to be simple buildings, similar in size and design to schools, churches, and other buildings in the community. Others combined in a grand and imposing edifice several different functions – public markets, police stations, fire halls, courtrooms, opera houses, sometimes even the administrative offices for town staff. Good early examples of these multifunction halls survive at Liverpool, Nova Scotia, Stratford, Ontario, and Chilliwack, British Columbia. Some multifunction town halls reached monumental proportions, frequently becoming a town's chief focal point and landmark.

In many locales the town hall was the only major building project directly un-

Single-function town halls tended to be simple buildings, similar in size and design to schools, churches, and other buildings. Pontiac, Quebec (CIHB)

dertaken by the municipality and its council. Architecturally, the eclecticism of the type follows from the variety of communities and times. Despite generally consistent functional requirements, the results were strikingly different from place to place, even between those a few miles apart.

In some communities, town halls were deliberately built on a scale that far surpassed the needs or indeed the financial capabilities of the residents at the time they were built. Such buildings tended to be both elaborately designed and prominently sited, constructed in the name of 'progress' by town councils with high ambitions for future expansion. Other

Some multi-function town halls were monumental – a town's chief focal point and landmark. Chilliwack, BC (CIHB)

Victoria Hall, Cobourg, Ontario. Perhaps Canada's grandest pre-Confederation municipal building (John Blumenson, OMCC)

centres built exceptionally modest structures that did no more than provide basic accommodation for their current needs. Such buildings were characterized by their plain design, by the fact that they faded insignificantly into the streetscapes that surrounded them and by the claims of their sponsoring councils to fiscal responsibility.[6]

THE HISTORICAL CONTEXT

Growth and Resources
Development of an infrastructure to support public services is essential in community- and nation-building. Yet much of the early funding for public services must come from tax revenues – often at a time when citizens have to address basic survival needs. Only in a relatively mature state would there be sufficient resources to keep public in-

vestments reasonably well synchronized with the private development that it serves.

Capital development in New France, British North America, and the fledgling Canadian nation was limited, first by the financial interests of the colonial powers and subsequently by the private investors of Europe and North America. Capital formation was marked early and often by competition for finance between private and public projects. Indeed, one of Britain's principal interests in Confederation was to stop its investments in colonial infrastructure.[7]

Colonial growth and expansion were driven almost entirely by immigration from abroad, and all 'civilized' goods had to be imported until well into the 19th century. With economies based almost exclusively on extraction and ex-

New City Hall (1874), Montreal. High-fashion public architecture, reflecting French heritage and national railway boom, orchestrated from Montreal; *Canadian Illustrated News* 9 (27 June 1874) supplement (NA c-67532)

port of primary staple resources, the colonies' needs for physical infrastructure were correspondingly modest, confined to waterway improvements until well into the 19th century. The colonies nevertheless required buildings to house their judicial and other public administrative functions. The chief beneficiaries of public-building construction were ports, capital cities, and major county towns.

Most pre-Confederation public buildings were simple, though ambitious and grand examples, even from the earliest days of settlement, still survive. The more complex and ornate facilities appeared only when sufficient wealth had been generated – either internally or through the munificence of the central government – to afford the improvements required for urban upgrading and expansion.

The arrival of the railways in the mid-19th century began to bind communities more closely together, enabling larger public facilities such as courts and administrative offices to serve wider regions and permitting realization of national dreams of western expansion and links to the Pacific. Growth was nevertheless uneven, contingent on external relations, particularly with Britain and the United States. Immigration came not steadily but in waves that reflected changes in British fortunes up until Confederation, and broader, global events afterward. Further, cyclical changes in world business and trade gave Canada and its regions alternating boom and decline along with the general tendencies toward bigger and better things for the future.[8]

The pace of developments varied over time and region. The look of public buildings varied further with the tastes and preferences of local authorities, inhabitants, and construction agencies and with available resources. A conspicuous example of serendipitous timing and local ambition is Kingston's city hall, built in the 1840s, when the rapidly growing town served briefly as the colonial capital, a position it soon lost.

The conspicuousness of public facilities has followed economic cycles and changing political and architectural fashion. Federal and provincial party politics has directed the timing and location of public building and to some extent its architectural character. Governments have increasingly used public-building construction as a conscious tool of economic policy. Economic cycles have had more overt influence on the timing and location of public building since the 1920s than previously. Yet, within these broad patterns, local variation has been considerable.

Over the last century the demand for public services has grown a great deal, and with it the specialization of function and building type. The earliest public buildings were simple but adaptable to many diverse needs, from courts to farmers' markets. The earliest post-Confederation federal buildings housed customs, tax collection, and postal service under a single roof, conspicuously signalled by a clock tower. But in the 20th century post offices, for instance, have been built separately, and the growing complexity and demand for space of even small regional offices have

fragmented governments' presence, physically and symbolically.

In national and provincial capitals, administrative offices were originally housed within the legislatures or in purpose-built structures adjacent to but easily identifiable with them. The public-access elements of newer facilities maintain the symbolic role of government, while most administrative and technical functions are housed in separate buildings, whether leased or owned, that look like private commercial buildings.[9]

Expansion and specialization of government services have also created wholly new building types. The need to regulate immigration formally led to development of immigration and quarantine stations after Confederation. Government's role in improving agricultural prospects produced experimental model farms and weather observatories. The nation's military interests diversified and led to new types of building, such as urban drill halls and convalescent hospitals. Provincial governments developed new types of social and educational facilities in response to their mandates. Municipalities erected chains of fire halls and police stations to serve their own responsibilities.

Public buildings introduced features of both style and function that led to improvements in private construction, through emulation and development of building codes based on public-building practice. For instance, fireproof construction was but one 19th-century advance incorporated into major public buildings, even into modest land registry offices, well in advance of commercial construction. But most innovations of type or technique were clothed in conservative historic styles to fit better into their communities. Many truly innovative public buildings may appear retrograde until examined closely.

Political Dimensions

Partisan loyalty has always figured in the distribution of government contracts, and its influence on the timing and location of public buildings can be traced in statistics and historical accounts. Its more material effects, on design and construction, came through selection of one or another architect or builder to take charge. Public works officials could not resist such influences if they were persistent. In federal construction, 'local political pressure as well as the interests of client departments held considerable influence over the minister of Public Works, not just in his decision to take on certain public works projects in the first place, but in determining the exact location of the structure, its style, scale and functional layout.'[10]

During the early years of Confederation, as the fledgling nation tried to establish an identity through its buildings, the two governing parties, Liberal and Conservative, maintained fairly consistent, if opposing, ideas about what visual impression their buildings ought to convey: 'The final design[s] for public buildings in both Brantford and Guelph (which were among the first undertaken entirely by branch staff [1876]) were for years criticized by Conservative members of Parliament. The Guelph Post Office, only two stories high, was deemed barely in keeping with the existing architecture that surrounded it. From the midst of a later period of Conservative expansion in public construction, government members criticized the previous Liberal administration for its "gaudy and cheap style of architecture of which the country would be ashamed," and in particular for the "dwarf and squatty" buildings foisted upon the unsuspecting citizenry of Guelph and Brantford.'[11]

The cycles of political taste reflected the deeper economic problem of reconciling the need for public facilities of all types to facilitate revenue-generating local growth where that growth had not yet produced sufficient wealth to pay for such facilities. Even in the pervasive climate of economic laissez-faire in the 19th century, national and provincial governments recognized the political value of public building at the right time in certain regions. For instance, the federal government built or expanded customs and immigration facilities that favoured some ports of entry over others, based on the regional loyalties of the party in power.[12]

Municipalities could not be so flexible. Many had to suffer inadequate facilities for decades until property taxation could pay for services that property owners wanted. Even in the wake of epidemics and fires, local public works necessary to prevent further disasters could be built only when economic conditions improved sufficiently. Senior authorities seldom permitted local governments to borrow heavily, fearing, with some justification, municipal bankruptcies. Just as immigration came in waves, so did local public building, but often much later than the first waves of demand.[13]

Economic Indicators

The surviving major public buildings of the later colonial period reflect the prosperity (or at least optimism) of their towns: Montreal's ambition to be the gateway to the North American interior, Kingston's temporary success as Canada's capital city, Cobourg's more modest claims to regional dominance, and so on. The boom in post-Confederation public building, especially in the 1880s, is seen best in eastern and central Canadian towns and cities, reflecting a tentative spreading out of the economic benefits of nationhood.

A second wave of completions in the boom years before 1914 is visible right across the country, most vividly in the prairie provinces. These structures embodied a more mature realization of Canadian ambition. The more modest public buildings of the Depression, built to ease unemployment, are most conspicuous in the west, testimony to the severity of economic conditions and to realization that a nation-wide network of public facilities was at last complete. Subsequent growth has taken place in the form of waves of redevelopment and consolidation relatively consistently across the country – often through abandoning or even destroying much of the architectural heritage.

SELECTING DESIGNERS

The process of selecting architects and engineers to carry out public building projects obviously influences the nature of the final product. Governments have commissioned private practitioners directly; they have held open or restricted competitions among private architects; and they have used, where available, the services of their own technical staff. The construction of the Ontario Legislative Buildings in Toronto will provide a brief case history of differences, strengths, and weaknesses among all three approaches; the history of the chief architect's branch in the federal Department of Public Works will illustrate the use of technical staff and, more recently, of private architects.

A Case History
Ontario established its own Department of Public Works in 1869. Kivas Tully had the duties of both architect and engineer, until the duties were separated in 1874. Tully reported in 1873 on the poor condition of the existing Legislative Building, which the province had inherited, and

advocated a more satisfactory structure. The chief architect's office was preparing in-house all plans and specifications for public buildings, and Tully accordingly began plans for a new legislative building. Elected representatives decided instead to hold an open competition to select a design, perhaps because they felt that the importance and size of the project placed it beyond the capabilities of the department, perhaps because they believed that the province needed the public attention that press coverage of such a competition would draw.

After years of discussion, an open competition was announced on 26 April 1880, with a capital budget of $500,000. Only Canadian products were to be used, and architects were instructed to economize, 'avoiding extreme or superfluous ornamentation.'[14] The competition jury was unable to select a satisfactory design from among 16 submissions. Though it did award prizes and directed three firms to rework their proposals (at their own expense), it still failed to turn up a scheme that met the legislature's budget and architectural aspirations.

In 1885 Buffalo architect R.A. Waite, one of the jurors, suggested that he himself would be best capable of producing a sophisticated and attractive design that would meet both requirements. To much surprise, the legislature agreed, and Waite was commissioned. The finished product, opened in 1893, was criticized heavily for the long and questionable commissioning process, for the ultimate selection of an American architect, for the awkwardness of some of the design, and for substantial delays and cost overruns during construction. The criticism helped bring about formation of the Ontario Association of Architects soon afterward.

Ontario's experience reveals many of the difficulties inherent in the process of public building. Public design is often

Ontario Legislative Buildings, Queen's Park, Toronto. Detail drawing from R.A. Waite's final design (AO)

viewed as just that: public. Large projects are seen as choice plums which any architect ought to have a chance to win, on merit, in open competition. A process that excludes the private sector or limits selection to a politically predetermined few provokes heavy criticism. However, definitive and rigorous guidelines must be used to run an open contest, or it too will become a subject of criticism, regardless of the results. Public-building competitions remain difficult to handle well. Those in 1957 for Toronto's city hall and in 1984 for a new hall for adjacent Mississauga have been cited in both the national and international press as exemplars of an open process that produced exciting and innovative – albeit controversial – designs and finished buildings while treating all competitors fairly.

A Model Branch

Given the large number and constant flow of similar types of project, governments able to afford the cost have maintained permanent departments of public works for some or all of the public-building process, from design to construction to maintenance. The experience of the federal Department of Public Works provides a useful model of the influences on, and the processes of, public-service building in Canada.[15] Confederation bequeathed the federal government a number of buildings and the urgent need to construct many more. The government established a position of chief engineer, responsible for all public buildings and public works. But by 1872 it had created a post of chief architect as well. This new office developed and maintained an architectural branch capable of preparing designs for a full range of public buildings and of superintending much of its construction by local builders. Up to the First World War, governments continued to encourage this self-sufficiency in design.

This policy created an imposing government presence across the country which displayed consistently high standards of design. It also provided project control and economy. The federal government developed over time a group of professionals familiar with the functional requirements of government departments: time-consuming consultations could be streamlined and designs for similar needs and situations refined and perfected. Though the era's principal building journal, *Canadian Architect and Builder*, criticized the chief architect's branch for some designs and for its exclusion of private-sector architects, the central government long maintained confidence in a system that provided it with control over every project.[16]

As the branch accumulated wide-ranging experience, it developed consistent approaches – a standard plan – that could be modified to meet regional variations. Consequent efficiencies of time and labour became crucial during the First World War, when manpower was in short supply, and during the Depression, when construction funds were limited. Post offices were particularly suitable candidates, and successful plans were repeated in many locales with minimal changes.[17]

While the names of the branch's chief architects are known, it is difficult to attribute individual designs to architects within the branch, in part because many were but temporary employees. And it has proved difficult to determine the chief architect's influence on the work of his staff. Each chief operated the office much like a private firm, where design accreditation is usually awarded only to the firm's principals.

However, the actual practice of architecture generally requires a co-operative approach, with individuals developing expertise either in specific areas of the design process – such as working drawings, presentation drawings, or project supervision – or in specific types of buildings. This was certainly true for the chief architect's office. Historical analysis of administrative papers reveals the development of a high degree of specialization.[18] The branch was notable for the long-term service of its staff and the in-house training and apprenticeship that could take an operative from draughtsman to senior architect. The cohesiveness and consistency of federal designs may have been as much a product of training and long-term association with the branch as of the influence of a single chief architect.

From Confederation until the First World War, the federal government pursued an active, extensive, and high-profile program of construction, and the position of chief architect itself was initially one of considerable power and influence. Thomas Fuller, chief architect 1881–96, was one of Canada's foremost architects and maintained that high regard during his public career.[19] Successors were usually appointed from within the department, and staff turnovers were infrequent. As long as the department was involved in design and construction of prominent public buildings, it attracted highly qualified professionals both as staff and chiefs and produced results of high quality.

By the First World War the chief architect's large-scale building activities had peaked. Shortages of manpower during the war curtailed construction, and during the 1920s repair and upkeep of the extensive inventory kept much of the budget away from new projects. During the Depression, the government allocated special funds under the Public Works Construction Act, 1934, to stimulate the economy, but the spirit of the legislation and the large number of public building projects (76 in all) forced the chief architect to turn to the private sector for assistance. The department never regained its design monopoly.

In the years following the Second World War, the government's policy on public design radically changed its earlier promotion of a strong central presence. In-house design largely fell from favour. Design by private firms became the norm, as the government continued to stimulate the private sector and divert attention from itself with small-scale, modest structures.

Today, public architects undertake little design themselves but act instead as client representatives, explaining government requirements to private architects. Public leasing of private space has also become a constraint on public architecture, as the government, like many other large organizations, often prefers to leave operation of physical facilities to private companies expert in building management. The historic mandates of departments of public works have changed radically, with dramatic changes to their organization, personnel, and, ultimately, the buildings they produce.

THE EVOLUTION OF DESIGN

After the larger cities in Quebec and Ontario had been provided for, as warranted by their large populations and returns of government revenue, with public structures in keeping with the finest facades along their main streets, the smaller centres requested and received like treatment – albeit in structures reduced both in size and grandeur.

In all its manifestations public architecture bespoke good government: responsiveness to particular national interests, concern for specific public needs, and above all faith in local enterprise and in the revenue that it would hopefully continue to generate.[20]

The success or failure of any public work is based on how well it performs and on whether it satisfies an important public need. For public architecture, the assessment is less consistently measurable

Scarborough Water Filtration Plant, Toronto. One of several public works in Toronto by Works Commissioner R.C. Harris; its architecture and engineering are inseparable. (Jean Simonton, OMCC)

Osgoode Hall, Toronto. Colonial Classicism, based on then-current fashions in the imperial capital, London (AO 51232)

(perhaps less obviously objective) than, say, the physical capacity and durability of a public utility. Yet buildings that serve administrative and social functions are often judged more by appearance than by structure and utility. Appearances may be absolutely crucial for their political and community acceptance, as we saw in the cycles of political influence on public buildings in the late 19th century.

Indeed, the façade of every public work carries the image and reputation of its sponsors and builders. Visual style is far from a frivolous aesthetic exercise or an afterthought; it may get the work accepted and built. The bridges and water-treatment facilities of Toronto Works Commissioner R.C. Harris display the positive role of conscientious visual design.

The requirements fulfilled by public building design have varied greatly with government, place, and time. Styles and designs of public building have varied accordingly. But there are a few underlying fundamentals. Every public building offers up for view its own unique resolution of some of these: whether its design ought to mould fashion, or follow it; whether it should stand proudly apart from its context, or sink discreetly into it; whether it can or should present a strong, even standardized, image readily identifiable as a branch of a particular authority, or follow surrounding tastes.

The history of public building design is a series of attempts to resolve each of these issues for every project. In general, that history seems to be a series of oscillations from one side of each question to the other.

A Changing Federal Presence
While most surviving historic Canadian public buildings (even in Quebec) can be considered 'conservative' derivatives of British or American models, borrowing

was selective. The earliest public administrations were housed in Georgian-style quarters, domestic in scale, out of necessity. When colonial wealth began to permit more ornate residences and public buildings, the questions of which models to borrow from became somewhat vexing, even contentious. Osgoode Hall (1829–57) in Toronto bears witness to changes in attitudes, both subtle and overt, about the best contemporary 'classical' model for the principal symbol of British justice in Upper Canada. There seemed little question of borrowing from the classical originals themselves.[21]

Thomas Fuller's Dominion Parliament Buildings (1859–66) and his subsequent urban post offices were not pioneers in Gothic Revival or Romanesque but did represent the full flowering of those styles early enough to be considered important and influential on both public and private buildings. The taste for rusticated Gothic and Romanesque in the mansions of the wealthy and in many town halls from the 1880s to the 1920s may be tentatively traced to Fuller's buildings. There was a nice Scots-Canadian virtue in that rustication. The style aged gracefully, saved time and money on the job, and contrasted with the smoothly polished classicism of much contemporary American public building.[22] But Fuller's strong role as public designer was seldom followed, and, despite their recognition, the Parliament Buildings did not inspire provincial legislatures in the same way as the US Capitol inspired American state legislatures. In Canada, borrowing and influence in public-building style were matters of detail rather than overall symbolism.

As private architects have taken over much of the practice of public architecture in Canada, and seek to satisfy committees and standard programs rather

Pictou County Court House, Pictou, Nova Scotia. The best Victorian public buildings fitted in with neighbours while declaring the government's presence. (CIHB)

than individual clients, their designs have generally become less distinguishable from private or corporate architecture. Design innovations in public building have become rare events. Only open architectural competition has produced innovative designs for traditional functions, but few of these have been built.[23]

Despite a long-term tendency toward less innovative public buildings, attitudes to the physical relations of public facilities to their immediate contexts have swung back and forth more frequently. Colonial public buildings tended to follow the lead of modest domestic neighbours or of well-known and comfortable British antecedents. They fitted well into their urban streetscapes, with proportions and details similar to those of their neighbours, even where their scale and siting were more dramatic.

Post-Confederation architecture followed this good-neighbour policy, but in a more self-confident, even exuberant, High Victorian eclecticism. If Fuller was particularly blessed with design skill, his times also tolerated and even encouraged his boldly sited and detailed post offices – they fit in by standing out. Small federal public buildings maintained this strength of identity on Canadian main streets well into the 1930s, even with the restrained and almost anonymous classicism of Depression design. They still had two- or three-storey frontages, with subtle shifts in massing and materials that let them look 'modern' while following the standard arrangements of elements and functions proved over 40 or more years.

But as federal social and economic activity expanded after 1950, the country became especially sensitive to the central government's presence. In the words of Deryck Holdsworth, 'The ornamental visibility of government is a low priority in an era of assertive province-building and persistent anti-Ottawa sentiment.'[24] Post offices of the 1950s and 1960s became standardized products radically different from Fuller's model. Fuller's plans had been tailored to each situation. Modern standards were completely off-the-rack, even down to each elevation. Between 1959 and 1967, more than 750 almost identically modest suburban 'bungalows' replaced main-street facilities, leaving older communities to deal with a now-empty landmark structure as they struggled to revitalize main street.

Provincial Restraint

The shuffle between standing out and fitting in produced especially interesting court-house architecture. Court houses were and are relatively few compared to other public building types and display an overall uniform aspect, reflecting shared assumptions about the nature of justice, while presenting considerable variety because of local clientele, wealth, and taste: 'The overwhelming characteristic of court houses built by county agencies is originality. They are diverse in exterior design, interior space allocation, siting and use of materials because they have been constructed to meet the needs of a specific situation as expressed by a group of local citizens ... [They] can also appear curiously whimsical in the functions they combine.'[25] But specific influences motivating the range of local varieties have been hard to trace: 'What has proven awkward to identify in Canada is the means by which they [architectural influences] entered the country; such vague explanations as "through the experience of immigrants and travellers," and "in the pages of international magazines" are unsatisfy-

Public Building, Maple Creek, Saskatchewan. Standardized features proclaim federal presence. (NA PA-46547)

ing unless they can be linked to specific people, articles and buildings. Indeed, although some court houses clearly follow the modes set by international arbiters, many more do not. Apparently other, more immediate factors were often a determining influence.'[26]

As the authorized court-house construction agencies after Confederation, provincial governments sought to restrain that local originality by developing standardized plans, as did the central government for territorial courts. By the end of the 19th century, the standard design became the rule. Since then, even though private firms have taken over most of the design work, the standard plan has been the real designer. Only in the larger regional complexes of recent years have court facilities, for instance, begun to reacquire some distinction. Even so, their quality and contribution to their settings have been uneven, from the impenetrable block of Ottawa's new provincial court building to the gracious public spaces in Vancouver's complex.

Local Pride

Town halls (and some associated police and fire stations) present a far less restrained sense of evolution from place to

City Halls (1965 and 1898), Toronto. Cities often build 'the most flamboyant of public buildings.' These two, contentious in their day, are major civic landmarks. (Mark Fram)

City Hall, Ottawa. Elegant and modernist, threatened with demolition; a heritage site (Mark Fram)

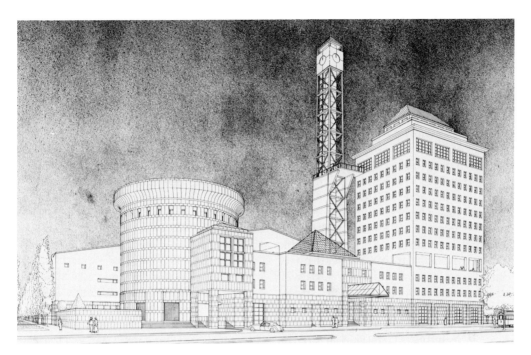

City Hall, Mississauga. Strikingly post-modern and assertive, still in flamboyant civic tradition (Rendering courtesy of Jones and Kirkland Architects)

place and more faithfully reflect architectural fashion. In the 19th and early 20th centuries, the town hall was a less abashed expression of public pride than any building erected by a more senior government, often in the face of budgetary difficulties and even scandals. The almost mythical traditions of town-hall democracy emphasized use of monumental architectural elements to evoke British and even classical antecedents. Traditional local functions of marketing and public debating allowed Victorian stonecarvers riotous opportunities to engage in naturalistic and even satirical renderings of animals and people as architectural elements.

The municipal council chamber has always offered an opportunity to add prominent ceremonial attributes beyond mere functional requirements, from the enlarged windows and extra ceiling height of early Victorian halls to the separate 'organic' structures evident in larger city halls since the 1950s.[27] Towns and cities have built both the most modest and the most flamboyant of public buildings, sometimes sober, sometimes playful. There may even be a modest renaissance of the playful tradition in the guise of the 'post-modern': 'The Mississauga City Hall tries to be a small city unto itself. It does manage to achieve a representational public stature by virtue of its allusive and metaphoric symbolism, and by the more explicit expression of parts of the facility. Symbolism is a fickle creature, however, and once created is likely to generate a host of meanings to the susceptible public that might never have been anticipated.'[28]

CONCLUSION

Variety and differentiation have overwhelmed any symbolic consistency in

Canada's public architecture. The nation's public style is a multitude of expressions, local and regional, not even sufficiently coherent to identify a single province. If there is anything approaching an identifiable public style, it should be discernible in the national capital, but even Ottawa cannot offer more than its own set of regionally specific styles, tied to its own particular eras of growth, only inadvertently corresponding with any other city or town: 'To the extent that Ottawa was a special medium for the cross-fertilization of French and British fashions – a picturesque northern Gothic that comfortably fronts a backdrop of Shield, mountains, and oceans, as well as integrates solidly into main streets large and small – then there has been a fabrication and diffusion of images that hint at a hybrid Canadian style. Its tentative presence is perhaps appropriate for a society so thinly stretched across a vast land, and one whose federalism has been in a state of flux, but, as an effort to cohere, join, and provide a focus for the country, its varying expression is an important element of the Canadian state.'[29]

From this evidence it is not possible to identify enough shared characteristics to define a distinctive Canadian public-building style or technique, either in the past or today. These public buildings do have some prototypical and consistent aspects, but not enough to exhibit direct influences that would overcome the overwhelming variety of their local execution. The public face of Canadian public building, indeed of Canadian public works, has many guises, some classical, some rusticated, some glazed, some grey, some multi-coloured. Its variety guarantees continuing interest in scholarship and preservation and may encourage other efforts to recover the interest it once had in order to produce the major public landmarks of the next century.

NOTES

1 Diana Bodnar 'The Prairie Legislative Buildings' *Prairie Forum* 5:2 (fall 1980) 143–56
2 The provinces in 1867 included New Brunswick, Nova Scotia, Ontario, and Quebec. The remaining provinces entered Confederation afterward: Manitoba in 1870, British Columbia in 1871, Prince Edward Island in 1873, Alberta and Saskatchewan in 1905, and Newfoundland in 1949.
3 See Randy Rostecki and Leslie Maitland 'Post Offices by Thomas Fuller, 1881–1896' unpublished report prepared for the Historic Sites and Monuments Board of Canada, June 1983; Margaret Carter ed *Early Canadian Court Houses* (Ottawa 1983); and Marc de Caraffe, C.A. Hale, Dana Johnson, G.E. Mills, and Margaret Carter *Town Halls of Canada* (Ottawa 1987).
4 For a detailed study of the architectural operations of the federal Department of Public Works, see Margaret Archibald *By Federal Design: The Chief Architect's Branch of the Department of Public Works, 1881–1914* (Ottawa 1983).
5 Other building types whose planning was progressively standardized included registry offices, court houses, drill halls, and armouries.
6 Carter *Court Houses* 9
7 See A.W. Currie 'Public Finance' *Canadian Economic Development* 4th ed (Toronto 1963) 342–61.
8 See Kenneth Buckley *Capital Formation in Canada, 1896–1930* (Toronto 1974).
9 See Deryck Holdsworth 'Architectural Expressions of the Canadian National State' *Canadian Geographer* 30:2 (1986) 167–71.
10 Archibald *By Federal Design* 34

11 Ibid 35–6
12 See Douglas Owram *Building for Canadians* (Ottawa 1979) especially chap 7.
13 See Buckley *Capital Formation* and de Caraffe et al *Town Halls* chap 4.
14 'General Instructions for the Guidance of Architects ...' Department of Public Works, Government of Ontario, 1880. Open competitions can be contrasted with competitions that are restricted in one manner or another. The competition for Manitoba's legislature, for example, was confined to British subjects; that for Saskatchewan's was by invitation only.
15 Archibald *By Federal Design*
16 *Canadian Architect and Builder* 7 (1894) 31; 14 (1901) 2
17 There are also many examples of standard plans for provincial facilities, such as Tully's Ontario registry offices and Rubidge's Quebec court-house plans, as well as for municipal types such as schools and branch libraries.
18 See both Owram *Building for Canadians* and Archibald *By Federal Design*.
19 Fuller, along with Chilion Jones, provided the winning design for the Parliament Buildings in Ottawa in 1859. There were also a few notable provincial chiefs, such as Kivas Tully, chief architect for Ontario, who moved to the public office from a successful private practice that had already included such notable public buildings as Victoria Hall, in Cobourg, and the Leeds and Grenville County Court House, in Brockville.
20 Archibald *By Federal Design* 6–7
21 Dana Johnson and Leslie Maitland 'Osgoode Hall and the Development of Public Architecture in Canada' *SSAC Bulletin* 10:4 (Dec 1985) 14–18
22 Rostecki and Maitland 'Post Offices by Fuller'; also B.C. Chattopadhyay 'Government Buildings in Canada and the USA' MARCH thesis, University of Toronto, 1964, 194
23 Since early in this century, public agencies have actively sought out adventurous designs for only one sort of program – the very theatrical architecture of exhibition pavilions (such as Ontario Place in Toronto) and world's fairs (such as Expo '67 in Montreal, or Expo '86 in Vancouver).
24 Holdsworth 'Architectural Expressions' 171
25 Carter *Court Houses* 15
26 Ibid 19
27 de Caraffe et al *Town Halls* chap 5
28 Anne M. de Fort-Menares 'Issues of Hierarchy and Social Ritual: Mississauga City Hall' *SSAC Bulletin* 10:4 (Dec 1985) 29
29 Holdsworth 'Architectural Expressions' 171

JULIE HARRIS

Airports

Transportation system technology may be divided into two broad categories: vehicles and ground services. With air transportation the latter are concentrated at airports, where facilities are designed to handle the safe take-off, landing, and servicing of aircraft and to connect airplanes and other modes of transportation. These functions have remained constant since the first Canadian public airport was licensed in 1920, but the design of airports and the procedures followed for their safe use and maintenance have changed significantly as aircraft have evolved and commercial services become more sophisticated.

Airport engineers have designed and built airports to meet changing aircraft characteristics, provided air services in remote areas, constructed airports quickly in response to military needs, and balanced commercial efficiency and cost. Public criticism of airport development, especially during the past two decades, has focused on the integration of airports into complex transportation networks and on the environmental and economic consequences of intensive, large-scale building programs. In this chapter 'airport' refers to the area, associated buildings, equipment, and installations licensed by the government of Canada for the arrival, departure, movement, and servicing of aircraft.

The responsibility for aviation legisla-

tion rests with the federal government, which has also played a large role in operating and funding urban airports.[1] By means of ownership, not jurisdiction, Transport Canada operated 122 airports in 1985; another 1,133 were operated by provincial agencies, municipalities, and private interests, some of which entered into cost-sharing agreements with the federal government. About 49 per cent of all airports had a public licence.[2] Today 80 per cent of aviation activity takes place at only 10 airports, all managed by Transport Canada.

Historically, federal airport programs have focused on establishing national standards, providing national services, and addressing international aviation concerns. The goal has been to maintain national routes, not simply to encourage inter-urban air transport. The first airway and its feeder routes stretched across the country from Vancouver to Halifax through Canada's southern population belt, thereby creating a transcontinental network which also served international operations. Subsequent air routes either advanced into frontier areas previously served only by float and ski planes or were developed or upgraded for military purposes and later integrated into Canada's civil airport network.

Commercial aircraft used by airlines today are completely dependent on

A transatlantic airfield: horse and buggy and airplane, 1917, near Harbour Grace,
Newfoundland. Neighbours helped pay for the strip of packed sand in hope of prosperity.
(NA PA-127541)

modern airports for operation, so airport engineers must address changing aircraft characteristics. Airliners can use only smooth, hard-surfaced, long runways with clear markings and lights distinguishing the runways from taxiways, holding aprons, and terminal areas. Aircraft weights largely determine thickness of landing surfaces and length of runways. Aircraft dimensions influence the width of runways and taxiways and the size of parking areas, which in turn influence the design of terminal buildings. The passenger and cargo capacities of aircraft are important considerations in the design of terminal buildings and in the choice of services the airport will offer. The configuration of an airport, namely the number and orientation of runways and the location of the terminal area relative to the runways, is designed to ensure that air traffic oper-

ates safely without unnecessary delays. Commercial airlines, which pay landing fees and other tolls for the use of airports, also require, among other things, air terminal buildings, freight warehouses, customs services, fuel depots, servicing centres, and public amenities, such as restaurants and hotels.

FROM LANDING FIELDS TO AIRPORTS

The airfields used by pioneer aviators at the beginning of the century were rarely more than relatively flat pieces of land free of tall hazards such as power lines and buildings. In 1903 the Wright brothers' historic first flight of a powered, heavier-than-air aircraft began from sand dunes near Kitty Hawk, North Carolina, and in 1909 Alexander Graham Bell's Aerial Experiment Association tested Canada's first aircraft on the frozen surface of Bras d'Or Lake in Nova Scotia. As aviation technology improved and flying became more popular, purpose-built airfields were constructed and maintained. Until the 1930s, however, most were all-way landing fields usable only in daylight. There were no marked runways; pilots simply landed and took off from the airfield, heading into the wind as marked by a wind sock. Other markings indicated the centre of the field, and services were usually limited to a fuel tank, a telephone, a small shed, and water.

Canada's earliest purpose-built, publicly funded aerodromes were developed for military purposes by the British government during the First World War. In 1917 Canada granted Britain's Royal Flying Corps (RFC) permission to recruit in Canada and to establish five military training aerodromes on Canadian soil. The first flying unit was formed at Long Branch on Lakeshore Road, Toronto, where Canada's first commercial airfield had been built in 1915 by Curtiss Aeroplanes and Engine Co. Additional RFC schools were established in Ontario at Armour Heights (north of Toronto), Beamsville, Camp Borden, Desoronto (two separate aerodromes, Rathburn and Mohawk),[3] and Leaside.[4] Each aerodrome was equipped with a large all-way grass landing field and basic services such as water, electricity, and wooden hangars, but there were no landing or navigation aids.

The Canadian government agreed to set up RFC air stations during the First World War, but until 1919 and 1920 it lacked the bureaucratic institutions and laws to establish aviation policies or regulate aeronautics. In 1919, after Canada had attended the meetings of the International Commission on Aerial Navigation at the Paris Peace Conference, John Armistead Wilson, whose 35-year career in aviation included the

positions of controller of civil aviation from 1927 until 1941 and director of air services until 1945, was asked to oversee the drafting of an Air Board Act based on Britain's air navigation acts. The Air Board, under the control of the Department of Militia and Defence until 1923, was responsible for military and civil air regulations and policies, borrowed from many sources and adapted to the Canadian situation.[5]

Officials such as Wilson recognized that inter-urban air transport could not be a primary objective of government aviation policies like it was in Europe. Canada lacked the infrastructure required by a national airway, and the federal government was not prepared to support a national public works program, especially in areas already served by railways and roads. In 1919 A.L. Sifton, Air Board chairman, stated:

An attempt on the part of the government to assume the responsibility for the general provision of aerodromes would, in view of the small amount of money available, result, (by the discouragement of local initiative) in the retardation of the development of air navigation, which, to a degree still little understood, depends upon ground organization rather than upon mere flying capacity. Terminal landing grounds for every urban area must necessarily be provided by the inhabitants of that area. Every city and town must have one within a very short time. Every village should. An urban municipality without an aerodrome will not be on the air map.[6]

The government would, however, provide emergency landing fields along 'recognized' air routes.

The Air Board established standards for licensing airports for safety purposes, controlled air operations for government departments, and also ran aerial defence programs, but it was pro-

Airmail routes encouraged the growth of municipal airports in the 1920s. Many, such as this one in Regina, were associated with flying clubs. (NA PA-139000)

hibited from constructing and operating airports 'on the same basis as wharfs and harbour facilities.'[7] Under its obligation to control government air operations, the Air Board was given responsibility for 'all government aerodromes and air stations.' Four government airports were built and licensed in 1920: a landplane base at Morley, Alberta, which supported fire surveillance activities on the eastern slopes of the Rockies; seaplane bases at Roberval, Quebec, and Vancouver, operated for the Geological Survey of Canada's mapping and aerial photography programs, which used HS2L flying boats; and a combined land and seaplane base at Rockcliffe, in Ottawa, employed initially by Militia and Defence but used subsequently for government transportation services, aerial

photography, and experimental aeronautics.[8] In addition, the former Royal Air Force seaplane base at Dartmouth, Nova Scotia, was reactivated to support aerial survey work, and Camp Borden, originally built by the RFC in 1917, served as a school for the Canadian Air Force.

In 1922 the Air Board identified 37 'airharbours' in Canada: 23 landplane facilities; 12 seaplane airharbours; and 2 combined bases. Of these, 7 were government facilities; 23 were private/commercial; and 7 were public airports licensed by the Air Board.[9] The number of airports increased very slowly in the 1920s, although private aviation and resource companies like Imperial Oil and Laurentide Air Services operated private airports. The construction of municipal airfields, usually no more than a cleared area with some markings, relied on the support of local governments and aviation companies. The Edmonton Municipal Airport, known earlier as Blatchford Field, was established in 1926. It was the first municipal aerodrome to receive a federal licence and played a very significant role in opening the Canadian north.[10]

Boards of trade also became involved at an early date and even today contribute to the identification of commercial needs associated with airports, because they consider a strong public works infrastructure important for a healthy local economy. The airport built in 1921 in Virden, Manitoba, for instance, was owned and managed by the local board of trade, which saw economic benefits in using the facility as a port of entry for customs purposes. The town probably hoped to gain commercial importance and additional government services. The airport was modestly equipped, with an all-way landing field featuring a sandy-loam surface of about 800 sq yd (669 sq m) and a surplus Bessoneau hangar loaned by the Air Board.

BUILDING AIRPORTS

St Hubert
The government of Canada built its first civil airport and the country's first large-scale airport at St Hubert, near Montreal, between 1927 and 1930. Prime Minister Mackenzie King had made a commitment at the 1926 Imperial Conference to improve 'Empire' communications by providing a landing base for an experimental transatlantic dirigible service.[11] Senior officials in the Civil Aviation Branch seized the opportunity to construct a fully equipped airport for landplanes in conjunction with the dirigible base, even though some questioned the technical feasibility of the dirigible program.

At a cost of nearly $2 million, St Hubert was built by the Department of National Defence with assistance from British Air Ministry staff. The dirigible base included a mooring mast and buildings to contain a hydrogen-generating station and meteorological facilities, while the airport was equipped with two hard-surfaced runways, a large hangar, and an administrative building housing facilities for airport staff, meteorology and telegraph offices, a passenger waiting room, a post office, and customs services. The dirigible base was used only once, in August 1930, by the British R-100; it was demolished in 1938 because it was unused and the tall tower was a hazard to aircraft.

St Hubert was also used as a terminal point for airmail service between Montreal and Rimouski. This route was intended to increase the speed of postal service between England and Canada by transferring mail carried on transatlantic vessels to and from airplanes at Rimouski. The contrast between the facilities at Rimouski and St Hubert was striking; the Rimouski airport was located on leased land and was equipped simply with grass landing strips in a T-shaped configuration, a gasoline pump, and a single hangar.[12] When other municipalities sought funds for construction of airports, the federal government insisted that St Hubert had been supported to meet national objectives, not local ones.

Transatlantic Airports: Newfoundland
The dirigible program for which St Hubert was built was cancelled in 1930 after the crash of the British R-101, but the commitment to developing commercial transatlantic air routes continued. Earlier attempts to cross the Atlantic by heavier-than-air aircraft started in Newfoundland, including the first successful non-stop flight to Ireland by Alcock and Brown in May 1919. They began from

Lester's Field, a rolling piece of land 400 yd (366 m) wide and 600 yds (548 m) long located west of St John's, which had been quickly converted into a provisional airfield by levelling the worst bumps, removing stumps, and filling a ditch.[13]

Throughout the 1920s most pilots venturing across the ocean started with a rough take-off from similar temporary and make-shift airfields, but, beginning in 1927, some took advantage of an aerodrome located near Harbour Grace, which 'claimed to be the only one in Newfoundland suitable for landings of trans-Atlantic planes.'[14] It was built 'from rough country at considerable cost' for Brock and Schlee, Americans who made the first direct flight from Newfoundland to English soil. With a $2,000 contribution from Brock and Schlee, $2,000 from Harbour Grace residents, who believed that it would help ensure the town's place on the air map of the world for commercial transatlantic flying, and $8,000 from the colonial government, a runway 200 ft (61 m) wide, 4,000 ft (1,219 m) long, and covered with packed sand was constructed.[15] Donations from local contributors and transatlantic aviators such as Amelia Earhart, who began her famous Atlantic crossing from Harbour Grace, helped maintain the field.

While Harbour Grace served occasional pioneer aviators, the governments of Canada, Newfoundland, Britain, and the Irish Free State, along with both Pan American and Imperial airlines, planned a commercial transatlantic air route with airports in Canada and Newfoundland. Agreements signed in 1933 and 1935 called for co-operation in experimental flights and eventual establishment of regular commercial air services.

From 1935 until 1939 experimental flights used flying boats, the most suitable type of aircraft for transatlantic crossings. Because they could land and take off from water, flying boats were initially seen as a safer and less expensive temporary alternative to landplanes, which required extensive ground services, such as terminal airports, alternative airports, and emergency landing fields. For England-to-New York service, seaplane bases consisting of a fuelling facility, a small office building, and a wooden slipway were constructed at Botwood in Newfoundland, Boucherville in Quebec, and Shediac in New Brunswick.[16]

The transatlantic agreements aimed for regular landplane service as soon as suitable long-range aircraft were developed. Newfoundland was an intrinsic part of the plan, serving as the main refuelling stop between Britain and North America. British engineers surveyed the island and chose a site near Gander Lake, about 100 mi (161 km) inland from the coastal fogs. When completed, it was to be one of the largest in the world; as the only transatlantic airport in Newfoundland, it had to be usable at all times under all weather conditions.

Construction of the Newfoundland Airport, at Gander, began in 1936, and by the following year it boasted 'the world's largest area of paved runways.'[17] Size created the potential for drainage problems, which engineers addressed with an impervious bituminous surface on the runways to remove surface water and concrete gutters punctuated by offtakes to convey water to main ditches. During peak rainfalls of up to $1\frac{1}{2}$ in (3.8 cm) per hour, 8 million gallons (40.9 million l) of water was drained off the runways in 60 minutes. The four paved runways, over 4,500 ft (1,372 m) in length, included one used for instrument flying which was 4,800 ft (1,463 m) long and 1,200 ft (366 m) wide.[18] The British Air Ministry specified a lighting system for both night-instrument and bad-weather flying, including boundary lights, contact lights, flush marker lights, range lights, landing field lights, a revolving beacon, an illuminated wind indicator, and traffic signals.

Shortly before construction was completed, the British government cancelled the Albatross project, the landplane for which the airport was built. Thus the first year of operation saw only meteorological services, experimental flights, and the testing of runway conditions in snow and ice.[19] With the outbreak of war, Newfoundland Airport, renamed Gander, assumed a central role. Under special wartime agreements, Canada expanded Gander for military purposes, extended three runways to 6,000 ft (1,829 m), and used it for ferrying bombers and troops to Britain and as the home of several squadrons and a us Air Force base.

Wartime improvements equipped Gander to handle long-distance commercial aircraft such as the Constellations and DC4s used by major North American and European airlines. Eight airlines, including Trans-Canada, were using Gander in 1946. Landing fees were relatively high in the 1940s, and some improvements were financed directly by the airlines. The cost of converting a Royal Air Force hangar into a terminal building, for instance, was shared by the airlines, while Pan American installed a ground control approach system in 1946. With Confederation in 1949, Gander passed from the Newfoundland government to the Canadian Department of Transport.

Trans-Canada Airway

When Gander was opened in 1938, scheduled cross-Canada passenger air service was several months away, but the pace of airport construction had accelerated since airmail flights between Rimouski and Montreal began in 1927. During the late 1920s the growth of northern air services in Canada and the success of commercial inter-city us air traffic had brought civil aviation into greater prominence among Canadian politicians, business leaders, and aviation officials. Some leaders feared that Canadian inter-urban services would become mere northern extensions of us airways. By 1925 the United States already had regular national airmail using airways served by a national weather service, radio beacons, and airports equipped with lights for night flying, and American airlines were asking for permission to fly into Canadian cities.

John A. Wilson and industry representatives recognized that a large amount of money would be necessary to construct a Canadian airway. Existing municipal airfields lacked navigation and communication systems and were too far apart to support commercial services. Previous Canadian transportation projects, like the Canadian Pacific Railway, had been supported by governments concerned about maintaining independent Canadian transport systems, but few politicians were willing to risk the subsidization of another system over territory already covered by roads and railways.

Little direct funding was offered to municipal airports by the federal government until 1936, but construction was encouraged through airmail contracts and from 1927 by a flying club program to promote training of pilots and develop public support for aviation. At a time of federal-provincial disputes over control of aviation, these programs allowed Ottawa to assert an interest in all aspects of civil aviation, not just licensing airports, aircraft, and pilots. National Defence offered two light aircraft to any community agreeing to provide a licensed flying instructor, an air mechanic, and a licensed airport with facilities for housing and maintaining aircraft. In addition, upon completion of training, newly licensed pilots received $100.[20] Enthusiasm for the program surpassed expectations, and in 1928 and 1929, 24 flying clubs were established, many with new airports. The Toronto Flying Club, organized in 1927, just months before the details of the program were announced, was the largest and most active. The club used the former RAF Leaside training field near Eglinton Avenue until 1931, when a new club airport, now part of Downsview Airport, opened on the northeast corner of Wilson and Dufferin avenues.

Representatives from the Post Office and the Civil Aviation Division of National Defence also agreed to establish experimental airmail routes using municipal airports and to build airfields in 'unorganized territory' such as northern Ontario.[21] Many municipalities, including Calgary, Edmonton, Hamilton, Lethbridge, and Regina, either built or upgraded airports for airmail services, and some received grants for lighting improvements.[13] Airmail contracts were awarded to private carriers such as Canadian Airways in 1929 to fly 10 airmail routes between Winnipeg and Moncton; the long stretch between Windsor and Winnipeg was initially flown by an American company over American territory.

The airports and navigation services along the eastern part of the airmail route were limited in number and sophistication. Before radio navigation systems were installed in the early 1930s, railway station agents reported weather changes to one another and placed large strips of white canvas on their platforms that were visible to pilots. A square meant 'Good –go ahead'; a triangle, 'Fair – go ahead at your own discretion'; and a cross, 'Bad – turn back.'[22] Runways at some major centres such as

Belleville, Hamilton, and Kingston were located on level grass fields and identified by standard painted markers such as the 100-ft (30.5-m) circle and 20-ft (6.1-m) arms.

Many other airports, however, were poorly drained, inadequately marked, and dangerously situated in the midst of power lines and other obstructions. Airport standards were hard to enforce and, in the absence of adequate funding, almost impossible to encourage. A Canadian Airways pilot who landed at Saint John in 1930 with the routine problem of a stalled engine had been told that the airport was small and the approaches were very poor, but he was still taken aback by a field that seemed carved out of rock, with an even more solid-looking rock face at one end. Only by touching down at the boundary edge was he able to avoid overrunning the field and hitting the rocks.[23]

The airmail service and the flying club program helped increase airport revenues and convinced some municipalities to build airfields. According to a US government report published in 1930, Canada's progress in aeronautics since 1920 had 'been slow but constant and firmly based.'[24] The report included descriptions of 125 public and private land and seaplane aerodromes, about half of which were licensed by the Air Board. Landing fees at most public airports ranged from $1 to $3 depending on the weight of the aircraft, and further charges were levied for storage of aircraft in and out of hangars. Most airports were equipped with repair and maintenance facilities, but the extent of services varied greatly. Calgary's public airport, for instance, had four small hangars and one large one, which housed up to 15 small aircraft and featured cement foundations, heating, electric lighting, plumbing facilities, offices, repair shops, a pilots' room, and even a classroom.[25]

In contrast, the Fort William airport, owned and operated by the local Aero Club, had one frame hangar that could store two planes.[26] Numerous smaller airports with marked landing fields and a few services such as water and a telephone could be found in every province.

The largest airports built or under construction in 1930, in terms of facilities offered, were those in Calgary, Edmonton, Hamilton, Moncton, Regina, St Hubert, Toronto, and Winnipeg. Runways at these airports were built on either sandy loam or sandy clay soil and covered with sod. They ranged from 2,000 ft (610 m) in length at Moncton to 3,850 ft (1,173 m) at Hamilton. Before hard-surfaced runways were built in the late 1930s, natural drainage was often used for airports on the prairies and a combination of natural and tile drainage in other areas. The Calgary, Regina, and Winnipeg airports were equipped with beacons and floodlights for night navigation and landing, while other airports were installing runway lighting after already having been equipped with beacons.

One facility under construction in 1930 was Vancouver's Sea Island Airport, a combined land and seaplane facility on 475 acres (192 ha) purchased by the city. Ambitious pre-Depression plans called for four runways, a seaplane channel, and a wide variety of associated facilities, such as administration and maintenance buildings, hangars with concrete aprons, extensive drainage works, and modern maintenance equipment.[27] In 1930 and 1931, a scaled-down program constructed one runway, together with an administration building, two hangars, a post office and mail-handling building, a pumping station, a seaplane base, a slipway connecting the seaplane base to the hangar apron, and a trench allowing flying boats to pull up close to the terminal building. Vancouver nonetheless had created an impressive and fully integrated airport, which by the mid-1930s was used for scheduled passenger, mail, and cargo services by Alaska Washington Airways, United Airlines, and Canadian Airways.[28]

Well-equipped municipal airports such as Vancouver's and successful frontier and airmail operators like Canadian Airways led the Royal Commission on Railways and Transportation in 1932 to report 'good progress' in developing commercial aviation in Canada, particularly in the north, 'without the large capital expenditures which are inseparable from roads and railways.'[29] John A. Wilson and other aviation officials in government and industry were keenly aware, however, that more was needed. To follow its traditional policy of building independent transportation and communication systems, the Canadian government would have to sustain airmail and passenger services with a comprehensive airway equipped with good airports and navigation aids which would be operated for one or more strong national airlines. All this seemed possible after 1932, when the Supreme Court ruled that the federal government had sole power over aviation regulations, including licensing of airports and aviation companies.

In 1932, the fledgling airway construction program suffered a setback, when the Post Office dropped airmail contracts, but National Defence started to use unemployment relief schemes to construct and improve what had become known as the Trans-Canada Airway. In 1932 and 1933 this program employed nearly 2,000 people on construction and upgrading of intermediate airfields at 100-mi (161-km) intervals between major terminal airports such as Calgary and Dorval and on emergency landing fields, situated 35 mi (56.3 km) apart. Most projects were located in eastern Canada, where labour-intensive components of

During the Depression, the Department of National Defence used relief workers to construct much-needed small and intermediate airfields across Canada. Here horse teams grade a landing field at Madawaska, Ontario, in August 1934. (DND/PA PA-037310)

Relief workers clearing and grubbing land for an airstrip in Hope, BC, 1934 (DND/NA PA-035078)

Airstrip at Lake of Two Rivers, Ontario, carved out of the forest, ploughed, and graded
(DND/NA PA-037320)

airway development, namely levelling of fields and construction of runways, were required. Except in the Rocky Mountain area, most of this kind of work had already been accomplished in the west. Western Canada needed better lighting and navigation aids, but such technical improvements fell outside the program.

By 1934, nearly 8,000 men were engaged on construction of the Trans-Canada Airway. The prairie sections were already completed, and work was well under way in northern Ontario through to Winnipeg. Work progressed eastward gradually, preceded by surveys of intermediate and emergency landing fields, a particularly difficult task in New Brunswick and Nova Scotia. After one survey, John Wilson quipped that there was not 600 yards of level ground between Halifax and Moncton and described some sites for intermediate fields such as Stanley and Shubenacadie as being 'no prizes.'[30] He often expressed concern about the slow pace of construction – one of the consequences of using only manual labour. At Charlottetown,

district engineers explained that many problems were encountered because workers were both 'inexperienced' and 'undernourished.'[31]

The planned route was to be supported by 20 municipal and 101 intermediate airfields. In January 1935, 32 of the latter were completed, 49 were under construction, and most of the other sites had been chosen. Except for major facilities such as Vancouver and St Hubert, airports and landing fields were sod-covered. The Bishopton, Quebec, intermediate airfield was a typical relief project. It was built in the winter and spring of 1934 with the labour of 200 single, homeless men and 12 teams of horses. They cleared the site, grubbed stumps in uncleared portions, ploughed the field, graded it, and seeded the runways.

Federal Responsibility
The public works program of airway construction acquired a much-needed focus and a federally sponsored user in the late 1930s. In 1936 the newly created Department of Transport (DOT) acquired all the civil aviation responsibilities of

National Defence, and civil aviation emerged clearly as a federal concern. Construction quickened as DOT established an airport grant program for municipalities along the Trans-Canada Airway and other points 'where it appeared to be in the national interest to do so.' This national public works program provided essential infrastructure for the formation in 1937 of the publicly owned Trans-Canada Air Lines (TCA). Airports and navigation systems between Winnipeg and Vancouver permitted TCA to begin its training and testing program; airmail services were inaugurated over this section in March, and a complete mail, passenger, and cargo service was started in April. DOT emphasized that the Trans-Canada Airway was a service available to all aviation companies, but as the primary user TCA exerted considerable influence over development and maintenance.[32] Other airlines were more influential elsewhere, notably Canadian Pacific in the north in the 1940s and 1950s.

Hard-surfaced runways at major municipal airports were one of the first major upgrading programs needed by TCA. Vancouver received new paved runways, improved drainage systems, and a $20,000 lighting system.[33] Ottawa Airport runways were surfaced in the summer of 1938 and officially opened the following spring after harsh winter weather testing. The paving contract typified other upgrading projects, with grading, gravelling, and surfacing of two runways and a taxi strip. A description of this five-week project appeared in 1939:

The runways are 3,300 and 3000 feet long, ... each 200 feet wide. Approximately 20,000 cubic yards of earth were moved by a LeTourneau power scraper in grading operations. Then 22,000 cubic yards of crushed gravel, spread by means of power graders, was laid four inches thick, followed by rolling and an application of binder oil. The final operation, apart from grading and seeding 40 foot strips at either side of the runways, was the laying of the hard surface. It took about 15,000 tons of 'Dibcoe' paving material to complete the work, laid two inches thick all the way and done by a machine known as an asphalt paver. The result was the transformation of a rough and bumpy landing field into a smooth modern airport, capable of providing all year round facilities for the heaviest types of aircraft without fear of disturbing the smooth level surface.[34]

Asphalt provided dependable, all-weather landing surfaces for heavy aircraft and facilitated runway marking. TCA also asked for passenger terminals at busy airports and improved lighting at all fields.

Prior to the Second World War, airport owners – usually municipalities – supplied terminal facilities, often little more than a hangar lean-to quite unsuitable for scheduled passengers. TCA made passenger service an important element of airport development, and in 1938 DOT built its first air terminal at North Bay Airport, hoping that the centres served by TCA would use it as a model. The building stood a safe distance from hangars, workshops, and fuelling facilities and boasted a public waiting room, administration offices, and facilities for radio and meteorology services. Its two-storey airside observation bay would be repeated in dozens of military airports constructed during the war.

Pilot information is a key to airport safety, and new lighting systems guided pilots to airports, provided information on runway conditions, and aided in touching down on the runway.[35] Rotating searchlight beacons, with 550-to-1,000-watt lamps, guided pilots to airports; some flashed an identifying Morse-code signal. At the controlled airports portable searchlights signalled

Airstrip side of London's airport terminal, built in 1940, handsomely designed in the Bauhaus style, with stucco over a wood frame. One of the earlier terminals designed to accommodate passenger service (NA PA-164632)

permission to land. Boundary lights, obstruction lights, and range lights informed pilots about runway configuration, favoured angles of approach, and dangerous obstacles. Radio, lighted wind socks, and tees provided weather information. Prior to paved runways, floodlights for night landings were arranged so that pilots never landed toward the light source. Paved runways needed contact light systems, instead of floodlights, for use with instrument landing systems. Two rows of contact lights, one on each side of the runway, enabled pilots to line up at the proper landing angle and proceed along the centre of the runway. Special winter lighting units were developed to allow light bulbs to sit on top of the snow and

retract as the snow melted.

The Trans-Canada Airway improved dramatically between 1939 and 1944. Initially it stretched from Vancouver to Montreal. Major municipal airports at Moncton, St Hubert, Ottawa, Toronto, Winnipeg, Lethbridge, Calgary, Edmonton, and Vancouver boasted 'hard surfaced runways averaging 3,000 feet [914 m] in length and capable of extension, when necessary to 5,000 feet [1,514 m].' The approach to each runway was 'at an angle of not less than 50 to one, and airport vicinities [had] been zoned so that this safety factor [could] be maintained' if the airports were enlarged.[36] In 1940 additional intermediate airports and emergency fields built in Kimberly and Penticton, British Columbia, made the crossing of the Rockies safer. In April 1941 the airway was extended to Halifax, and in May 1942 to St John's, where the Canadian government built Torbay Airport under a special wartime agreement with Newfoundland. In 1944 the airway was served by 29 municipal airports, 24 intermediate airports, and 42 emergency landing fields.

THE SECOND WORLD WAR

Airports and the War

In both military and commercial terms, the Trans-Canada Airway played an important part in Canada's national transportation system during the Second World War, when thousands of airmen were trained, a Canadian air force was equipped and deployed, and a large aircraft industry was established. Military and civil airport construction rose to a frantic pace to meet the requirements of military training programs, to ferry aircraft to Europe, to accommodate increased commercial activity, and to support ever larger and heavier aircraft. New airways were developed, airports were enlarged, and navigation and traffic control systems were upgraded. At Vancouver Airport in 1942, for example, runways were extended and widened and concrete was laid over existing asphalt to carry Canadian and American military transport aircraft weighing up to 40 tons.[37] With air links to the United States, DOT and National Defence rigorously enforced (North) American standards for airport planning, zoning, lighting, weather information, and air traffic control.[38] As of 1 January 1942, for instance, DOT required all licensed airports to use the US system of marking runways according to the reciprocal of their magnetic bearings.[39] More detailed guidelines were prepared to ensure effective winter use of airports. In dry and cold regions, snow was compacted with rollers to create a hard surface; elsewhere it was cleared from runways.

Increased traffic and larger airports made air traffic controllers a necessity, and in 1939 they were licensed and Canada's first control tower was built at St Hubert. At one time less than 500 registered aircraft had shared about 200 airports, and airport staff had had a relatively clear view of the landing field by standing at ground level on the operation side of the airport or looking from the second storey of a terminal building. By the end of the war, however, several airports were accommodating over 100 aircraft movements per day on runways almost 1 mi (1.6 km) in length, and so control towers became imperative.

Air Training

The largest military airport construction program was undertaken for the British Commonwealth Air Training Plan (BCATP). Through the Royal Canadian Air Force (RCAF), Canada provided air observer, bombing, gunnery, air navigation, and pilot training schools for servicemen from Australia, Britain, Canada, and New Zealand. In December 1939, the program initially called for 64 training schools, but within six months the total number grew to 96 and construction time was halved. Subsequent increases would lead to over 150 schools in operation by 1943, an amazing achievement: when the war started the RCAF had only five operational airports and six more under construction.

Responsibility for selecting airport sites and developing airfields fell on DOT, which worked with National Defence to plan and construct aerodromes 'from the airman's point of view.' The experience gained by DOT officials on the Trans-Canada Airway was used effectively and supplemented by specialists in areas such as hydrology, pavements, and production of turf.

With the assistance of provincial high-way departments, DOT selected 150 sites worthy of development from nearly 2,000 identified during an initial reconnaissance program in early 1940. The survey found 153 airports completed or under development, including small facilities located in towns not served by the Trans-Canada Airway. Eighteen airports were chosen for immediate use by the BCATP because they needed little more than new buildings; another 75 needed further development. Once again, immediate needs were met with an eye to the future. The prairies could have easily accommodated the entire program, but choosing sites in every region of Canada spread immediate economic benefits and put in place improvements that would assist a large portion of Canada's civil aviation network after the war.[40]

The service flying training schools, for pilot and gunner training, were demanding in terms of number, cost, and physical facilities. They required large and convenient sites, with safe approaches; level, well-drained, and firm ground; and easily accessible public utilities, including water and electricity. Engineers paid special attention to the quality of hard surfacing, because 'the abuse war airports [would] get ... [was] entirely out of proportion to the wear and tear experienced on any commercial airport.'[41] Each training school needed a main airfield, featuring three to six hard-surfaced runways laid out in triangular form, to allow for 2,500-ft (762-m) runways in six directions of wind, and two relief fields built a few miles away for emergency landings and practice.

Northern Airports

The construction of the BCATP airports substantially increased DOT's work-load, but engineers there relied on relatively standard solutions and found few opportunities for new construction and design techniques. Other wartime airports, particularly those constructed for joint defence programs, such as the North West Staging Route, the Crimson Route, and the Goose Bay Airport, were more challenging.[42]

Yukon's North West Staging Route was initially planned during peacetime and became an integral part of Canada's civil aviation network following the war. It was originally seen as part of the 'Great Circle' route, which many air transport enthusiasts believed would become the most important transportation link between North America and Asia. More modestly, aviation companies and DOT officials hoped that it would help to maintain and encourage northern settlements. Although bush planes had been flying into the area as early as the 1920s, lack of airports precluded scheduled service. Aircraft equipped with skis and floats could land only during periods of complete thaw and complete freeze-up, leaving communities without air services for long periods each year. Scheduled service using larger aircraft was needed to transport passengers and mail, to assist in exploration and mapping, to provide transportation for building roads and power projects, and to deliver northern products to other markets. Year-round airfields needed hard-surfaced runways, meteorological facilities, proper lighting, and navigation equipment.

Planning for the route began in 1935, when DOT surveyed a United Air Transport route through Grande Prairie, Fort St John, Fort Nelson, Watson Lake, and Whitehorse. In 1939, before the start of war, DOT decided to build minimum-standard airfields, with emergency lighting, radio aids, and meteorological aids, but still suited only to daylight and good-weather operation. At the outbreak of war, the project was reconsidered; it was continued because of poten-

Truck-mounted snow blowers clearing airfield at Whitehorse, December 1942. The same type was used on the Alaska Highway Project. (NA PA-130468)

tial military uses, particularly if the United States were to become involved in hostilities.

When the United States entered the war in December 1941, Canada offered use of the airway to the American government to transport military personnel to strategic locations in Alaska and to assist in construction of the Alaska High-

way. Runways had been built, lighting installed, and service buildings and houses erected. In 1942 the United States requested that the airports be enlarged and improved to handle large transport planes. Runways were resurfaced and lengthened, and new fuel facilities were constructed, all at American expense, and some with US military labour.

Airport at Tuktoyaktuk, NWT, one of several built by the federal government in the 1950s as part of its growing commitment to the north (NA PA-164635)

The Canol Project, an American oil pipeline constructed between Norman Wells and Whitehorse in 1942 and 1943, was accompanied by the secret upgrading or construction of airfields at Peace River, Fort McMurray, Fort Simpson, Fort Smith, and Norman Wells by American contractors. The airfields, later acquired and licensed by the Canadian government, conformed to US Ferry Command specifications. Most runways were built of compact earth, which was continually graded and backfilled to receive heavy aircraft. The Norman Wells runway was constructed on a glacial esker which kept it above the permafrost on a well-drained base.[43]

Military programs continued to push airport construction northward in the 1950s. The construction of the Distant Early Warning Line in the mid-1950s added an Arctic dimension to the northern airport network. Airports such as Tuktoyaktuk, Frobisher, and Cambridge Bay received gravel runways and good communication and navigation facilities.

Today, northern public airports are administered under a memorandum of understanding between the federal and territorial governments establishing responsibility for commercial regulatory matters. Airports are classed A, B, or C, according to scale, location, and strategic economic importance. Class A airports, such as Yellowknife, serving air carriers operating on a regular scheduled basis, are equipped to the same standards as many inter-urban airports and are managed by Transport Canada. Territorial governments are largely responsible for class B and C airports, such as Dawson and Old Crow.

Tuktoyaktuk airport (background) and supply ships (foreground) underscore reliance on outside supplies. (NA PA-164636)

Dorval

Some wartime developments, such as the building of Dorval Airport, in Montreal, reflected the heightened economic and industrial activities that strained all transportation networks. St Hubert had served Montreal since 1927, but by 1940 it appeared inadequate for both BCATP requirements and increased domestic and international air traffic. Negotiations between DOT and National Defence led to the decision to maintain St Hubert for military purposes and to build a new combined military/civil airport at Dorval. Fifteen hundred acres of land were purchased for this purpose, and part of the cost of the airport was borne by the British Ministry of Aircraft Production, which used the airport for the Transatlantic Ferry Command, the biggest operation at Dorval during the war.[44]

Only 11 months after the land purchase, Dorval opened, in September 1941, as Canada's best-equipped airport.

The $4.5-million complex featured three paved runways, about 5,000 ft (1,524 m) long by 200 ft (69.6 m) wide, six large hangars, administration buildings, and a passenger terminal. The latter was a two-storey, arc-shaped building, longer on the air side than on the ground transportation side. Atop it sat the now essential control tower.

The runways were a model of modern construction: a stabilized base of screening on a clay subsoil, topped by a 5-inch (12.7-cm) layer of macadam surfaced by a 1-inch (2.54-cm) sheet of asphalt. Special features included v-shaped trenches with catch basins and buried drains to collect surface water, as well as a 7-inch (17.8-cm) concrete layer to reinforce high-stress areas on aprons and the ends of runways.

Dorval Airport was planned to allow future expansion by construction of parallel runways. In 1946 it was the busiest airport in Canada; 246,359 passengers passed through its doors to fly with TCA, BOAC, Canadian Pacific Air-Lines, Quebec Airways, and smaller carriers.[45]

THE POST-WAR PERIOD

Toward the end of the war, the federal government faced two major problems with regard to airports: nearly all the training fields had to be returned to civil use or abandoned, and major airports required upgrading to accommodate larger aircraft ordered by TCA and other airlines. Many 'progressive' towns with small airfields, most constructed for training purposes during the war, considered expanding their facilities, while others investigated new sites. DOT officials were kept so busy advising municipalities that they embarked on an active public information campaign in 1944 about the planning and design of small airports. In an article directed toward small communities, the chief inspector

of airways, A.D. McLean, emphasized selection of a site suitable for expansion, even if it meant abandoning a developed field.[46] Advice was given about runway surfaces, drainage, buildings, control towers, communication services, utilities, and lighting. Drawings illustrated site plans that would allow conversion of a two-runway airport into one with six runways when traffic increased.

The conviction that private flying would grow quickly after the war fuelled the desire to enhance small airports. In 1944 John A. Wilson wrote: 'Private flying must necessarily play a most important part in our future organizations. It is probable that every normal boy and girl will, in a few years, wish to learn to fly, just as they now wish to learn to drive a motor car. Not all of them will continue flying, but many will ... This will call for an immense expansion of our airport facilities.'[47]

This expansion did not envision 'million-dollar' airports in many communities – simply 'a strip half a mile long and 600 feet [183 m] wide, adjacent to a highway, well drained, graded and sown to turf.' Larger towns might consider 'an all-way field, with diagonals of 3,000 ft [914 m]' to accommodate 'all normal private aircraft and the smaller types of transport aircraft used on feeder-line airways,' while major cities and refuelling points would require concrete runways of 8,000 to 10,000 ft (2,438 to 3,048 m) to handle larger aircraft.[48]

Air industry representatives encouraged enthusiasm, but many recognized the danger that 'public opinion has been unduly stimulated ... and may expect almost too much from aviation. In peacetime, financial considerations inevitably have a greater weight than in wartime.'[49] They feared that expectations would not be met, interest not sustained, and unrealistic goals pursued as communities tried to establish and upgrade airport facilities.

The Aeronautical Institute of Canada actively promoted private aviation, but it also challenged DOT's air policies and airport licensing standards. In 1944 a large number of businessmen and local politicians attended the institute's second annual convention. Motivated by concern for returning military airmen and by business considerations, they investigated strategies whereby 'they could get their community on the Air Map of Canada.'[50] The institute advocated the construction of small airports for every community in Canada and asked DOT to change minimum licensing standards and to contribute funds for building small airports. The institute argued that a community with a population of 1,000 to 5,000 could develop a small field with a sod surface to accommodate light aircraft, which would create a market for private airplanes and jobs for civilians and returning service personnel.[51] DOT countered that long-term considerations strongly influenced government policies and regulations. Lower standards could lead to more accidents, higher insurance rates, and lessened public confidence in aviation, which would affect the aviation industry from both domestic and international perspectives. Existing regulations were a compromise to maintain safety without requiring rigorous training for every pilot, which would make licences so difficult to obtain as to deter flying in itself.[52]

Most communities wanted airports established or upgraded during the war to be maintained but were not prepared to pay. Of the 291 publicly owned airports in operation in 1945, 281 were leased or owned by the federal government during the war. DOT planned to abandon 74 of these and retain 207, either permanently or temporarily for defence or commercial aviation. Those to be retained included main airports, improved

intermediate airports originally developed for the Trans-Canada Airway, and existing municipal fields. Only a few communities such as Calgary chose to operate airports; most let DOT operate and manage them.

Transportation officials judged that every airport along the Trans-Canada Airway, except Dorval, required upgrading, and many needed to be relocated before expansion. The largest plane in domestic service in 1945, the DC4, had a gross take-off weight of between 62,000 and 73,000 lb (28,150 and 33,140 kg), but modified DC4s already ordered were expected to increase this weight to 80,000 lb (36,320 kg), and some engineers predicted aircraft take-off weights of about 130,000 lb (59,020 kg) within five years. Runways at major airports had to be extended from about 3,500 ft (1,067 m) to 4,500 ft (1,372 m). One professional journal, *Roads and Bridges*, could see 'that a great deal of airport construction and reconstruction still remains to be done in Canada,' especially 'in view of recent discoveries that the damage both to subgrades and to pavements resulting from the operation of modern aircraft is more serious than engineers had anticipated.' Many engineers believed that previous studies had allowed for too much absorption of impact stresses by rubber tires and shock absorbers.[53]

Dorval and Malton (outside Toronto) illustrate how increased passenger and cargo traffic due to improvements in air services, general prosperity, and changing aircraft characteristics affected postwar civil airport development. Between 1946 and 1956 the number of passengers annually at Dorval rose from 246,359 to 1,092,000 and at Malton from 180,307 to about 900,000.[54] Terminals became overcrowded – particularly the building serving transatlantic passengers at Dorval, which was expanded in 1946 to accommodate travellers staying overnight.[55]

Forms being laid for foundations of apron building, Malton Airport, Toronto, 1948
(Pringle & Booth/NA PA-164630)

Between 1946 and 1956 BOAC, KLM, Air France, and Lufthansa were granted traffic rights at Dorval, adding to the services already offered by TCA.

DOT began planning expansion at Dorval in 1948, but work on a new terminal did not begin until 1956. Even then, plans had to be altered during construction to accommodate larger aircraft, such as the DC8, scheduled for service in 1960, and expanded airline needs, such as those created by TCA's decision in 1957 to consolidate its maintenance, overhaul, engineering, and stores facilities at Dorval. The $30-million Dorval terminal building opened in December 1960. It was one of the largest in the world, with 39 aircraft gates and 800,000 sq ft (74,300 sq m) of floor space, accommodating domestic, transborder, and international airline operations, airport management offices, US and Canadian customs and immigration services, weather services, and air traffic control. The car park held 2,800 vehicles, and for the first time DOT planned restaurant and shop concessions to increase non-aviation revenues.[56]

The growth of Malton Airport paralleled Dorval. A new one-storey brick terminal opened in 1949 adjacent to the 1939 wood frame terminal building, which was converted for operations and administration. Originally designed to handle 400,000 passengers per year, the new building was enlarged in 1954 and 1959. Sunday visitors contributed to the congestion, as the terminal's observation deck became one of Toronto's most popular attractions in the 1950s. In 1962, Malton's hopelessly overcrowded terminal handled 1,480,000 passengers, to surge ahead of Dorval as Canada's busiest airport.[57]

The explosive post-war growth of air cargo in Canada from 23,838,762 lb (about 10.8 million kg) in 1946 to 319,260,401 lb (about 144.9 million kg) in 1956, boosted airport improvement costs.[58] In 1955 DOT granted Timmins Aviation Ltd the first long-term lease on land for a private hangar at a Canadian government airport. Built at Dorval, the hangar was the first air cargo building erected at a DOT airport and marked a change in policy, which led to more private hangars at government airports and to the sale and lease of hundreds of surplus government-owned hangars built during the war.[59]

Growth in air cargo and passenger traffic made possible by larger aircraft and improved air traffic control substantially increased aircraft movements at major airports. One important advance was the installation of instrument landing systems (ILSS), which consisted of two radio beams transmitted to cockpit instruments that guided the pilot's approach. ILSS were installed on the busiest runways at major Canadian airports, beginning in 1948 on Dorval's runway 11, followed by runway 32 at Malton. TCA lent experienced technical advisers to supplement DOT staff during planning and installation of systems between 1946 and 1951, because the airline had a great stake in a system that could substantially decrease flight delays and cancellations.[60] ILSS were accompanied by improved lighting systems, and in 1954 Malton and Dorval were equipped with ALPA-type high-intensity approach lighting systems.[61]

THE JET AGE

Transition

Acquisition of civil jet aircraft in the late 1950s and early 1960s brought important changes to Canadian airports. During the mid-1950s, discussions regarding the effect of jets on airports filled professional aviation journals. Engineers anticipated that some jet aircraft characteristics would affect the design and configuration of runways and associated ground facilities, others would require changes in air traffic control procedures, and some would lead to readjustments in the distribution of traffic over airways. New jet aircraft, such as Douglas DC8s and Vickers-Armstrong Vanguards, had much greater flying ranges than piston-engine aircraft, consumed almost five times as much fuel, doubled landing weights and the number of passengers per aircraft, travelled at much greater speeds, and created serious noise problems. While jets could perform the same manoeuvres as piston-engine aircraft, the increase in fuel consumption made many procedures, such as laddering and maintaining holding positions over airports, prohibitively expensive.

In 1957 J.T. Dyment, chief engineer of TCA, presented a paper to the Royal Aeronautical Society about the impact of jet aircraft on air transportation systems.[62] Like other engineers, Dyment recognized that many changes would have to be made in the design of airports and in operating and maintenance procedures. Runways would have to be lengthened and more concrete used in their construction, for ruggedness and clarity of markings. Concrete would also be needed for refuelling points and for aprons, where spilled fuel would damage asphalt surfaces. Better visual aids, such as lighting and surface markings, would now be necessary to distinguish clearly

Pearson International Airport, Toronto, 1977. Modern airports need massive amounts of land as well as complex facilities for truck, bus, and automobile traffic. (TC)

approaches, thresholds, and runways. Because objects could be sucked up into and seriously damage turbine engines, methods for clearing and maintaining runways would have to be changed, and use of sand and calcium chloride for icy conditions stopped. The increase in the number of passengers per aircraft would require improvements to air terminal buildings and increased mechanization for some tasks, such as baggage handling. Noise and fumes associated with operating jets would demand insulated and air-conditioned buildings, as well as the end of emplaning and deplaning passengers directly to and from the airport apron. Further, little time would be available for necessary changes, and the pace of adjustment would continue for many years, as aircraft companies refined and improved aircraft designs.

Redevelopment of Malton into Toronto International Airport – formally Lester B. Pearson International – stands out as the single most ambitious project in the transition to the jet age. John B. Parkin and Associates of Toronto won a $23-million design contract for a 'new jet age aeroquay.'[63] Publicized as an 'entirely new design concept,' the terminal building opened in 1964, the same year that the airport site was enlarged to its present 4,272 acres (1,730 ha). Engineers and architects departed from the traditional linear building because the space required for the air side would have required a structure of impractical length. Instead, they designed a circular passenger building around a central administration building and a multi-storey parking garage, to keep walking distances to a minimum. Within two years, the terminal was operating beyond its designed capacity of 1,400 passengers per hour. Unfortunately, the circular form did not allow extension of the air side.

Introduction of jets required extended air traffic control systems to handle more aircraft movements at higher speeds. Solutions came through introduction of approach control centres, more air traffic control towers, radar equipment, altitude assignment apparatus, direct control-pilot communications, flight data displays, and computerized data processing to handle information such as flight paths and weather and runway conditions.[64] In 1957 DOT ordered radar systems capable of seeing transport aircraft at 60,000-ft (18,300-m) altitudes up to 150 mi (241 km) away, for 15 airports, and began evaluating a Dectra system for Gander. New control towers were built at major airports, and control centres designed to handle traffic out of the range of airport control towers were established. By the end of the 1950s, Canada had 26 control towers and 8 control centres.

Predicting and Planning
Beginning in the 1960s, skyrocketing land and airport construction costs plus increased demands for public involvement and government accountability led to substantial expenditures on airport planning. It was no longer sufficient simply to choose a relatively flat and well-drained field on the edge of town. Planners were called on to fit an airport into an overall transportation network, to predict future needs, and to assess social, economic, and environmental factors. During the planning process, conflicting political, economic, and technical pressures emerged: some created difficulties that were never resolved and led to the abandonment of projects such as the international airport that was to be built at Pickering, about 22 mi (35 km) east of Toronto.

The successful prediction of future traffic needs proved to be elusive. During the late 1960s, aircraft movements, passengers, and cargo increased substantially. While growth was fully expected, its pattern suggested that existing facilities would soon become obsolete and that it would be economically sound to consider long-term needs, possibly 20 or 30 years ahead, when planning new facilities. This approach was followed for the largest projects undertaken in the early 1970s, including the new Montreal International Airport, at Mirabel.

The planning of Mirabel began after a study published in 1968 about Dorval predicted that great increases in air traffic would require expansion of operations from 3,900 acres (1,580 ha) to 7,500 acres (3,040 ha) by 1985, with an additional 2,500 acres (1,010 ha) needed for future development.[65] Compounding this was noise that had led to a night curfew on jet operations. The study recommended a new airport on another site, with Dorval maintaining short-haul inter-city traffic, general aviation, and aircraft servicing.

In 1969 a site for the new airport was chosen, at Mirabel, and 88,000 acres (35,640 ha) of land, covering 14 small towns and affecting nearly 10,000 people, was expropriated. The site, 55 km (34.2 mi) from the city centre and 52 km (32.3 mi) from Dorval, was large enough to meet predicted future needs without infringing on residential or industrial development. Only 17,000 acres (6,885 ha) was needed for airport operations; the rest was planned as a controlled buffer zone of low-rise light industrial and warehousing enterprises, which would contribute to business at the airport without interfering in its operation. The master plan included six passenger terminals, six runways – four 12,000 ft (3,658 m) long and two 10,000 ft (3,048 m) long – and associated taxi strips, and aircraft aprons with a total of 150 aircraft gates designed to accommodate over 50 million passengers annually by 2025. Phase 1, the only part of the plan executed so far, occupies 5,200 acres (2,106 ha).

Construction began in 1970 and cost about $300 million: nearly 50 per cent was spent on land acquisition, 23 per cent on the air terminal building, and 22 per cent on the airfield.[66] Planning and design required the services of about 30 consulting firms. The design work was divided into 70 packages, and over 60 major construction contracts were awarded. Phase 1 included two 12,000-ft (3,658-m) cement runways and taxiway systems, the air terminal building, the control tower, a car parking garage, service buildings, and utilities. Aviation companies constructed an advanced underground refuelling system and an air cargo terminal. The airport operates 24 hours per day because it has no noise restrictions.

The terminal is a remote-gate type, requiring international passengers to use transfer vehicles between the building and aircraft parked at servicing clusters located about 1,500 ft (522 m) away; domestic flights use a connected aeroquay. This type of facility avoids aircraft congestion at the terminal, minimizes walking distances, and decreases capital costs while allowing greater flexibility in handling fluctuating traffic loads.

Traffic has never met projections. In 1973 DOT predicted that Mirabel would see 15.5 million passengers and Dorval 3.7 million in 1984.[67] The actual figures for that year were 1.5 million at Mirabel and 5.5 million at Dorval. In the same year, 14.7 million passengers used Toronto International Airport.[68]

The projected figures for Mirabel were overly optimistic, to justify an intensive building program, but they illustrate the difficulties faced by airports in a competitive transportation environment and reveal the powerful influence of airlines and general economic conditions on airport use. Although the number of international passengers at Canadian airports – 90 per cent of whom pass through Montreal, Toronto, and Vancouver – doubled between 1970 and 1984, new bilateral air agreements in the early 1970s between Canada and several European countries allowed more international carriers to deplane in Toronto, in exchange for access to European gateways by Canadian airlines. Passengers no longer had to land in Montreal and transfer to a domestic carrier for a flight to Toronto.[69] Longer-range aircraft like the Lockheed L1011-500 also made it possible to fly directly from European points to Toronto, Winnipeg, Edmonton, and Vancouver without stopping in Montreal. Mirabel, like other Canadian airports, has also been affected by unforeseen economic conditions, including dramatic fuel-price increases in the mid-1970s, which led airlines to streamline operations, and the economic recession in the early 1980s, which witnessed serious declines in almost all sectors of the aviation industry.

In 1986, airports became busy again, and there were renewed pressures to improve facilities. Nevertheless, the era of acquiring new airport sites has passed. Since the 1970s, limits to airport growth have affected aircraft design. While commercial aircraft now being developed will carry more passengers and cargo and travel at greater speeds, they will use existing runways. Airport expenditures are now focused on upgrading passenger and cargo facilities and air traffic control systems, as in Toronto's third air terminal building, being constructed by a private consortium. Thus the story of public works infrastructures in Canadian aviation has entered a new era. In the future, changes will be less visible but just as important as in earlier eras. But, as in the case of most public works, they will be rarely thought about by the public as long as they are working well, which is most of the time.

NOTES

1 The most comprehensive history of federally operated airports is T.M. McGrath *History of Canadian Airports* (Ottawa 1984).
2 Statistics Canada *Aviation in Canada* (Ottawa 1986)
3 McGrath *History* 24
4 The first official airmail flight, from Montreal on 24 June 1918 in a JN–4 by Capt. Brian Peck of the RAF, terminated at Leaside; ibid 25.
5 William J. McAndrew 'The Evolution of Canadian Aviation Policy Following the First World War' *Journal of Canadian Studies* 16:3 and 4 (fall 1981) 89
6 As quoted in McGrath *History* 746
7 Statistics Canada *Avaiation in Canada* 119
8 McGrath *History* 95
9 The list included in the 1922 annual report of the Air Board can be found in ibid 96.
10 Ibid 274
11 See Renald Fortier 'Technologie et politique: la participation canadienne à un programme impérial de transport par dirigeables, 1924–1931' *HSTC Bulletin* 7:3 (Sept 1987) 135–71.
12 McGrath *History* 520
13 Ibid 49
14 Lawrence Ring *Airports in Canada and Newfoundland* (Washington 1930) 41
15 Archives of Newfoundland and Labrador, AG/15, Harbour Grace Airport, Letter to R. Manning, Secretary, Department of Public Works, from Harbour Grace Airport Trust Company, 20 Nov 1936
16 Other seaplane bases were located at Port Washington, NY, Foynes, Eire, and Hythe, Southampton, England. McGrath *History* 124
17 'The Newfoundland Airport' *Canadian Engineer* (7 March 1939) 6
18 McGrath *History* 324
19 Ibid 326
20 Frank H. Ellis *Canada's Flying Heritage* (Toronto 1961) 290
21 National Archives of Canada (NA), MG 30, E243, Vol. 3
22 W. Woollett 'Introducing Cross-Canada Airmail Services' *CAHS Journal* 24:2 (summer 1986) 45
23 Ibid 46
24 Ring *Airports* 1
25 Ibid 9
26 Ibid 22
27 Ibid 16
28 McGrath *History* 670
29 Canada *Report of the Royal Commission to Inquire into Railways and Transportation in Canada* (Ottawa 1932) 57
30 NA, MG 30, E243, Vol. 2
31 NA, RG 12, Vol. 5151, File 176, pt. 2
32 NA, RG 12, Vol. 1601, File 5158-6
33 'Vancouver's Sea Island Airport' *Canadian Aviation* 10:12 (Dec 1937) 45
34 'Runways Awaiting Spring Inspection' *Canadian Aviation* 12:3 (March 1939) 29
35 A.H. Clarke 'Airport and Airway Lighting' *Canadian Aviation* 12:6 (June 1939) 14 and 16
36 'Canada's Airway System Shows Results of Two Years Intensive Development' *Canadian Aviation* 12:1 (Jan 1939) 8
37 'Plan Expansion at Vancouver Airport' *Canadian Aviation* 15:7 (July 1942) 63
38 J.A. Wilson 'Air Transport in Canada' *Civil Aviation in Canada* (Ottawa n.d.) 30

39 'New Runway Numbering Plan for Runways Here' *Canadian Aviation* 15:2 (Feb 1942) 88

40 J.A. Wilson 'Aerodrome Construction for the British Commonwealth Air Training Plan 1940' *Civil Aviation in Canada* (Ottawa n.d.) 30

41 NA, RG 12, Vol. 1836, File 5158-8, pt. 2

42 Ibid pt. 5

43 P.S. Barry *The Canol Project: An Adventure of the U.S. War Department in Canada's Northwest* (Edmonton 1985) 171

44 McGrath *History* 426

45 'Airport Building Major Industry' *Canadian Aviation* 14:11 (Nov 1941) 27; McGrath *History* 427

46 A.D. McLean 'Fundamentals of Airport Planning and Construction' *Roads and Bridges* 82:9 (Sept 1944) 61–6, 92, 94–6

47 Stuart Graham 'Airfields for Postwar Aviation' *Roads and Bridges* 82:11 (Nov 1944) 60

48 Ibid

49 Ibid 61

50 NA, RG 12, Vol. 1837, File 5304-A8, pt. 1

51 Ibid

52 Ibid

53 'Disposition of Canada's Airfields' *Roads and Bridges* 83:12 (Dec 1945) 57

54 McGrath *History* 431 and 646

55 DOT *Annual Report, 1946–47* (Ottawa 1947)

56 McGrath *History* 431 and 433

57 NA, National Film, Television and Sound Archives 'Airports in the Jet Age' 1962, 01V1CV 8201 075-3

58 Statistics Canada *Aviation in Canada 1971* (Ottawa 1972) 28

59 McGrath *History* 432

60 Philip Smith *It Seems Like Only Yesterday: Air Canada, the First 50 Years* (Toronto: McClelland and Stewart 1986) 151

61 DOT *Annual Report, 1954–55* (Ottawa 1955)

62 J.T. Dyment 'The Problems of Jet Transport Operations' *Journal of the Royal Aeronautical Society* 61 (Sept 1957) 594–608

63 'New Jet Age Aeroquay' *Roads and Engineering Construction* 98:12 (Dec 1960) 38

64 DOT '10 Year Plan, 1958–1968' unpublished report, Transport Canada Library, Ottawa

65 McGrath *History* 432

66 G.Y. Sebastyan 'The New Montreal International Airport' *Journal of the Construction Division: Proceedings of the American Society of Civil Engineers* 101:2 (June 1975) 327

67 Transport Canada *Keeping Canada One Step Ahead: The New Montreal International Airport at Mirabel, Quebec* (Ottawa 1973) 7

68 Statistics Canada *Aviation in Canada* 135

69 Ibid 141 and McGrath *History* 443

ALAN F.J. ARTIBISE

Building Cities

Human settlements are complex phenomena that develop from a wide variety of forces. Studies of Canadian city-building have examined most of these influences – social, economic, political, and institutional – and quite comprehensive understanding has been achieved during the past two decades.[1] But there has not been sufficient appreciation of the role of public works in providing the essential physical infrastructure for urban development. Indeed, it is no exaggeration to state that public works make towns and cities possible. The planning, design, construction, operation, maintenance, and administration of public works are central to any story of Canadian urban development.

Canadians have, of course, recognized achievements by their engineers, but largely by focusing on major transportation, water, and communications projects – hardly surprising in a country with vast distances to span and innumerable natural resources to tap. There is, however, another – perhaps less heroic – story that needs to be told. It is the history of the building of Canada's thousands of towns and cities. And the role of public works professionals is central; without them Canada could not have developed as one of the most highly urbanized nations in the world.[2] As city-building proceeded, public works professionals were called on to

put into place – and maintain – a complex urban infrastructure of streets, sewers, water systems, power grids, and public buildings. Their work was often unrecognized; a sewage system rarely captured the public imagination in the same way as construction of a canal, dam, or bridge. Occasionally, however, when the urban infrastructure was neglected or broke down, the essential nature of public works could be clearly recognized.

The contribution of public works professionals to city-building involves two distinct but interrelated elements. It includes most obviously the design and construction of a wide range of public works but extends far beyond this purely technical context to include the planning and administration of urban space. In other words, any analysis of the contributions of engineers must include more than purely technical capacities. Although these capabilities are critical, they are insufficient in and of themselves to the task at hand, which includes the overall planning and administration of a public works system, operating in a context of rapidly changing and complex social, economic, environmental, and political forces. Not surprisingly, the story of public works planning and administration in Canada contains both successes and failures, in almost four centuries of challenges.

THE COLONIAL/MERCANTILE ERA, 1608–1820s

Until the early 19th century, Canada's urban settlements were tiny outposts of imperial and mercantile expansion, and this fact determined their planning and administration, function and form.[3] Urban settlements were central elements in French and British imperial expansion from the 17th to the early 19th centuries. Most towns were consciously conceived to precede and stimulate more general settlement. In this regard, the imperial nations' military and administrative needs were of paramount concern. Quebec and Montreal were founded by fur-trading companies for business and missionary purposes, but in the 1660s Louis xiv's government took over direct control of these and other settlements. This imperial connection is best seen in Louisbourg, designed as the Atlantic bulwark in the bitter French-English rivalry for control of the northern portion of the continent, but it is also evident in most other settlements in what was to become Canada.

The form of Canada's early settlements was determined by imperial needs and designs, whether French or British. As Gilbert Stelter has noted, 'During the seventeenth century, the French state became more directly involved in the building or redesigning of towns, as in Colbert's founding of Rochefort as an arsenal and naval base, or in the rebuilding of La Rochelle, the main port for Canada, as a fortified site along the lines recommended by the great military planner, Sebastian Vauban.'[4] The most striking example of the role of military engineering in urban planning in Canada, however, is Louisbourg. Patterned after the plans of Sébastien le Prestre de Vauban, marshal of France, Louisbourg was a fortified settlement that housed not only a permanent garrison but a large fishing and trade centre as well.[5] Engineers were also central to the development of Canada's other major settlements. Jean Bourdon, who arrived in Quebec City in 1634, surveyed the land and produced the first maps of the city. He was succeeded by military engineer Jacques Levasseur de Nere – who trained under the great Vauban himself – and Gaspard-Joseph Chaussegros de Léry.[6]

These and other engineers initially designed defence installations and fortifications. But beyond the considerable influence that these projects had on city-building, military engineers were also involved in other activities. In New France, engineers designed not only the fortifications surrounding the settlements, but their internal layouts as well.

Under the British regime, military engineers began to lose their influence on general public works but continued to play a key role in defence installations, which in many cities –notably Quebec and Halifax – weighed heavily on general planning issues. But if the military were less involved, government planners were still much in evidence. The British-built towns, such as Halifax and Charlottetown, were characterized by the regularity and symmetry of their Georgian plans, with their central squares for parades and their grid-iron layout drawn up by imperial officials. Individual houses and streets were subordinated on general schemes both in Atlantic Canada and in Upper Canada (Ontario).

With the exception of defence planning and an overall concern for street systems and patterns – and the placement of important public buildings within the system – public works planning was not far advanced prior to 1850. As a result, Canada's towns and cities were not pleasant places in which to live. 'In the years before mid-century, the cities

TABLE 1
Urban population in Upper and Lower Canada, 1851

Population	No. of centres	Population	Percentage
100,000 and over	–	–	–
25,000–99,999	3	130,542	49.4
10,000–24,999	2	25,697	9.7
5,000–9,999	2	14,795	5.6
2,500–4,999	13	47,769	18.1
1,000–2,499	29	45,403	17.2
Total	49	264,206	100.0

SOURCE: George A. Nader *Cities of Canada* I (Toronto 1975) 170

and towns of central Canada achieved some degree of maturity before iron rails and smoke-belching locomotives disrupted them anew. But it would be wrong to romanticize the typical urban community of the time. It was dirty, untidy, and cluttered, with jammed-in or half-built streets, miserable shanties in back lanes, few gas lights or sewers, and much drunkeness and hardship.'[7]

THE COMMERCIAL ERA, 1820S–1870S

The lack of a system of public works planning and administration, so evident in the 18th century, continued well into the 19th. Indeed, in many ways there was less direction and control in the commercial era than in the colonial phase. At the same time, city-building was rapidly becoming more dependent on the skills and services of engineers. As both the size and number of settlements grew (see Table 1), it became increasingly apparent that the most successful would be those settlements that could best exploit their natural and locational advantages (or overcome their disadvantages) through construction of roads, canals, and railroads. Similarly, ambitious city-builders became aware of the need to accommodate growing populations through provision of water, power, and other urban services. In all these areas, public works rarely moved

beyond the rudimentary level by the 1870s, but there was growing recognition of the value of planning public works.

The key characteristic of cities in the commercial era was the absence of any central direction in planning. No imperial official or municipal officer planned or regulated development; rather, the town was determined by the decisions of thousands of individuals or, in some cases, by private corporations. Yet there was a remarkable degree of order and regularity. Original pathways were usually perpetuated as streets; in Montreal, for example, new street patterns followed the 17th-century division of agricultural land into long, narrow strips laid out perpendicular to the river. In Toronto, suburban expansion was framed by the north-south lines of original lots. Transportation routes into settlements also shaped development. Subdivisions were drawn to these corridors, and internal transportation – the horse-drawn streetcar – followed. Private or public provision of services such as water and sewers also influenced the direction and density of development.[8]

But public works were still rare. In most instances, services – whether gas, water, or transportation – were provided by private companies rather than by municipalities, a situation that would not be altered significantly until the great

TABLE 2
Urban population in Quebec and Ontario, 1881 and 1921

Population	No. of centres		Population		Percentage	
	1881	1921	1881	1921	1881	1921
100,000 and over	1	4	140,747	1,362,393	17.1	48.1
25,000–99,999	4	5	212,234	249,184	25.8	8.8
10,000–24,999	3	28	46,351	452,541	5.6	15.9
5,000–9,999	18	34	131,353	238,580	16.0	8.4
2,500–4,999	40	74	140,380	257,257	17.1	9.1
1,000–2,499	98	176	151,489	274,543	18.4	9.7
Total	164	321	822,554	2,834,498	100.0	100.0

SOURCE: Nader *Cities of Canada* 1 226

urban boom of the industrial era. Engineers did play a key role in urban development, but from outside any organized system of public works planning, usually as agents of private companies or senior governments. The redevelopment of the Lachine Canal in the 1840s, for example, was undertaken by Montreal's Harbour Board engineers, positioning Montreal to become the industrial cradle of Canada. These same engineers later initiated a wide variety of works to develop the port of Montreal, assuring supremacy over the city's rival – Quebec. Engineers also had a major influence on the cityscape, as railroad rights of way and tunnels were planned and railroad stations sited. Yet, in this era, engineers did not yet concern themselves with actual city planning. Only as population grew did formerly individual problems – such as water supply, refuse disposal, fire protection, and transit – become public ones that demanded collective solutions and, more important, systematic planning. But this 'modern' approach was not everywhere evident until around the turn of the century.[9]

In the mean time, public works developments were few and far between. In Ontario, for example, 31 municipalities developed gasworks prior to 1900, but none was publicly owned; the first public system was begun in Brockville in 1900. Similarly, private companies dominated the development of urban electrical systems, and municipal organization and ownership of power systems did not advance rapidly until after 1900.[10] Waterworks and sewerage systems were also developed relatively late. Prior to 1880, only three Ontario urban centres had sewerage systems, only 21 had water services, and some of these were very small. Indeed, until the 1880s, the main reason for a water system was to provide fire protection; a more general service was usually not developed until municipal governments were forced by some crisis, such as an epidemic.[11]

In short, while some progress had been made between the 1820s and the 1870s, it was at best uneven and at worst marginal. But the Canadian city – and public works engineering – were on the verge of a revolution in public works administration and planning.

THE INDUSTRIAL ERA, 1870S–1920S

Canada's cities underwent dramatic transformations between the 1870s and the 1920s. New cities were founded and grew rapidly, established cities expanded, and the complexities of urban life were everywhere evident (see Table 2). Indeed, during this era the 'modern city' emerged, characterized by a professional, public system of public works administration and planning.[12] Both the extent and the nature of urban development in this era depended significantly on Canada's technological capacity. 'Science and engineering were systematically applied to transportation, communications, building methods, and production.'[13] The use of structural steel, for example, led to the high-rise building and made possible the rapid concentration of office space in central cities. The development of public transit systems allowed workers to commute, thus permitting the development of segregated residential, commercial, and industrial districts. The rapid expansion of electricity as an energy source transformed internal transportation by increasing the speed and carrying capacity of street railway systems.

The achievement of the modern system involved more than technology, however. It also called forth new attitudes toward technical problems, such as the provision of urban services, which would eventually result in entirely new administrative structures for municipal governments, including prominent roles for municipal engineers. The boom atmosphere of the industrial era raised expectations for extensive urban service networks, and this demand, coupled with the rapid professionalization of engineers, resulted in an era very different from the past.

The scale and extent of change were overwhelming. In western Canada, for example, an entire system of cities sprang up in three decades, and by the 1920s the region boasted municipal services that could match those of central Canada.[14] And the challenges faced by engineers were rarely easily solved. In Winnipeg, the development of an efficient and safe water-supply took over 40 years, but the problems were conquered brilliantly.[15] Engineers also played essential roles in developing public utility

and service systems and in structuring urban space.

The story of these critical years is complex and cannot be told in its entirety here. Rather, a few well-chosen examples must make the case. Perhaps most notable in this era is the rapid growth in the number of publicly owned urban services, administered and operated by municipal engineers. In Ontario alone, for example, over 170 urban places started waterworks systems between 1880 and 1920, and over 110 of these were municipally owned. Similarly, some 400 urban places in Ontario had electric systems by 1920, and most of these were municipal. The cities' professional engineers were also involved in the extensive development of streets, street railways, and interurbans and the construction of hospitals, public libraries, municipal halls, and other public buildings.[16]

Equally impressive was the extent of services in some of Canada's larger cities. Toronto's experiences illustrate this point. In 1900, Toronto had almost 260 mi (418 km) of streets, but only 30 mi (48 km) were paved in asphalt. By 1930, the city boasted of 571 mi (919 km) of streets, 483 mi (777 km) – or 91 per cent – of which were paved. In 1900 the city had 429 mi (690 km) of sidewalk, 400 mi (644 km) of which were wooden planks. By 1930 there were almost 900 mi (1,448 km) of concrete sidewalks.

The general physical environment of the city was further enhanced by the extension of sanitation services, including the collection and disposal of garbage, street watering and snow removal, and the construction and maintenance of sewers and sewage disposal facilities. By 1900 Toronto was long past the days when garbage was burned in backyards or fed to the hogs ... Garbage was collected semi-weekly and disposed of in two crematories ... Moreover, since the city had doubled in size through annexation ... it was necessary to organize the city into twenty-four districts averaging 900 acres [365 ha] each to ensure efficient collection in every area. Likewise, street watering to reduce dust on the main thoroughfares and snow removal has entered the motorized age.[17]

These experiences were repeated across Canada in the era, in cities large and small, old and new. And Canada's engineers provided the basic infrastructure for rapid urbanization.

But public works professionals also played another, less well understood role. As several commentators have noted, the period saw the zenith of planning for orderly growth, following master plans that incorporated 'city beautiful' concepts.[18] Across Canada, engineers, surveyors, and other professionals not only built the urban infrastructure but also argued for acceptance of planning as an everyday public function. And, for a time at least, they achieved a measure of success. Provincial and municipal planning agencies and departments were established, master plans were started, and zoning, slum clearance, and public housing were undertaken. Yet, by the 1920s, the planning professionals had failed to measure up to the larger task they faced, that of achieving a high standing in the public debates of the day. Prestige, direction, and cohesion were not achieved in this period; instead, engineers simply became technical facilitators for growth-oriented city councils. The professionals tried to be more than technicians, but four cataclysmic events damaged their prospects: 'the frenzied boom and its subsequent collapse; the trauma and totality of the Great War; the strife, uncertainty and disillusionment which haunted the peace; and the catastrophe of the Great Depression. Between them, they left Canada in turmoil and bereft of social resources, self-assurance and agreed goals.'[19]

This is not to say that public works professionals had not achieved much; indeed, their accomplishments in so short a period have never been matched. But their hopes of becoming recognized and respected partners in the city-building process were still-born. Once services were provided and plans made, they were often forgotten. By the 1920s, the engineers were identified with the values and aspirations of growth-oriented city councils, giving practical and institutional form to an entrenched utilitarianism. Not until the 1980s would another opportunity arise for moving beyond this rather narrow role.

THE CORPORATE ERA, 1920S–1980S

The 1910s and 1920s marked a high point in the prestige, authority, and affluence of Canadian municipalities and, hence, of public works professionals. Since then, Canadian cities have been in a long period in which municipal autonomy and prestige have been seriously eroded.[20] Yet municipal services continued to be demanded at a rapidly increasing rate and in ever more complex forms. The corporate era was characterized by the technology of the truck and automobile, an economic orientation away from industry to service functions dependent upon high technology, and massive spatial decentralization of population and activities.

The new corporate city was characterized by five types of development: the corporate-suburb, private-enterprise town; high-rise apartments; suburban industrial parks; downtown office towers; and shopping centres. With this 'corporate city' came a set of policies drawn up and implemented by newly established planning departments that legitimized and regulated an overall urban form; and municipal engineers accepted these new directions almost without question:

The classic [post-1945] city plan called for a sectorized city, with the major functions – low density residential, industrial, office-commercial, and retailing – allocated to physically separate sectors of the city. It established the density extremes of the corporate city as the norm ... It assumed almost universal car ownership ... and it accepted what could be termed the 'corporatization' of public space: ownership by the development corporation of the street and sidewalk in the shopping centre prototype, in office towers and high-rise apartments. City planners [and engineers] laid out the public-sector supporting facilities required for the corporate city: the sewers, watermains, roads, expressways.[21]

The achievements of the corporate city were considerable. Canada's urban population grew from less than 50 per cent of the total in 1921 to more than 75 per cent in 1981, and Canada became known around the world for its unequalled urban environment.[22] Municipal engineers were simultaneously faced with the old challenges of providing for new growth and the new challenges of new forms of growth such as suburbs, shopping centres, and expressways. The transformation of downtown cores under pressures from promoters, followed by the proliferation of urban renewal and urban redevelopment projects in the 1970s, also posed complex problems. The work was rarely mundane; indeed, it often involved exceptional projects, such as preparing for major events like Expo '67 in Montreal and Expo '86 in Vancouver.

To meet these challenges, the profession itself changed. Beginning in the 1960s, the development of electronic data processing provided powerful tools for streamlining certain routine tasks.

And engineers increasingly found themselves working with multidisciplinary teams of architects, urban planners, surveyors, computer scientists, and technologists. In all these areas, the public works professionals acquitted themselves well, continuing to provide the vital services necessary to maintain Canada's high quality of urban life, while at the same time meeting the special needs of major public events and spectacles.

Public works professionals also had to cope with problems of overlapping jurisdiction caused by often-uncontrolled suburban growth after 1945. The contradiction between the essentially metropolitan character of many services, such as transit, water-supply, and sewage disposal, and the proliferation of independent jurisdictions was a powerful impetus toward metropolitan government. In these circumstances, the engineers again acquitted themselves well; in Winnipeg, for example, the transition from 13 separate municipalities to one 'Unicity' was generally handled smoothly in the urban services areas.[23]

Building on this strong record, public works professionals began to emerge in the 1980s as a new force in Canadian cities. As quality-of-life issues gradually replaced growth as the force behind municipal politics, engineers were increasingly consulted about traffic, air quality, water-supply, and recreation space. Whereas in the past cities had measured success almost purely in terms of growth, the new politics stressed environmental quality. Engineers were called upon to solve urban service problems in new and innovative ways, designing, for instance, new forms of waste disposal and public transportation. These challenges, appearing first in the late 1970s, will continue to preoccupy the profession for the coming decade.[24]

A far more immediate challenge arose in the 1980s that will test the power and prestige of public works professionals as never before. For well over three centuries, engineers had served the city-building process by providing the infrastructure necessary for growth. Spurred on by growth-conscious municipal governments, they had had little time to maintain and rehabilitate what had been built. Few politicians saw maintenance and rehabilitation as a 'high-profile,' 'vote-getting' activity. Glamorous new projects, such as buildings, parks, expressways, and rapid transit systems, outshone routine infrastructure activities. Fiscal retrenchment and cut-backs came at a time when the ageing and deterioration of the existing infrastructure first became readily apparent.

Public works professionals therefore face the challenge of shifting the funding priorities of governments toward maintenance and rehabilitation at a time when funding is difficult to obtain for any project. Municipal engineers thus face their greatest challenges ever, and ones – unlike most in the past – not exclusively or even largely technical. Rather, they involve new modes of management and persuasion, and new techniques for raising revenue. In short, they require a far more active role in policy formulation. Evidence that the profession is up to this challenge can be seen in the role it played in the First Canadian Conference on Urban Infrastructure, held in Toronto in February 1987.[25] Municipal engineers were prominent in the program, and for the first time the public was made aware in dramatic terms of the extent of the problem. But much remains to be done before the priorities of government budgets reflect the needs of urban infrastructure maintenance and replacement.

Yet the new confidence of the public works professionals suggests that this situation, like so many in the past, can be met. The public may finally come to realize that the services that it has so long taken for granted need constant care and attention. The role of those who design, build, and maintain those services may finally receive the standing and general public approbation it deserves.

NOTES

1 For a general overview of Canadian urban studies see Alan F.J. Artibise and Paul-André Linteau *The Evolution of Urban Canada: An Analysis of Approaches and Interpretations* (Winnipeg 1984).

2 By 1851, the proportion of Canadians living in urban centres was 13 per cent. It reached 52 per cent by 1931 and 75 per cent by 1981. In any ranking of nations, Canada always appears as one of the most urbanized.

3 The best studies of urban development in Canada prior to 1870 have been prepared by Gilbert Stelter. See especially 'The Political Economy of Early Canadian Urban Development' in Gilbert A. Stelter and Alan F.J. Artibise eds *The Canadian City: Essays in Urban and Social History* (Ottawa 1984); 'The City-Building Process in Canada' in Gilbert A. Stelter and Alan F.J. Artibise eds *Shaping the Urban Landscape: Aspects of the Canadian City-Building Process* (Ottawa 1982); and 'Urban Planning and Development in Upper Canada' in W. Borah, J. Hardoy, and G.A. Stelter eds *Urbanization in the Americas* (Ottawa 1981).

4 Stelter 'The City-Building Process'

5 Paul-André Linteau 'Planning and Management of Urban Space' *Forces* No. 78 (summer 1987) 49–51

6 Ibid. See also A. Charbonneau, Y. Desloges, and M. Lafrance *Quebec, the Fortified City: From the 17th to the 19th Century* (Ottawa 1982).

7 J.M.S. Careless *Urban Development in Central Canada to 1850* Canada's Visual History Series No. 7 (Ottawa 1974) 5

8 Stelter 'The City-Building Process'

9 Linteau 'Planning and Management'

10 Elizabeth and Gerald Bloomfield *Urban Growth and Services: The Development of Ontario Municipalities to 1981* (Guelph 1983) passim

11 Ibid

12 John C. Weaver 'The Modern City Realized: Toronto Civic Affairs, 1880–1915' in Alan F.J. Artibise and Gilbert A. Stelter eds *The Usable Urban Past: Planning and Politics in the Modern Canadian City* (Toronto 1979) 39–72

13 Stelter 'The City-Building Process'

14 See, for example, Alan F.J. Artibise 'The Urban West: The Evolution of Prairie Towns and Cities to 1930' in Stelter and Artibise *The Canadian City* 138–64, and Alan F.J. Artibise ed *Town and City: Aspects of Western Canadian Urban Development* (Regina 1981).

15 The long and complex story of Winnipeg's water-supply is told in Alan F.J. Artibise *Winnipeg: A Social History of Urban Growth* (Montreal 1975).

16 Bloomfield and Bloomfield *Urban Growth and Services*

17 Roger Riendeau 'Servicing the Modern City, 1900–1930' in Victor L. Russell ed *Forging a Consensus: Historical Essays on Toronto* (Toronto 1984) 157–80

18 See, for example, Walter van Nus 'The Fate of City Beautiful Thought in Canada, 1893–1930' in Stelter and Artibise *The Canadian City* 167–86.

19 For the best account see M. Simpson *Thomas Adams and the Modern Planning Movement: Britain, Canada and the United States, 1900–1940* (Mansell 1985) chap 4 and 5. See also articles by Thomas Gunton and P.J. Smith in Artibise and Stelter *The Usable Urban Past* (Toronto 1979).

20 John Taylor 'Urban Autonomy in Canada: Its Evolution and Decline' in Stelter and Artibise *The Canadian City* 478–500

21 James Lorimer 'Citizens and the Corporate Development of the Contemporary Canadian City' *Urban History Review* 12:1 (June 1983) 3–10

22 Alan F.J. Artibise 'Canada as an Urban Nation: Reflections on City-Building in Montreal, Toronto and Vancouver' *Daedalus* (forthcoming 1989)

23 See, for example, H. Kaplan *Reform, Planning and City Politics: Montreal, Winnipeg, Toronto* (Toronto 1982).

24 The importance of environmental issues and the concept of 'sustainable development' can be expected to grow. See, for example, *Report of the National Task Force on Environment and Economy* (Ottawa 1987), Canada's response to *Our Common Future: The World Commission on Environment and Development* (New York 1987).

25 The conference, held at the University of Toronto, was organized by the Federation of Canadian Municipalities (FCM) and the universities of Toronto and Alberta. The papers presented are to be published by the FCM.

Index